RESIDENTIAL INTERIOR DESIGN

RESIDENTIAL INTERIOR DESIGN
A GUIDE TO PLANNING SPACES

Maureen Mitton, CID, IDEC

Courtney Nystuen, AIA, CSI

With CAD Illustrations by Melissa Brewer

BICENTENNIAL
1807
WILEY
2007
BICENTENNIAL

JOHN WILEY & SONS, INC.

Published by John Wiley & Sons, Inc., Hoboken, New Jersey

Published simultaneously in Canada

For general information about our other products and services, please contact our Customer Care Department within the United States at (800) 762-2974, outside the United States at (317) 572-3993 or fax (317) 572-4002.

Wiley also publishes its books in a variety of electronic formats. Some content that appears in print may not be available in electronic books. For more information about Wiley products, visit our web site at www.wiley.com.

Library of Congress Cataloging-in-Publication Data:

Mitton, Maureen.
  Residential interior design : a guide to planning spaces / Maureen Mitton, Courtney Nystuen ; with CAD illustrations by Melissa Brewer.
    p. cm.
  Includes bibliographical references and index.
  ISBN-13: 978-0-471-68473-2 (pbk.)
  ISBN-10: 0-471-68473-2 (pbk.)
  1. Interior architecture. 2. Dwellings—Planning. 3. Dwellings—Specifications. I. Nystuen, Courtney. II. Brewer, Melissa. III. Title.
  NA2850.M56 2006
  728' .37—dc22
                                                                            2006013278

Printed in the United States of America

10 9 8 7 6 5 4 3

CONTENTS

ACKNOWLEDGMENTS

Having worked in the design portion of the construction industry for many years, I am well aware of the collaborative nature of the entire industry. Throughout the duration of every project (conception to occupancy), everyone needs to rely on the competence of those whose work precedes one's own. Short of that, it all starts to fall apart.

There is a list as long as my arm of people I have worked with and learned from over the years. You know who you are; you have made a de facto contribution to this book and you have my ongoing gratitude.

I must make mention of a few individuals who made direct contributions to this book: Melissa Brewer has consistently been the "go-to-gal," competent, diligent, organized, and thorough; William P. Halgren and Todd Armstrong contributed their expertise; and Gail Kann, a friend and colleague, is the hardest-working woman south of Duluth.

And, of course, the prime mover, the leader of the pack, et cetera, et cetera, in this entire enterprise—the results of which you hold in your hands—has been Maureen Mitton. Absent her vision and tenacity, it would not have happened, period!

And then, there is always a family that sticks with you through thick and thin; in my case, J / S,T,K,H / P,M,E / A,N,K,S.

CourtneyNystuen
April 2006

We live in times in which the word *teamwork* is used often, in many cases by people who are not very good at it. In the case of this book, I have been a very happy member of a working team of three.

Working with Courtney is delightful; he works hard, he delivers, he makes me laugh, and most importantly, he always makes me think. This book would not exist without Courtney, who taught this subject matter for years and educated so many interior design students over his academic tenure. He has influenced the design community a great deal over the years. He has also kept a full range of professional projects going throughout his academic career and into his alleged retirement. His ability to consider the information and content most useful to students and present it in an approachable manner made this book happen. Courtney contributed all of the hand-drawn illustrations in this book; his wonderful hand is evident and makes the drawings a pleasure to view.

Melissa Brewer, the other member of this team, has been a miracle worker, taking messy, sometimes undecipherable sketches and turning them into easy-to-read figures; she contributed all of the CAD illustrations contained in this book. Her positive attitude, talent, kindness, incredible organizational skills, and round-the-clock hard work have made this project happen— color-coded paper clips and pristine files were simply an added bonus.

Two of my colleagues at UW-Stout have been very helpful and supportive. Thanks to Shelley Pecha for understanding, and hanging in there, without much first-year support from me, and a special thank-you to Kristine Recker-Simpson for doing all the FIDER/CIDA work cheerfully and well. My students always suffer when I work on a big project like this, due to my lack of time for preparation, and I thank all of them for the ongoing support and energy they provide.

My family, as usual, paid the price on this project. Thank you, Anna and Luc, for putting up with many weeks of a distracted, frazzled mother. Thank you to the Mitton parents and siblings for your support and understanding, and as always, thank you to Roger Parenteau, the husband who makes everything possible.

MaureenMitton
April 2006

INTRODUCTION

> *"Every cubic inch of space is a miracle."*
>
> WALT WHITMAN (*Leaves of Grass,* "Miracles")

WHAT THIS BOOK IS ABOUT

This book has a very specific focus: the space planning of individual rooms in homes. Many current publications are available that offer an overview of the principles of residential design combined with information about materials, finishes, and furnishings. Also available are beautiful books that provide lavish photographs and descriptions of residential design projects. Unlike those books, this one is meant to serve as a primer on space planning for major rooms/spaces in a home, and to offer related information regarding codes, mechanical and electrical systems, and a variety of additional factors that impact each type of room/space. In addition, this book includes information about accessible design in each chapter in order to provide a cohesive view of residential accessibility.

This book is meant to serve as a reference for use in the design process, and as an aid in teaching and understanding the planning of residential spaces. For purposes of clarity, most chapters follow a similar format, starting with an overview of the particular room or space and related issues of accessibility, followed with information about room-specific furnishings and appliances. Chapters continue with information about sizes and clearances, organizational flow, related codes and constraints, and issues regarding electrical, mechanical, and plumbing. At the end of each chapter, basic information is provided about lighting the specific room.

This book describes the minimum requirements for specific spaces and rooms so that students and designers can get a sense of the amount of space that is minimally necessary in order for rooms to function usefully. Examples of larger spaces are also given, but at its heart, this book is intended to show students how to use space wisely and make good use of space throughout the dwelling. Put another way: The book is about meeting the minimum standards required to create spaces that work functionally. Such minimum standards are dictated by building codes and manufacturers' recommendations, and/or reflect good design practice. With clear knowledge about minimums, designers and students of design can learn when it is appropriate to exceed such standards for a variety of reasons that reflect specific project criteria based upon clients needs, budget, site, and other constraints.

This book is meant as an introduction to the topics covered with the intention of getting the reader comfortable with basic concepts so that he or she might move forward in design education or on to additional research in certain areas. To that end, an annotated bibliography section is provided at the end of each chapter. Thinking of the information provided in each chapter as basic building blocks that allow for the discovery of the basic issues involved is a helpful approach to this book. We state this because there is much that goes into the design of a dwelling that is not covered in this book; our intent is to focus on the use and design of individual rooms (again, a building-block approach) so that the reader will have the core information required to understand the design of these individual spaces. See Figure 1-1.

This building-block or basic informational approach may bring up questions about the role of the interior designer versus the role of the architect. Clearly, the design of the totality of the structure is the role of the architect (or engineer); however, in many cases, the interior designer is taking an increasingly larger role in the design of rooms and spaces. Interior designers engaged in renovation work can take a lead role in the design of the interior architecture of a space, with a significant hand in the design of a room or many rooms. This is in contrast to notions of the interior designer as the person in charge of materials and furnishings selections only.

Home renovation and remodeling continues to be a multibillion-dollar industry providing continuing work for interior designers, architects, builders, and others in the construction trades. Home remodeling and improvements reached a record of $275 billion in 2005, with industry experts predicting continued growth for the next several years. The most common home remodeling jobs continue to be kitchen and bathroom projects. Readers will note that the detailed kitchen and bathroom information contained in this book is applicable to remodeling as well as new construction.

In new custom-home design, interior designers may take on a variety of roles from materials and furnishings selection to the design of the interior architecture of the dwelling. New-home construction has also shown continued strength, with a decade of incredibly strong sales, providing continued work for those in design, construction, and related industries. The authors believe that interior designers and design students must be well versed in the aspects of residential design covered in this book.

AN OVERVIEW: QUALITY AND QUANTITY

Readers may note that throughout the book, the authors mention the evolution of the use of rooms, room sizes, and growth of the overall size of the American home. It's worth noting that the authors have a bias toward careful consideration of the *quality of design* rather than the *quantity of space* in a given home. We hope to make clear that the successful design of space requires careful consideration of the real needs of clients measured against budgetary, code, climate, and site restrictions—all of which require careful development of a project program prior to the beginning of the actual design of the project.

The last hundred years have brought dramatic changes related to the public perception of the design, furnishing, and size of the American house. According to the National Association of Home Builders (NAHB), the "typical" American house built in 1900 was between 700 and 1200 square feet, with two or three bedrooms and one or no bathrooms (2006). The average home built in 1950 was 983 square feet, with 66 percent of homes containing 2 bedrooms or fewer. These earlier homes are quite a contrast to the 2349-square-foot average found in new single-family homes sold in 2004. A majority of these new homes (those built since 2004) have three or four bedrooms, two and one-half bathrooms or more, with at least one fireplace. A visual representation of the ever-expanding North American home can be found in Figure 1-2.

Interestingly, family size has decreased in this period to the point where the average American household size in 2004 was 2.57 persons—in contrast to 3.67 in

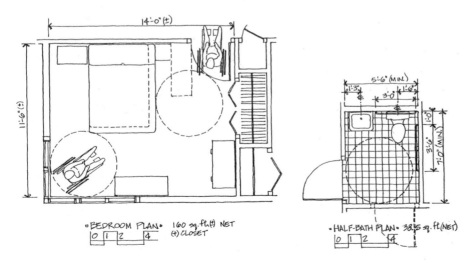

Figure 1-1 This book covers the design of houses using a room-by-room approach as an aid in understanding the use and design of each room.

Figure 1-2 The average new home in the United States has grown in size over the last 50 years—despite the fact that family size has grown smaller. However, larger is not necessarily better, and well-planned spaces need not be excessively large. Given land and construction costs, as well as environmental concerns, smaller, well-designed houses may be a future trend. Numbers for square footage shown do not include garage spaces.

1940 (according to the U.S. Census). Based on a review of available figures, new homes are larger than ever, and yet they house fewer people per building than houses held, on average, in the past. The authors argue that a larger house is not necessarily a better house, and that designing a house that works well on a functional level is more important than mere size in creating a useful and pleasant environment. Additionally, large single-family homes are currently out of the financial reach of many citizens and are seen by some as wasteful in a time when issues of sustainability are increasingly engaging the national consciousness.

Consideration of housing size and use of related resources is not unique to this publication. Architect Sarah Susanka's book *The Not So Big House* has proven very popular, has helped many people to consider quality over quantity of space, and has certainly had an impact on the design of many homes (1998). *A Pattern Language*, by Christopher Alexander and colleagues, an earlier book and one considered seminal by many, has at its core the notion that spaces should be designed for the way people really live and that good design can be accessible for all (1977).

The notion of seeking quality of design, rather than quantity of space, is shared by many, and yet larger and larger houses continue to be built to house very small family groups. This dichotomy suggests that two opposing popular views of space exist. Although the architect Phillip Johnson was once quoted as saying "architecture is the art of wasting space," clearly that was a bit tongue-in-cheek, and we concur more with Walt Whitman's notion that "Every cubic inch of space is a miracle"—or should be.

HUMAN BEHAVIOR AND HOUSING

Environmental designers—including interior designers—benefit from gaining an understanding of human behavior as it relates to privacy, territoriality, and other issues related to the built environment studied by social scientists. Privacy can be defined as having to do with the ability to control our interactions with others. According to Jon Lang: "The ability of the layout of the environment to afford privacy through territorial control is important because it allows the fulfillment of some basic human needs" (1987). Lang goes on to state that the single-family detached home "provides a clear hierarchy of territories from public to private."

Lang also states that "differences in the need for privacy are partially attributable to social group attitudes." He continues, "Norms of privacy for any group represent adaptation to what they can afford within the socioeconomic system of which they are a part." From Lang's comments we can learn that the need for privacy is consistent but varies based on culture and socioeconomic status.

The notion of territory is closely linked to privacy in terms of human behavior. There is a range of theories about the exact name and number of territories within the home. One, developed by Claire Cooper, describes the house as divided into two components: the intimate interior and the public exterior (1967). Interestingly, Cooper (now Cooper Marcus) later wrote *House as a Mirror of Self: Exploring the Deeper Meaning of Home* (1995), which traces the psychology of the relationship we have with the physical environment of our homes, and in which she refers to work being done by Rachel Sebba and Arza Churchman in studying territories within the home. Sebba and Churchman have identified areas within the home as those used by the whole family, those belonging to a subgroup (such as siblings or parents), and those belonging to an individual, such as a bedroom or a portion of a room or bed (1986). Figures 1-3a and 1-3b illustrate various theoretical approaches to territory and privacy.

The term *defensible space,* coined by Oscar Newman, refers to "a range of mechanisms—real and symbolic barriers . . . that combine to bring an environment under the control of its residents." Defensible space as described by Newman includes public, semi-public, semi-private, and private territories (1972).

For the most part, Newman's *public* spaces, such as streets and sidewalks, are those not possessed by any individual. Semi-public spaces include those areas that may be publicly owned but are cared for by homeowners such as planted parkways adjacent to sidewalks. *Semi-private* spaces can include yards or spaces owned in association (some theoreticians include porches and foyers in this category). *Private* territory is the interior of one's home or fenced areas within a yard, or, for example, the interior of a student's dorm room.

Newman's notions of defensible space and related territories have significant implications for planners, architects, and interior designers because taking them into account in designing homes can help to create spaces in which residents feel safe and have a genuine control over their immediate environment. See Figures 1-3a and 1-3b.

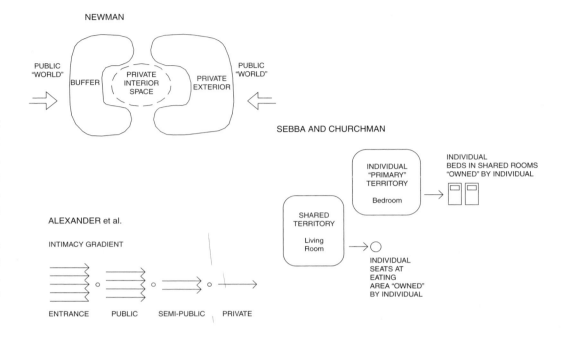

Figure 1-3b An illustration of territories related to interior space as identified by theoreticians. Newman describes the need for a buffer between the public world and private interior territories. Sebba and Churchman describe areas within a home as "shared territory" when used by all, with limited privacy; "individual primary territories" are those seen as belonging to individuals, such as a bedroom, which becomes the private sanctuary of the individual. Alexander et al. describe an intimacy gradient with the most public spaces related to the entrance leading to a sequence of increasingly private spaces.

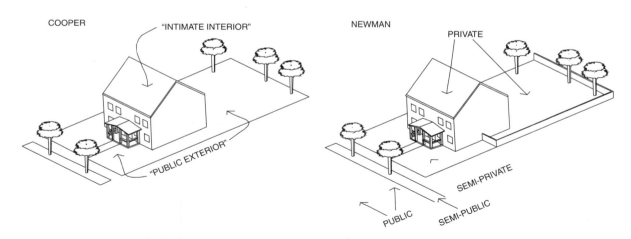

Figure 1-3a An illustration of territories as identified by theoreticians. Cooper identifies a public exterior and an intimate interior. Newman identifies public territories, which are not possessed or claimed; semi-public territories such as sidewalks, which are not "owned" but are seen as being possessed, nonetheless; semi-private territories, which are shared by owners or seen as being under surveillance by neighbors, such as front yards or shared swimming pools.

Figure 1-3c Sommer's *personal space* and Hall's *body distances*.

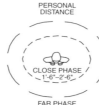
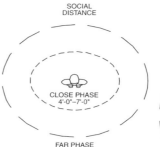
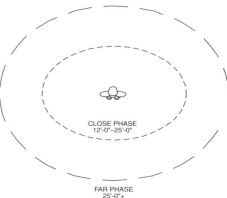

SOMMER PERSONAL SPACE

HALL INTIMATE DISTANCE
CLOSE PHASE 0"–6"
FAR PHASE 6"–18"

PERSONAL DISTANCE
CLOSE PHASE 1'-6"–2'-6"
FAR PHASE 2'-6"–4'-0"

SOCIAL DISTANCE
CLOSE PHASE 4'-0"–7'-0"
FAR PHASE 7'-0"–12'-0"

PUBLIC DISTANCE
CLOSE PHASE 12'-0"–25'-0"
FAR PHASE 25'-0"+

In *A Pattern Language*, mentioned earlier, Christopher Alexander and his colleagues describe territories as falling along an "intimacy gradient," which is a sequence of spaces within the building containing public, semi-public, and private areas. The bedroom and bathroom are the most private, and the porch or entrance space are the most public. Alexander writes, "Unless the spaces in a building are arranged in a sequence which corresponds to their degrees of privateness, the visits made by strangers, friends, guests, clients, family will always be a little awkward." See Figure 1-3b. Chapter 8 provides additional information about public and private spaces as they relate to the entry spaces.

Personal space is a term introduced by Robert Sommer in the 1960s. According to Sommer, "personal space refers to an area with an invisible boundary surrounding the person's body into which intruders may not come" (1969). See Figure 1-3c.

A similar sounding term expresses a different concept and comes from work done by Edward Hall, an anthropologist who coined the term *proximics*—for the "interrelated observations and theories of man's use of space as a specialized elaboration of culture" (1966). Hall identified four distinct body *distances* or boundaries that people will maintain in varying social situations: *intimate* (0 to 18 inches), *personal-casual* (1 foot, 6 inches to 4 feet), *social-consultative* (4 to 12 feet), and *public* (12 and beyond). Hall found that while actual spatial boundaries vary based on cultural differences, the concepts of intimate, personal, social, and public distances are consistent cross-culturally. Figure 1-3c also illustrates the spatial boundaries identified by Hall.

Hall's term *personal distance* refers to the distance maintained between friends and family members for discussion and interaction, whereas Sommer used the term *personal space* to refer to the invisible, territorial boundary around each person. Similarly, Hall's *intimate space* is a "bubble" of space around a person that can only be entered by intimates, whereas *social-consultative spaces* are those in which people feel comfortable engaging in routine social interaction for business or in conversation with strangers. *Public space* is that where there is little interaction and people are generally comfortable ignoring one another; this distance also allows one to flee when danger is sensed.

Considering Hall's spatial boundaries can be useful for designers in planning living spaces. For example, most casual social interaction takes place within personal distances. Later portions of this book focus on specific room-related dimensional information for encouraging interaction and creating privacy. It is also worth noting that in designing public and commercial spaces that encourage interaction and help users attain privacy, the designer will find it helpful to reference the work of social scientists such as Hall, Newman, Lang, and others. For those seeking additional information about environmental psychology and the related work of other social scientists, the bibliography section of this chapter includes related bibliographic information.

BASIC RESIDENTIAL BUILDING CONSTRUCTION AND STRUCTURE

Interior designers are not responsible for the design of structural or mechanical systems; however, practicing interior designers must understand the basic structural and mechanical building systems in order to work well within them. Our discussion here is limited to *common* standards of current residential construction and is a brief overview of the basic components of construction intended to supply the reader with the knowledge required to begin to gain an understanding of this topic. This book does not examine any of the myriad alternative, less common modes of construction that are used in residential construction, such as straw bale, adobe, timber frame, rammed earth, geodesic domes, and others. These and others have a place in the construction of homes, in special circumstances, and are covered in detail in specialty publications.

Houses sit on some type of concrete or wood *platform,* which together with the foundation, supports the portions of the house that rise above it. These include the following:

1. A *concrete slab* platform that sits directly on the ground. Concrete can resist termites, moisture, and rot and can serve as a suitable substrate for a wide variety of finish floor materials. The platform (slab) is most typically on a single plane, but it can be designed as a multilevel platform—a more complicated and more expensive option. In some cases, a very slight indentation in the slab is created to accommodate floor finishing materials of varying thicknesses, such as wood flooring, or to provide slopes for drainage (for example, a roll-in shower). In geographic areas subject to frost upheaval due to low temperatures and/or soil conditions (such as water-retaining clays), it is necessary to augment the concrete slab platform with a perimeter foundation wall that extends deep enough into the ground to reach stable soil. Figure 1-4 illustrates slab foundations.

2. A *wood platform* that sits off the ground to avoid rot and/or termite infestation. It can sit off the ground far enough to form a crawl space or a basement. Figure 1-5 illustrates wood-frame floors over crawl spaces and basements, and Figure 1-6a shows a basement foundation.

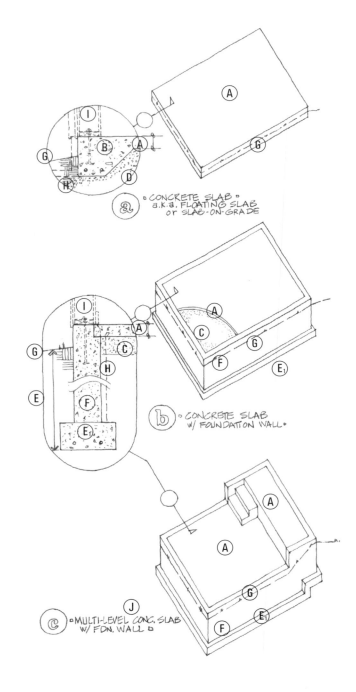

Figure 1-4 Houses sit on some type of a platform. One type is a concrete slab.

A. Slab is typically 4-inch-thick reinforced concrete and serves as suitable substrate for a full range of floor materials.

B. Perimeter of slab is thickened and reinforced.

C. Compacted granular fill (6 inches plus or minus).

D. Well-drained compacted substrate under floating slab.

E. Depth of footings (E1) (below grade) is a function of climate (frost depth) and soil conditions (some layers of soil may be more stable—under load—than others).

F. Foundation wall(s) are commonly 8-inch-thick concrete or concrete blocks (called CMUs), less commonly are brick or stone.

G. Ground line.

H. Rigid insulation (dashed line) required in cold climates.

I. Walls of the building envelope (walls and roof) are anchored to the concrete slab or foundation wall.

J. This is an uncommon multilevel slab, which can be costly but can provide for an interesting ground floor.

Figure 1-5 Another type is a wood platform that sits off the ground (on some type of foundation wall). It can sit off the ground far enough to form a crawl space or a basement as shown. Figure 1-6a also shows a basement foundation.

A. Floor joists. Floor structure is typically constructed of wood joists (the longer the span, the deeper the joist) and structural sheets (A1) (4 feet by 8 feet) of plywood or oriented strand board (OSB) that is ¾ inch plus-or-minus thick.

B. Frame walls. The floor serves as the platform for the construction of the building envelope (walls and roof) above.

C. Sill plate. Floor joists rest on this "plate" (typically 2 by 6 inches) that rests on and is anchored to the foundation.

D. Foundation wall. Typically reinforced concrete (8 to 10 inches) or concrete block, known as CMU (10 to 12 inches). The higher the foundation wall, the thicker the wall must be.

E. Insulation (shown with a dashed line). Required in colder climates.

F. Footing. Reinforced concrete. Typically the width is twice the thickness of the foundation wall and thickness (depth) is half the width.

G. Grade. Ground line, 8 inches (minimum) below the wood structure.

H. Crawl space. 18-inch height (minimum) with vapor barrier (H1).

I. Full basement. 8-foot-high foundation wall (minimum) (I1) with a 3- to 4-inch-thick concrete slab floor (I2).

J. Look-out and walk-out basements require a site that slopes sufficiently to accommodate the required change of grade and yet drain properly—away from the building.

K. Look-out basement can provide legal egress windows (K1), allowing bedroom(s) without requiring changing the footing depth.

L. Walk-out basement requires stepping down the footings and associated foundation walls in colder climates.

M. Door(s).

N. Drain tile to carry away excess groundwater and reduce the pressure of groundwater against the foundation wall.

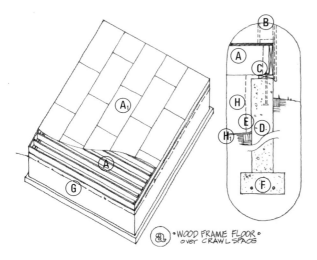

a •WOOD FRAME FLOOR•
over CRAWL SPACE

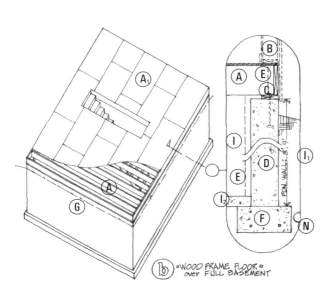

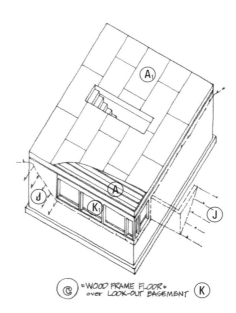

b •WOOD FRAME FLOOR•
over FULL BASEMENT

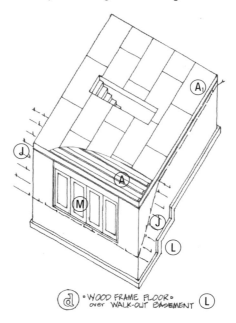

c •WOOD FRAME FLOOR•
over LOOK-OUT BASEMENT K

d •WOOD FRAME FLOOR•
over WALK-OUT BASEMENT L

There are methods of support for the wood platform apart from foundation walls. These include piers (posts) of wood, steel, or concrete supporting beams that, in turn, support the platform. While this method is less common, it is useful on hillsides or sites that are prone to flooding.

Major construction elements of a wood-frame building system are illustrated in Figures 1-6a and 1-6b. These include elements that combine to form the roof and walls, including structural and insulating elements and related finish materials, as shown in Figure 1-6a. Electrical, plumbing, heating, and air-conditioning elements are shown in Figure 1-6b, with detailed notes. Information about doors and windows are shown in Figures 1-7a to1-7c.

Figure 1-6a This is a "peel away" exploded view of a wood frame house meant as an illustration of the most common residential construction techniques currently used in the United States.

A. Roofing. Commonly asphalt shingles; less commonly clay tile, wood (cedar shingles), sheet metal (includes copper and other metals), fiber reinforced cement, and slate.

B. Roofing felt. Commonly #15 asphalt-impregnated paper.

C. Roof sheathing (also known as the roof deck). Typically 4-foot-by-8-foot-by-⁵⁄₈-inch-thick (plus or minus) sheets of structural plywood or oriented strand board (OSB).

D. Roof trusses. Commonly 2 feet on center; shown in this case as attic trusses (see Figure 2-11). Most commonly prefabricated off-site using dimensional lumber (such as 2 by 4 inch, 2 by 6 inch, etc.); less frequently fabricated of light gauge steel.

E. Subfloor. 4-foot-by-8-foot-by-¾-inch-thick (plus or minus) structural plywood or OSB; provides a walkable surface in the unfinished attic (as shown); serves as the structural base (support) for the finished flooring materials.

F. Attic insulation. Commonly fiberglass (batts, blankets, or blown-in); see Figure 2-11.

G. Gas fireplace. Requires venting to the outdoors (G1); shown here, venting to the roof.

H. Chimney. The chimney (in this case a gas vent); the chimney housing can be of light frame construction, as shown, or masonry, such as brick or stone.

I. Interior wall material. Commonly gypsum board, ½ inch thick (also called drywall) serves as a suitable surface for application of paint or wall covering. Alternatives include wood or composite paneling (boards or sheets); composite options include Homasote and medium density fiberboard (MDF).

J. Vapor barrier. Polyethylene sheet, placed on the room side of the insulation in cold climates in order to prevent water vapor from entering (from the interior) and condensing within the insulation.

K. Wall insulation. Commonly fiberglass blanket (batts) fills the entire wall stud cavity.

L. Studs. Commonly 2-by-4-inch or 2-by-6-inch wood 1 foot, 4 inches on center. An alternative is steel (C-studs). These carry roof loads to the floor and/or foundation and serve as a structural entity to attach interior and exterior sheeting/sheathing materials. Exterior studs shown here are 2 by 6 inches; interior studs are commonly 2 by 4 inches.

M. Wall sheathing. Structural sheets (commonly 4-feet-by-8-feet-by-½-inch-thick (plus or minus) fastened securely to the studs (L) to resist lateral forces (such as wind or earthquake).

N. Infiltration barrier (also known as building wrap). Resists air (wind) penetration; does not (and should not) impede water vapor transmission.

O. Exterior finish (also known as siding). Cedar shingles are shown; wood, vinyl, and metal products are used for lap or vertical siding. Alternatives to items mentioned are stucco (and stuccolike products), brick, stone veneers, and so on.

P. Underlayment. ¼-inch- to ⁵⁄₈-inch-thick wood fiber material (4-foot-by-8-foot sheets); used to level substrate under finish floor materials such as carpet; plywood is used under vinyl; cement based products are used under ceramic tile.

Q. Subfloor. ¾-inch-thick (plus-or-minus) sheets of structural plywood or OSB.

R. Floor joist. I joist is shown; dimensional framing lumber such as 2 foot by 10 foot can also be used. Allowing 12 inches for the total thickness of a structural wood floor system is a good preliminary rule of thumb.

S. Sill. Floor joists sit on a sill plate (commonly a treated 2 by 6), which is anchored to the foundation wall. A rim joist caps the ends of the floor joist and serves as edge support for the subfloor.

T. Foundation wall. Commonly concrete is 8 inches, 10 inches, or 12 inches thick and 8 feet, 9 feet, or 10 feet high (the higher the wall, the thicker the concrete required). Common alternatives include 10- or 12-inch-thick concrete masonry unit (CMU). Treated wood is used less frequently. Liquid or sheet damp-proofing is applied to the exterior prior to backfilling with soil. T1 footing, in most cases, is poured concrete; minimally twice as wide as the thickness of the wall it supports; spreads building loads over more ground surface for support.

U. Concrete slab (also known as basement slab). 4-inch-thick concrete commonly over a membrane vapor barrier (polyethylene).

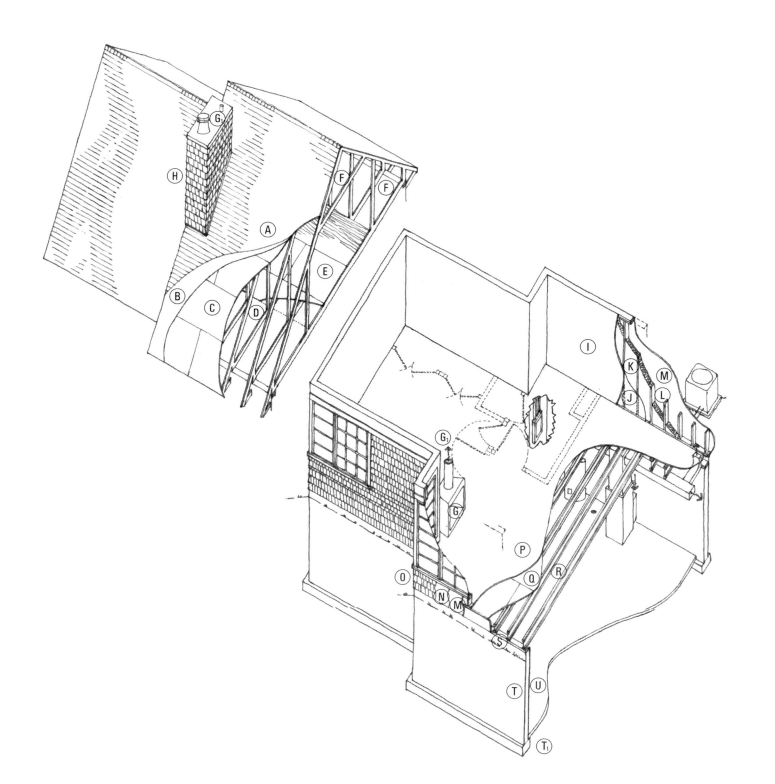

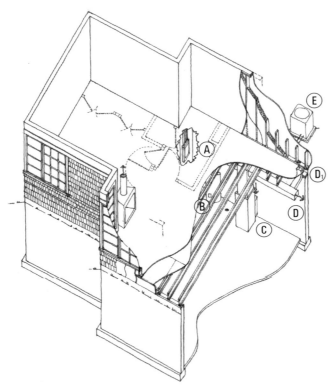

Figure 1-6b A "peel away" exploded view of a house meant as an illustration of building systems.

A. Electrical service panel. 100-amp service is minimum; a 200-amp panel is common. Service is brought to the house by underground or overhead wire, through a meter mounted at an exterior location (typically the exterior wall of the house) and then to the service panel; branch circuits feed from the service panel to a variety of outlets (also known as receptacles), light fixtures, switches, and appliances throughout the house. The International Residential Code requires 3 feet by 2 feet, 6 inches and 6 feet, 6 inches (height) of clear space in front of the service panel.

B. Water heater. Should be located near a floor drain to minimize the length of the hot-water lines that serve sinks and appliances. Heaters that burn a fuel (as compared to electric models) require a vent to the exterior.

C. Furnace/air-handling unit. Designed to heat, clean air (filter), move air (blower), and mix indoor with outdoor (fresh) air—and, with the addition of refrigeration coils and condensing unit, cool and dehumidify air. Located in this example in the basement. For houses without basements, this equipment can be located on any floor or in an accessible attic. Forced-air furnace systems, as shown, are very common because of the ability to integrate the variety of functions listed above. However, other heating unit types are available, such as radiant in-floor heating systems and baseboard convectors. Both can be accomplished with either electricity or hot-water heat systems.

D. Supply air. The furnace blower moves air through ducts to diffusers (D1) located throughout the house. Return air is ducted from the rooms back to the furnace, ideally mixing with ducted outside (fresh) air before it arrives back at the furnace to be recirculated.

E. Compressor/condensing unit. Supplies cold refrigerant to the evaporator coils at the furnace. Unit is commonly located on a concrete slab near the house and requires adequate air circulation space around the unit.

Figure 1-7a Door types and styles. Door types can be classified by operation and include swinging (these swing on hinges or pivots and are the most common), bypass sliding, pocket sliding, surface sliding (not used commonly in residences), and bifold. Door style designs include flush, panel, French, and louvered. Flush types may be solid core (1¾ inch thick) or hollow core (1⅜ inch thick). French-types include single glass panels and those divided by muntins (called divided lights).

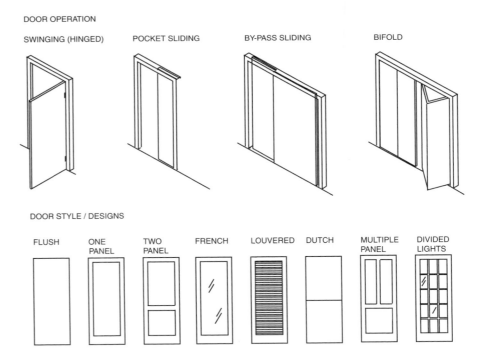

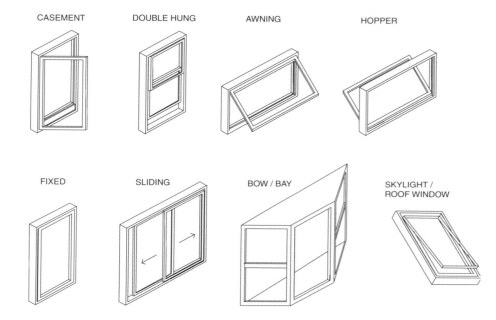

CASEMENT DOUBLE HUNG AWNING HOPPER

FIXED SLIDING BOW / BAY SKYLIGHT / ROOF WINDOW

Figure 1-7b Window types and styles include the following:

- Casement windows are hinged at the side and open outward.
- Double-hung windows open by sliding vertically.
- Awning windows are hinged at the top and open outward.
- Hopper windows are hinged at the bottom and open inward (very limited applications)—must be well protected from weather.
- Fixed windows are stationary and can be used in combination with other types—particularly double-hung and casement types.
- Sliding windows open by sliding horizontally.
- Bow and bay windows use types in combination and project outward from the building.
- Skylights and roof windows are designed for installation on sloped surfaces.
- There are also a variety of specially shaped windows that employ curved shapes or angles other than 90 degrees.

Figure 1-7c Window construction and terminology (applicable to fixed windows).

A. Rough opening
  A1. Header
  A2. Double stud at jamb(s)
  A3. Sill
B. Frame
  B1. Head
  B2. Jamb(s)
  B3. Sill
C. Trim (casing)
D. Fixed stop
E. Glass
F. Removable stop

Note: Door frame construction is similar but would contain no glass and no removable stop or sill. Additional information on doors and door framing can be found in Figure 3-11.

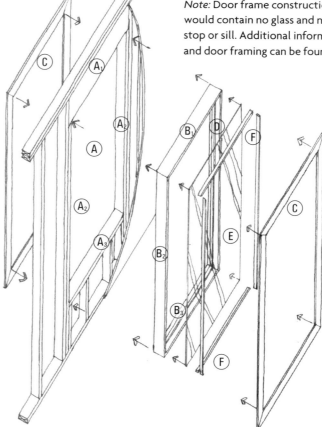

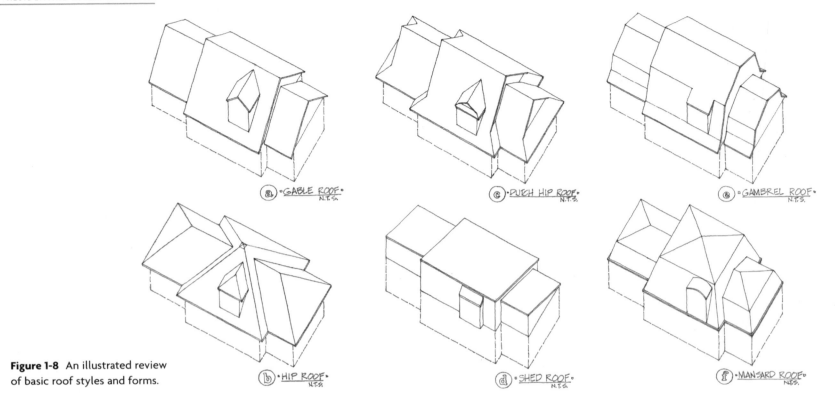

(a) ·GABLE ROOF·
N.T.S.

(c) ·DUTCH HIP ROOF·
N.T.S.

(e) ·GAMBREL ROOF·
N.T.S.

(b) ·HIP ROOF·
N.T.S.

(d) ·SHED ROOF·
N.T.S.

(f) ·MANSARD ROOF·
N.T.S.

Figure 1-8 An illustrated review of basic roof styles and forms.

Roof design and form have a significant impact upon the visual characteristics of the exterior and can also impact how the interior spaces are formed. The primary function of a roof is to shed water and to shade the interior, as well as to protect walls and windows from the ravages of the elements. Much in the way an umbrella shields a person from the weather, a roof serves to shield and protect a building. In addition, the roof of a house contributes a great deal toward the visual qualities of the building, as do the design and placement of window and door openings. Complex plan shapes generally require complex roof forms, which can be wonderful but typically add to the building cost. Figure 1-8 is a review of simple roof styles and forms.

Roofing materials and configurations for residential construction include shingles, tiles, and sheets. Shingles rely on the redundancy of at least two layers, as well as lapped joints, whereas sheets and tiles are laid as single layers with lapped joints. Asphalt is the most commonly used material for shingles; wood (common-

ly cedar) and slate are also used. Materials used for roofing tiles include concrete, clay, cement fiber, and metal.

Sheet materials used for roofing include sheet metal with standing seams (including galvanized steel, aluminum, and copper). This type of roof is constructed of interlocking panels that run vertically from the roof's ridge to the eaves. Two materials used for very flat roofs include built-up types (made from multiple layers) and single-ply roofing membranes (ethylene propylene diene monomer, or EPDM).

AN OVERVIEW OF CHAPTER TOPICS

Generally, the remainder of this first chapter is organized in a manner that is similar to later chapters covering individual rooms and spaces. The only chapter that differs organizationally is Chapter 2, which serves as an introduction to design graphics and therefore has its own unique focus. This chapter serves as an introduction to the definitions, concepts, and organizing principles that will be used throughout the book. Topics are as follows:

Accessibility, universal design, and visitability

Ergonomics and required clearances

Organizational flow

Related codes and constraints

Electrical and mechanical

Lighting (While lighting is clearly part of the electrical system, we have separated it merely for purposes of organization.)

Accessibility, Universal Design, and Visitability

Initially used to describe environments that do not present physical barriers for people with physical limitations, such as wheelchair users, the term *accessible* now describes design, including graphics and Web design, that considers the needs of users with a wide range of both physical and cognitive abilities and limitations. According to Dr. Edward Steinfeld of the Center for Inclusive Design and Environmental Access (IDEA), "Accessible design allows people with disabilities to demonstrate that they have capabilities—to work, manage a household, marry and raise children [—that] they can play a vital role in the community" (1996).

Generally, the design of private, single-family homes is not mandated by any current accessibility regulations except as noted later in this chapter. However, many homeowners seek residences that are accessible, either because they plan to "age in place" in the home (that is, grow old in one's home without having to relocate) or because they or a family member have current needs that warrant the design of accessible spaces. These two distinct scenarios present two distinct design criteria. In cases where current physical or other limitations create the need for accessible spaces, the design should address the specific needs of the owner or family member. For example, designing a home for a specific person who uses a wheelchair requires meeting a set of appropriate criteria and guidelines, whereas designing a home for a person with a vision impairment requires considering a different set of standards and guidelines.

In contrast, designing a home for aging in place or for general accessibility requires making design decisions based on basic accessibility standards and guidelines. These are presented throughout this book as part of the body of each chapter. Incorporating accessibility information for each area is intended to provide readers with a comprehensive view of accessible design. Information about regulations and standards for accessibility is provided in the "Related Codes and Constraints" section of this chapter.

The concept of *universal design* grew, in part, out of the accessible design movement but is not synonymous with accessibility. Ron Mace, an architect, product designer, and educator, is credited with coining the term; he also established what is now the Center for Universal Design at North Carolina State University.

According to the IDEA Center (SUNY at Buffalo), universal design can be defined as "an approach to the design of all products and environments to be as usable as possible by as many people as possible regardless of age, ability or situation…" and that "…results in better design and avoids the stigmatizing quality of accessible features that have been added on late in the design process or after it is complete." In "Accessible Design Can be Beautiful," Nancy Mannucci, a designer living with Multiple Sclerosis, writes, "Universal design takes into account multigenerational needs, namely the needs of children, the needs of elderly people, and those who, for whatever reason, have sensory or mobility impairments" (1988).

Universal design is an approach that is becoming increasingly embraced in product design, architecture, interior design, and urban design, as well as in graphic and Web design, that considers usability. One approach to universal design in the home is the notion of *adaptable* elements that may be designed to offer greater flexibility for a range of occupants. For example, counters that can be made so they are adjustable to adapt for users of varying heights (including those using seats and wheelchairs). Adaptable cabinets can be designed with fronts and bases that can be removed to create a clear area underneath for use by someone in a wheelchair. Illustrations of both of these examples can be found in Chapter 5, "Kitchens."

Visitability is a concept that shares some commonalities with universal design concepts; it refers to creating homes that can be visited or accessed by people with physical disabilities. Visitable residences must meet three important criteria:

1. There must be one zero-step entrance into the home.
2. All main-floor interior doors, including the bathroom, must provide 32 inches of clear passage space.
3. There must be at least a half bath (preferably a full bath) on the main floor.

Eleanor Smith is a founder of a group of advocates for this approach that is seeking to have visitability ordinances adopted by various jurisdictions or to be federally mandated. To date, a number of jurisdictions, such as Pima County, Arizona, have adopted visitability ordinances, while others, such as Urbana, Illinois, have adopted visitability ordinances for residences built using city funds.

Of the three criteria for visitability, the most difficult to achieve nationally is the zero-step entrance requirement. This could prove problematic in parts of the country where basements are commonplace. Typically, the main floor of a house with a basement is 18 to 20 inches above ground level, which could require a significant ramp for a zero-step entry. In some cases, through careful building placement and site grading, the driveway and sidewalk to the entrance can be designed with a slope of not more than 1:12 for a zero-step entry. There continues to be controversy within the building community as to the feasibility of making all new houses visitable.

Ergonomics and Required Clearances

The field of study known as *anthropometrics* provides detailed information about the dimensions and functional capacity of the human body. According to authors Julius Panero and Martin Zelnick, anthropometry is "the science dealing specifically with the measurement of the human body to determine difference in individuals, groups, etc." (1979). *Ergonomics* is the application of human-factors data, including anthropometric data, to design. An overview of basic anthropometric data, helpful in residential design, can be found in Appendix A, whereas specific ergonomic information is included in each chapter.

The last chapter of this book is devoted to circulation space; the focus of that chapter is movement from room to room. The discussion of room-specific circulation is covered within each chapter.

The introductory discussion of proximics earlier in this chapter described Edward Hall's finding that human spatial boundaries vary from one culture to another; readers should note that the clearances and ergonomic information provided throughout this book represent North American norms rather than reflecting a world view. This is particularly true of dining and leisure spaces. Many chapters also provide furniture and appliance sizes; these too are based on items currently available in North America.

Organizational Flow

The authors use the term *organizational flow* to refer to the use of activity areas or elements within a room in relationship to traffic flow. For example, in design-ing a kitchen, one must consider the various activity areas (such as cooking, cleanup, and preparation) and the ease of their use, as well as circulation within the room and to other areas within the residence. Each room in a home serves a distinct purpose, and the design of the room must support that purpose in order for the room to function well. When considering organization flow, a designer must consider the range of uses of the room and make design decisions that support those purposes. For example, bedrooms are used for sleeping but also have other uses such as clothing storage (in closets and dressers); the flow of the room should support both sleeping and accessing stored items, as well as additional activities that occur within the room, such as watching television or working on a computer. Such issues of organizational flow are discussed in detail in the various chapters of this book.

Related Codes and Constraints

Building codes, zoning regulations, and fire, health, and safety codes all influence the design of buildings and their interior elements and provide constraints to the overall design. A basic understanding of the codes and regulations that affect residential design is required as projects are undertaken.

Building codes generally govern the construction of buildings based on the type of occupancy intended for the building. This means that residences are generally regulated by standards different from those regulating public spaces, and public spaces are regulated in varying ways based on intended use. Building codes are adopted by cities, states, and/or municipalities and, in rural areas, often by county agencies. In some cases, states adopt a statewide residential building code; however, often codes adopted within states can vary. Additionally, states and municipalities can add local requirements or amendments to generally adopted model codes to allow for incorporation of regional variation or geographic factors.

Prior to 2000, three model codes were used widely throughout the United States: the Uniform Building Code (UBC), the Building Code Officials and Code Administration National Building Code (BOCA), and the Standard Code. In 2000 these code entities came together to prepare the International Building Code (IBC), which was written to serve as a consolidated model code for commercial and public buildings Many states and municipalities have adopted the IBC, although it is not currently as consistently adopted as the name implies. Many code jurisdictions have intentions of adopting the IBC in the future, however.

IBC also publishes related codes including the International Residential Code (IRC)—which is used in the regulation of single-family homes, the International Mechanical Code, and the International Plumbing Code. Please see the "Electrical and Mechanical" section of this chapter for related information about electrical-code requirements called for by the IRC, Section E. The IRC does not cover multi-family dwellings, dorms, apartments, nursing homes, or assisted-living facilities; these are covered by the IBC.

Throughout this book the International Residential Code is the code that is referenced. Referencing this single code is useful for purposes of clarity; however, not all locales or code jurisdictions have currently adopted this code, and this code does not regulate multifamily housing. Therefore, prior to beginning any project, the designer must research the local code and all related regulations where the project is intended to be built.

Zoning regulations control building size, height, location, setbacks, and use. These regulations are adopted by local municipalities and vary greatly throughout the United States. In some areas, there are very strict zoning codes that control many facets of a building's design, while in others, there are few zoning restrictions. As with the building code, zoning regulations should be researched prior to beginning the design of any project.

Additional codes and regulations that govern the design of buildings include energy codes as well as fire and flammability standards. There are also additional standards developed by testing and other agencies that are incorporated into model codes and federal regulations. Such testing agencies include the American National Standards Institute (ANSI) and the American Society for Testing and Materials (ASTM).

Federal regulations that govern the design of multifamily dwellings include the Fair Housing Amendments Act (FHAA), a civil rights law requiring that privately and publicly funded multifamily dwellings (those on the first floor and all in buildings with elevators) provide limited accessibility. In addition, the Uniform Federal Accessibility Standards (UFAS) require a percentage of units within federally funded multifamily dwellings to be accessible.

Early residential accessibility standards were published in 1980 in the ANSI A117.1 standards, which included bathroom and kitchen accessibility standards. The most current version, ANSI A117.1-2003, which was approved in 2003, provides standards for two types of accessible units: Type A and Type B. In brief, Type A units (Section 1003) are fully accessible, while Type B (Section 1004) provide limited accessibility.

Type B units are consistent with Fair Housing Act Requirements, while Type A units are consistent with UFAS. A review of Type A and Type B standards will show that Type B standards are less strict—however, Type B standards are also more broadly applied. ANSI A117.1-2003 also sets standards for accessible communications features for dwelling and sleeping units (Section 1005). Information about kitchen and bath layouts that meet ANSI standards for Type A and B units may be found in Appendix B.

The Americans with Disabilities Act (ADA) is also civil rights legislation that includes federal accessibility guidelines (known as ADAAG). The ADA requires that *public* buildings (including those owned privately) are designed so that they accommodate people with disabilities. ADA guidelines share many similarities with ANSI standards. While the ADA has significant implications for the interior design of public places and should understood by the practicing designer, it does not directly impact the design of single-family homes— except in a small portion of housing built with public funding.

Electrical and Mechanical

These issues are covered in each chapter as they relate to individual rooms and spaces. With that said, there are some general rules for locating electrical switches and convenience outlets, with typical exceptions being in kitchens, bathrooms, and utility spaces. In most other locations, the on/off switches for overhead or general lights are best located close to the room entry door on the latch side of the doorway when possible. In larger rooms with more than one entrance, a second on/off switch can be employed in another convenient location; this is called a "three-way switch." Where a number of light fixtures are used for general lighting, a single switch can be used to control several fixtures and outlets.

The International Residential Code (IRC, section E3893.2) requires that "at least one wall-switch-controlled lighting outlet shall be installed in every habitable room and bathroom." One exception to this requirement is "in other than kitchens and bathrooms, one or more receptacles controlled by a wall switch shall be considered equivalent to the required lighting outlet." The IRC (section E3803.3) requires additional locations for a wall-switch-controlled lighting outlet in hallways, stairways, and attached and detached garages with electric power. This section of the code also requires that a wall-switch-controlled lighting outlet be installed on the exterior of egress doors with grade-level access.

The on/off switch should be mounted at 44 to 48 inches off the floor. Because there are two receptors, typical household electrical outlets are referred to as

Figure 1-9 Switching and outlet locations for standing adult and seated (wheelchair) users.

1. Standard switch placement is convenient to latch side of door and centered at 48 inches above the floor.
2. Standard wall outlet placement is one outlet for each 12 feet of wall area in general living spaces. Actual locations in individual rooms will vary based on room design and possible furniture arrangement.
3. For wheelchair users, switches are best located centered 42 to 44 inches above the floor and never higher than 48 inches above the floor.
4. For wheelchair users, wall outlets are best placed 15 to 17 inches above the floor and never lower than 15 inches above the floor.

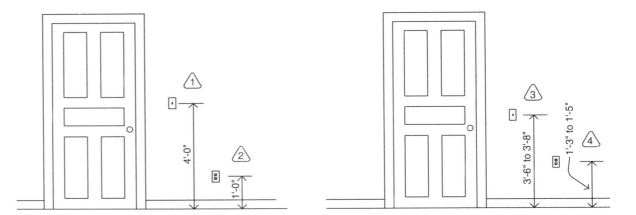

duplex outlets or *duplex receptacles*. These outlets are commonly placed about 12 inches off the floor, as shown in Figure 1-9.

This is rather low for wheelchair and other users. For these users, outlets are best placed between 15 and 17 inches off the floor and wall switches should be placed no higher than 48 inches off the floor, as shown in Figure 1-9. The Center for Inclusive Design and Environmental Access indicates "wall outlets should be located no lower than 15 inches from the floor" and controls "that will be used frequently should be within the 24–48 in. 'comfort range.'" Such controls include thermostats and alarm systems. It is worth noting that placing controls in this comfort range and locating receptacles between 15 and 17 inches above the floor makes rooms meet universal design criteria and adds no extra expense, making them worth considering on many projects.

A general rule of thumb for electrical outlet placement is one duplex receptacle per 12 feet of wall space in order to avoid the use of extension cords (standard appliance cords are often 6 feet long). Following such rules can be a good starting point; however, the placement of outlets must be considered in relation to the design and layout of the room. It is also important to consider the various possibilities for furniture placement so that the outlets can be designed in a way that is useful for a variety of scenarios.

The term *mechanical* is an umbrella term used to describe the heating, ventilation, air-conditioning (known together as HVAC), and plumbing elements of a building. With very few exceptions, all residences in the United States are required

by code to be heated; for example, the International Residential Code calls for heating to a minimum of 68°F when the winter temperature is below 60°F. Cooling may not be required by code, but it is seen as necessary by most people in many parts of the country.

The most common solution for providing heat is a furnace that burns a fossil fuel (such as natural gas, liquid propane, or heating oil) and less commonly wood, charcoal, and in some cases coal, or the furnace will derive heat from electric resistance coils or a heat pump. In almost all cases, the furnace uses a fan that moves air, via ducts, to the various rooms where heat is required. This type of system can be equipped to clean (with filters), humidify, and—with the addition of a compressor or condensing unit—cool the air (which in the process dehumidifies the air).

Other heating systems are available, such as a boiler that heats water in tandem with a pump that moves the heated water to a baseboard convector unit; a similar result can be achieved with electric resistance baseboard units. Hot water can also be delivered to radiant-heating pipes located in the floors of a residence, with similar results achieved with resistance heating in the floors. All of the methods described do not work to accomplish the cooling, cleaning, and dehumidifying that forced-air systems allow; these must be achieved through the use of separate equipment.

Air-to-air heat pumps are commonly used in temperate climates; these remove heat from the inside air in warm weather and work in reverse to provide heat to the interior during colder weather. In these systems, air is delivered much like the forced air described previously.

Increasingly, consumers are seeking alternative sources for heating and cooling homes. Geothermal heat pumps use the relatively constant temperature of the soil or surface water as a heat source for a heat pump that can provide heating (and cooling). These use buried tubing submerged in soil or a nearby lake or pond. Many consumers find the initial higher cost of geothermal heat pumps offset by energy savings and special energy and possible tax incentive programs. For years solar energy has been used to heat homes, and a number of passionate advocates see this as a realistic solution to energy independence and cost reduction. A great deal of additional information is available on designing solar heating and geothermal heating and cooling systems. These areas are clearly not the purview of this book, but designers are encouraged to seek additional information about these systems.

While interior designers are not responsible for the design of such heating, ventilation, and air-conditioning systems, they should understand the various types of systems and their impact on the design of interior spaces. For example, knowing that hot-water heat may require the use of baseboard convector units and that the location of such units will have a direct impact on the design and layout of interior spaces is useful.

Forced-air systems require the use of return-air grills and supply-air registers/diffusers. These are available in a range of styles and in types such as baseboard, wall, and floor units. Location of these items has an impact on the layout of a room and the level of comfort found there; for example, a favorite seating location that receives a constant blast of air will not remain a favorite for long. In addition, the visual qualities of grills, diffusers, and registers should be in keeping with the overall design intent of the project—a Victorian-style grill placed within a mid-century modern interior may look ridiculous. Placement of grills, diffusers, and registers in relationship to trim and architectural details is also worth careful consideration.

Lighting

Information about lighting specific rooms and spaces is provided in this book as a means of acquainting students with basic concepts related to planning and design. In no way is the information provided intended to be a significant source of a student's lighting design education. Instead, information offered is introductory in nature and related to the overall design of rooms and spaces. So that the student can understand and work with the information provided in each chapter, an overview of terminology and basic lighting concepts is provided here. The bibliography at the end of this chapter includes lighting design publications helpful for more in-depth study.

Types of lighting discussed for various rooms include ambient, accent, task, and decorative lighting. *Ambient light* is general illumination that provides a uniform light level throughout the area or room. According to Randall Whitehead (2004), in residences "the best ambient light comes from sources that bounce illumination off the ceiling and walls." This type of lighting is referred to as *indirect lighting*, which means that light arrives at a given surface after being reflected from one or more surfaces, which tends to cause less glare than *downlights* (defined as those sources that direct light downward). Whitehead adds that dark ceilings make this type of lighting ineffective. There are also a number of direct-light sources that provide ambient lighting. Figure 1-10 illustrates ambient light sources.

Figure 1-10 Ambient light is general illumination that provides a uniform light level. Task lighting aids in performing work such as reading or preparing food. Accent lighting functions to illuminate objects or special features, and decorative lighting tends to draw attention to itself in the form of a decorative element such as a chandelier or wall sconce (decorative elements can add to a room's ambient lighting).

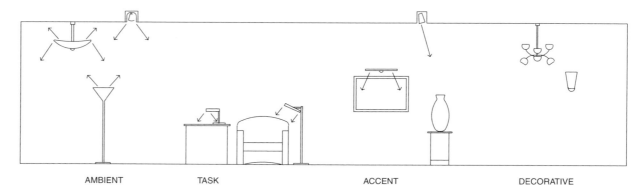

AMBIENT   TASK   ACCENT   DECORATIVE

Also referred to as *focal lighting*, *accent lighting* illuminates features, objects, and/or specific areas. This type accents items or creates focal points and can add a level of interest to the general or ambient lighting. Well-planned accent lighting puts the focus on the desired objects rather than the light source or fixture. Generally, using only accent lighting in a room without giving thought to ambient lighting creates clusters of darkness within rooms. Figure 1-10 illustrates some accent light sources.

As its name implies, *task lighting* has a job to do; it aids in performing work and specific tasks. In a residence, many of these tasks are performed at table or counter height, requiring that the work surface is illuminated. Considering the type of task performed and the body positions required to complete them helps the designer make task-lighting choices; for example, at kitchen counters and work tables, light coming directly from the ceiling is blocked by the human body (or head), creating shadows at the work surface rather than illumination. Figure 1-10 illustrates some task light sources.

Decorative lighting is ornamental in nature and provides interest based on its design and material qualities. Unlike accent lighting, decorative lighting functions to show itself off and make a visual statement. Decorative lighting can be used to accent elements and spaces or to add interest to ambient lighting, yet its function is typically secondary to the visual impact of the light source itself. Figure 1-10 illustrates some decorative light sources.

Basic lighting design requires an understanding of *glare*, which is defined as "loss of visibility and/or the sensation of discomfort associated with bright light within the field of view" by the Lighting Research Center (at Rensselaer Polytechnic University). There are two types of glare: *direct glare*, which results from bright light in the field of view, and *reflected glare*, which results from reflections in the field of view (including surfaces and reading material). Locating light sources out of the line of vision or shielding them in some manner can prevent direct glare. Reflected glare can be minimized by using less reflective surfaces and placing the light source so that it is not directly above but rather at an angle to the surface and/or viewer.

The term *luminaire* is used to describe the complete lighting unit consisting of (1) a lamp or lamps (the general public calls these lightbulbs) and (2) the parts (housing) necessary to distribute the light, position and protect the lamps, and connect the unit to the power supply. *Light fixtures* are luminaires that are permanently affixed to the architecture of the building. Portable luminaries are, as the name implies, easily moved; these include what the general public calls table lamps, desk lamps, floor lamps, and so on. A range of luminaires and fixtures may be used to create ambient, accent, task, and decorative light; some of these are shown in Figure 1-11. Recessed luminaires are illustrated in Figure 1-12.

Daylight is a term that correctly refers to what most people call natural light; it is light produced by solar radiation and includes direct sunlight as well as reflected light. The term *daylighting* refers to the process of designing buildings to utilize daylight. True daylighting requires careful consideration of the totality of the architecture of the building, so that the orientation of the building to the site, the location and size of building openings, and adequate shading devices are incorporated into the building design. Daylighting is a useful component of sustainable design because it does not require electricity and can save energy on building cooling as well, when done properly Currently daylighting is a strategy employed more commonly for public buildings than for private homes.

Regardless of how well daylighting is incorporated into a building design, electric light (referred to by the general public as artificial light) is required when it becomes dark outside. The appearance of electric light is rated by the *color rendering index* (CRI), which according to a glossary produced by the Lighting Research Center (at Rensselaer Polytechnic University) is

"A technique for describing the effect of a light source on the color appearance of objects" being illuminated, with a CRI of 100 representing the reference condition (and thus the maximum CRI possible). In general, a lower CRI indicates that some colors may appear unnatural when illuminated by the lamp."

For residences, a CRI of 80 to 89 provides color rendering where color quality is important in residential applications, such as spaces where the visual quality of colors, materials, finishes, artwork, and accessories are an important part of the experience of the room. In some cases, such as residential, utility, and storage spaces, a CRI lower than 80 is acceptable.

Another measure of color appearance called *color temperature* or *correlated color temperature* (CCT) "describes the color appearance of the actual light produced in terms of its warmth or coolness," according to the Lighting Research Center. Color temperature is measured using the Kelvin (K) temperature scale, with lower temperatures (3000 K and lower) used to describe a warm source and high temperatures (4000 K and above) to describe a cool source. Typical incandescent lamps and warm fluorescent lamps are lower than 4000 K.

Figure 1-11 Luminaire is a term used to describe a complete lighting unit. Luminaires may be portable, pendant-mounted (also known as suspended), surface-mounted on walls or ceilings (decorative luminaries mounted on walls are often called sconces), or track-mounted (the track can be mounted on the ceiling or suspended and can include track heads or pendants). Other options include recessed and semi-recessed fixtures, as well as other architectural lighting options (this term applies to lighting permanently affixed to the architecture of the building) such as cove and valance lighting. More information on recessed luminaries can be found in Figure 1-12.

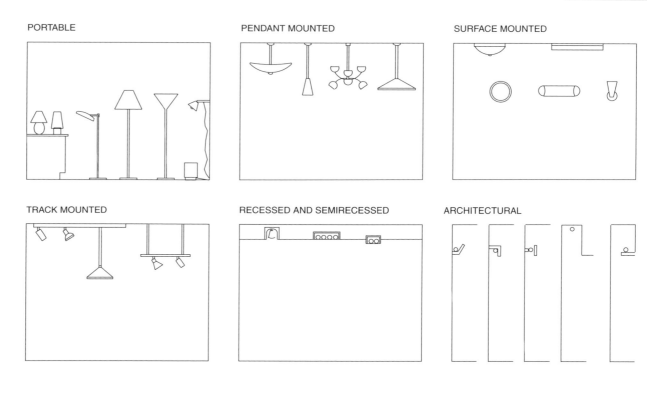

PORTABLE

PENDANT MOUNTED

SURFACE MOUNTED

TRACK MOUNTED

RECESSED AND SEMIRECESSED

ARCHITECTURAL

RECESSED DOWNLIGHTS

RECESSED WALL WASH   ADJUSTABLE RECESSED

RECESSED TROFFERS

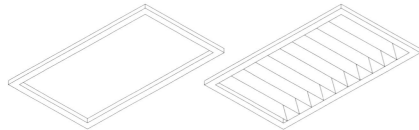

Figure 1-12 Recessed luminaires include recessed downlights, and recessed adjustable downlights can be used for ambient lighting. Another type, recessed wall washers, direct light down at an angle and are used for accent lighting. Recessed troffers are square or rectangular luminaries that house fluorescent lamps. They are available with diffusers or with louvers. Those with diffusers are used to provide ambient light, whereas louvers can direct light for tasks such as computer work. Surface-mounted versions with diffusers are used more commonly in residential settings.

Designers must understand the roles of lamps in lighting design (remember, these are called lightbulbs by the general public). Lamps are divided into three broad categories: incandescent, fluorescent, and high-intensity discharge. Within each category there is variety in how the lamps look and perform and the quality of light produced. Incandescent lamps create light as electricity flows through a filament, heating it and making it glow. Incandescent lamps are popular due to the color quality of light they create (remember the CRI and CCT). However, they use a great deal of energy to produce limited light. Only 10 to 15 percent of the energy that goes into the filament is emitted as light; the remainder is generated as heat.

Incandescent lamps come in a range of shapes and sizes, with a letter designating shape and a number indicating the maximum diameter of the lamp (in eighths of an inch). For example, for a common A19 household lamp, the *A* refers to a standard bulb shape (A for "arbitrary") and the *19* stands for 19 eighths of an inch (or 2 3/8 inches). Figure 1-13 illustrates the shapes of other incandescent lamps. Other terms referred to in code have to do with the glass used in the lamp, such as clear or frosted types. The frost effect is referred to as *inside frost* based on the location of the glass treatment.

There are also *reduced-wattage* incandescent lamps, which are shaped similarly to other incandescent types but use a different gas inside the lamp that

Figure 1-13 Lamps are divided into three broad categories: incandescent, fluorescent, and high-intensity discharge (not shown). Incandescent and fluorescent are used most commonly in residences. Incandescent lamps come in a range of shapes and sizes, with a letter designation referring to shape and a number indicating the maximum diameter of the lamp (in eighths of an inch). Halogen lamps are another type of incandescent lamp. PAR, R, and ER lamps are incandescent reflector lamps that create directional beams. A range of fluorescent lamp shapes and types are available, including straight tubular (or linear), u-shaped, twin-tube, and circular (properly called circline) lamps. In addition, there are compact fluorescent lamps.

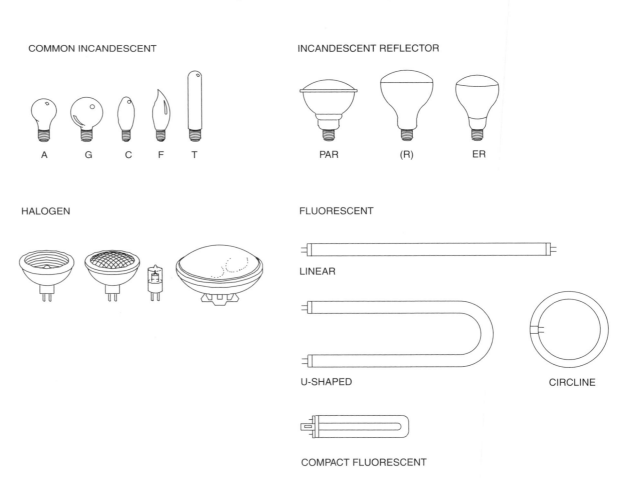

COMMON INCANDESCENT

A   G   C   F   T

INCANDESCENT REFLECTOR

PAR   (R)   ER

HALOGEN

FLUORESCENT

LINEAR

U-SHAPED

CIRCLINE

COMPACT FLUORESCENT

allows different wattages or, in some cases, a longer lamp life. *Halogen* lamps (also called *tungsten-halogen*) are another type of incandescent lamp in which the filament is inside a halogen-filled capsule. The use of halogen gas allows lamps of a similar wattage to produce more light. These can become quite hot, requiring special care or lamp protection. Dimming these lamps changes the color dramatically and can shorten lamp life.

Specialized *incandescent reflector* lamps have reflective coatings that create a directional light source and are available in a range of beam spreads from spot to flood. PAR lamps (for parabolic aluminized reflector), R lamps (for common reflector), and ER lamps (for ellipsoidal reflector) types are all incandescent reflector types.

Incandescent lamps are also available in *low-voltage* versions, which require transformers to change primary power (120 volts) to the required low voltage (often 12 volts). This type includes MR16 (the *MR* is for mirrored reflector; the *16* is for 16 eighths of an inch, or 2 inches) and PAR 36 lamps, which are often used for accent or display lighting. Figure 1-13 shows some halogen lamps.

Fluorescent lamps are coated glass tubes filled with gas; light is produced when the gas reacts to electrical energy, producing ultraviolet light, which in turn is absorbed by the coating and produces visible light. Fluorescent lamps require ballasts within the luminaire or lamp. These provide the starting voltage and control the current when in use. Compared to standard incandescent lamps, fluorescent lamps produce minimal heat and are more energy-efficient. Lamp color, such as "cool white" or "warm white," is created by the chemicals (called *phosphors*) used to coat the lamps and is controlled by the manufacturer.

A range of fluorescent lamp shapes and types are available, including *straight tubular* (or linear), *u-shaped*, *twin-tube*, and *circular* (properly called *circline*) lamps. In addition, there are *compact fluorescent* lamps, which, as the name implies, are smaller in size (allowing them to fit in smaller locations). Compact fluorescent lamps also require the use of a ballast, which may be integral to the lamp or may be part of a separate module that can be replaced separately. Figure 1-13 includes illustrations of some fluorescent lamps.

Another type of lamp, known as *high-intensity discharge* (HID), operates using a current and gas or vapor under high pressure to produce light. These also require a ballast. While highly energy-efficient, these are not widely used in residential interiors except for applications where lights are left on for extended periods of time, such as for security or in multifamily stairway applications.

Additional issues that relate to residential lighting involve lamp bases, which come in a range of sizes and types and are referred to by name. For example, a standard A lamp with a screw-in base is referred to as a *standard* base, whereas a smaller flame-tip shaped lamp (for use in a chandelier) may have a *medium* or *candelabra* base. Also, compact fluorescent lamps are available with an integral ballast and a standard screw-in base for use in a standard socket.

Controls for lighting include switches, dimmers, timers, sensors, central controls, and motion detectors. This large family of controls can be divided into two categories: manual and automatic controls.

Switches and dimmers are commonly used manual controls, with switches used to turn lamps on and off and dimmers used to control the light output of some lamps. Timers are automatic controls that are intended to control lamps based on a designated time period. Controls vary a great deal in complexity and cost, with the more advanced and costly options used in many cases as part of a complete home security system.

BIBLIOGRAPHY

(Annotations where appropriate.)

Alexander, Christopher, et al. *A Pattern Language*. New York: Oxford University Press, 1977. A seminal work and part of a series that is based on the notion that people can design and build their own structures. Urban planning, the design of dwellings, and details and ornament are covered. Spatial hierarchy, issues related to privacy, and the design of spaces that take advantage of daylight are all described and illustrated. The quotations from this chapter are from page 127.

Ching, Francis. *Home Renovation*. New York: Van Nostrand Reinhold, 1983. A good general guide to residential design as it relates to renovation. Out of print but available from used booksellers.

Ching, Francis, and Cassandra Adams. *Building Construction Illustrated*, 3rd ed., Hoboken, NJ, John Wiley & Sons, 2001.

Cooper, Clare. "The Fenced Back Yard—Unfenced Front Yard—Enclosed Porch." *Journal of Housing*, 1967. For additional information please see the notes under Jon Lang below.

———. "The House as a Symbol of the Self." In *Designing for Human Behavior*. Edited by J. Lang, C. Burnette, W. Moleski, and D. Vachon. Stroudsburg, PA: Dowden, Hutchinson & Ross, 1974.

Hall, Edward. *The Hidden Dimension*. New York: Doubleday, 1966. While this book is often quoted, it is also rarely read, but it should be by more designers and educators. Although some current theorists disagree with Hall, this pivotal book has many concepts worth considering.

Lang, Jon. *Creating Architectural Theory: The Role of the Behavioral Sciences in Environmental Design*. New York: Van Nostrand Reinhold, 1987. An excellent overview covering exactly what the subtitle implies: a description of the work of psychologists, anthropologists, sociologists, and others as it relates to the built environment. The discussion of interior and exterior territories from early work by Claire Cooper Marcus comes from Chapter 14, which covers privacy and territoriality in detail. This title is currently out of print but available from used booksellers.

Rensselaer University Lighting Research Center. Web Glossary. 2006. http://www.lrc.rpi.edu/programs/nlpip/glossary.asp

Mannucci, Nancy. "Accessible Design Can Be Beautiful." *Inside MS: The Magazine for Members of the National MS Society* 16(3), 1998.

Marcus Cooper, Clare. *House as a Mirror of Self: Exploring the Deeper Meaning of Home*, Berkeley, CA: Conari Press, 1995.

National Association of Home Builders. *Facts, Figures, and Trends*. March, 2006. www.nahb.org/publication_details.aspx?publicationID=2028. Information about housing size and homeowner preferences discussed throughout this book was first found easily within the pages of this publication (free download).

Newman, Oscar. *Defensible Space: Crime Prevention through Urban Design*. New York: Macmillan, 1972.

———. *Design Guidelines for Creating Defensible Space*. National Institute of Law Enforcement and Criminal Justice. Washington, DC: US Government Printing Office, 1976.

———. "Defensible Space." *Journal of the American Planning Association* 61(2): 149, 1995.

Panero, Julius, and Martin Zelnik. *Human Dimension and Interior Space*. New York: Whitney, 1979. A quintessential guide to human dimensions.

Preiser, Wolfgang, and Elaine Ostroff, eds. *Universal Design Handbook*. New York: McGraw-Hill, 2001. A huge (literally) compilation of articles, presentations, and research papers; international in scope, with contributions from leaders in the movement.

Russel, Leslie, and Kathryn Conway. *The Lighting Pattern Book for Homes*. Troy, NY: Rensselaer Polytechnic Institute, 1993. This publication provides excellent information about luminaires, lamps, color quality, and efficacy and includes a useful glossary of lighting terms—with a clear focus on energy efficiency. Published by Rensselaer's Lighting Research Center, an entity with a helpful lighting research Web site at www.lrc.rpi.edu/index.asp.

Sebba, Rachel, and Arza Churchman. "The Uniqueness of the Home." *Architecture & Behaviour* 3(1): 7–24, 1986. Journal archives from this organization can be found at www.colloquia.ch/en/journal.htm.

Sommer, Robert. *Personal Space: The Behavioral Basis of Design*. Englewood Cliffs, NJ: Prentice Hall, 1969.

Steinfeld, Edward. *A Primer on Accessible Design*, v. 1.0. Buffalo: Center for Inclusive Design and Environmental Access, SUNY at Buffalo, 1996. A little pamphlet full of helpful information that can serve as an introduction to accessible design.

Susanka, Sarah. *The Not So Big House: A Blueprint for the Way We Really Live*. Newtown, CT: The Taunton Press, 1998. This book started a bit of a revolution as a practical guide to thinking about how people really live.

Whitehead, Randall. *Residential Lighting: A Practical Guide*. Hoboken, NJ: John Wiley & Sons, 2004. An easy-to-follow lighting primer that describes using "layered" lighting in residences.

Whitman, Walt. *Leaves of Grass*. New York: Oxford University Press, 2005.

CHAPTER 2

VISUAL THINKING AND DESIGN GRAPHICS

A range of types of drawings, sketches, and diagrams are used in the design of buildings and spaces within buildings and are used to explore and refine ideas and information as the design process takes place. Each type of drawing has a specific role or roles in the design process.

Writing in *Interior Design Illustrated*, Francis Ching identifies three basic stages of design process: analysis, synthesis, and evaluation. According to Ching, *analysis* involves defining and understanding the problem, *synthesis* involves the formulation of possible solutions, and *evaluation* involves a critical review of the strengths and weaknesses of the proposed solutions and alternatives. To these three stages, Ching adds *design development*, a generally accepted phase of architectural and interiors practice, which is the portion of the process when the design is fully refined, detailed, and ready for incorporation into construction drawings and documents.

To properly introduce readers to the various types, design graphics are covered in two ways in this chapter: first, in general terms with simple introductory graphics and, second, in relationship to a specific sample project with more detailed drawings and graphics.

Project analysis involves identifying requirements, constraints, limitations, and conditions. The identification of these items is generally referred to as *project programming*. Pat Guthrie, writing in *The Interior Designer's Portable Handbook*, states "programming is a process leading to the statement of an architectural problem and the requirements to be met in offering a solution" (2004). As Peña et al. write in *Problem Seeking: An Architectural Programming Primer,* programming has been referred to as "problem seeking," while the actual project design has been referred to as "problem solving" (1987). Residential programming requires a careful analysis of all project criteria and constraints, as well as research into site conditions and local zoning and codes, and often results in written lists, problem statements, and basic diagrams.

Diagrams are used to bring quantitative and qualitative information together with visual information so that the designer can understand and synthesize it more easily. It could be said that diagrams aid the designer in the movement from the analysis to the synthesis phases of a project, or stated another way, diagrams can serve as a bridge between programming and preliminary project design.

One type of diagram, commonly used as designers begin the preliminary design of residential projects, is known as the *bubble diagram*. These diagrams serve to visually represent project adjacency requirements and can also represent very rough proportional information. For example, client requirements for an addition that adds a painting studio, with a small bathroom, that is attached to the house through a gallerylike space with a separate entrance could be represented with a bubble diagram in which the bubbles represent not only room locations and adjacencies but rough proportional information as well. See Figure 2-1a.

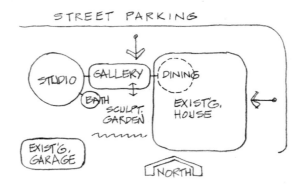

Figure 2-1a A bubble diagram representing client requirements for an addition requiring a painting studio and a small bathroom. The addition must be attached through a gallerylike space with a separate entrance. The bubbles represent not only room locations and adjacencies but rough proportional information.

Generally, designers create many bubble diagrams as a means of generating multiple ideas. Later, the diagrams are reviewed and evaluated. They may be shown to the client for evaluation, and on some occasions, another round of diagrams is generated, while in other instances, the designer begins more refined project planning based on a successful diagram or a series of diagrams. Other diagrams and images may be employed as well, including sketches and doodles drawn by the designer to represent some visual imagery suggested in programming or client interviews. Figure 2-1b is a massing sketch of the painting studio shown in Figure 2-1a.

It is worth noting that sketches, such as the one shown in Figure 2-1b, perspective drawings, and three-dimensional models are used throughout the design process in order to help the designer visualize and refine the design, and communicate the design (or design options) to clients and other interested parties, such as investors and board members. Such drawings and models are incredibly important to the overall success of any design project. They are not covered in this book because they fall outside its scope, but they should be seen as integral to the design process and used for every project.

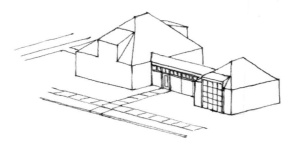

Figure 2-1b A preliminary sketch for the project represented in Figure 2-1a.

ORTHOGRAPHIC PROJECTIONS

More refined project planning and design, which takes place as the designer moves through the design process, requires very specific drawings known as *orthographic projections*, which include plans, elevations, and sections. These drawings are created by projecting visual information onto an imaginary plane known as the picture plane. This direct projection of an object's dimensions allows for orthographic projections to retain true shape and proportion, making these drawings accurate and precise and allowing them to be scaled to exact measurements.

Orthographic projection creates fragmentary views of an object, resulting in the need for multiple drawings. This means that, because of their fragmentary nature, orthographic projections become parts of a system and are mutually dependent on one another. By their nature, orthographic projections appear flat and lack the three-dimensional quality of perspective drawings.

One way to visualize orthographic projection is to imagine a small building (in this case a writer's studio) enclosed in a transparent box. Each transparent plane of the enclosing box serves as the picture plane for that face of the object as the drawings are created. See Figures 2-2a, 2-2b, and 2-2c.

The view through the top plane of the enclosing box is called a *plan* (in this case a roof plan). In a plan view, only those elements seen when looking directly down at the object through the picture plane are drawn, as shown in Figure 2-2a. The views through the picture planes that form the sides of the enclosing box are called elevations. *Elevations* depict only what is visible when viewed directly through the picture plane on that side or portion of the building (Figure 2-2a).

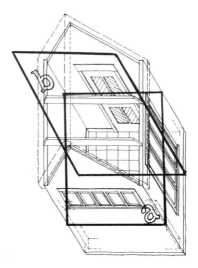

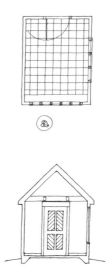

Figure 2-2b Some orthographic projection drawings are sectional views drawn as though the picture plane slices through the building, exposing the structure. Item **a** is a floor plan drawn as though the picture plane has made a horizontal slice, and item **b** illustrates a building section drawn as though the picture plane has been inserted vertically.

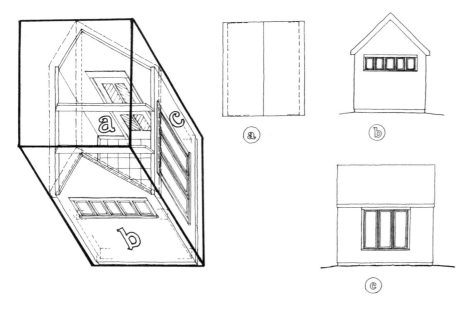

Figure 2-2a Orthographic projection drawings are drawn as though seen through a clear glass box, in which each plane of the box serves as a picture plane for each drawing. Item **a** represents a roof plan, drawn as though traced directly from above using the top plane of the enclosing box as the picture plane. Item **b** represents the elevation (rear of the building as seen through the front of the box), drawn as though traced directly using the side (rear) plane of the enclosing box as the picture plane. Item **c** represents a side elevation, drawn as though traced directly using the side plane of the enclosing box as the picture plane.

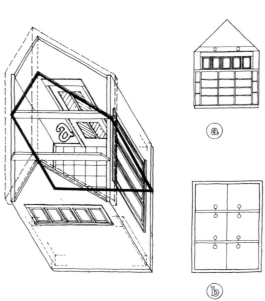

Figure 2-2c An interior elevation **a** is drawn as though the picture plane has been inserted inside the building/room, exposing interior architecture and details. Only interior elements are included in these drawings, as opposed to building sections, which expose structural elements. A reflected ceiling plan is drawn as though a giant mirror were on the floor, reflecting the elements located on the ceiling as shown in **b**.

A *section* portrays a view of the object or building with a vertical or horizontal plane sliced through it and removed. One way of understanding section views is to imagine that a very sharp plane has been inserted into the object or building, cutting neatly into it and revealing the structure and complexity of the object's form. Most building sections are drawn as though the picture plane has been inserted into the building vertically, neatly exposing structural elements and interior details, as shown in Figure 2-2b.

Floor plans are drawn as though a horizontal cut has been made in the building (typically between 3 feet, 6 inches and 5 feet, 6 inches above the floor), as shown in Figure 2-2b. Cutting into the building at this location exposes the thickness of walls and other structural elements, and shows windows, doors, and sometimes floor finishes and furnishings—all of which are located below the location of the cut.

One way to understand the creation of *interior elevations* is to picture yourself inside the room you are drawing. Imagine standing inside a room facing one wall directly, with a large sheet of glass (the picture plane) inserted between yourself and the wall. The interior elevation can then be created by outlining (projecting onto the picture plane) the significant features of the wall, as shown in Figure 2-2c. Each wall of the room can be drawn in elevation by means of projecting what is visible as you face that wall directly.

Reflected ceiling plans are specialized drawings used in interior design (more often for commercial projects than for residential). Reflected ceiling plans communicate important information about the design of the ceiling, such as height and materials, layout, and locations of fixtures. A reflected ceiling plan is drawn as though a giant mirror were on the floor, reflecting the elements located on the ceiling, as shown in Figure 2-2c. The use of reflective imagery allows for the ceiling plan to have exactly the same orientation as the floor plan.

Orthographic projection drawings are clearly an abstraction of reality and use specific conventions to delineate space and materials. Unlike some other forms of drawing, orthographic projection drawings require adherence to conventions, proportional scale, and accuracy of line; these design drawings are highly standardized so that they carry universal meaning. Therefore, items such as walls, doors, windows, property boundaries, references to other drawings, and other items are represented by very specific graphic symbols or combinations of lines. Figure 2-3 illustrates some graphic notations used in these types of drawings, such as wall lines and door and window symbols.

Figure 2-4a illustrates graphic symbols used for notes and references. Figure 2-4b shows graphic symbols used for electrical and lighting. These are standard drawing conventions used to show the items indicated. Figure 2-5 shows additional graphics used to describe construction materials.

Figure 2-3 Common graphic devices used in orthographic projection drawings. These are standard drawing conventions used to show the items indicated.

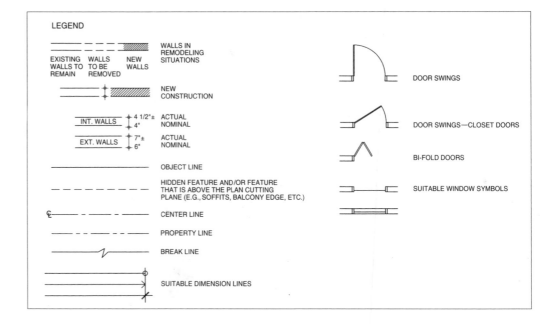

LEGEND

EXISTING WALLS TO REMAIN   WALLS TO BE REMOVED   NEW WALLS   WALLS IN REMODELING SITUATIONS

NEW CONSTRUCTION

INT. WALLS   4 1/2"±   4"   ACTUAL NOMINAL

EXT. WALLS   7"±   6"   ACTUAL NOMINAL

OBJECT LINE

HIDDEN FEATURE AND/OR FEATURE THAT IS ABOVE THE PLAN CUTTING PLANE (E.G., SOFFITS, BALCONY EDGE, ETC.)

CENTER LINE

PROPERTY LINE

BREAK LINE

SUITABLE DIMENSION LINES

DOOR SWINGS

DOOR SWINGS—CLOSET DOORS

BI-FOLD DOORS

SUITABLE WINDOW SYMBOLS

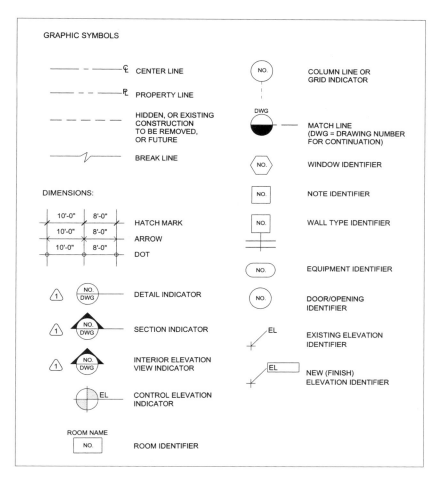

GRAPHIC SYMBOLS

— — — ℄   CENTER LINE

— - — - — Ⓛ   PROPERTY LINE

— — — —   HIDDEN, OR EXISTING
CONSTRUCTION
TO BE REMOVED,
OR FUTURE

———⟋\——   BREAK LINE

DIMENSIONS:

10'-0"	8'-0"	HATCH MARK
10'-0"	8'-0"	ARROW
10'-0"	8'-0"	DOT

① ⟨NO./DWG⟩   DETAIL INDICATOR

① ⟨NO./DWG⟩   SECTION INDICATOR

① ⟨NO./DWG⟩   INTERIOR ELEVATION
VIEW INDICATOR

⟨EL⟩   CONTROL ELEVATION
INDICATOR

ROOM NAME
⟨NO.⟩   ROOM IDENTIFIER

(NO.)   COLUMN LINE OR
GRID INDICATOR

DWG ●—   MATCH LINE
(DWG = DRAWING NUMBER
FOR CONTINUATION)

⟨NO.⟩   WINDOW IDENTIFIER

⟨NO.⟩   NOTE IDENTIFIER

⟨NO.⟩   WALL TYPE IDENTIFIER

⟨NO.⟩   EQUIPMENT IDENTIFIER

⟨NO.⟩   DOOR/OPENING
IDENTIFIER

EL   EXISTING ELEVATION
IDENTIFIER

⟨EL⟩   NEW (FINISH)
ELEVATION IDENTIFIER

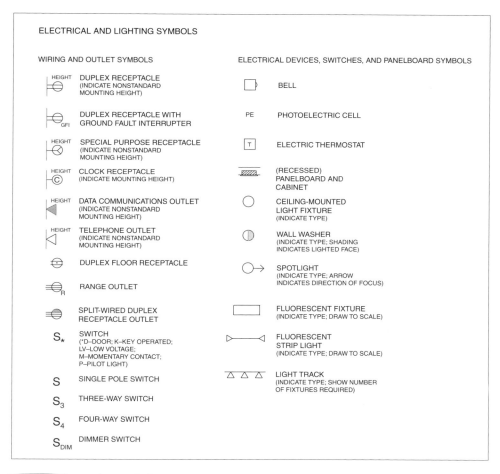

ELECTRICAL AND LIGHTING SYMBOLS

WIRING AND OUTLET SYMBOLS

HEIGHT ⊖   DUPLEX RECEPTACLE
(INDICATE NONSTANDARD
MOUNTING HEIGHT)

⊖GFI   DUPLEX RECEPTACLE WITH
GROUND FAULT INTERRUPTER

HEIGHT ⊖   SPECIAL PURPOSE RECEPTACLE
(INDICATE NONSTANDARD
MOUNTING HEIGHT)

HEIGHT ⓒ   CLOCK RECEPTACLE
(INDICATE MOUNTING HEIGHT)

HEIGHT ◀   DATA COMMUNICATIONS OUTLET
(INDICATE NONSTANDARD
MOUNTING HEIGHT)

HEIGHT ◁   TELEPHONE OUTLET
(INDICATE NONSTANDARD
MOUNTING HEIGHT)

⊖   DUPLEX FLOOR RECEPTACLE

⊖R   RANGE OUTLET

⊖   SPLIT-WIRED DUPLEX
RECEPTACLE OUTLET

S*   SWITCH
(*D–DOOR; K–KEY OPERATED;
LV–LOW VOLTAGE;
M–MOMENTARY CONTACT;
P–PILOT LIGHT)

S   SINGLE POLE SWITCH

S₃   THREE-WAY SWITCH

S₄   FOUR-WAY SWITCH

S_DIM   DIMMER SWITCH

ELECTRICAL DEVICES, SWITCHES, AND PANELBOARD SYMBOLS

▢   BELL

PE   PHOTOELECTRIC CELL

T   ELECTRIC THERMOSTAT

▨   (RECESSED)
PANELBOARD AND
CABINET

○   CEILING-MOUNTED
LIGHT FIXTURE
(INDICATE TYPE)

◑   WALL WASHER
(INDICATE TYPE; SHADING
INDICATES LIGHTED FACE)

○→   SPOTLIGHT
(INDICATE TYPE; ARROW
INDICATES DIRECTION OF FOCUS)

▭   FLUORESCENT FIXTURE
(INDICATE TYPE; DRAW TO SCALE)

▷—◁   FLUORESCENT
STRIP LIGHT
(INDICATE TYPE; DRAW TO SCALE)

△ △ △   LIGHT TRACK
(INDICATE TYPE; SHOW NUMBER
OF FIXTURES REQUIRED)

Figure 2-4a Graphic symbols used for references and notes. These are some standard drawing conventions used to show the items indicated.

1. These symbols include a number on top of another number. The number on top refers to the individual drawing number; the lower number refers to the sheet the individual drawing may be found on. Figures 2-9a and 2-9b illustrate some of these symbols in use.

Figure 2-5 Common graphic symbols used to indicate construction materials. These are some standard drawing conventions used to show the items indicated.

Figure 2-4b Graphic symbols used for electrical and lighting. These are some standard drawing conventions used to show the items indicated.

ARCHITECTURAL MATERIAL SYMBOLS

EARTH   CAST-IN-PLACE CONCRETE   WOOD; ROUGH WOOD FRAMING   WOOD; (FINISH BOARDS)   COARSE POROUS FILL (GRAVEL)   PLYWOOD   BRICK   BATT/FIBROUS INSULATION   RIGID INSULATION BOARD   STEEL

In addition to graphic conventions and symbols, design drawings often contain written notes. Over the years certain abbreviations have become commonplace for use in design practice. Use of abbreviations can save time in drawing production and space on the actual drawings; however, such use also requires that standard abbreviations be used—as opposed to some creative use of letters that may have no meaning to the reader. A partial list of some common abbreviations is shown in Figure 2-6.

ABBREVIATION	STANDS FOR		
ADJ.	Adjacent or Adjustable	INCAND.	Incandescent
A.F.F.	Above Finished Floor	KIT.	Kitchen
BLDG.	Building	LAV.	Lavatory
BM.	Benchmark	℄	Line of Center
BR.	Brick	MAS.	Masonry
BRG.	Bearing	MAX.	Maximum
CER.	Ceramic	MECH.	Mechanical
CLG.	Ceiling	MIN.	Minimum
C.M.U.	Concrete Masonry Unit	MO.	Masonry Opening
CONC.	Concrete	MTD.	Mounted
DIA.	Diameter	N.T.S.	Not To Scale
DN.	Down	N.I.C.	Not In Contract
D.	Dryer	O.C.	On Center
DBL.	Double	OPG.	Opening
DET.	Detail	OH.	Overhead
DW.	Dishwasher	PLAST.	Plastic or Plaster
EXIST.	Existing	P.LAM.	Plastic Laminate
EXT.	Exterior	PL.	Plate
FIN.	Finished	RM.	Room
FL.	Floor	RAD.	Radius
FLUOR.	Fluorescent	R.	Riser
FDN.	Foundation	REF.	Refrigerator
FTG.	Footing	SQ. FT.	Square Foot / Feet
GL.	Glass	T.	Tile
G.F.I.	Ground Fault Interrupter	TOIL.	Toilet
GYP. BD.	Gypsum Board	TR.	Tread
HC	Handicapped	TYP.	Typical
HT.	Height	U.G.	Underground
HTG.	Heating	V.	Vinyl
INT.	Interior	W.	Washer

Figure 2-6 Common abbreviations used in construction notes and drawings and, in some cases, used throughout this book.

THE SAMPLE PROJECT

As a means of illustrating the design graphics discussed to this point, this section reviews a sample project. This project consists of the design of a cottage, to be built on a city lot with an existing home, and is the intended residence for a grandparent—hence, the project title, "the Granny Cottage." Project programming notes and information for this project are shown in the sidebar titled "Programming Information for the Sample Project." Figure 2-7 shows a finalized, complete bubble diagram reflective of program requirements.

Figure 2-7 Bubble diagrams for the sample project. Two preliminary approaches (a and b), and a final complete diagram incorporating elements from earlier versions (c)

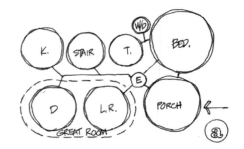

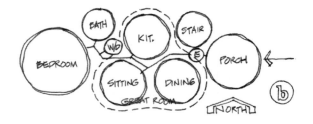

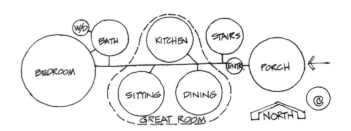

PROGRAMMING INFORMATION FOR THE SAMPLE PROJECT

Occupant:
71-year-old female, recently widowed, physically able at this time.

Owner:
Daughter (39 years old) and son-in-law (40 years old), who are parents to two young children.

Problem Statement:
The owners wish to create/build a backyard cottage for grandma, for use throughout the rest of her life and/or for future rental. The cottage design should fit within the context of the existing house and neighborhood of well-cared-for older homes.

Additional Information and Requirements:
The existing house on the lot, currently owner occupied, was built in 1924. Local ordinances allow one and two family dwellings in R-1 zones. To build the second dwelling on the property requires a zoning variance because the new dwelling will not be attached to the existing house; the variance has been approved.

Budget:
$175,000

Square Footage:
600 to 800 square feet of finished living space (gross), plus porch and attic.

Basement:
The existing house was built without a basement; the owners want the Granny Cottage to have a basement not only for the resident of the cottage but for the entire family to use as a storm shelter. The basement will also be used for HVAC equipment, water heater, water treatment, electrical panel, and so on, and dead storage as well as overflow storage for the main house.

Front Porch:
120 square feet with a roof to protect from sun and rain. A place to sit and enjoy outside air, it should also serve as the entrance porch providing some protection from the elements for the main entrance.

Site Considerations:
Separate access (sidewalk) to the public street.
Use cottage to create a more private backyard and patio area for the owner's family.
Grandma will park her car in the garage; the second family car will park in the driveway.

Room and Space Requirements:

Sq. Ft (net +/−10%).	Room/Area Notes
200 sq. ft.	GREAT ROOM: Dining area to seat four max. Living area to seat four comfortably View of the garden Lots of natural light/daylight Flat-screen TV Hardwood floors
80 sq. ft.	KITCHEN Dishwasher, compact range, double sink with garbage disposal, refrigerator/ freezer Two 24-inch-high stools at a 36-inch-high counter Work/prep area that is 42 inches wide (minimum)
150 sq. ft.	BEDROOM 10 lineal feet of clothes rod Linen closet Queen-size bed Small desk for laptop and personal business
45 sq. ft.	BATHROOM Ceramic tile floors 4-foot sit-down shower module
As required	LAUNDRY
As required	CIRCULATION Stairs, hallways
150 sq. ft.	ATTIC LOFT Playroom; carpet over pad

SITE PLANS

A site plan generally includes a roof plan of the building as well as the surrounding property and site boundaries, along with adjacent street information and topographic information as required. Site plans require the use of a north arrow and are generally drawn in a scale that permits including the necessary information. In some cases, site plans are drawn at engineer's scales of 1 inch = 20 feet or 1 inch = 30 feet, while in other instances, a standard architectural scale such as 1/16 inch = 1 foot, 0 inches may be used. Figure 2-8 is a site plan for the sample project drawn using CAD (computer-aided drafting). A hand-drawn version appears later in this chapter.

When reviewing the site plan shown in Figure 2-8, you might find it helpful to consider site-related issues involved in building design. There are, of course, myriad issues to consider related to any building site. The following list provides only an introductory overview of some site planning issues:

- Local ordinances govern site design and building occupancy; check local zoning prior to beginning the design of any project. Frequently those areas zoned for single-family occupancy will allow for duplexes, although often the building of a separate residence (as shown in Figure 2-8) requires a variance.
- Setbacks are key issues in residential site design. *Front setbacks* can vary widely, with 20 to 40 feet the most common. *Side setbacks* are often 6 feet. *Rear*

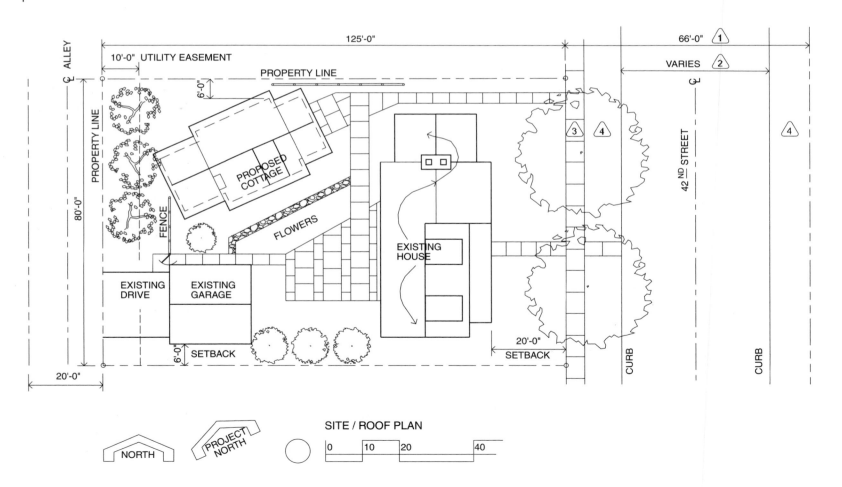

SITE / ROOF PLAN

setbacks can be a percentage of lot depth or a percentage of green space (green space is discussed in the caption for Figure 2-8).

■ Site design should encourage water away from building structures, and water should be viewed as an enemy of construction materials. Therefore, positive drainage away from buildings is required and no standing water should gather immediately adjacent to buildings.

■ Orientation to the elements is a significant issue in building/site design. Sunlight and protection from the elements should be considered and reviewed with clients.

■ The location of utilities is another important consideration in site design. When possible, electrical service should be buried. Water service is buried and the depth is a function of climate. Sewer depth is also deeper in cold climates. The lowest drain in the house should be sufficiently above the sanitary sewer main in the street to allow gravity flow to carry away the house waste. This avoids having to pump the waste up to the sewer main.

■ Site design involves planning for the movement of vehicles onto the property in most cases. Local ordinances may require on-site/off-street vehicle parking and/or storage.

■ The site should be a major consideration in the design of the building from the very first moment work begins on the project. Site design is about context; the next larger context must be considered. For example, in the design of a building, not only should the immediate site (owner's property) be considered, but the larger neighborhood as well.

Figure 2-8 An AutoCAD-generated site (and roof) plan for the sample project. The lot size for this project is 80 by 125 feet = 10,000 square feet. Percentage of green space (uncovered ground that will absorb rainfall) is 55 percent, with the proposed building on the lot (local ordinance is 50 percent minimum).

1. Street right-of-way (R.O.W.) width is local jurisdiction; very frequently it is 66 feet.
2. Street width (curb to curb) is dependent on whether or not it is a through street and whether or not there is parking on one side or two sides, or no parking.
3. Public sidewalk, generally located within the public R.O.W. The width is up to local jurisdiction, frequently 4 to 6 feet wide.
4. "Boulevard" strip, generally landscaped with grass or other ground cover and maintained by the property owner, even though it is within the public right-of-way. Municipality often maintains trees.

FLOOR PLANS

As noted previously, floor plans are drawn as though a horizontal cut has been made in the building (typically between 3 feet, 6 inches and 5 feet, 6 inches above the floor). The floor plan is generated as though the portion above the cut has been removed, allowing the viewer to see the thickness of walls, understand door and window locations, and see additional elements such as cabinetry and flooring materials as required.

Figure 2-9a is a main-level floor plan for the sample project, 2-9b is a dimensioned main floor plan, Figure 2-9c is a partial dimensioned floor plan, and Figure 2-9d is a main-level floor plan that includes furnishings. Figure 2-10a is a basement floor plan, and Figure 2-10b is a loft floor plan for the project.

When drawing floor plans, the designer must convey significant spatial relationships with consistent graphic conventions. Various line weights are used to convey depths and qualities of form. In standard floor plans the boldest line weight is used to outline those elements that have been cut through and are closest to the viewer (such as full-height wall lines). An intermediate line weight is employed to outline objects that lie below the plane of the cut but above the floor plane, such as fixtures, cabinetry/built-ins, and furnishings. A finer line weight is used to outline surface treatment of the floors and other horizontal planes such as tile and wood grain. Objects that are hidden, such as shelves, or above the plane of the cut are dashed or ghosted in; this must be done in a manner that is consistent throughout the drawing or set of drawings.

Standard doors are generally drawn open at 90 degrees to the wall and are most often shown with the arc of their swing. The door frame and the space it requires must be considered in the drawing of the door system (this means the dimensions of the frame must be considered). Windowsills are typically outlined, often with a lighter line weight at the sill only. Window frames and sheets of glass are shown in various details as scale allows. Stairs are generally shown as broken off past the height of the plane of the cut; this is signified with a special break line. An arrow should be included indicating the direction of the stairs from the level of the floor plan being shown, with the word *up* (UP) or *down* (DN) adjacent to the directional arrow.

A title, a north arrow, and some type of scale notation should be included on all floor plans. Scale notation can be stated numerically, for example: ¼" = 1-0". Current practice often requires the use of a graphic scaling device, which allows for reduction, enlargement, and electronic transmission of the drawings. Symbols relating the floor plan to additional orthographic views or details are often drawn on the floor plan and serve as cross-references, as shown in Figure 2-9a.

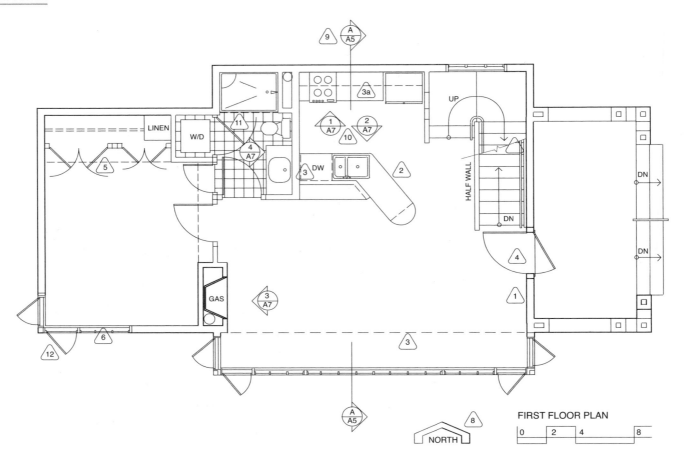

LINEN

W/D

GAS

DW

UP

HALF WALL

DN

DN

DN

DN

NORTH

FIRST FLOOR PLAN

0   2   4   8

Figure 2-9a An AutoCAD-generated, main-level floor plan for the sample project, with appropriate reference symbols.

1. Boldest lines indicate the location of cut, meaning full-height walls are bold.

2. Fixtures, cabinetry, and finish materials are drawn with progressively lighter lines as they recede from the cut location.

3. Elements that are above or below the cut line, such as cabinets (3a) and soffits, or hidden, such as dishwashers, are indicated with dashed lines.

4. Standard doors are drawn open at 90 degrees with the arc of swing shown. The full swing can be shown to ensure that nothing impedes the full swing of the door.

5. Specialized doors, such as smaller closet doors (shown), bifold doors, sliding doors, and pocket doors, are drawn in a way that indicates size and construction.

6. Window glass and sill lines are shown, often with lighter-weight lines than walls.

7. Stairs are drawn as broken off past the line of the cut; a special break line is used.

8. A title, north arrow, and scale notation are required on all plans. Because this drawing was reduced, a standard written scale was omitted. Instead, a graphic scale device is included. A north arrow should appear on all plans.

9. This is a section reference symbol. The arrow indicates the direction of the view of the section. The top number within the symbol indicates the individual drawing number, while the bottom number indicates the sheet number the drawing is on, in this case sheet A5.

10. These are elevation reference symbols. The arrow indicates the direction of the view of the elevation. The top number within the symbol indicates the individual drawing number, while the bottom number indicates the sheet number the drawing is on, in this case sheet A7.

11. Flooring materials may be shown as required (using a light line weight).

12. Egress window.

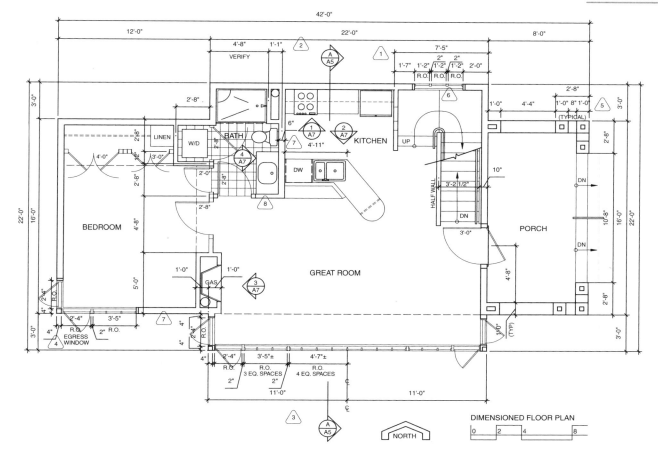

DIMENSIONED FLOOR PLAN

NORTH

Figure 2-9b An AutoCAD-generated, main-level floor plan for the sample project, with dimensions. This type of drawing is required for construction.

1. Dimension lines and leader lines should be lighter than wall lines or objects measured.

2. Horizontal written dimensions sit above the dimension lines—so they are underlined by the dimension line—as shown, or they are written in a break in the dimension line.

3. Note the location of dimensions. They should not read by rotating the sheet counterclockwise (as in reading from the left side of the sheet), and one absolutely should not have to turn the sheet upside down to read these dimensions.

4. Leader lines run from the building location being dimensioned to the dimension lines. Leader lines should not touch the building; instead, they should be drawn slightly away.

5. Dimensions are written in feet and inches unless less than 1 foot.

6. Dimensions measured from centerlines must be clearly indicated. Windows are commonly measured to centerlines or rough openings as shown.

7. Exterior walls (and plumbing walls) are shown as nominal 6 inches thick (actual: 6 ½ inches to 7 ½ inches).

8. Interior walls are shown as nominal 4 inches thick (actual: 4½ inches, typically).

Figure 2-9c An AutoCAD-generated room dimensioned with interior finish-to-finish dimensions. In some cases dimensions are shown from interior wall finish to interior wall finish (called paint-to-paint dimensions by some) as shown. This is most common in interior renovation/remodeling projects. Generally, rules for dimension lines, leader lines, and text are consistent with those listed in Figure 2-9b, with only the location of leader and dimension lines different from exterior or centerline dimensions.

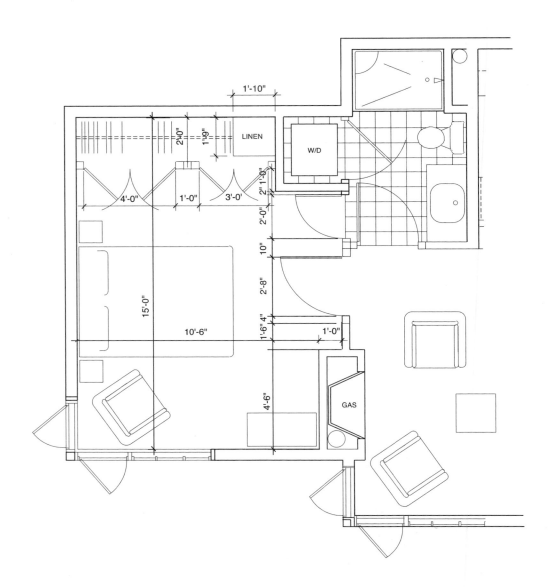

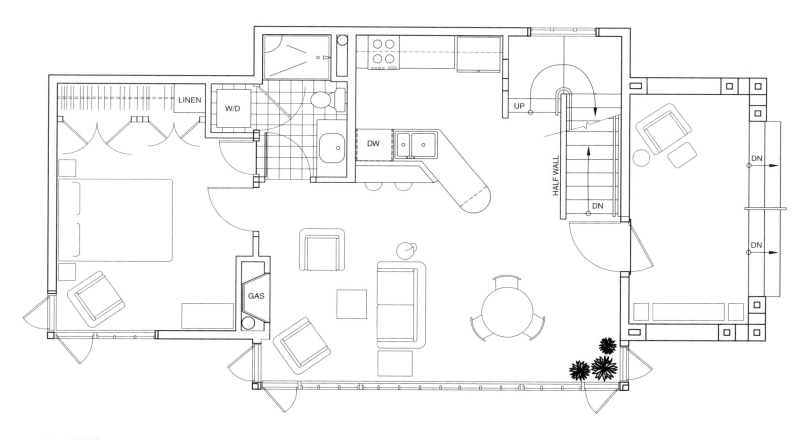

LINEN

W/D

DW

UP

HALF WALL

DN

DN

DN

GAS

Figure 2-9d An AutoCAD-generated main-level floor plan for the project with furnishings included. Furnishings should be drawn in lighter line weight than those used for walls. This drawing is geared toward a client design presentation or to communicate furniture locations rather than for construction. Current AutoCAD programs allow for furniture to be imported as "blocks," but these often are quite dark when printed and the furniture included is rather generic and is best used for planning purposes. Furniture, fixtures, and appliances are covered in detail in individual chapters throughout this book.

NORTH

FIRST FLOOR PLAN

0   2   4   8

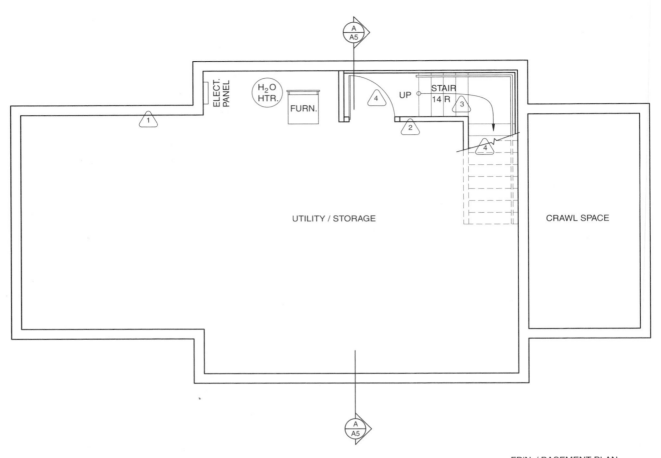

Figure 2-10a An AutoCAD-generated basement floor plan for the project. Conventions for drafting line weights and symbols are consistent with those listed in Figure 2-9a.

1. Foundation walls are typically 8-inch-thick concrete.
2. Interior walls are 4-inch-thick wood frame walls.
3. Stairs are framed with wood.
4. The "UP" run terminates with a break line: steps that are above the plan cut line are shown as dashed, hidden lines; often they are not shown.

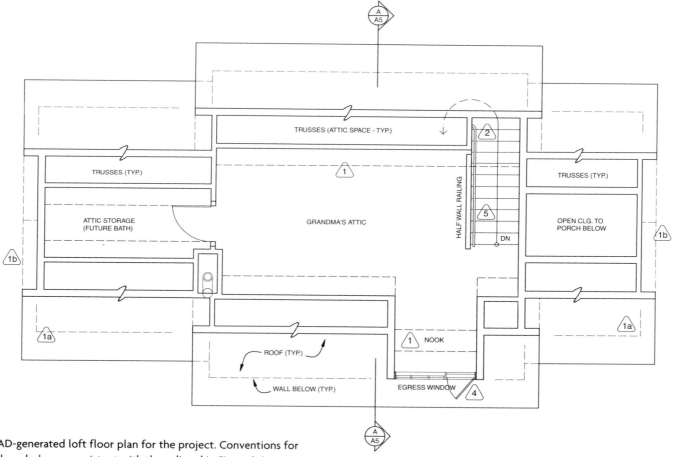

TRUSSES (ATTIC SPACE - TYP.)

TRUSSES (TYP.)

TRUSSES (TYP.)

ATTIC STORAGE
(FUTURE BATH)

GRANDMA'S ATTIC

HALF WALL RAILING

OPEN CLG. TO
PORCH BELOW

DN

ROOF (TYP.)

NOOK

WALL BELOW (TYP.)

EGRESS WINDOW

Figure 2-10b An AutoCAD-generated loft floor plan for the project. Conventions for drafting line weights and symbols are consistent with those listed in Figure 2-9a.

1. Dashed line represents a change of plane in the ceiling or:
   1a. Exterior wall line below the roof.
   1b. Roof edge above the "cut" plane.
2. Down portion of stair run disappears under the roof and does not end in a break line as in item 4 in Figure 2-10a.
3. See section shown in Figure 2-11 for information about location of cut used to create this plan.
4. Egress window.
5. Stair treads shown at 10 inches deep; see Chapter 8 for information on stairs.

NORTH

ATTIC / 2ND FLOOR PLAN

0   2   4   8

DIMENSIONS

Dimensions are included in a wide range of drawings at various points in the design process (such as in both preliminary and design development drawings) and in construction drawings (as shown in Figure 2-9b). When included in drawings, dimensions are always listed in feet and inches; for example 2'-4" is written, rather than 28", except for those dimensions that are less than a foot, for example, 11" or 0'-11". Dimensions should be placed on top of the dimension line, so that they are underlined by the dimension line, and should be placed so as to not require being read by rotating the sheet counterclockwise (reading from left to right) or upside down.

Generally, for standard construction, dimensions and dimension lines are placed outside of the object (such as the building), as shown in Figure 2-9b. In terms of organizing a series of dimensions, specific dimensions are placed close to the particular object they are related to, while the overall distances are placed in the position farthest from the constructions.

Dimensions typically run from the outside of exterior walls to the centerline of interior walls. Where interior tolerances are critical, dimensions can be run from the face of the finished wall to the face of the other finished wall (paint-to-paint, so to speak), as shown in Figure 2-9c. This type of dimension is often used for interior design projects created within existing architecture. For example, when dimensioning walls for an interior renovation of an existing office or retail space, designers commonly dimension only the paint-to-paint dimensions, rather than exterior-to-center dimensions.

Openings such as windows and doors are dimensions to centerlines or to rough frame openings (R.O.), with the exception of masonry openings (M.O.), which are not drawn to centerlines. Another rule of thumb is to dimension things once and only once; repetition from one drawing to another can lead to discrepancy errors.

SECTIONS

As described earlier, a building section is a view of a building created as though a vertical plane has cut through the building and been removed. Unlike interior elevations, which depict only what occurs inside the interior, sections can expose the structure of the building. In drawing sections, the designer must include the outline of the structural elements as well as the internal configuration of the interior space. Sections require varied line weights as a means of describing depths and spatial relationships. It is typical to show what is cut through, and therefore closest to the viewer, in the boldest line weight. Receding features and details are drawn using progressively lighter line weights. A section for the project is illustrated in Figure 2-11.

It is important to consider carefully the most useful location (or locations) of the building to show in section. The section should, preferably, be cut through the building as a single continuous plane. Sections should expose and convey important interior relationships and details such as doors, windows, changes in floor level, ceiling heights, and, in some cases, finish material locations. Sections require symbols for cross-referencing located on the plan and called out in the section title, as shown in Figures 2-9a and 2-11.

INTERIOR ELEVATIONS

Interior elevations are used extensively in professional practice. Successful elevations must clearly depict all interior architectural elements in a consistent scale. Interior elevations are typically drawn in a scale ranging from $1/4$"=1'-0" to 1"=1'-0". Elevations drawn to depict accessories, equipment, cabinetry, fixtures, and design details are often drawn at $3/8$"=1'-0" or $1/2$"=1'-0". Millwork and other highly complicated elevations are often drawn at $1/2$"=1'-0"or larger. All elevations require the use of differing line weights to clearly communicate spatial relationships. Typically, any portion of walls cut through and those closest to the viewer are drawn using a bold line weight. Receding elements become progressively lighter in line weight as they move farther from the picture plane. Some designers draw the line representing the floor line as the boldest line, with the lines representing the top and sides of the wall drawn just slightly lighter in weight. Figure 2-12 depicts kitchen elevations for the sample project.

Interior elevations can be difficult for beginning students to master. However, they deserve a student's full attention because accurate elevations are necessary to successfully communicate key elements of a design. Like floor plans and sections, elevations used for design presentations vary greatly from those used for construction. Elevations used for construction drawings must necessarily contain significant dimensions as well as appropriate technical information. Elevations used for presentations can be drawn more freely and often contain less technical information, but they must be drawn accurately and in consistent scale.

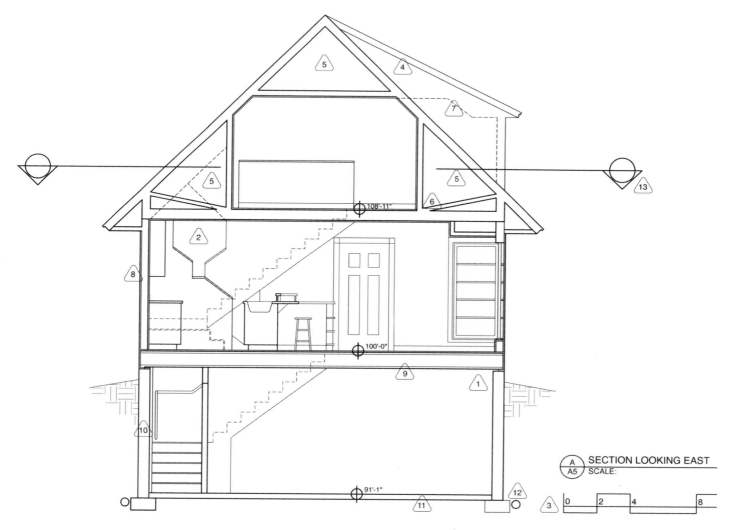

SECTION LOOKING EAST
SCALE:

Figure 2-11 An AutoCAD-generated section for the sample project.

1. Boldest lines indicate relative location of cut.
2. Receding elements are drawn with progressively lighter lines; important hidden elements are shown as dashed lines.
3. Sections require titles, reference symbols keyed to a floor plan (names or numbers), and scale notation.
4. Dormer beyond.
5. Dead attic space.
6. Structural members (wood frame) that comprise attic trusses, which are 2 feet, 0 inches O.C.
7. Ceiling profile at nook (hidden line).
8. Exterior wood frame wall.
9. Wood floor joist (I joist in this example). Commonly 16 inches O.C.; alternative spacings, when appropriate, are 19.2 inches O.C. or 24 inches O.C.
10. 8-inch-thick concrete foundation wall with 2-inch-thick furred finish wall in the stairwell.
11. 4-inch-thick concrete slab (basement floor).
12. Drain tile, where required by groundwater presence.
13. A section symbol is not typically drawn to reference floor plans; however, in this case, one is shown to depict the location of the cut for the attic/loft floor plan shown in Figure 2-10b.

Figure 2-12 AutoCAD-generated interior elevations for the sample project.

1. Portions of walls cut into or closest to viewer are bold.
2. Receding elements are drawn with progressively lighter lines.
3. In elevations including cabinetry and or millwork, details such as countertops, door frames, and hardware should be included.
4. Interior elevations require titles, reference symbols (names or numbers), and scale notation.
5. Mirror with wall sconces at each side.
6. Flat-screen TV.

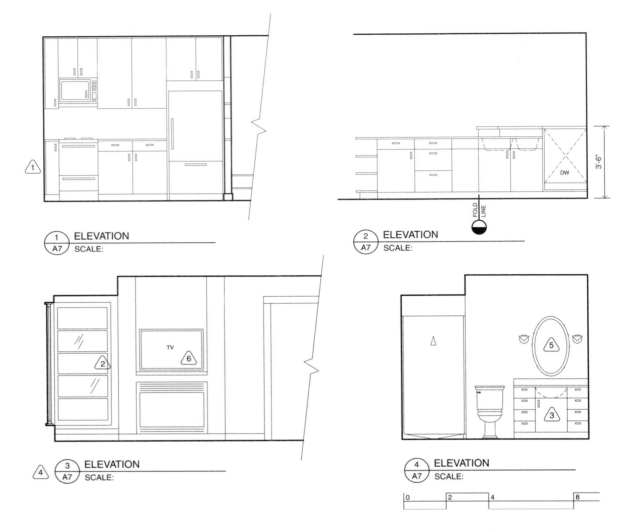

REFLECTED CEILING PLANS

Reflected ceiling plans are often used in conjunction with floor plans, elevations, and sections to communicate interior design. Reflected ceiling plans communicate important information about the design of the ceiling, such as materials, layout and locations of fixtures, and ceiling heights. A reflected ceiling plan is drawn as though a giant mirror were on the floor, reflecting the elements located on the ceiling. These are used commonly for commercial interior design projects and are used less often for residential projects, although one is included in

Figure 2-13 for the example project as a means of communicating the concepts covered.

Reflected ceiling plans are typically drawn in the same scale as the corresponding floor plan, although for complex designs, larger-scale partial reflected ceiling plans are prepared. More complex ceiling designs also may require that dimensions be included, which is not the case with simple ceiling plans. In addition to ceiling heights, finish materials, light fixtures (those located on the ceiling), and diffusers/registers (those located on the ceiling) are included and switching information may be included.

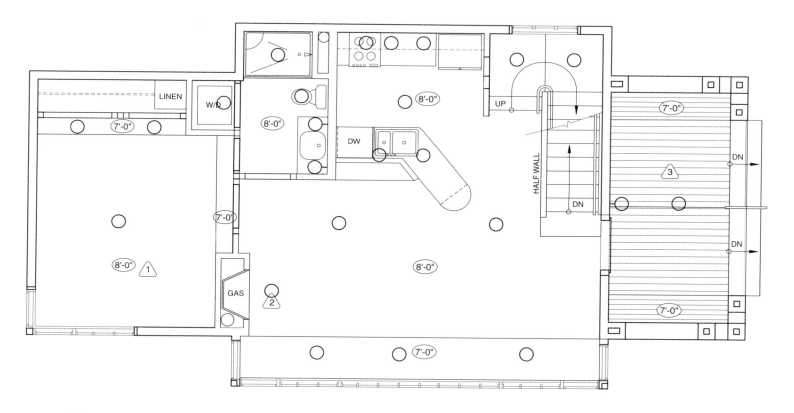

Figure 2-13 AutoCAD-generated simple reflected ceiling plan for the sample project.

1. Ceiling heights are noted and enclosed in a symbol.
2. Light fixture locations at ceiling are shown.
3. Finish materials such as wood are indicated in scale; in this case the wood ceiling on the porch is indicated, whereas other ceiling locations are shown as gypsum board (also called drywall or Sheetrock).
4. Reflected ceiling plans require titles, north arrows, and scale notation.

REFLECTED CEILING PLAN

NORTH

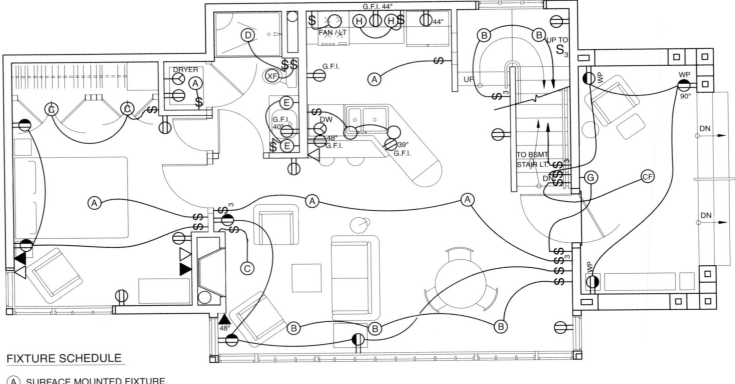

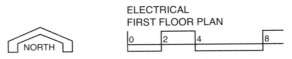

FIXTURE SCHEDULE

- (A) SURFACE MOUNTED FIXTURE
- (B) RECESSED DOWN LIGHT
- (C) RECESSED, ADJUSTABLE DOWN LIGHT
- (D) RECESSED WATER PROOF SHOWER LIGHT
- (E) WALL SCONCE
- –(G) EXTERIOR, WALL MOUNTED GLOBE
- (H) UNDER CABINET "PUCK LIGHT"
- (CF) SURFACE MOUNTED CEILING FAN
- (XF) EXHAUST (CEILING) FAN

Figure 2-14 An AutoCAD-generated electrical and lighting plan for the sample project. Detailed information about lighting can be found in Chapter 1 and at the end of each chapter.

NORTH

ELECTRICAL
FIRST FLOOR PLAN

0   2   4   8

Often for residential projects, light fixtures, electrical outlets, and switching information are all included directly on a standard plan—not a reflected plan. These are referred to as *electrical and lighting plans* or *power and lighting plans*. Figure 2-14 is an example of a electrical and lighting plan for the sample project. Throughout this book, electical and lighting plans are included to convey information about lighting, switching, and outlet locations.

For purposes of reference and comparison, a freehand drawn version of the site plan, floor plan, and exterior elevations of the sample project are shown in Figures 2-15a, 2-15b, and 2-16. These were drawn on ⅛-inch "fade-out-grid" paper.

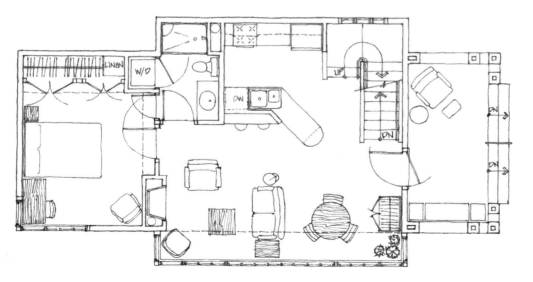

Figure 2-15a A manually drawn preliminary site plan for the sample project; drawn freehand on ⅛-inch "fade-out" grid paper.

Figure 2-15b A manually drawn floor plan for the sample project; drawn freehand on ⅛-inch "fade-out" grid paper.

Figure 2-16 Manually drawn exterior elevations for the sample project; drawn freehand on ⅛-inch "fade-out" grid paper.

A. Asphalt shingles
B. Cedar shingle siding
C. Chimney housing for gas fireplace vent and other household venting
D. Cedar fascia
E. Rough-sawn plywood with cedar battens
F. Attic louver
G. Egress window
H. Roof pitch 12:12; dormer roof pitch 6:12
I. Profile of porch ceiling (hidden line)

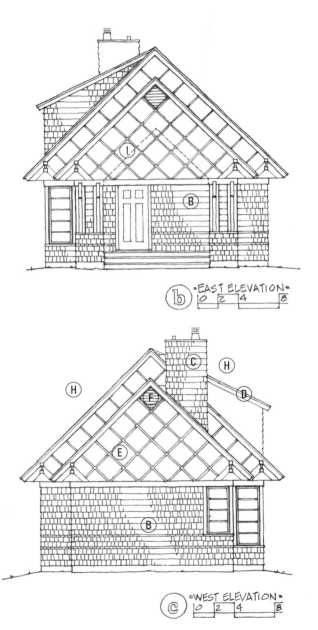

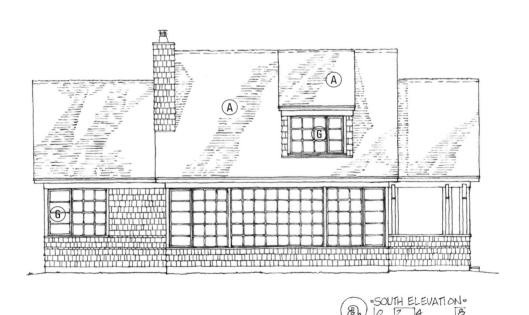

TABLE 2-1 Room Finish Schedule

| Room Name | Floor | Base | Walls | Finish | Ceiling | | Remarks |
					Material	Height	
BASEMENT							
Utility/Storage	CONC	NONE	CONC	UNFINISHED	UNFINISHED	7' 9½" (±)	
Stair	CARPET	HARDWD	GYP. BD.	PAINT	GYP. BD.	VARIES	
1ST FLOOR							
Bedroom	CARPET	HARDWD	GYP. BD.	PAINT	WOOD	8' 0"/ 7' 0"*	*GYP. BD. SOFFITS/CLOSET CEILING
Bath	CER. TILE	CER. TILE	GYP. BD./ CER. TILE	PAINT/CER. TILE**	GYP. BD.	8' 0"/ 7' 0"*	*GYP. BD. SOFFITS **CER. TILE AT TUB ENCLOSURE AND 36" WAINSCOT
Great room (kitchen/dining/sitting)	HARDWD	HARDWD	GYP. BD.	PAINT	GYP. BD.	8' 0"/ 7' 0"*	*GYP. BD. SOFFITS
Stair	CARPET	HARDWD	GYP. BD.	PAINT	GYP. BD.	VARIES	
Porch	WOOD	NONE	CEDAR*		WOOD	VARIES	*SEE EXTERIOR ELEVATIONS
ATTIC							
Grandma's attic and nook	CARPET	PINE	PINE/GYP. BD.*	OIL/PAINT*	PINE	7' 0"	*(EAST) END WALL ONLY
Stair	CARPET	HARDWD	GYP. BD.	PAINT	PINE/GYP. BD.*	VARIES	*AT LANDING

ABBREVIATIONS: CONC—CONCRETE   GYP. BD.—GYPSUM BOARD   CER. TILE—CERAMIC TILE   HARDWD—HARDWOOD

FINISH SCHEDULES

A finish schedule may be included in residential construction drawings. These show the materials and finishes to be applied to walls, floors, and ceilings in the various rooms of a building. Typically, a finish schedule includes a column that lists the various rooms by name or number, as well as column headings for floors, walls, base, and ceilings. Also included are remarks or notes for any comments necessary to clarify information or details. Finish schedules vary greatly in terms of complexity and in the information conveyed depending on the complexity of the project or situation. Table 2-1 is a very simple finish schedule for the sample project.

BIBLIOGRAPHY

(Contains both works cited and recommended reading. Annotations where appropriate.)

Ching, Francis. *Architectural Graphics*. 2nd ed. Hoboken, NJ: John Wiley & Sons, 2002. An excellent introductory text.
———. *Interior Design Illustrated*. 2nd ed. Hoboken, NJ: John Wiley & Sons, 2005.
Guthrie, Pat. *The Interior Designer's Portable Handbook*. New York: McGraw-Hill, 2004, p. 29. A helpful resource for students and professionals.
Kilmer, W. Otie, and Rosemary Kilmer. *Construction Drawings and Details for Interiors*. Hoboken, NJ: John Wiley & Sons, 2003. A good, basic guide to construction drawings for interior design/interior architecture.
Peña, William, Steven Parshall, and Kevin Kelly. *Problem Seeking: An Architectural Programming Primer*. Washington, DC: AIA Press, 1987. A seminal work on programming.

CHAPTER 3

BEDROOMS

The last hundred years have brought dramatic changes related to the public perception of the design, furnishing, and quantity of bedrooms in the American house. In contrast to the house of the1950s with an average of two bedrooms, the American house built in 2002 was on average 2,230 square feet; 52 percent had three bedrooms, and 36 percent contained four bedrooms or more (only 11 percent of those contained two bedrooms or fewer). Today's houses have more bedrooms on average than before and can contain large owner's suites that serve as the adult luxury enclave in some homes.

There is a range of experience, but it can be said that roughly one-third of our lives are spent sleeping, which for many of us takes place in the bedroom. In addition to being a room for sleep, the bedroom also serves as a private sanctuary or retreat and, as such, it is a place to take refuge from the world outside. As stated in the introductory chapter, various zones of privacy can be identified in homes. The bedroom is unique in that it serves a variety of purposes far more private than any other in the home, with the possible exception of the bathroom. Because of this need for privacy, a bedroom's placement within the residence must be well considered as it relates to family circulation patterns and outside noise.

If we break the bedroom down into its most essential functions, it is used for sleeping, dressing, sexual intimacy, and as a place of recovery from illness. In terms of space, at the most minimal extreme, a bedroom consists of a place to lie down, store clothing, and get dressed. Figure 3-1 illustrates the absolute minimum space required by most codes for a single bedroom. While this minimal approach may meet certain building standards, it is certainly less than ideal in terms of the access space required to make the bed and dress comfortably, and navigate within the room.

In simple terms, bedrooms are ruled by bed size and location. Beds are quite large and therefore tend to dominate the use of the room both in terms of circulation and in the related placement of additional furnishings. Most bedrooms include a bed, some furnishings for various types of storage, and some sort of closet.

Many bedrooms go well beyond the minimal to include various ancillary functions such as entertainment, study, and reading and therefore can include an array of furnishings, including items used for storage such as dressers, chests, shelves, night tables, and clothing or media armoires. Seats or chairs, lamps, and mirrors are often included, as are desks. It is especially common to include desks in rooms meant for children or students, as the bedroom commonly serves as a study area.

The overall square footage and general layout will dictate the amenities that can be found in a given bedroom. A king-size bed, two night tables, two or more dressers, a small office nook, a sitting area, a fireplace, an entertainment console or armoire, and two walk-in closets, or some combination of these items can be found in some of the larger custom homes popular today. Figure 3-2 shows a very large, fully furnished bedroom, which serves as an extreme contrast to the minimal bedroom shown in Figure 3-1.

It is often the smaller dwelling, found in denser settings and/or in less costly housing, that necessitates that the bedroom serves multiple functions such as sleeping, entertainment, and office/study area. This means that a smaller room is fulfilling multiple functional requirements, a situation that requires careful planning and design. In larger houses, on the other hand, specialized rooms are used for home offices and study areas, allowing the bedroom to serve fewer functional requirements.

A thorough review of the project, including careful client interviews, enables the designer to uncover the functional requirements as well as the reality of the

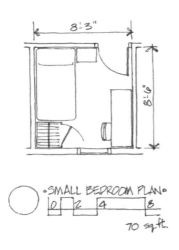

Figure 3-1 This floor plan represents a minimum of space and includes minimal functional elements required for a bedroom. At 70 square feet, it meets the absolute minimum code requirements of square footage for habitable rooms.

Figure 3-2 This floor plan represents what could be called the maximum bedroom. It includes substantial room around the king-size bed, a study/library area, a sitting area with fireplace, a large bathroom with luxurious plumbing fixtures (with an additional fireplace), as well as a large closet with an island adjacent to a laundry room.

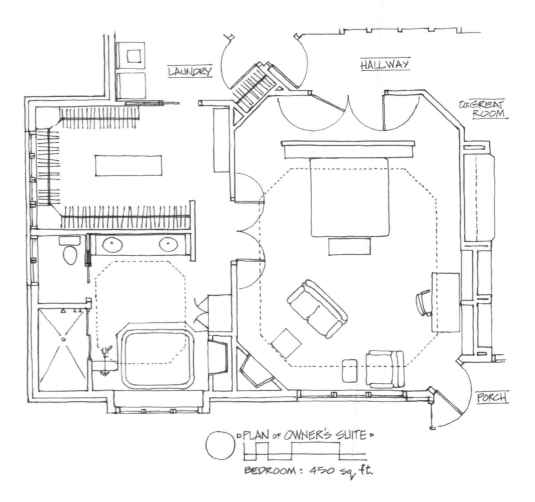

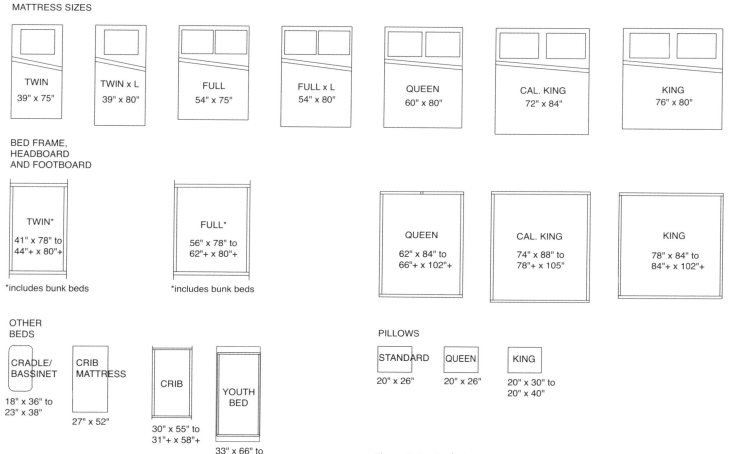

MATTRESS SIZES

TWIN 39" x 75"
TWIN x L 39" x 80"
FULL 54" x 75"
FULL x L 54" x 80"
QUEEN 60" x 80"
CAL. KING 72" x 84"
KING 76" x 80"

BED FRAME, HEADBOARD AND FOOTBOARD

TWIN* 41" x 78" to 44"+ x 80"+
FULL* 56" x 78" to 62"+ x 80"+
*includes bunk beds

QUEEN 62" x 84" to 66"+ x 102"+
CAL. KING 74" x 88" to 78"+ x 105"
KING 78" x 84" to 84"+ x 102"+

OTHER BEDS

CRADLE/BASSINET 18" x 36" to 23" x 38"
CRIB MATTRESS 27" x 52"
CRIB 30" x 55" to 31"+ x 58"+
YOUTH BED 33" x 66" to 36" x 76"+

PILLOWS

STANDARD 20" x 26"
QUEEN 20" x 26"
KING 20" x 30" to 20" x 40"

Figure 3-3a Bed sizes

budget and square footage limitations, thus leading to the design of the best bedroom for a given situation. With that said, it is worth noting that most design solutions should not only meet short-term requirements but should in addition be able to withstand changes in the needs of the client or resale of the home.

This chapter provides detailed information about furnishings, closets, organizational flow, required clearances, and ergonomics, and is meant as a general aid in the planning of bedrooms for a range of clients with varying needs. Figures 3-3a, 3-3b, 3-4, 3-5, and 3-6 detail the sizes of furnishings commonly found in bedrooms.

The closet, much like the rest of many homes, has become larger to accommodate an increase in the quantity of clothing, personal belongings, and leisure activities of current homeowners. Anyone having lived in an American home built before 1920 can attest to the minimal closet space in individual bedrooms. Closet space has not only grown in terms of quantity, but the arrangement and organization of closets has evolved to the point that closet design and fabrication is now a billion-dollar industry. Various storage systems and organizational elements are employed to create closets that allow appropriate, accessible storage for all of one's personal items.

SOFA BEDS

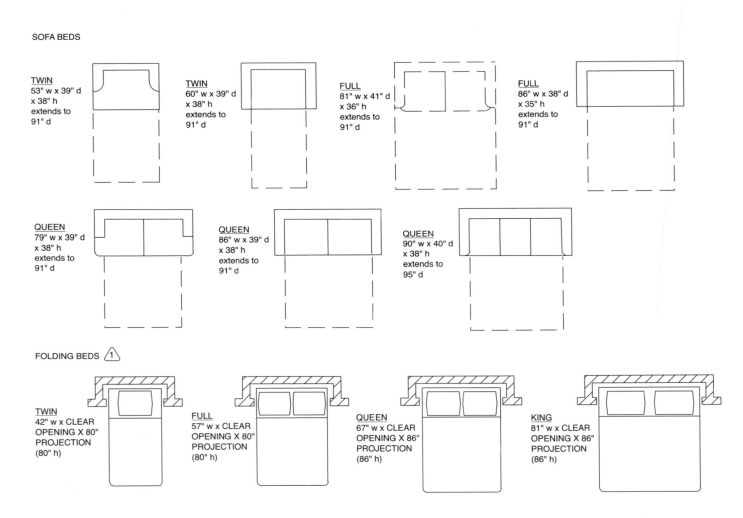

TWIN
53" w x 39" d
x 38" h
extends to
91" d

TWIN
60" w x 39" d
x 38" h
extends to
91" d

FULL
81" w x 41" d
x 36" h
extends to
91" d

FULL
86" w x 38" d
x 35" h
extends to
91" d

QUEEN
79" w x 39" d
x 38" h
extends to
91" d

QUEEN
86" w x 39" d
x 38" h
extends to
91" d

QUEEN
90" w x 40" d
x 38" h
extends to
95" d

FOLDING BEDS ⚠1

TWIN
42" w x CLEAR
OPENING X 80"
PROJECTION
(80" h)

FULL
57" w x CLEAR
OPENING X 80"
PROJECTION
(80" h)

QUEEN
67" w x CLEAR
OPENING X 86"
PROJECTION
(86" h)

KING
81" w x CLEAR
OPENING X 86"
PROJECTION
(86" h)

Figure 3-3b Sofa beds and folding bed sizes.

1. These beds are often built into cabinetry or closetlike
   enclosures.

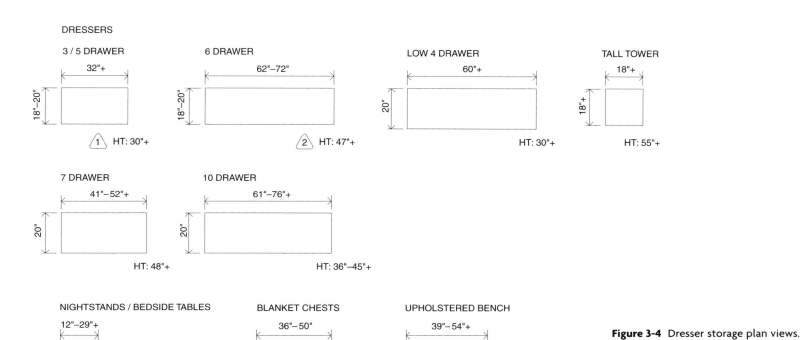

DRESSERS

3 / 5 DRAWER
32"+
18"–20"
1 HT: 30"+

6 DRAWER
62"–72"
18"–20"
2 HT: 47"+

LOW 4 DRAWER
60"+
20"
HT: 30"+

TALL TOWER
18"+
18"+
HT: 55"+

7 DRAWER
41"–52"+
20"
HT: 48"+

10 DRAWER
61"–76"+
20"
HT: 36"–45"+

NIGHTSTANDS / BEDSIDE TABLES
12"–29"+
12"–20"+
HT: 22"–29"

BLANKET CHESTS
36"–50"
18"–20"

UPHOLSTERED BENCH
39"–54"+
16"–20"

Figure 3-4 Dresser storage plan views.
1. Taller, six-drawer versions are 36 inches (w) x 20 inches (d) x 50 inches (h).
2. Taller versions are available.

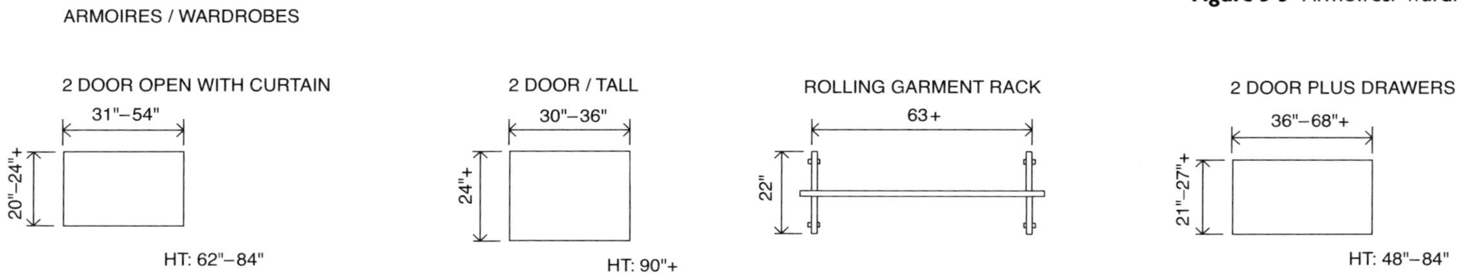

Figure 3-5 Armoires/wardrobe storage sizes.

ARMOIRES / WARDROBES

2 DOOR OPEN WITH CURTAIN
31"–54"
20"–24"+
HT: 62"–84"

2 DOOR / TALL
30"–36"
24"+
HT: 90"+

ROLLING GARMENT RACK
63+
22"

2 DOOR PLUS DRAWERS
36"–68"+
21"–27"+
HT: 48"–84"

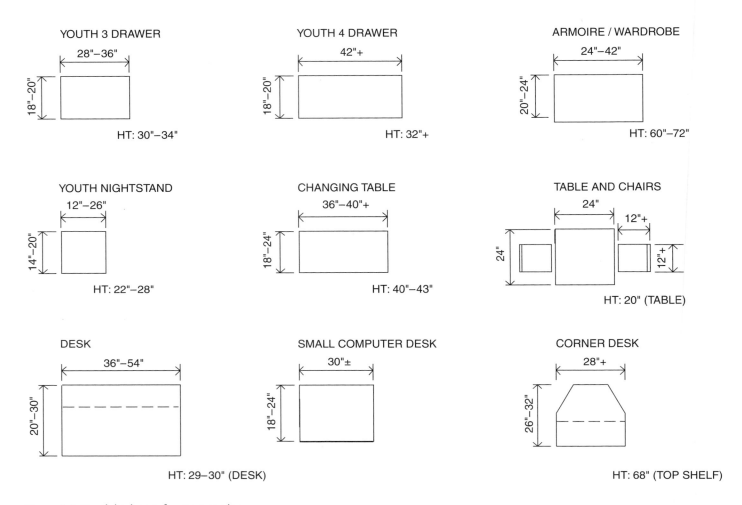

Figure 3-6 Youth bedroom furniture in plan.

Some firms specialize in designing and building closets outfitted with fine hardware, stone countertops, specialized lighting, and beautiful custom cabinetry. Such luxurious elements do not necessarily improve the functional qualities of the closet. They do, however, appeal to some homeowners. Closets need not be outfitted with such luxurious elements to serve the homeowner well; a suitable and useful closet is a matter of design and careful planning, which is covered in detail in the "Ergonomics and Required Clearances" section.

ACCESSIBILITY

Accessible bedrooms require access to the room through a door with a 32-inch minimum clear opening, as well as clear circulation space for a wheelchair (also 32 inches minimum) for access to the bed, closet, and additional clothing storage. Providing clear turning space for the wheelchair within the room is also recommended. In addition to providing clear circulation space for movement of the wheelchair, space must also be provided for opening doors and drawers. The following section of the chapter covers more specifics related to circulation and clear spaces required for wheelchair users.

Consideration of mounting heights for clothing rods, shelves, and additional storage elements is important in order to provide useful storage space for wheelchair users and those individuals with limited mobility. This information is also provided in the following section of the chapter.

Figure 3-7 Standard circulation space and bed access.

A. Circulation occurs at the entrance and most traveled areas; major circulation areas require 30 to 36 inches of clear floor space.

B. Minor circulation areas—those less traveled—are most comfortable designed at 24 inches. However, they can function at 22 inches and can be tightly sized at 18 inches.

C. The area required to make the bed is a minimum of 18 inches and is more comfortably designed at 24 inches.

ERGONOMICS AND REQUIRED CLEARANCES

The specialized nature of bedrooms requires that designers consider several ergonomic factors in order to design useful, successful rooms for sleep. Figures 3-7 and 3-8 depict bedroom circulation area requirements. The work of making and cleaning around the bed requires a minimum of 18 inches but is most comfortably designed at 24 inches. Making and accessing the bed using a wheelchair requires a minimum of 36 inches.

Figure 3-8 Circulation space and bed access for wheelchairs. The solid lines at the bed area indicate a queen-size bed; dashed lines at the bed indicate a full bed.

A. Major circulation areas require 36 inches for wheelchairs.

B. For wheelchair users, all circulation space is best kept at 36 inches (or more), with 32 inches the minimum required for wheelchairs.

C. A clearance of 36 inches around beds is required for wheelchairs, with 48-by-36-inch clear space next to closet.

D. The minimum turning radius for wheelchairs is 60 inches.

E. Clear space is required on the latch side of doors opening in (as shown) for wheelchair access to the door when opening and closing the door (minimum of 18 inches x 48 inches as shown with dashed lines at E).

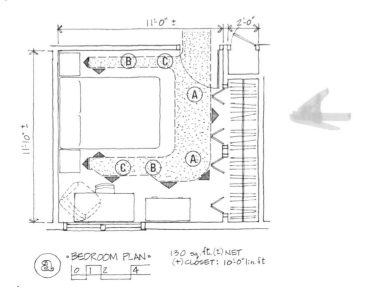

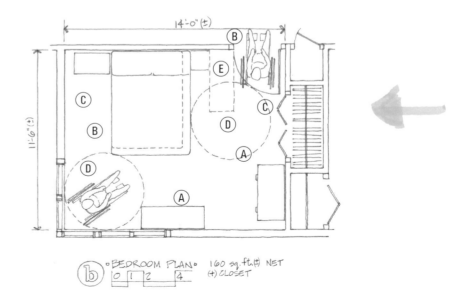

Storage furnishings such as dressers, dressing tables, shelves, and nightstands often require the user to bend down rather low to use the furniture and require clearance for drawers to pull out. For access to storage items from a wheelchair, a 30-inch-by-48-inch clear space adjacent to storage furnishings with doors and drawers is necessary. Figure 3-9 illustrates requirements for using bedroom storage furnishings.

As stated previously, closets present specific dimensional requirements related to reaching and retrieving items and influenced by the sizes of garments and accessories. Figures 10a and 10b illustrate reaching heights and storage information. Because closets are generally enclosed by some sort of door or visual screen, the type of door selected requires serious consideration. Doorjambs and frames can strongly influence the ease with which the closet is accessed, as illustrated in Figure 3-11.

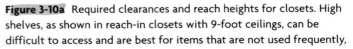

Figure 3-10a Required clearances and reach heights for closets. High shelves, as shown in reach-in closets with 9-foot ceilings, can be difficult to access and are best for items that are not used frequently,

1. Two-row (-rod) hanging clothing storage.
2. Single rod for long coats, gowns, and dresses.
3. Closets deeper than 24 inches offer limited benefits as shown.
4. Very deep closets may offer additional shelving storage behind hanging clothes; this can be awkward to access and useful only for storage of items that are seldom accessed.

Figure 3-9 Required clearances for bedroom storage.

1. In some cases a bed can be located closer than indicated; this requires that users use the drawers while sitting on the bed.

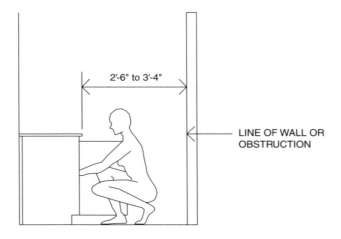

2'-6" to 3'-4"

LINE OF WALL OR OBSTRUCTION

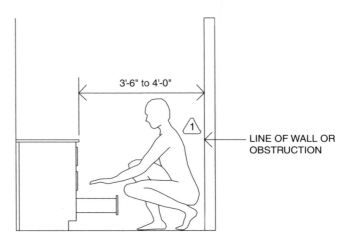

3'-6" to 4'-0"

LINE OF WALL OR OBSTRUCTION

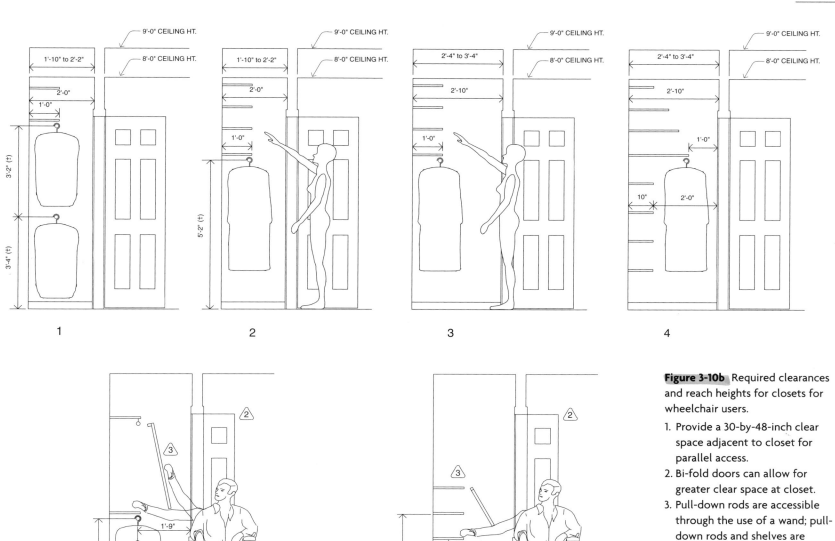

1

2

3

4

KIDS WITH CHAIR REACH RANGE
36"–44"

Figure 3-10b Required clearances and reach heights for closets for wheelchair users.

1. Provide a 30-by-48-inch clear space adjacent to closet for parallel access.
2. Bi-fold doors can allow for greater clear space at closet.
3. Pull-down rods are accessible through the use of a wand; pull-down rods and shelves are available.

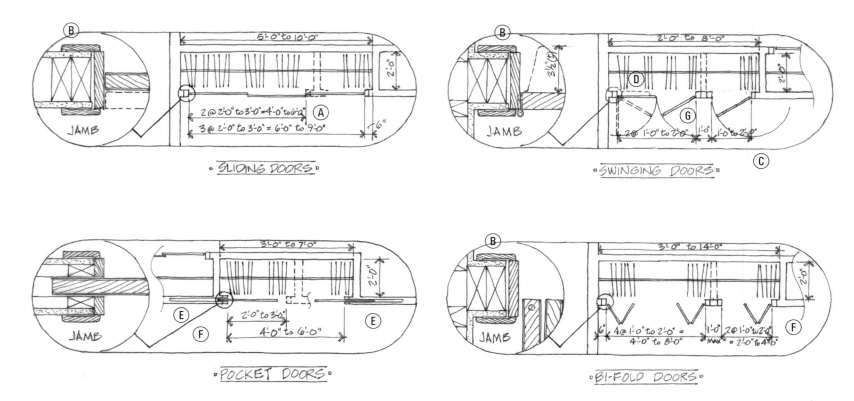

Figure 3-11 Closet doors.

A. Three door example shown. Additional doors can be added. Standard double track allows for only 33 percent opening. The addition of a third track allows for 66 percent opening.

B. In all of the door examples shown, there must be an allowance for door trim, which varies in width from 1½ inches to 5½ inches, with 2¼ to 3½ inches the most common. In budget installations, sliding and bi-fold doors can be installed without a door frame/trim.

C. Unlike sliding doors, swinging doors require no track, creating less maintenance problems.

D. Swinging doors permit the back of the door (closet side) to be used for lightweight shallow storage, much like a refrigerator door.

E. There may not be wall space available for the location of a pocket on two sides. With adequate room in the adjacent walls for pockets, this type of door can allow up to a 95 percent opening.

F. Pocket and bi-fold doors can allow for a great percentage of open area, with limited floor space taken up by door swings, making them helpful for some wheelchair users.

G. These doors (maximum of 2 feet) grant a large opening (90 percent), with minimal door swings.

Note: The construction of doors and door frames for other interior locations is similar to that shown in this figure.

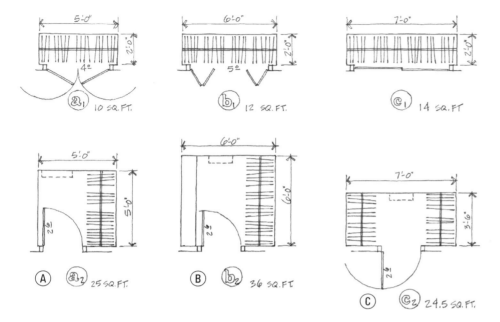

Figure 3-12 Closet type comparison. Generally, reach-in closets are more efficient because they share circulation space with the actual room rather than requiring internal space. This is illustrated in the following drawings:

A. Closets a1 and a2 contain the same lineal footage of clothing rod space; however, due to the need for circulation space in closet a2, far more square footage is required. a2 does offer an area for shelving (dashed lines), but this is a minimal advantage when weighed against the additional square footage. a1 will work using bi-fold, swinging, and sliding doors, while a2 would generally use a swinging, and less commonly a pocket door.

B. Closets b1 and b2 contain the same lineal footage of clothing rod space; however, due to requirements for circulation space in closet b2, far more square footage is required. b2 does offer an area for shelving (dashed lines), but this is a minimal advantage when weighed against the additional square footage. b2 will work using bi-fold and sliding doors, while at this size, swinging doors (2-feet, 6-inches each) would project into the room excessively.

C. Closets c1 and c2 contain the same lineal footage of clothing rod space. Unlike the previous walk-in examples on this page, c2 offers the advantage of "double-loaded" rod or storage areas sharing one circulation aisle, which offers a better economy of space than the single-loaded examples. This type of double-loaded walk-in closet can be extended quite aways, as the depth of the closet increases and additional width of 8 feet or more proves helpful. As the width expands, accessing the closet through double swinging doors becomes possible, which appeals to some clients. c1 will work using bi-fold and sliding doors, while at this size (3 feet) swinging doors would project into the room excessively.

Note: This figure illustrates the comparative square footage in the various types of closets. In some instances walk-in closets may be seen as preferable based upon the overall room design. For example, walk-in closets may provide more wall space for locations of furnishings and artwork within the room.

While many homeowners prefer the idea of a walk-in closet, such closets do not always provide the most effective clothing storage. This has to do with the fact that clothing rods generally run in a line and require access space for clothing retrieval. Reach-in closets use space efficiently because they share circulation space with the bedroom. In some cases, walk-in closets can limit actual clothing rod space because they require that the access to the rod be contained within the closet area, while in other instances, walk-in closets may be preferable in that they can provide more wall space for placement of furniture and artwork in the bedroom because they require a narrower door opening. Therefore, it is important to discuss storage requirements and spatial constraints in detail with the individual client and to adjust closet location and type to the specific project plan. Figure 3-12 illustrates the use of floor space requirements relative to clothing storage in a range of closets.

As with all types of home storage, it is important to inventory items that will be stored in individual closets. Those items used least frequently can be placed in less accessible areas (typically on a top shelf or an area that requires a bit of reaching). The most accessible portions of the closet (this varies based on door type)

should contain the most commonly used items. Rods placed at varying heights allow for the appropriate amount and type of hanging space and free up space for racks and shelves.

Specialized closet storage systems are available. These run from simple shelves and rods to custom cabinetry. Within quite a range of options and costs, there are some common elements shared by many closet storage systems. Rods arranged at various heights, including areas of double rods, are part of most well-designed closets. Shelves, baskets, and drawers are used to store folded clothing and other

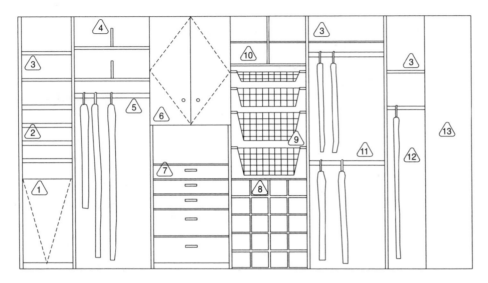

ELEVATION

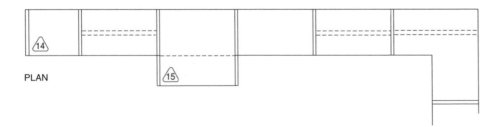

PLAN

Figure 3-13 Closet storage elements.

1. Bottom-hinged door, useful as hamper. Coated wire inserts are available.
2. Angled shoe shelves.
3. Open shelves, generally adjustable. Available in wood, laminate, glass, and coated wire.
4. Vertical acrylic/plastic shelf dividers.
5. Clothes rod for full-height clothes.
6. Doors available in a range of styles including wood panel, laminate, wood with glass window, and clear acrylic panels.
7. Drawers available in a range of styles (similar to doors). Drawers range in depth and width from 5 inches to 10-plus inches deep.
8. Shoe cubes.
9. Coated wire baskets available in a range of widths and depths from 4 inches to 12-plus inches deep.
10. Shelves with dividers create "cubbies."
11. Double clothes rod area (for shirts, blouses, jackets, some skirts, etc.).
12. Clothes rod for medium-length dresses and trousers hung by the cuffs.
13. Corner unit usually employs shelves or rods. In some cases a corner is created by a corner shelf placed at the top of two tower units.
14. Depth of many storage units ranges from 14 to 18 inches.
15. Some storage units are deeper, running from 20 to 24-plus inches. There are also combined units that are deeper at the base and narrow above.

accessories. These are often open but can be concealed behind doors as desired. Most shelves are adjustable, and some can pull out the full dimension of the shelf. Shoes are commonly stored on shelves, angled racks, hanging racks, or "shoe cubes." Other closet accessories include forward telescoping rods, tie racks, belt racks, and bottom-hinged doors with hamper inserts. Figure 3-13 provides information about elements used with various closet-organizing systems.

Larger, more elaborate closets may include an island with a finished top placed in a central location and used for folding and arranging clothes. Such islands are often roughly 36 inches high and require significant circulation space so that one may access both the island and the adjacent clothes storage areas. Closets may include specialized lighting, windows, or mechanical ventilation systems (useful where hampers are located), dressing tables, and vanities. These items can all be combined to create an entire dressing enclave that often includes or is adjacent to the bathroom area. Such an area is detailed in the previously discussed Figure 3-2.

ORGANIZATIONAL FLOW

As stated, the bed and its placement tend to dominate the layout of the room. Therefore, as a bedroom is designed, the location of the bed is best considered first. As stated previously, circulation space in a bedroom directly relates to the bed and to those spaces considered ancillary, such as the closet, additional storage, other furnishings, and sometimes a bathroom, as well as access space to the main entry to the room.

When considering how elements in a room are used, the designer must also imagine the traffic flow. Circulation space is required as one approaches the bed, but traffic also must flow to the closet and additional clothing storage areas (such as dressers), as one requires a change of clothing. This means that on some occasions, people enter the room with no intention of approaching the bed and instead are attempting to retrieve an item of clothing or to change clothes. With this in mind, it is generally most useful to place the closet close to the entry of the room instead of on the wall farthest from the room entrance. Figure 3-14 depicts a bubble diagram detailing the relationship between the room entry and closet area.

Because dressers and chests of drawers are used to store clothing and are often used at the same time as closets, it is helpful to place dressers relatively

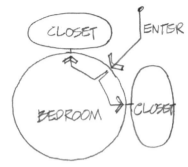

Figure 3-14 Bubble diagram depicting the entrance and its relationship to closet space. Closets placed adjacent to the room entrance allow for easy retrieval of clothing and accessories.

close to closets when possible. This helps with room layout relative to traffic flow as well. Those places used most often require more circulation space. As one moves from the dressing areas toward those areas less frequently accessed, less circulation space is required, as discussed previously.

Note that the location of the bedroom entrance relative to the location of exterior walls (and therefore windows) is a primary determinate of the form of the room. The authors have identified four basic bedroom form types based on relationships to exterior walls.

In one type, the exterior wall is opposite the entrance, as shown in Figure 3-15 (Room A). A similar situation occurs when there are two exterior walls in a room, with of those walls opposite the entrance. This has the potential to create a "corner room," as shown in Figure 3-15 (Room B).

Another room form is created when one exterior wall is adjacent to the room entrance, as shown in Figure 3-15 (Room C). This room form is rare because it typically requires that a hallway terminate at the bedroom entrance, which can involve some wasted space in new construction. In other, also rare cases, a "bedroom wing" is created, with the entrance being flanked by three exterior walls, as shown in Figure 3-15 (Room D). This room form is often found in suites in custom homes and offers the possibility of taking great advantage of views, as it allows for daylight on three sides. The discussion of room form to this point relates to generic room types and is meant to be helpful as one plans the general disposition of rooms. Room size, furniture layout, closet design, window placement, and orientation are additional issues that must be considered as the room is developed further.

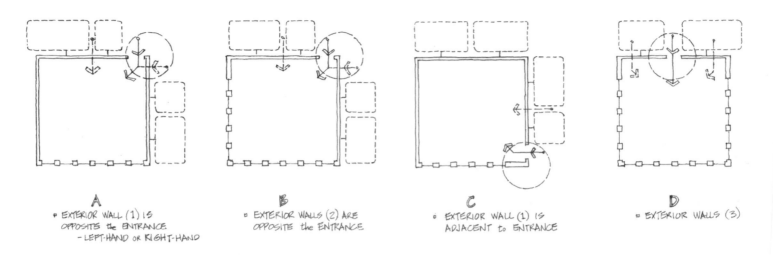

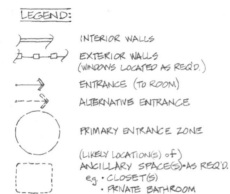

Figure 3-15 Generic room forms. Drawings A, B, C, and D show generic bedroom plans based upon the relationship between the room, the exterior walls, and the entrance. While exterior walls are shown using lines that represent windows, this is only an indication that windows may be placed at points along these walls. Actual window placement will vary based upon a series of factors including site orientation, aesthetics, climate, budget, and building context and style.

Room A. The exterior wall is opposite the entrance, offering one wall for window location and creating two possible locations for closet placement and a range of possibilities for furniture placement. The door is best placed in an offset position, as centering it can cause traffic flow problems and limits furniture placement.

Room B. Two exterior walls are opposite the entrance, offering two walls for window location, allowing daylight from two sides (highly prized by some), creating two possible locations for closet placement and multiple possibilities for furniture placement. Window placement on each exterior wall must be well considered so that the most advantageous use of light and views takes place while at the same time not limiting furniture placement options. The door is best placed in an offset position, as centering it can cause traffic flow problems and limits furniture placement.

Room C. The exterior wall is adjacent to the entrance. This is rare, as it requires that a hallway terminate at an exterior wall (as shown). Although somewhat rare, this type of room can be found in two-story houses, with a central stair creating a second-floor hallway with room entrances on opposite sides.

Room D. Three exterior walls are opposite the entrance, offering three walls for window location, allowing daylight from three sides (highly prized by some), and taking great advantage of available views. This room form is often found in suites in custom homes. It limits the placement of the closets, as there is only one location adjacent to the entry door, forcing the closets and ancillary spaces into a more remote location than is often desired (centering the door can aid in closet placement). As with the previous room form, the placement of windows in such rooms requires careful thought in order to provide flexibility for furnishings.

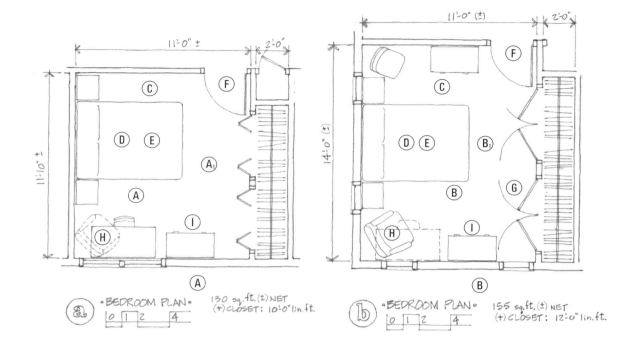

11'-0" ± 2'-0"

11'-0" ±

C   F

D   E

A₁

A

H   I

A

·BEDROOM PLAN·
0 1 2   4

130 sq.ft. (±) NET
(+) CLOSET: 10'-0" lin.ft.

11'-0" (±) 2'-0"

F

C

14'-0" (±)

D   E   B₁

B   G

H   I

B

·BEDROOM PLAN·
0 1 2   4

155 sq.ft. (±) NET
(+) CLOSET: 12'-0" lin.ft.

Figure 3-16 Room size, circulation, and furniture layout.

A. This room size allows for furniture to be placed on only two walls with adequate major circulation space provided. See Figures 3-8a and 3-8b for information on spatial requirements. Major circulation space: A1

B. This larger room size allows for furniture to be placed on three walls with adequate major circulation space provided. See Figures 3-8a and 3-8b for information on spatial requirements. Major circulation space: B1

C. Minor circulation space. To areas less traveled. See Figures 3-8a and 3-8b for information on spatial requirements.

D. It is often best to locate the bed off of the exterior wall at the windows due to climate, the nature of furnishings (headboards), and in the case of small children, safety.

E. Shown with a queen-size bed, currently the most popular bed size in the United States. Wheelchair access at the sides of the bed of 36 inches as well as a turning radius may require a reduction in bed size. Use of king-size beds requires a larger room area or the elimination of some additional furnishings. Use of twin or full-size beds allows for smaller room size or the addition of furnishings.

F. Doors shown are 2 feet, 8 inches; 3-foot doors are required for wheelchairs in order to provide 32 inches of clear space. Doors should be placed so that the arc of their swing works functionally and the door swings to an appropriate location and is kept out of the way.

G. Swinging closet doors require adequate swinging space. For additional information on closet doors, see Figure 3-11.

H. Area shown for a variety of furnishings and uses.

I. Adequate area should be provided for opening doors and drawers. See Figure 3-9.

The overall size of the room will dictate where furniture may be placed and therefore where the circulation aisles and spaces are located, so that more than one major circulation space is created. A room that is roughly 130 to 140 square feet—and relatively square in shape—allows for placement of major furniture (queen-size bed and dressers) on two walls. This two-wall placement creates a single major circulation aisle and one minor circulation space used for the secondary bed approach. Given this room size, it is not possible to load furnishings on additional walls, unless the bed size is reduced, as shown in Figures 3-16 to 3-18.

As the dimensions of the room are expanded, particularly in one direction, a more rectilinear room form is created. In this form, at roughly 150 square feet or more, placement of storage furniture and bed(s) can occur on three walls—or more depending upon closet location. Furniture located in this manner requires space for major traffic flow to all three walls as shown, which is accommodated easily in a room this size. This is shown in Figures 3-16 to 3-18. For a bedroom suite, the room sizes and configurations discussed to this point must be increased with considerable square footage to accommodate a walk-in closet and/or bathroom.

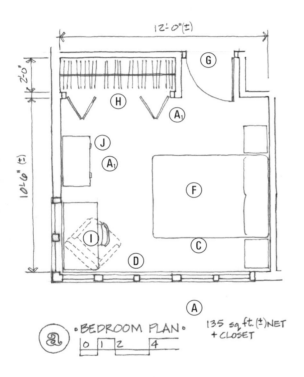

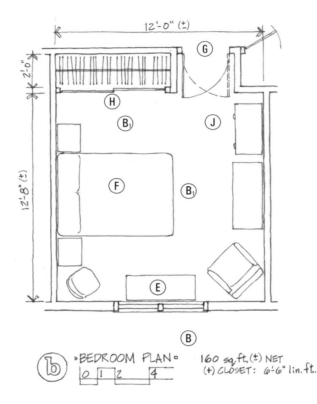

Figure 3-17 Room size, circulation, and furniture layout.

A. This room size allows for furniture to be placed on only two walls with adequate major circulation space provided. See Figures 3-8a and 3-8b for information on spatial requirements. Major circulation space: A1

B. This larger room size allows for furniture to be placed on three walls with adequate major circulation space provided. See Figures 3-8a and 3-8b for information on spatial requirements. Major circulation space: B1

C. Minor circulation space. To areas less traveled. See Figures 3-8a and 3-8b for information on spatial requirements.

D. It is often best to locate the bed off of the exterior wall at window due to climate, the nature of furnishings (headboards), and in the case of small children, safety.

E. While this window is shown as centered, this is not necessarily the best placement relative to room layout, window style, and overall building design.

F. Shown with a queen-size bed, currently the most popular bed size in the United States. Wheelchair access at the sides of the bed of 36 inches as well as a turning radius may require a reduction in bed size. Use of king-size beds requires a larger room area or the elimination of some additional furnishings. Use of twin or full-size beds allows for smaller room size or the addition of furnishings.

G. Doors shown are 2 feet, 8 inches; 3-foot doors are required for wheelchairs in order to provide 32 inches of clear space. Doors should be placed so that the arc of their swing works functionally and the door swings to an appropriate location and is kept out of the way.

H. Swinging closet doors would require adequate swinging space. For additional information on closet doors, see Figure 3-11.

I. Area shown for a variety of furnishings and uses.

J. Adequate area should be provided for opening doors and drawers. See Figure 3-9.

Figure 3-18 Room size, circulation, and furniture layout.

A. This room size allows for furniture to be placed on only two walls with adequate major circulation space provided. See Figures 3-8a and 3-8b for information on spatial requirements. Major circulation space: A1

B. This larger room size allows for furniture to be placed on three walls with adequate major circulation space provided. See Figures 3-8a and 3-8b for information on spatial requirements. Major circulation space: B1

C. Minor circulation space. To areas less traveled. See Figures 3-8a and 3-8b for information on spatial requirements.

D. It is often best to locate the bed off of the exterior wall at windows due to climate, the nature of furnishings (headboards), and in the case of small children, safety.

E. While this window is shown as centered, this is not necessarily the best placement relative to room layout, window style, and overall building design; in this case it may preclude locating the bed on that wall (see D above).

F. Shown with a queen-size bed, currently the most popular bed size in the United States. Wheelchair access at the sides of the bed of 36 inches as well as a turning radius may require a reduction in bed size. Use of king-size beds requires a larger room area or the elimination of some additional furnishings. Use of twin or full-size beds allows for smaller room size or the addition of furnishings. Two twin beds are shown with dashed lines (F1).

G. Doors shown are 2 feet, 8 inches; 3-foot doors are required for wheelchairs in order to provide 32 inches of clear space. Doors should be placed so that the arc of their swing works functionally and the door swings to an appropriate location and is kept out of the way.

H. Swinging closet doors require adequate swinging space. For additional information on closet doors, see Figure 3-11.

I. Area shown for a variety of furnishings and uses.

J. Adequate area should be provided for opening doors and drawers. See Figure 3-9.

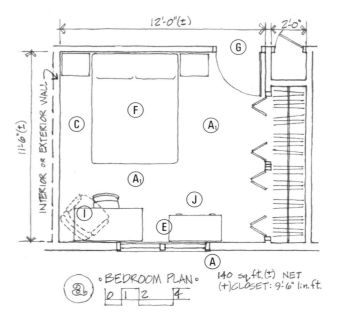

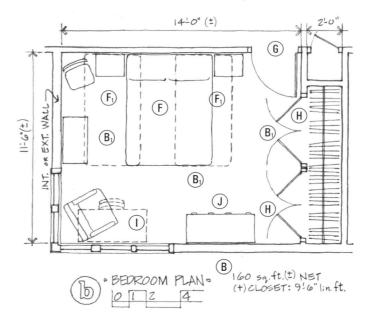

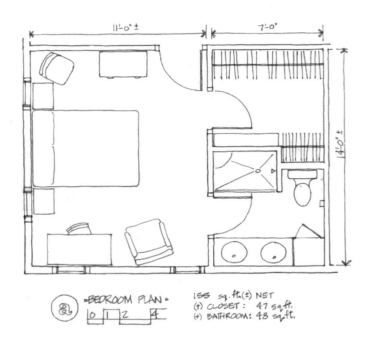

•BEDROOM PLAN•
0 1 2 4

155 sq.ft.(±) NET
(+) CLOSET: 47 sq.ft.
(+) BATHROOM: 48 sq.ft.

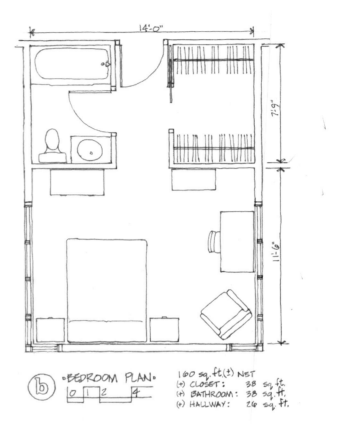

•BEDROOM PLAN•
0 1 2 4

160 sq.ft.(±) NET
(+) CLOSET: 38 sq.ft.
(+) BATHROOM: 38 sq.ft.
(+) HALLWAY: 26 sq.ft.

Figure 3-19 depicts basic room sizes shown previously with the areas for the larger closet and bathroom added to create owner's suites. While these designs only suggest some of the many possibilities of suite design, they do point to the need for the actual bedroom area to retain its relative size, which is augmented significantly with a large closet or closets and bathroom. A poorly designed room that does not take into consideration the many issues covered thus far is shown in Figure 3-20. This illustration depicts a room of 130 square feet containing a poorly considered walk-in closet. While one can walk into the closet, it provides limited clothing rod space. Also, the location of the closet is not convenient to the entry door, and it limits options for window placement in the room. Additionally, the room design creates a good deal of wasted space, little access space for furnishings, and poor traffic flow.

Figure 3-19 Bedroom suites. The addition of a generous walk-in closet and bathroom add considerably to a room's square footage. The rooms shown were covered in Figures 3-16 item b and 3-17 item b (plan rotated) and have been kept intact to demonstrate that as suite size increases, basic room requirements can remain consistent. Bathrooms and large closets necessarily add to the room area and should not decrease the quality or function of the actual bedroom. When considering the options, the designer should keep in mind that all bedrooms require some form of closet and bathrooms can be seen as optional.

Figure 3-20 Unsuccessful bedroom plan.

A. The closet location is very remote from the room entrance, requiring traveling the entire distance of the room to retrieve clothing. Additionally, the room is long and narrow and the closet is located in a way that narrows the room further.

B. The closet occupies a prime room location on the exterior wall, eliminating possible window locations and limiting furniture placement options.

C. Closet door (bi-fold) is drawn too small, thereby giving a false impression of how much space the door takes up.

D. Entry door at 2 feet, 4 inches is too small. The recommended minimum is 2 foot, 8 inches. The door swing is awkward and would be better placed on the other side, where it would be out of the way when open.

E. The room contains adequate square footage, but the narrow design/closet location creates significant problems with circulation and furniture locations.

F. Closet contains only 4 lineal feet of rod space; a similarly located reach-in with appropriate doors would allow 7 lineal feet of rod space.

G. There is no good place for a queen-size bed and no room for adequate side clearances and circulation.

H. This is wasted space, while other portions of the room are too tight to function (such as item G).

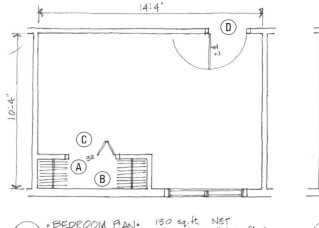

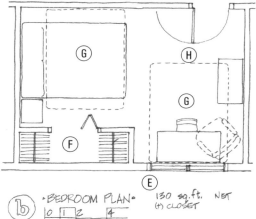

RELATED CODES AND CONSTRAINTS

Section R303 of the International Residential Code (IRC, 2004) covers light, ventilation, and heating. This section (R303.1) states that "all habitable rooms shall be provided with aggregate glazing area of not less than 8 percent of the floor area of such rooms. Natural ventilation shall be through windows, doors, louvers, or other approved openings to the outdoor air. Such openings shall be provided with ready access or shall otherwise be readily controllable by the building occupants. The minimum openable area to the outdoors shall be 4 percent of the floor area being ventilated."

The IRC defines habitable space as "a space for living, sleeping, eating or cooking," which means that bedrooms must follow the guidelines listed above with some exceptions, such as rooms that are provided with acceptable mechanical ventilation systems. In addition, there may be exceptions or broader requirements in some state and local codes. Regardless of possible exceptions, it is a good general rule to meet or exceed the ventilation and light requirements by providing the window area called for in bedrooms.

Section R304 of the IRC (2004) covers minimum room areas and states that "every dwelling unit shall have at least one habitable room that shall have not less than 120 square feet (11.2 m²) of gross floor area." This largest required room is not typically the bedroom, although in some instances that could be the case. The code goes on to state that after the required 120-square-foot room, "other habitable rooms shall have a floor area of not less than 70 square feet (6.5 m²)." In addition: "habitable rooms shall not be less than 7 feet (2143 mm) in any horizontal dimension." The previously discussed minimal bedroom shown in Figure 3-1 represents a room meeting these minimum standards. According to this section of the code, "portions of a room with a sloping ceiling measuring less than 5 feet or with a furred ceiling measuring less than 7 feet from the finished floor to the finished ceiling shall not be considered as contributing to the minimum required habitable area for that room."

Section R305 of the IRC covers ceiling height in detail and reads, "Habitable rooms . . . shall have a ceiling height of not less than 7 feet (2134 mm). The required height shall be measured from the finish floor to the lowest projection from the ceiling." There are some notable exceptions listed in the section on ceiling height, including beams and girders "placed not less than 4 feet (1219 mm) on center may project not more than 6 inches (152 mm) below the required ceiling height." It is also noted that "not more than 50% of the required floor area of a room or space is permitted to have a sloped ceiling less than 7 feet (2134 mm) in height with no portion of the required floor area less than 5 feet (1524 mm) in height." Figure 3-21 illustrates the ceiling heights relative to room areas required by the IRC.

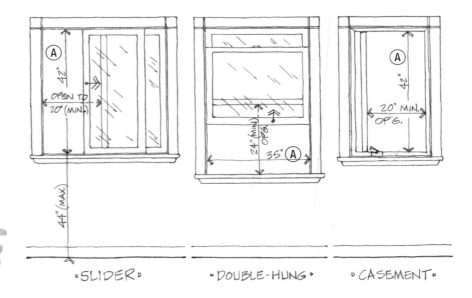

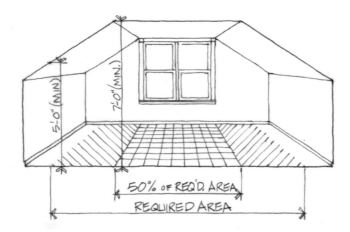

Figure 3-21 International Residential Code (IRC) Required Floor Area and Ceiling Heights. The International Residential Code calls for habitable rooms (including bedrooms) to have a ceiling height of "not less than 7 feet (2134 mm)." It also states that "not more than 50% of the required floor area of a room or space is permitted to have a sloped ceiling less than 7 feet (2134 mm) in height with no portion of the required floor area less than 5 feet (1524 mm) in height."

Figure 3-22 International Residential Code (IRC) Emergency Escape and Rescue Openings (Egress Windows). The International Residential Code states that "every sleeping room shall have at least one openable emergency escape and rescue opening . . . where emergency escape and rescue openings are provided they shall have a sill height of not more than 44 inches above the floor (118 mm) . . . minimum opening area of all emergency escape and rescue openings shall have a minimum net clear opening of 5.7 square feet (0.530 m²)," with the exception of grade floor openings, which "shall have a minimum net clear opening of 5 square feet (0.465 m²)." The code further states "the minimum net clear opening height shall be 24 inches (610 mm)" and the "minimum net clear opening width shall be 20 inches (508 mm)." The dimension (A) shown in each case is required to meet the 5.7 square foot opening requirement when paired with the horizontal or vertical dimensions shown.

Issues related to bedrooms are also covered in the IRC under "Emergency Escape and Rescue Openings" in Section R310. This section starts with "Basements with habitable space and every sleeping room shall have at least one openable emergency escape and rescue opening. Where basements contain one or more sleeping rooms, emergency egress and rescue openings shall be required in each sleeping room, but shall not be required in adjoining areas of the basement. Where emergency escape and rescue openings are provided they shall have a sill height of not more than 44 inches above the floor (118 mm)." The section continues to state that the "minimum opening area of all emergency escape and rescue openings shall have a minimum net clear opening of 5.7 square feet (0.530 m²)" with the exception of grade floor openings, which "shall have a minimum net clear opening of 5 square feet (0.465 m²)."

Opening height and width are also covered as follows: "The minimum net clear opening height shall be 24 inches (610 mm)" and the "minimum net clear opening width shall be 20 inches (508 mm)." In terms of operation the code states that emergency, ". . . escape and rescue openings shall be operational from the inside of the room without the use of keys or tools." Figure 3-22 illustrates minimum opening areas.

The code issues mentioned to this point relate to single-family homes, which are governed by the IRC. For introductory information regarding codes related to multifamily housing, please see the "Related Codes and Constraints" section of Chapter 1.

ELECTRICAL AND MECHANICAL

Unlike other rooms in the home, bedrooms are not typically influenced to any large degree by plumbing or significant electrical requirements. Mechanical provisions for bedrooms are rather straightforward. Because the International Residential Code (Section R303.8) calls for heating to a minimum of 68°F when the winter temperature is below 60°F, most bedrooms in the United States are required to have some form of heat source.

The location for the heat source or its registers or diffusers, as well as those used by any air-cooling source, must be considered by the interior designer as lighting, furnishings, window, and door locations are planned. The actual engineering of the heating and cooling system are, of course, done by professionals other than the interior designer. For additional information on heating, ventilation, and air conditioning, please see the "Electrical and Mechanical" section of Chapter 1.

As with other general wall spaces, there are some general rules for locating electrical switches and convenience outlets in bedrooms. The on/off switches for overhead or general lights are best located close to the room entry door on the latch side of the doorway when possible. In larger suites with more than one entrance, a second on/off switch, known as a three-way switch, can be employed in another convenient location. Where a number of light fixtures are used for ambient lighting, a single switch can be used to control a number of fixtures and

outlets. Switch placement for bedrooms follows those described in Chapter 1 and illustrated in Figure 1-9.

Following general rules can be a good starting point; however, the placement of outlets must be considered in relation to the design and layout of the room. It is very important to consider the various possibilities for furniture placement in a bedroom so that the outlets can be designed in a way that is useful for a variety of scenarios. While a designer might have an initial plan for locating furnishings, years later the homeowner may wish to move the furnishings around. With this in mind, the outlets should be designed to accommodate a range of furniture layouts, not simply the one planned for the short term. See Figure 3-23 for drawings of outlet locations in a room with two different furniture layouts.

In addition to lighting and power outlets, bedrooms may require various communication lines. Telephone, cable, and stereo/audio may be required in bedrooms. Much like power outlets, these elements must be located in areas that work for a variety of furniture layouts. As stated in Chapter 1, interior designers often designate the locations for lighting, outlets, switches, and various communication systems, while the actual engineering of the power, HVAC, and communication systems is done by professionals in those fields. Just as with electrical outlets, designers must consider a range of locations for cable and communications outlets so that various furniture layouts can be accommodated. As wireless communication becomes more common, the location of communications outlets will likely become less of a concern. Figure 3-23 illustrates cable and communication outlet in a room with a variety of furniture layouts.

LIGHTING

Lighting for bedrooms has evolved and is now, in some cases, quite sophisticated. In years past a single overhead ceiling-mounted light fixture, with its light pouring downward, was seen as a standard design feature in residential bedrooms. This is no longer considered standard, and in most cases, pleasant ambient lighting is supplied by sources other than a downlight. Pendant-mounted uplights bounce light off the ceiling and wall, creating ambient light that softens physical features—an excellent choice for the bedroom. In addition, cove and cornice- and soffit-mounted luminaires can provide excellent, indirect ambient lighting.

Some rooms benefit from perimeter lighting as well as a ceiling-mounted fixture in the center for balance. Comfortable, adequate general lighting should be

Figure 3-23 Electrical plans depicting two different furniture layouts, with light, outlet, and switch locations. The location of outlets and switches permits flexibility in furnishing the room. Note that the overhead fixture and a wall outlet are switched to provide general room light, which would allow for the elimination of one of those sources. Also note that communication lines (phone and cable) are provided to two locations to allow for flexibility with furniture placement. For additional information on electrical symbols and lighting, see Chapters 1 and 2.

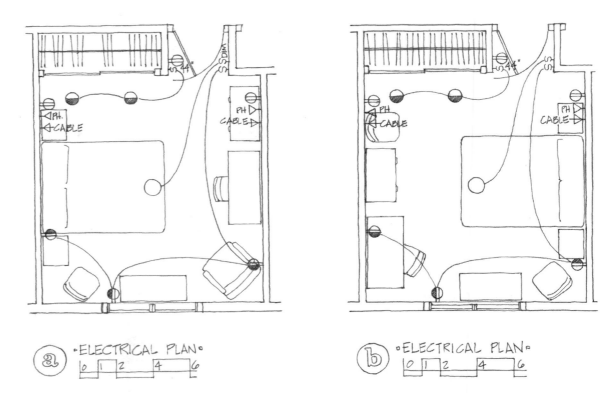

supplied in one manner or another, and the type of fixture used must be determined after careful discussions with the client so that the appropriate luminaires can be identified. Regardless of the type of fixture selected, the fixture or fixtures that supply general lighting should be switched at the wall adjacent to the room entry, as discussed previously.

In addition to adequate general lighting, the bedroom requires task lighting for reading, self-care, and in some cases, for work. Task lighting is often supplied by table, floor, or wall-mounted fixtures. Additionally, accent lighting can be used to create focal points, enhance artwork, and give focus to important objects or areas.

BIBLIOGRAPHY

(Contains both works cited and recommended reading. Annotations where appropriate.)

Ramsey, Charles George, Harold Reeve Sleeper, and John Ray Hoke, Jr. *Architectural Graphic Standards*. 10th ed. Hoboken, NJ: John Wiley & Sons, 2000.

Whitehead, Randall. *Residential Lighting: A Practical Guide*. Hoboken, NJ: John Wiley & Sons, 2004.

CHAPTER 4

BATHROOMS

A "typical" American bathroom, a room combining a toilet, bathtub and/or shower, and sink, is a relatively new development. It is only since the Victorian era that the functions of bodily washing and toileting have been brought together in one room inside the home. Until the advent of successful indoor plumbing, most bathing took place in a portable tub with water hauled, heated, and poured into the tub. The water closet, the ancestor to the modern toilet (still called water closet by some), was invented in England in the mid-1800s and was refined with varying success into the early 1900s.

As indoor plumbing and water-heating devices evolved, the activities of washing and toileting came together in a single room in the American home, often called the bathroom. New grand houses of the late 1800s often boasted large, elaborate bathrooms with plumbing fixtures encased in decorative wood cabinets. In older homes of the day, bathrooms were often added through renovation of existing rooms such as smaller bedrooms and storage rooms. Figure 4-1 is a photograph of the interior of a plumbing fixtures shop taken in 1890.

In 1927, Kohler introduced bathroom sets—a bathtub, toilet, and lavatory—in matching colors. The matching set with various design options and available color choices was a step in the progression toward the myriad of options available for the homeowner of today. Figure 4-2 shows the Purist™ Lavatory by Kohler.

Figure 4-1 Photograph of the interior of a plumbing fixtures shop taken in 1890. This photograph shows some of the many plumbing fixtures available in the late 1800s and indicates consumer interest in the most up-to-date fixtures of the day. Photograph courtesy of the Minnesota Historical Society.

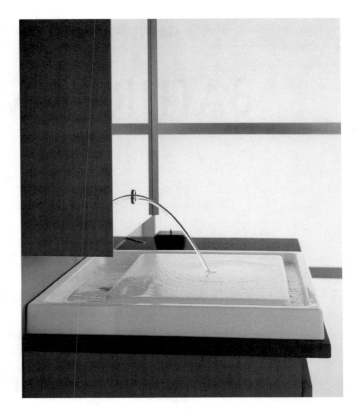

Figure 4-2 A photograph of the Purist™ Lavatory by Kohler. Current manufacturers continue to develop inventive products such as this one to satisfy ongoing customer interest in new, innovative plumbing fixtures. Photograph courtesy of Kohler Co.

According to the National Association of Home Builders (NAHB), 96 percent of American houses of the 1950s included one and a half bathrooms or fewer, whereas only 5 percent of homes built in 2003 included one and a half bathrooms or fewer, with 56 percent containing two and half bathrooms. The NAHB has also stated that as of 2004, the average 2,349-square-foot, single-family home contained three bathroom sinks, three toilets, two bathtubs, and one shower stall.

Bathrooms have proliferated in quantity in our homes because many homeowners prefer a bathroom for each bedroom or, at the very least, an owner's suite with bathroom, a youngster's and/or overnight guest's bathroom, and a partial bathroom—often called a powder room. Writing in *The Not So Big House*, Sarah Susanka urges homeowners to "cut back on the number of bathrooms," which can be done by considering "which bathrooms can be shared." Susanka states that most master baths are "typically more an expression of fantasy than reality, With its whirlpool or soaking tub the master bath implies a life of leisure and relaxation. The reality, in many families, is that the tub is used most often by children under the age of five." Susanka continues by stating that for some families, a large shared bathroom makes sense, while for others, a private bathing sanctuary for adults is best.

Susanka's plea for well-thought-out bathrooms, those that fit with the reality of daily living, makes sense given the fact that building and outfitting bathrooms is expensive and can lead to a significant use of natural resources, not only in the fabrication of fixtures but in the use of water, electricity, and natural gas. Issues of sustainability, cost, and use of space should be considered relative to the real needs of the family as bathrooms are designed. Some homeowners are willing to balance the fantasy of multiple elaborate bathrooms against the use of natural resources and/or budget and will opt for fewer bathrooms, while other homeowners will insist upon more bathrooms than there are household occupants and some of these may be quite elaborate, containing a range of specialized products.

A single well-designed bathroom can provide much of the privacy and comfort provided by two—or more—poorly considered bathrooms. Designing the bathroom to contain private chambers for differing activities, allowing more than one person to use the bathroom area at the same time, is a useful approach for lessening the overall number of bathrooms per home. For example, separating the sink area and/or the bathing areas from the toilet area allows one person to bathe or groom him- or herself while another person can use the toilet privately. Figure 4-3a illustrates a bathroom design that allows privacy for only one person. Figure 4-3b illustrates a bathroom design that provides private areas for more than one user.

In addition to considerations of privacy and efficiency of use, bathroom design is constrained by the basic nature of plumbing and the size and form of plumbing fixtures. All plumbing fixtures require water supply lines or pipes, as well

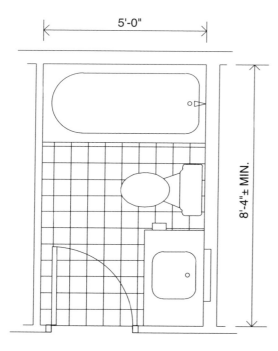

Figure 4-3a A plan of a commonly used single-wall bathroom design, which allows privacy for one user only.

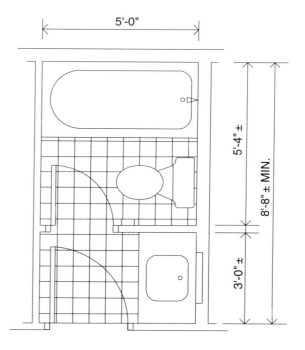

Figure 4-3b Illustrates a plan similar to that in Figure 4-3a, yet provides private areas for more than one user.

as drainpipes. The toilet requires a larger drainpipe known as a soil pipe. A network is formed as the independent branch drainpipes of other fixtures also lead to the soil pipe (also called a soil stack), and it is this larger pipe that leads sewage and wastewater out of the building.

The branch lines and soil pipes work using gravity and therefore require downward slopes (as called for in codes) for positive flow. In addition, the drainage system requires venting, which is generally supplied by an upward rising vent-line or pipe ultimately extending through the roof. Because the water supply system is under pressure, a continuous downward slope is not required by code. However, use of a continuous slope will facilitate the draining of the entire system, which is helpful in the prevention of frozen pipes in unoccupied homes. Figure 4-4 illus-

trates the water supply pipes in a standard bathroom, and Figure 4-5 illustrates the drainage pipes in a standard bathroom.

Understanding the basics of bathroom plumbing is helpful as a means of understanding the interrelationships of fixtures and drains. Each wall that contains a plumbing fixture is considered a *plumbing wall*, and minimizing the number of these plumbed walls per bathroom can save money. However, the overall ease of use and creation of privacy zones must be considered as equal in importance—if not more important—than the simple economy of minimizing plumbing walls. Bathroom design requires a consideration of the best layout of space and fixtures for the given client and project, balanced with a careful look at the economy of plumbed walls.

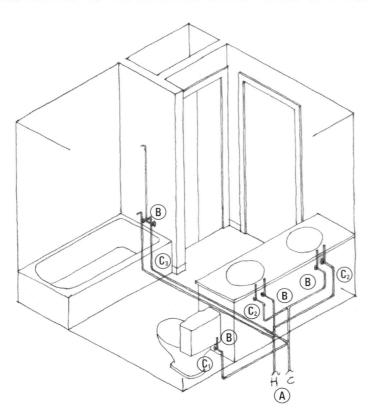

Figure 4-4 Bathroom supply pipes.

A. Water supply pipes can be fed from below or above and must be kept out of unheated spaces.

B. Each fixture requires a shutoff valve for each line (hot and cold). This facilitates the repair or removal of the fixture or faucet.

C. Pipe sizes (branch lines to individual fixtures).

  C1. Toilet (WC)—$\frac{3}{8}$ inch to $\frac{1}{2}$ inch. See manufacturer's recommendations.

  C2. Lavatories—$\frac{3}{8}$ inch. See manufacturer's recommendations.

  C3. Tub/shower—$\frac{1}{2}$ inch.

Water supply pipes fabricated of copper will meet most codes. Certain plastics will also meet some codes. Check local codes for clarification.

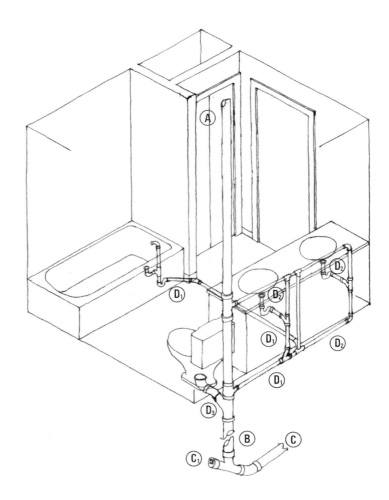

Figure 4-5 Bathroom drainage pipes.

Important rules of plumbing related to the waste system include the need to *trap all drains* and *vent all traps*. Wastewater must be trapped to prevent reentry of sewer gas, as methane can be lethal. There is no trap shown at the toilet because the fixture itself is shaped to form the trap. All traps must be vented in order to vent gas and to prevent siphoning action from pulling all of the wastewater out of the trap at times when a large quantity is released.

A. Vent stack—Goes through the roof. When possible, it is combined with plumbing vent pipes from other parts of the house to minimize the number of penetrations through the roof.

B. Soil stack—Goes to house sewer line; 3- to 4-inch size depending upon how many fixtures are draining into it.

C. House sewer line with cleanout (known as C.O., shown in C1). House sewer line runs to a municipal sanitary sewer main, most often in the street, or to an on-site private waste disposal system (septic tank and drainfield).

D. All horizontal waste pipes slope 1 to 2 percent. Size (diameter of pipe) is dependent upon length of run, number of fixtures serviced by the line, type, and distance from trap to vent. As shown:

  D1. (Tub)—2 inches.

  D2. (Lavatories)—$1\frac{1}{2}$ inches.

  D3. (Toilet)—3 inches.

Waste pipes are most often PVC (polyvinyl chloride) plastic; however, some codes require that certain pipes must be cast iron, such as the house sewer line and possibly soil and vent stacks.

ACCESSIBILITY

Bathrooms, along with kitchens, are rooms that have significant potential to create barriers for people with disabilities. Individuals using wheelchairs or with other mobility issues can be kept from using bathrooms with standard fixtures and standard clearances. As noted in Chapter 1, standards such as ANSI A117.1 and UFAS, as well as FHAA legislation, govern private multifamily housing units. In addition, some municipalities are governed by local visitability codes and/or guidelines, which require, at minimum, a ground-floor bathroom consisting of a toilet and sink that can be entered and used by a person using a wheelchair.

Although the Americans with Disabilities Act (ADA) covers bathroom design in detail, this legislation does not create guidelines for private residences. Some designers and students use the ADA guidelines as a default design standard for residential bathroom design, but doing this does not necessarily result in the best solution for a given client or situation. This is because the ADA guidelines are meant to serve as a standard for a wide range of individuals, whereas the design of private residences often requires special features designed for a particular client. For example, some homeowners require the use of personal aides and/or equipment for toileting and bathing, which will result in the need for clearance space not covered in the ADA guidelines.

Some advocates for the disabled argue that by creating residences that meet basic accessibility requirements for bathrooms (as well as other areas), designers not only serve the immediate need of wheelchair users in their homes but serve the future needs of an aging and mobile population. In addition to accessibility, designers should be aware of adaptability—those design features that can be changed to serve wheelchair users, such as removable vanity doors and toe-kicks that can accommodate wheelchair users.

With these considerations in mind, this chapter includes a discussion of accessibility as it relates to bathroom fixtures, clearances, maneuvering spaces, and grab bar placement. These items are included in the body of the chapter, rather than in a special section, in order to familiarize students and designers with accessibility and visitability as part of the totality of bathroom design.

FIXTURES

Because of the specialized nature of the various bathroom plumbing fixtures, it is important to understand each type of fixture in terms of size, construction, use, and required clearances, as well as issues of accessibility related to each fixture. The following is a review of the most commonly used fixtures.

Toilets

Toilets are made with *flush tanks* or *flush valves*. Those with flush valves are generally used in commercial applications because they require a larger water supply line. Most residential toilets are of the flush tank type, and these are available with integral tanks (one-piece), as well as the more common separate tank (two-piece) type. See Figures 4-6a and 4-6b.

In North America the most commonly used residential toilets use a siphonic action created in the trapway. This "pulls" the waste from the bowl. *Reverse-trap* toilets introduce water only through the rim, whereas others known as *siphon jet* types employ siphon jets in addition to the rim action. In residences, gravity flush tanks are most commonly used; however, there are also pressure and power-assisted toilets that provide powerful flushing action with less water use.

This discussion of toilet systems is important because the type of system selected significantly affects the convenience, noise, and water use of the toilet. The amount of water used by toilets varies a great deal based on the number of gallons consumed for each flush. According to the U.S. Department of Energy, "toilet flushing accounts for 45 percent of indoor water use, or approximately 32,000 gallons per year for a family of four. . . . By law, replacement or new construction toilets are restricted to flush a maximum of 1.6 gallons rather than the 3.5 to 7 gallons used by older toilets." In addition to conserving water, this reduction does a great deal toward reducing the amount of energy used to pump and treat water.

Figure 4-6a An integral (one-piece) toilet. Image courtesy of Kohler Co.

Figure 4-6b A two-piece toilet. Image courtesy of Kohler Co.

Another option in terms of reducing water use is the dual-flush toilet. Dual-flush toilets operate with two water use settings: a full 1.6-gallon flush for solids and a reduced-volume flush (often 0.8 to 1.1 gallons) for liquids only. Although a new system to North America, the dual-flush concept has been used in other parts of the world for quite some time. Some dual-flush models use tank-based power assistance, while others employ a gravity tank and "wash-down" bowl type—which washes the waste directly down a larger trapway, pushing it out, instead of using siphonic action. Wash-down-type toilets have not been widely used in North America because they have been seen as requiring more frequent cleaning of the toilet bowl. A few manufacturers now make dual-flush toilets for use in the American market.

In addition to the variety of tank types and flushing systems mentioned, toilets are available in a range of finishes, colors, and styles, from old-fashioned to sleek and minimalist in appearance. Toilets are most commonly available in round bowl or elongated bowl styles; many people consider the elongated bowl style to be the most comfortable. Toilet seats are available in a range of shapes to fit the various types of bowls. See Figure 4-7 for typical toilet sizes.

Standard toilet height is roughly 15 to 16 inches above the floor. However, there are toilets with higher seats available, allowing for greater ease of movement onto and off of the seat. In addition, devices are available that boost standard seat height by 5 or more inches for those users who have significant difficulty sitting or bending.

It is worth noting that the ADA calls for accessible toilet seats to be 17 to 19 inches to the top of the seat. However, as previously noted, single-family homes are not required to meet ADA guidelines and meeting the ADA does not necessarily accommodate a range of users in a way that could be seen as universal. In some rehabilitation settings, a seat as high as 20 inches may be used due to similarities with wheelchair seat height; however, this can cause some people's feet to dangle and also problems with balance. While 18 inches is seen as a compromise to the 17- to 19-inch standard set by the ADA, a height of 19 inches can prove better for those who have difficulty bending. Clearly, a bathroom designed for a specific client requires consideration of that particular person's limitations and stature. In addition, when planning accessible bathrooms, designers must also give careful thought to general floor clearance spaces at the toilet and other fixtures. More information about clearances is provided later in this chapter.

In order to allow for wheelchair transfers and to provide stability, grab bars are required when toilet areas are designed for use by those with physical limitations and disabilities. Grab bars come in a wide variety of shapes and configurations in order to accommodate a range of needs; horizontal, vertical, diagonal, and pivoting grab (or swing-away) bars can all be useful depending on the needs of the individual. Figures 4-8a to 4-8c show types of grab bars used at toilet and other locations.

Vertical and diagonal grab bars are useful for pulling from a seated position to standing position (and in moving into the seated position from standing) and therefore can be useful for some ambulatory people. However, according to the Center for Inclusive Design and Environmental Access (IDEA Center), vertical bars are "not as useful for preventing a fall or transferring to a wheelchair. They are also more difficult to use for stabilization. The horizontal bar provides the greatest safety."

Pivoting bars can be helpful in assisting semiambulatory people and can be moved out of the way as needed. They are also useful in situations where an assistant works as an aide in transferring, as they move out of the way as needed. However, pivoting bars can prove to be an obstacle to those using wheelchairs, so their use requires careful thought. Bars attached directly to toilets seats can be

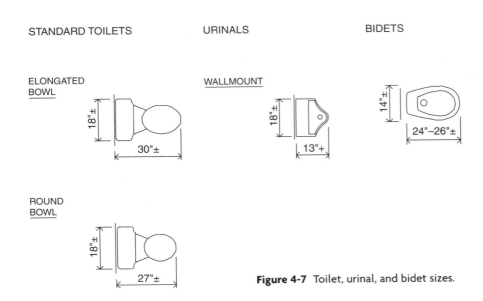

STANDARD TOILETS   URINALS   BIDETS

ELONGATED BOWL
18"±   30"±

WALLMOUNT
18"±   13"+

14"±   24"–26"±

ROUND BOWL
18"±   27"±

Figure 4-7 Toilet, urinal, and bidet sizes.

Figure 4-8a This photograph shows a range of grab bars made by Hewi, including a swing-away or pivoting grab bar (foreground) as well as a collection of horizontal bars and one rather short vertical bar (not for use at the toilet). Photograph courtesy of Häfele America.

Figure 4-8b This photograph shows a short horizontal bar that serves as an aid in balance; this bar does not meet ANSI standards but works to steady the user and is helpful for some people. Photograph courtesy of Häfele America.

Figure 4-8c A photograph depicting a bar similar to that shown in 4-8b in use. Photograph courtesy of Häfele America.

helpful for some, yet they do not project beyond the toilet seat and are most often mounted too low to easily facilitate a transfer. For additional information about the placement and location of grab bars, please see the "Ergonomics and Required Clearances" section of this chapter.

Urinals

While urinals are most commonly used in commercial applications, there are reasons to consider using them in a residential setting. Urinals use less water than toilets and can be quite convenient as well. Used by males, urinals are receptacles, attached and plumbed to the wall. Those models used in residential settings are directed to flush using a push button, whereas many used commercially have an automatic sensor that flushes them after a number of uses. Because they are wall mounted, urinal mounting height can vary. Some urinals are fitted with a sanitary lid, making them more appealing for some residential users. Figure 4-7 includes dimensions for urinals.

Bidets

Bidets are wash basins used for partial bathing. Typically the user sits astride the bowl facing the faucets to control water flow. Models are available with vertical or horizontal spray for water flow. Often bidets are manufactured in styles, colors, and finishes that are similar to toilets so that the two can appear to be a matching pair. See Figure 4-7 for typical bidet dimensions There are also bidet functions incorporated into some toilets, as well as add-on kits that outfit standard toilets with a bidetlike water spray.

Sinks (Also Known as Lavatories)

Sinks are currently available in a range of shapes, colors, and styles. Porcelain over steel, enameled cast iron as well vitreous china, stainless steel, glass, and other materials are currently used for sink fabrication. Shapes range from oval, round, square, rectilinear, and triangular (used in corner locations).

Lavatories can be wall hung, supported by pedestals, or placed into countertops—often as part of a vanity or storage cabinet. Of the countertop variety, there are four basic mounting types, in which the sink "mates" to the countertop in a different way. Types include self-rimming, rimless, under-mount, counter-over, tile-in, and integral. Often the choice of countertop material and overall design determines the mounting style used.

Self-rimming sinks have a rim or lip that fits over the top surface of the counter. This type works well in countertops made of plastic laminate, granite, marble, and solid wood and can also be used over tile. Self-rimming sinks are readily available in many styles, colors, and materials. The rim prevents this type of sink from allowing water to be drawn back into the sink bowl, which can cause water and soil to collect at the point where the rim meets the countertop and can be difficult to clean. See Figure 4-9a.

Rimless sink mounting requires the use of a separate mounting rim and clips attached below the countertop, which hold the sink in place. This mounting type works well with plastic laminate countertops. Much like the self-rimming sink, the edges of this type can be difficult to keep clean.

Under-counter sinks attach to the bottom surface of the countertop. They're often used with solid-surface counters and are also used with various stone countertops. Typically the countertop is cut so that it overhangs the sink, making for easy cleanup, as water and debris can be washed directly from the counter surface into the sink bowl. See Figure 4-9b.

Counter-over sinks have a lip that fits under the countertop yet on top of the counter's base material (often plywood, cement board, or particleboard). This type

Figure 4-9a Self-rimming sink. Photograph courtesy of Kohler Co.

Figure 4-9b Under-counter sink. Photograph courtesy of Kohler Co.

Figure 4-9c Tile-in sink. Photograph courtesy of Kohler Co.

of sink works well when the countertop itself is made of an uneven material such as tile. In such cases the tile often goes from the countertop surface directly over the sink's rim. The tile setter generally does this after the sink has been mounted.

Some manufacturers produce sinks known as *tile-in* sinks. These sinks allow tile to be taken flush to the edge of the sink. This type of sink does not typically require tile trim pieces to serve as a transition from the tile to the sink edge, allowing for a wide range of tiles to be used on the counter surface, as shown in Figure 4-9c.

Various manufacturers and craftsmen produce countertops with integral sinks. Synthetic marble, various solid surfaces, concrete, terrazzo, stainless steel, and stone slabs can be fabricated to create a counter in which the sink is one with the counter surface.

The mounting styles mentioned previously are all simply methods of mating the sink to the countertop. As stated, other types of sinks are available, such as pedestal, wall hung, and vessel. *Pedestal* sinks consist of a sink bowl that sits atop a pedestal base, which conceals supply and drain lines. Because they do not offer the storage found in sinks mounted in countertops or vanities, pedestal sinks are often used in powder rooms or are accompanied by adjacent shelves or some other storage device for holding toiletries and personal items. See Figure 4-10.

Figure 4-11 Wall-mounted sink. Photograph courtesy of Kohler Co.

Figure 4-10 Pedestal sink. Photograph courtesy of Kohler Co.

Wall-hung (also known as *wall-mount*) sinks feature a basin that is hung from the wall at a desired height. The drainpipe and supply lines are usually exposed on wall-mounted fixtures. However, some feature a matching cover placed beneath the basin to conceal the piping and to protect the legs of those using wheelchairs. Wall-mounted sinks are ideal for use by those in wheelchairs, as they allow for chair clearance directly under the sink, easing access to the sink bowl, faucet, and controls. This type of sink is also excellent for use by small children because of the ease of access to the sink bowl and the flexible mounting height. See Figure 4-11.

Like pedestal sinks, most wall-hung models provide very limited space for storage of toiletries and personal items. Adjacent shelves, built-in wall storage, medicine chests, and other storage devices can help eliminate clutter. In addition, some wall-hung models contain ledges to the side of the sink bowls, which can allow for very limited storage. Console table models are also available. These have legs that help support the unit and create a visual impression different from that of a wall-hung unit.

Figure 4-12 Vessel sink. Photograph courtesy of Kohler Co.

Vessel sinks are bowl-like basins that generally sit atop a counter or deck, exposing the full body of the bowl form. Vessel sinks often rest atop a counter that appears more like a tabletop than a traditional bathroom vanity countertop. Some vessel sinks are placed on a single-layer deck surface made of glass, wood, or stone and attached at the wall. Some vessel sinks can be used as wall mounts supported by rods or brackets. Although beautiful and interesting, such installations are not the most sturdy, easy to maintain, or long-lasting sink selections. See Figure 4-12.

Many vessel sinks are rather tall and require faucets that reach well past the vessel rim. Certain vessel sinks may be used in under-counter applications, while others can be used as self-rimming sinks when inset into the countertop surface.

Figures 4-13a and 4-13b illustrate a range of sink types and sizes.

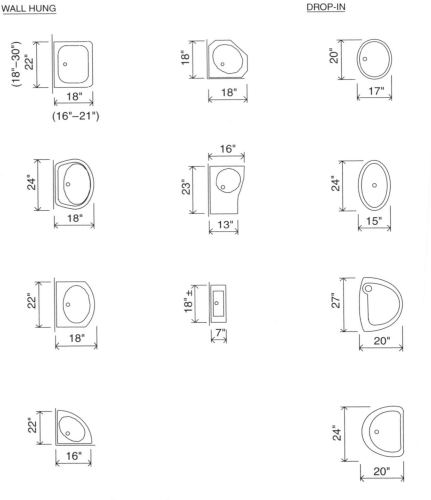

Figure 4-13a Sink types and sizes.

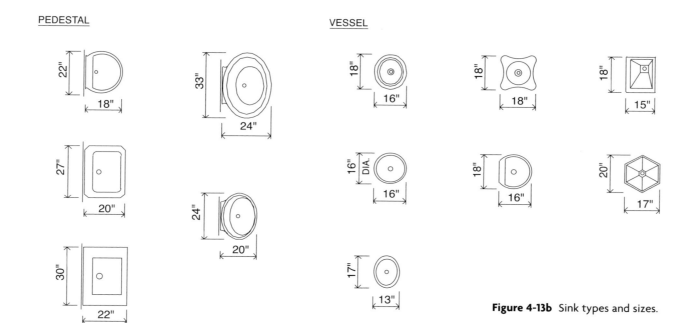

PEDESTAL

VESSEL

Figure 4-13b Sink types and sizes.

Faucets

Sink selection requires consideration of faucet selection because the two elements must be compatible. Faucets come in a vast range of styles and finishes. Additionally, types of faucets available include two-handled and single-handled models. Two-handled faucets require sinks with the appropriate number of holes. These are drilled with a distance of either 4, 8, or 12 inches between the hot and cold faucet handles. Single-handle-type faucets require that the sink be drilled with a single hole, as well as possible mounting holes.

Sinks are also available that do not have faucet holes. In this type the faucet is mounted directly on the countertop or to the wall. Vessel sinks rarely have predrilled holes, thereby requiring that faucets be mounted outside of the vessel, in walls or countertops. Wall-mounted faucet pipes typically must be installed before drywall is installed. Therefore, the decision to use them must occur early.

The designer must seriously consider the selection of lavatory faucets when designing bathrooms for use by individuals with disabilities, the elderly, and small children. According to the Center for Universal Design, faucet options available for universal accessibility include faucets with single-control levers, crosses, or loops (in place of other handle styles); faucets with non-slip textures; faucets with easy-to-control flow rate and/or temperature; pedal-operated options; faucets with motion-sensing activation; and side-mounted options.

The Center for Independent Living describes single-lever faucet handles as the best choice for bathroom use, as does the IDEA Center. These suggestions are in keeping with the ADA, which does not apply to single-family dwellings but which requires that "operable parts shall be operable with one hand and shall not require tight grasping, pinching, or twisting of the wrist. The force required to activate operable parts shall be 5 pounds (22.2 N) maximum" (Section 309.4, "Operation").

Bathtubs

Bathtubs are available in many shapes and installation types and in a range of materials, and can be surrounded by various interior finish materials. Tub materials include fiberglass, acrylic, enameled cast iron, and enameled steel. In addition, soft tubs made of polyurethane foam over fiberglass can be used for comfort and safety for individuals with special needs. Installation types include built-in and freestanding tubs.

Built-in units include the *alcove*-type tub, the most common type of bathtub in the United States. This type is enclosed on three sides, with only the front exposed, as shown in Figure 4-14a. Because there are fewer finished surfaces, these models tend to be more economically priced than other installation types. This type of tub is specified as left-hand or right-hand, terms describing the drain location as one faces the tub. Alcove-type tubs are also the most common installation types used in tub/shower combinations, which are covered in more detail in the "Showers" section later in this chapter. Most alcove units employ wall-mounted faucets with waste and overflow mounted within the tub. Alcove models can be purchased with matching shower doors. Shower doors may also be purchased separately. More information regarding shower doors can be found later in this chapter.

Another built-in bathtub variety is the *drop-in* installation type, mounted much like sinks are installed in countertops. The tub is mounted to a deck area that is framed independently. Because of the cost of framing and finishing the deck area, this type of installation is generally more costly than alcove models. In such installations tubs can be under-mounted or self-rimming in a manner similar to sinks. See Figure 4-14b.

Drop-in models may also be installed in walled alcoves similarly to alcove models; however, with drop-in models, a supporting frame and deck must be constructed. Occasionally drop-in models are installed in a floor-mounted sunken application, which requires space below the floor area and can be very difficult for a bather to get out of. Because the tub framing and decking conceal the plumbing pipes, drop-in tubs may be expensive or difficult to service, especially if access to the plumbing has not been considered by the designer. Under-mount installations may also be possible.

Freestanding tubs come in a range of styles, from the old-fashioned claw-foot tubs to pedestal-supported models to those that sit on an exposed frame. See Figure 4-14c. These tubs typically sit independently, often with exposed pipes that are easy to service. The old-fashioned claw-foot type is available in American models with holes drilled for faucets, drain, and overflow. European models do not have faucet holes drilled to the tub but do have drilled drain and overflow holes. This design allows for deeper filling levels. Such models with no faucet drilling require freestanding water pipes and faucets or wall-mounted faucets.

Figure 4-14a Alcove bathtub. This type of tub is most often set in an alcove of full height walls, rather than as shown here. Photograph courtesy of Kohler Co.

Figure 4-14b Drop-in bathtub. Photograph courtesy of Kohler Co.

A pedestal tub rests on a base that is typically oval in shape. Most of these tubs do not have faucet drilling—floor- or wall-mounted faucets are used with these tubs. In some cases, the pedestal tub rests on a base that is custom-made for the client. Wood or another appropriate material can be used for such bases. Some manufacturers are producing freestanding tubs that rest on an exposed framework. In most cases these are pedestal-type tubs resting on an exposed wood frame rather than an oval pedestal. It is possible to integrate a shower function using a freestanding tub. This is done through the use of both handheld showerheads and/or freestanding shower-height units, which generally require a shower curtain.

The installation types mentioned are available in various sizes and shapes. The most common bathtub size in American homes is 5 feet in length. Yet tubs are available that are only 4 feet long and that are more than 6 feet long. A standard American bathtub height is 14 to 17 inches, with European tubs at 18 inches. For a range of bathtub sizes and shapes, see Figure 4-15.

STANDARD ALCOVE AND DROP-IN TUBS

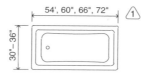

LARGER AND UNUSUAL-SHAPED
ALCOVE AND DROP-IN TUBS

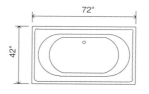

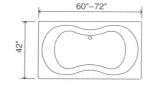

FREESTANDING

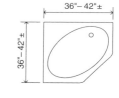

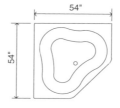

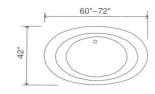

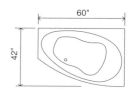

Figure 4-15 Bathtub types and sizes.

1. 30 by 60 inches is the most common bathtub size.

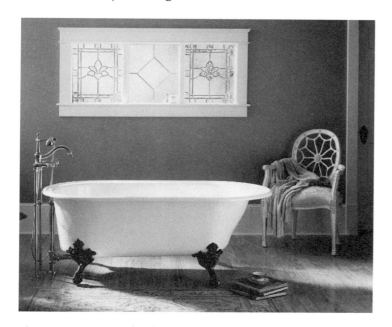

Figure 4-14c Freestanding bathtub. Photograph courtesy of Kohler Co.

Bathtub accessibility is highly dependent upon the specific needs of the individual client. When considering accessibility, the designer must assess current and future needs as well as a client's possible interest in visitability. For example, a particular homeowner may require the assistance of a caregiver in bathing as well as a hydraulic or mechanical lift, resulting in the need for clearance room for the caregiver, the bather, and the lift. Therefore, an understanding of the current and future needs of the given client is essential, rather than simply meeting ADAAG (Americans with Disability Act Accessibility Guidelines) or ANSI (American National Standards Institute) standards as a default position for creating an accessible bath.

Generally speaking, standard bathtubs present a series of obstacles to anyone except the average adult in possession of a good range of motion and strength. Entering a tub, bending to recline, and then standing to exit the tub creates a situation in which individuals with limited range of motion and flexibility, as well as other mobility issues, are not well served by a standard tub. Many people benefit from tub designs that include integral handles or rails (see Figure 4-16a) for entering and exiting the tub, whereas others require more extensive solutions to problems of balance, strength, and mobility. If wall-mounted grab bars are required, an alcove-type setting is often best, as it offers walls for bar placement.

The IDEA Center has stated that a shower stall is preferred over a tub; however, the center does list ways in which a tub can serve a more universal population. Those are the inclusion of a "seat; structural reinforcement for grab bars; controls mounted near the entry side of head wall; 30-in. by 60-in. minimum clear floor space; hand-held shower spray." Should they be required, grab bars should be provided at both ends of the tub, and two bars (of different heights) are required along the side of the tub. It is worth noting that there are various color and material options available to the designer when selecting and specifying grab bars. Homeowners are not limited to stainless steel or chrome. For homeowners with limited vision, grab bars of contrasting colors may prove helpful. Figure 4-16b shows a production, one-piece bathtub/shower module with a transfer seat and grab bars. Additional information about clearances and grab bar placement can be found in the next section.

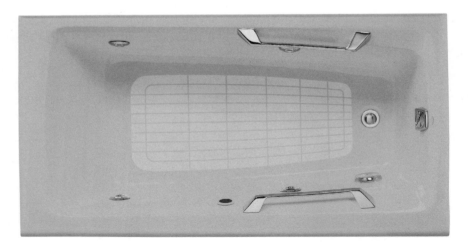

Figure 4-16a Bathtub with integral handles for ease of entry and exiting. Photograph courtesy of Kohler Co.

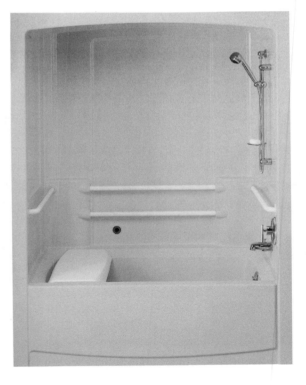

Figure 4-16b Prefabricated bathtub/shower module for wheelchair transfer with a seat, multiple grab bars, handheld shower spray, and controls mounted near the entry side of head wall. Many users prefer the addition of a vertical grab bar at the control side of tub. Showers are generally the best option for wheelchair users. Photograph courtesy of Kohler Co.

Some manufacturers produce bathtubs with an actual door that opens into the tub and then seals upon closing, allowing the bather to enter without climbing into the tub. Such models are often equipped with whirlpools and are most often available as alcove models. In addition, soft bathtubs (those covered in polyurethane foam) can be useful for individuals with limited mobility and issues with balance, as they provide a cushioned and more comfortable tub area. Some people with disabilities related to mobility can use bathtubs as long as a fixed seat, grab bars, nonslippery surfaces, and handheld shower sprays are included. However, as mentioned, for many individuals using a wheelchair, a shower unit is the best choice for bathing. Additional information about accessible showers can be found in subsequent sections of this chapter.

Soaking and Whirlpool Tubs

A soaking tub is typically a bathtub constructed in a manner that allows the bather to sit in a upright position and immerse his or her body more fully than in a standard tub, as illustrated in Figure 4-17a. Japanese and Greek baths both provide an extra-deep basin for soaking and are available in a range of sizes and materials at heights from 22 to 32 inches. These are also available in lengths shorter than standard bathtubs.

A whirlpool is a type of soaking tub fitted with pipes, an electric pump, water jets, and frequently a booster and heater. The pump is used to circulate water through the pipes, using several water jets, as shown in Figure 4-17b. Pumps must be installed in a location that allows access. Whirlpool tubs are available in alcove and drop-in models in standard 5-foot and much larger sizes, as well as in a range of shapes. Five-foot standard alcove models tend to be less expensive and can work as retrofits in existing rooms (as long as there is appropriate clearance in doorways).

Drop-in whirlpools are generally installed into an elevated deck and placed against a wall or corner or out in the open. Full whirlpools with occupant(s) can weigh as much as 1,500 pounds, requiring extra floor support. Larger whirlpools can require oversized hot-water heaters. Whirlpools can be difficult to enter and exit. For this reason, it is helpful to have homeowners sit in the tubs prior to purchase. See Figure 4-18 for sizes of soaking tubs and whirlpools.

Figure 4-17a A soaking or "Greek" tub. Photograph courtesy of Kohler Co.

Figure 4-17b A whirlpool tub. Photograph courtesy of Kohler Co.

GREEK AND JAPANESE SOAKING TUBS

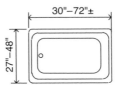

WHIRLPOOLS

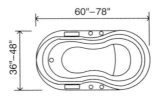

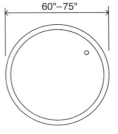

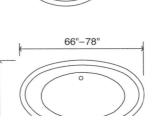

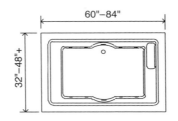

Figure 4-18 Soaking and whirlpool types and sizes.

Showers

According to *Plumbing and Mechanical* magazine, "all market trends point to the emergence of the shower as a hot point of interest for today's remodelers and homeowners." The magazine also describes the current trend toward open, airy showers and showers for two versus one bather.

Other design trends include luxurious showers with multiple showerheads or shower towers. Multiple-head showers require appropriate water pressure and use significant hot water. According to *Keidel's Planning Guide* (an online guide), larger multiple-head showers require a dedicated water heater for the shower alone: "A dedicated 50 gallon hot water heater will supply a four-outlet custom shower for approximately 8 minutes (assuming showerheads are restricted and all are turned on for the entire duration). For best performance, one manufacturer (GROHE) recommends a 100 gallon water heater as a minimum." Because of the water used, drain capacity must also be considered with this type of shower.

While these luxury showers are popular, they use significant natural resources, including large amounts of water as well as energy to heat the water, and they impact municipal water systems. Many of the multiple-head showers go against recent trends in water conservation and are not of interest to homeowners with a commitment to water conservation or for use in locations with water use restrictions. However, there are some recirculation systems available that conserve water and some multiple-head showers that have conservations settings such as the one shown in Figure 4-19.

Showers are available in two distinct types: prefabricated (also known as modular) and site-built. The prefabricated types are available as complete modules, which include the shower base and surrounding wall finishes. Of this type, some are *multipiece* units, in which the base, walls, and in some cases ceilings are separate entities, which are installed together to achieve a watertight seal and visual appearance of one unified element. This type is ideal for remodeling, as the various components can be easily maneuvered and installed. See Figure 4-20a.

Other prefabricated units are manufactured as *one-piece*, with walls, base, and sometimes a ceiling constructed as a single element, as shown in Figure 4-20b. These units are used in new construction more often than in remodeling. Both the multipiece and the one-piece units come in a range of options such as built-in seats, grab bars, and colors and are available in fiberglass and acrylic. Both types

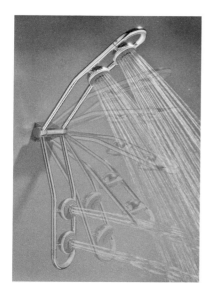

Figure 4-19 Photograph of the Freehander Shower System® by Grohe. This is one of the new shower systems that offer flexibility in the quantity of water used, allowing for water conservation when desired. The Freehander combines showerhead and body spread capabilities through the use of pivoting arm and rotating showerheads and allows one head to be turned off in order to conserve water and energy. Photograph courtesy of Grohe America.

Figure 4-20a Multipiece shower module. This type of shower module consists of separate pieces that are installed together. These work very well in remodeling situations, as they easily move through existing doors and other obstacles. This type is available in a range of sizes and styles. The version shown is a combination tub and shower module. Photograph courtesy of Kohler Co.

Figure 4-20b A shower/tub module. This type is also available in a range of sizes and finishes. Photograph courtesy of Kohler Co.

are available in various sizes and shapes, with most designs fitting into an alcove configuration much like an alcove bathtub. The advantages of prefabricated showers can include lower installation costs and, in some cases, ease of maintenance.

Bathtub/shower combinations are available in both one-piece and multipiece units. Bathtub/shower combinations are more economical in terms of space used and cost, yet they are being replaced in popularity by single baths or shower units as homes continue to increase in square footage. Figure 4-20b shows a prefabricated tub/shower combination.

Prefabricated shower bases (called *receptors*) are also available. This type of unit consists of the shower base only, with the surrounding walls and doors often treated in a manner similar to a site-built shower. These units are available in square, rectangular, and angled corner units (often called neo-angle units) in a range of sizes, with 3 feet by 3 feet the most commonly used size. With this type of unit, the surrounding walls are often finished with an appropriate material such as ceramic tile, and a glass shower enclosure and door are included to complete the shower. See Figures 4-21a to 4-21c.

Depending on size and design, most prefabricated shower units require a shower door, a curtain, or some form of screen, which work to keep adjacent areas dry. Glass shower doors are readily available in sliding or swing-type designs. Glass shower doors are available from manufacturers in standard sizes for tub/shower combinations, as well as for prefabricated shower modules and receptors, and are also commonly custom-designed for site-built showers. Shower manufacturers, glass suppliers, and art glass creators all supply glass shower enclosures. Shower screening devices need not be limited to glass only. Metal, stone, some plastics, and acrylic can be put to use as interesting and innovative shower screen devices.

Figure 4-22a Example of site-built shower, visible at far left in this image. Photograph courtesy of Kohler Co.

Figure 4-21a A receptor base. Photograph courtesy of Kohler Co.

Figure 4-21b A receptor base. Photograph courtesy of Kohler Co.

Figure 4-21c A receptor base. Photograph courtesy of Kohler Co.

Figure 4-22b Example of site-built shower—in this case, a roll-in shower with grab bars and a seat (grab bars and seat are Hewi/Häfele products). Photograph courtesy of Häfele America

Site-built showers are those that are constructed without the use of prefabricated modules or receptors. This type of shower is not restricted by the size or shape limitations of prefabricated units, which results in the creation of highly customized designs such as walk-in showers and shower rooms. Walk-in showers are those without a door and therefore must contain enough space so that splashing onto adjacent surfaces is not a problem. See Figures 4-22a and 4-22b.

In most site-built showers, the shower floor is sloped, typically ¼ inch per foot to the drain (for example, ⅝ inch in a 5-foot-by-5-foot shower stall with a center drain). This requires a depressed area in the construction below the stall or that the shower itself is raised above floor level and then sloped down to the drain, which in turn requires some form of step or ramped transition threshold at the entry to the shower.

In order to accommodate a perfectly flush transition (with no raised threshold) in homes with a wood floor structure, the area directly under the shower must contain a lower portion with shallower joists. Homes built on concrete slabs require a depressed area in the slab directly beneath the shower to accommodate the drain slope. This type of sloping shower floor is also used to create roll-in showers for use with wheelchairs. In such cases a flush transition from bathroom floor to shower floor is desirable. In those cases where a flush transition is not possible, a ramped threshold or rubber threshold can be employed to allow for wheelchair access. Figures 4-23a and 4-23b illustrate a range of shower types and sizes.

As previously stated, the Center for Inclusive Environments has described showers as preferable to tubs for wheelchair accessibility. The center describes two types of useful accessible shower stalls. A smaller 3-foot-by-3-foot stall called a *transfer stall* allows for transfer to a shower seat from a wheelchair. The relatively small size can help users maintain balance and allows them to catch themselves should they fall. This type of shower requires a folding seat because a fixed seat can make the shower difficult for ambulatory users (Figure 4-16b includes images of a shower seat). A larger 5-foot-long type known as a *roll-in* shower has enough space to allow a wheelchair to roll directly into the stall, thus eliminating the need for a transfer seat. The "Ergonomics and Required Clearances" section contains detailed information about the dimensional requirements and clearances required for wheelchair-accessible showers.

Although they take up more room, roll-in showers also create additional maneuvering room (within the shower) for people using wheelchairs, which can be helpful. In order to be fully accessible, roll-in showers must have a flush or very limited threshold, as discussed previously in the discussion on site-built showers. Most prefabricated base and modular shower units have at least a slight raised threshold; however, some manufacturers, such as Americh, produce a modular shower base with no raised threshold.

When designing both tubs and showers for people with disabilities, the designer must carefully consider the controls. According to Marc Mendelsohn, a

PREFABRICATED RECEPTORS

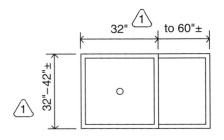

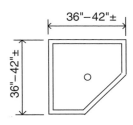

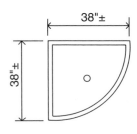

PREFABRICATED MODULES

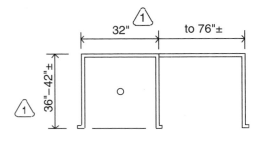

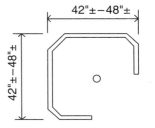

SHOWER/TUB COMBINATION

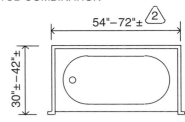

Figure 4-23a Modular shower types and sizes.

1. 2-foot, 8-inch showers are under the recommended minimum; while available, they are not comfortable. The recommended minimum, 3 feet by 3 feet, is the most common American shower size.
2. The most common American tub size is 2 feet, 6 inches by 5 feet.

designer with a specialty in universal home design and founder of the Bomarc Barrier Free Foundation, standard shower controls—those directly above a drain location—in a shower can present serious problems. Mendelsohn has stated "if a person's in a wheelchair, they need to be able to turn the shower on and let it warm up before they get in. You can plumb a shower valve anywhere. We normally install it close to the edge of the shower so if the person is either left-handed or right-handed, they can turn it on and let it warm up." It is also helpful to allow maneuvering room or additional clear space adjacent to the shower controls so that a wheelchair can access the controls. This is illustrated in the following section.

In terms of accessibility, as mentioned, controls in tubs and showers should be single-lever types in order to be universally accessible. Pressure-balanced valves and hot-water limiters are necessary for users who are not able to move out of the way should the water become too hot. Grab bars in showers are a necessity for

SITE-BUILT SHOWERS

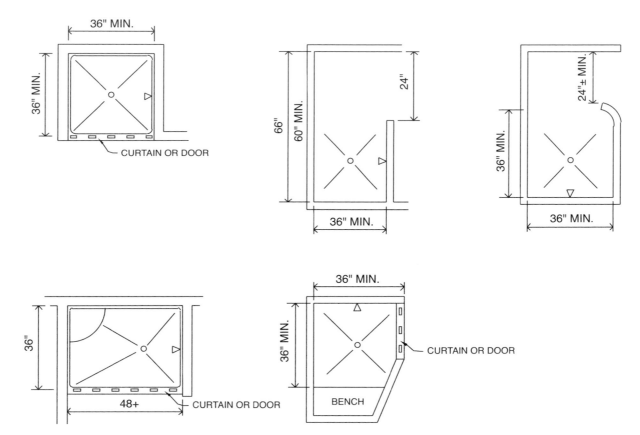

Figure 4-23b Site-built shower size option.

those with mobility issues. In a smaller transfer stall, bars should be located on all sides except the seat side, as that would interfere with using the seat. In roll-in showers, grab bars on all sides are useful. Depending on the needs of the homeowner or the desire of the builder for adaptability, wall reinforcement placed during the initial construction or major remodeling at potential future grab bar locations is worth considering. More information on control locations and grab bar placement can be found in the next section.

Water shutoff valves are required for all plumbing fixtures to facilitate the repair and maintenance of items such as faucets, showerheads, and toilet tanks, and access to the valves must be provided. Toilet shutoff valves are generally exposed under the tank. For tubs and showers the valves are generally concealed, often by being placed in an adjacent closet or cabinet—or, in some cases, an access panel in a wall or floor may be required to access valves.

STORAGE AND CABINETRY

Bathrooms require varied storage areas to house items that support the specialized activities taking place in the room. In planning bathroom storage, the designer should consider the various bathroom fixtures and activities related to their use and plan storage related to these activity areas. The sink, toilet, and shower/bathtub areas each require the use of specialized items, and housing these items requires a careful consideration of the use of each area.

The sink area requires storage for items used in washing hands and faces, shaving, brushing teeth, brushing hair, applying makeup, occasionally applying first aid, and in some instances, washing infants or delicate garments. Therefore, storage space for the items used in these activities should be placed in proximity to the sink area, with those items used most frequently placed closest to the sink (when possible). This is usually accomplished through the use of a vanity or some form of shelving directly adjacent to the sink and/or through the use of a medicine cabinet or some similar storage element. In addition, hand towels and washcloths should be placed in a convenient location for use in drying hands and faces.

Other items including medicines and toiletries that are used infrequently may be housed in a storage area such as a linen closet, where an inventory of towels and washcloths may also be located.

Vanities are bathroom cabinets that often contain sinks and—most often—faucets. The vanity is generally a smaller variation of the kitchen cabinet, available from many of the same manufacturers that produce kitchen cabinets. The design and fabrication of many vanities is similar to that of kitchen cabinets. Cabinet frames, doors, and drawers are available in the same styles, the same methods of construction, and generally the same materials as kitchen cabinets. For further information on materials, construction, and detailing of stock cabinets please see Chapter 5, "Kitchens."

While in many cases vanity construction is similar to that of kitchen cabinets, some of the heights and overall sizes vary, with bathroom vanities often smaller and lower than kitchen cabinets. Standard vanity bases are available from 18 to 21 inches deep and 12 (not recommended for actual sink locations) to 72 inches wide—usually available in 3-inch increments in units under 3 feet and 6-inch increments for units over 3 feet. Some vanities, which are currently popular, vary

Figure 4-24a Standard vanity bases. These are available from 18 and 21 inches deep (corresponding counter depths are shown in Figure 4-26b) and in widths from 12 to 72 inches. Standard base heights vary from 29 inches to 34 inches, with the countertop material adding to this height. Additionally, some vanities with more than one sink range in height to accommodate users of varying heights (not shown).

1. While 12-inch cabinets are available, these are not long enough to allow space for a sink.
2. Cabinets should be a minimum of 24 inches to allow for sink installation, which requires that top drawers are eliminated.
3. Drawer locations (as shown in the middle of this cabinet) do not allow space for a sink; sinks would be installed at either side of this cabinet. Sink mounting locations are illustrated in 4-26b.

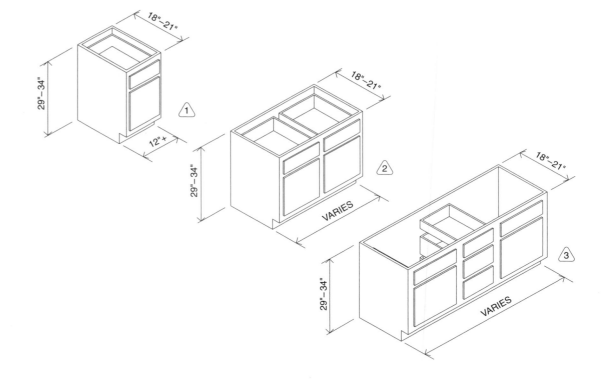

Figure 4-24b Some designers and homeowners prefer less traditional vanity designs such as those shown at left that are more consolelike and may rest on feet or legs rather than a traditional toe-kick. Some vanity bases range in depth within the vanity; the areas containing sinks are deeper and storage locations are shallow, as shown at right. Sink mounting locations are illustrated in Figure 4-26b.

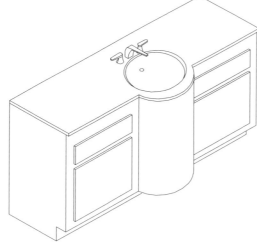

worth noting that because sinks and their related plumbing lines occupy the space a drawer might use, sinks are not mounted directly over an operable drawer. Instead, doors or false drawer fronts are often mounted to the front of the bowl. Using furniture such as an antique dresser or chest and outfitting it with a sink and related plumbing is becoming a popular alternative to a standard vanity. Some manufacturers of furnishings and cabinetry are now producing vanities that appear more like antique, vintage, or contemporary home furniture pieces.

Lavatory design and sink mounting height and location require careful consideration when bathrooms are designed for individuals with disabilities. The Center for Universal Design describes a preference for lavatories "with bowl mounted as close to front edge as possible." Knee space directly under the sink (29 inches high for most adults) allows someone to use the lavatory from a seated position, as shown in Figure 4-25. This space may be open knee space or accomplished through the use of fold-back or self-storing doors.

Figure 4-25 Wheelchair-accessible vanity design requires a clear area under the sink that is a minimum of 27 inches above the floor (29 inches recommended) and 30 inches of clear approach space. For additional information on required clear space, see Figure 4-27b.

1. Note: 40 inches is the maximum mirror height, when mirror is not tilted (tilted mirrors are preferred by many wheelchair users), and controls and outlets should be 15 to 48 inches above the floor (2). Accessible wall-hung sink-mounting information is shown in Figure 4-26c.

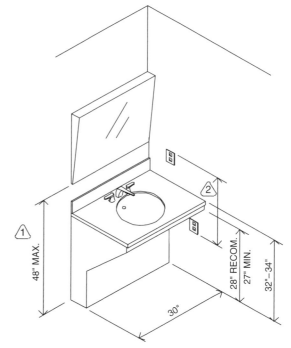

in terms of depth, with the sink located at the deepest portion of the vanity and storage areas located in narrow portions of the vanity. A vanity base of a minimum of 24 inches wide is recommended for sink locations, as this size will accommodate most drop-in sinks. Figures 4-24a and 4-24b illustrate vanity construction and dimensions.

Standard vanity heights vary from 29 to 34 inches (with countertops adding to that height), with 32 inches perhaps the most common height. Interestingly, there is a current trend toward higher vanities. In addition, some clients benefit from a two-tiered vanity system, with one counter higher for the taller partner. These cases generally employ two sinks at the two heights. More common are two sink bowls provided at a consistent single height.

Regardless of height, a vanity with two sink bowls requires appropriate clearance for two sink users, which will be discussed further in the next section. It is

Burns and scrapes may be caused when individuals with limited feeling in their legs come in contact with supply pipes and drainpipes. For this reason, the pipes must be wrapped with insulating material, or an angled panel or apron can be installed to conceal pipes. According to the Center for Inclusive Design and Environmental Access, ambulatory users prefer a lavatory height of 34 inches, whereas a "32 inch height is better for wheelchair users." The center also advocates using tilted mirrors above vanities used by individuals in wheelchairs so that they are accessible to view. In cases where the mirror is to be shared by ambulatory and wheelchair users, an adjustable mirror allows both types of users to view the mirror.

The toilet area requires far less storage than the sink area—at minimum a roll of toilet paper and one to serve as backup. Additional toilet paper and other similar items, as well as cleaning supplies, may be kept in the immediate toilet area or in a location outside the bathroom, such as a linen closet or supply pantry. All of the items mentioned may be located in a base cabinet, shelving unit, or some storage unit appropriate to the design of the space. Some homeowners prefer storage for reading materials immediately adjacent to the toilet. When a bidet is included in a toilet area, storage should be provided for soap and towels immediately nearby at a convenient height for the user.

The shower and/or tub area requires conveniently placed towel storage as well as areas provided to hang clothing or robes for use as one dresses and undresses. Storage for shampoo, conditioners, and lotions should be provided as well. Many homeowners find a laundry hamper placed in this area useful.

According to a survey entitled "What 21st Century Home Buyers Want" conducted by the National Association of Home Builders: "A linen closet topped the list of desired bathroom features, with 88% of the respondents categorizing it as essential or desirable. Other desirable features included an exhaust fan (86%), separate shower enclosure (69%), water temperature control (67%), a whirlpool tub (58%), ceramic tile walls (55%), and a dressing room/make-up area (52%)."

The listing of a linen closet as essential by many homeowners points to the necessity of adequate storage; a related question that could be posed to such respondents would involve the actual necessity of placing linen storage within the bathroom or merely adjacent to it.

In the design of storage areas for wheelchair users or with visitability in mind, some rules of thumb are helpful. According to the National Kitchen and Bath Association's Bathroom Basics, "Storage for toiletries, linens, grooming and general bathroom supplies should be provided within 15 inches to 48 inches (38cm–22 cm) above the floor." This allows wheelchair users access to the items and creates less need for bending in those with mobility issues. In the same publication, the National Kitchen and Bath Association states, "Storage for soap, towels, and other personal hygiene items should be installed within reach of a person seated on the bidet or toilet and within 15 inches to 48 inches (38cm–122 cm) above the floor."

Towel bars, soap and tissue holders, and other bathroom storage items are available in a number of finishes to match most faucets and are often available from the faucet manufacturers (and others). For homeowners in certain geographic areas, towel warmers are desirable, often resembling standard towel bars with heat circulated through use of an electric current or by a recirculating hot-water system. Such units can be quite costly to purchase and install but are prized by some homeowners.

ERGONOMICS AND REQUIRED CLEARANCES

Important dimensional information about toilet clearances includes the space to each side of the toilet as well as clearance in front of the toilet. See Figures 4-26a and 4-27a. Toilets designed for use by those in wheelchairs have distinct clearance and grab bars requirements, which can be found in Figures 4-26c, 4-27b, and 4-28a. Like toilets, bidets require appropriate clearance to each side and in front of the fixture. Those dimensions are shown in Figure 4-26a.

When planning sink areas, the designer should consider the space required to approach and use the sink. These dimensions are shown in Figures 4-26a, 4-26b, and 4-27a. Sinks intended for use by those in wheelchairs require specific clearances in approach as well as the ability to access the sink bowl by wheeling under the lavatory. See Figures 4-26c and 4-27b.

Bathtubs require space in which to enter and exit the tub comfortably. This is often an issue of distance from nearby fixtures. For standard tub clearance dimensions, see Figure 4-27a (whirlpool and soaking tubs require clearances similar to standard tubs). Wheelchair-accessible tubs require a clear space a minimum of 30 inches by 60 inches for parallel approach and 48 inches by 60 inches for a forward approach for transferring into the tub. Wheelchair-accessible tubs also require grab bars and a bench or seat. Dimensions for these are shown in Figures 4-27b and 4-28b, although clear space may overlap, as shown in Figure 4-29.

TOILET

WALL

1'-6" RECOM. MIN.
1'-3" ABSOL. MIN.

1'-3" RECOM. MIN.
1'-0" ABSOL. MIN.

ADJACENT FIXTURE LINE

SINK: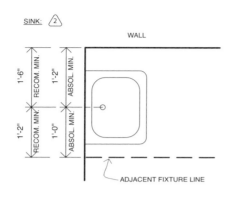

WALL

1'-6" RECOM. MIN.
1'-2" ABSOL. MIN.

1'-2" RECOM. MIN.
1'-0" ABSOL. MIN.

ADJACENT FIXTURE LINE

BIDET

WALL

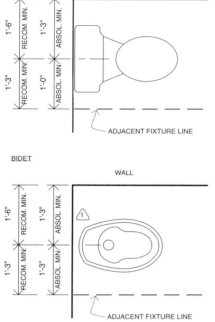

1'-6" RECOM. MIN.
1'-3" ABSOL. MIN.

1'-3" RECOM. MIN.
1'-3" ABSOL. MIN.

1

ADJACENT FIXTURE LINE

Figure 4-26a Toilet, bidet, and sink fixture mounting locations; fixtures require clearance and placement as noted.

1. Various models require 3 to 9 inches of clearance between fixture and wall.
2. Dimensions given are rules of thumb for sinks up to 2 feet wide. For oversized or unusual shapes and sizes, please consult manufacturer's recommendations.

TOILET

WALL

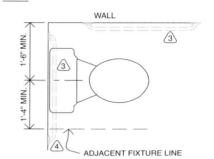

1'-6" MIN.

1'-4" MIN.

3

3

4

ADJACENT FIXTURE LINE

BIDET

WALL

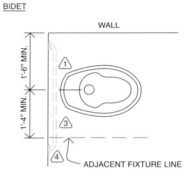

1'-6" MIN.

1'-4" MIN.

1

3

4

ADJACENT FIXTURE LINE

SINK:

WALL

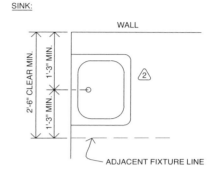

2'-6" CLEAR MIN.

1'-3" MIN.

2

ADJACENT FIXTURE LINE

Figure 4-26c Wheelchair-accessible toilet, bidet, and sink fixture mounting locations; fixtures require clearance and placement as noted.

1. Various models require 3 to 9 inches of clearance between fixture and wall.
2. For information on clear space for sink access, see Figure 4-27b.
3. For information about grab bar placement, see Figure 4-28a.
4. Could conflict with vanity.

Figure 4-26b Vanity/sink fixture mounting locations; sinks placed in vanities require clearance and placement as noted.

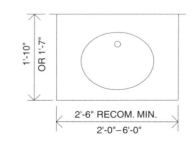

1'-10" OR 1'-7"

2'-6" RECOM. MIN.
2'-0"–6'-0"

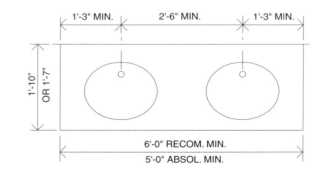

1'-3" MIN.   2'-6" MIN.   1'-3" MIN.

1'-10" OR 1'-7"

6'-0" RECOM. MIN.
5'-0" ABSOL. MIN.

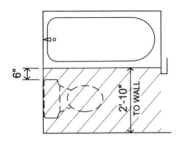

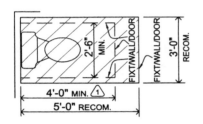

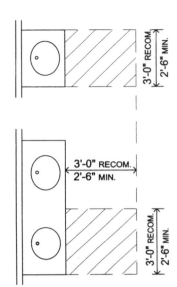

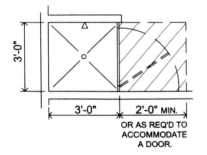

Figure 4-27a Standard bathroom fixture clearances required for comfortable use. Minimum dimension for round bowl models only. *Note:* Showerheads and curtain rods are often installed at 72 inches A.F.F. (above finished floor) or to meet the user's specific requirements.

CLEARANCES AND GRAB BAR LOCATIONS

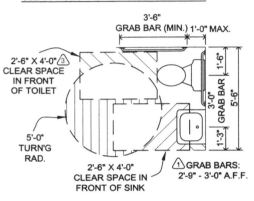

TRANSFER TUB: SIDE APPROACH

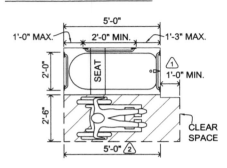

TRANSFER SHOWER

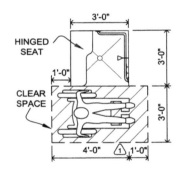

ROLL-IN SHOWER

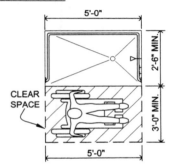

Figure 4-27b Wheelchair-accessible bathroom fixture clearances.

1. Required by some codes; easier to operate faucets before entry.
2. Up to 1 foot of the 4 feet required for forward approach can extend under a lavatory with clear access to knee space.
3. While 4 feet by 4 feet of clear space is recommended, in some cases, a clear space of 4 feet by 2 feet, 6 inches is used.

TRANSFER TUB: FORWARD APPROACH

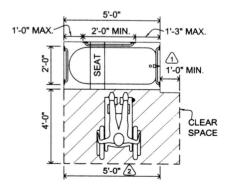

WHEELCHAIR ACCESSIBLE TOILET AND LAVATORY ELEVATIONS

WATER CLOSETS

LAVATORIES

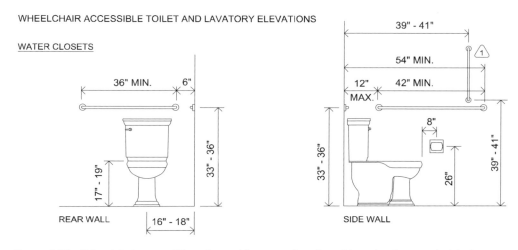

REAR WALL

SIDE WALL

KNEE CLEARANCE 8" MIN.　　6" MIN. TOE CLEARANCE

LAVATORY CLEARANCES

Figure 4-28a Wheelchair-accessible toilet and lavatory elevations. Note that lavatory height is listed as 34 inches maximum; however, the Center for Inclusive Design and Environmental Access recommends 32 for residences.

1. Vertical grab bar height is 18 inches minimum.

BATHTUB AND TUB/SHOWER COMBINATIONS

SHOWERS

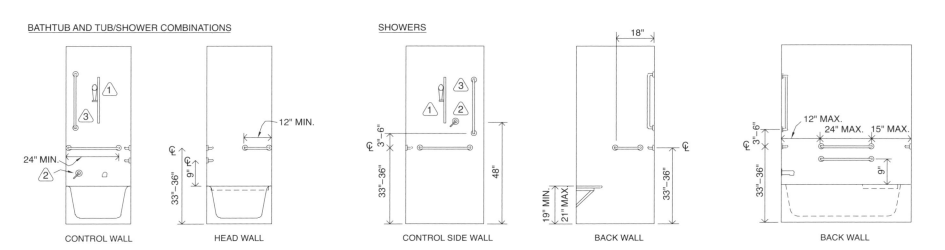

CONTROL WALL　　　　HEAD WALL　　　　　CONTROL SIDE WALL　　　　　BACK WALL　　　　　BACK WALL

Figure 4-28b Wheelchair-accessible bathtub and shower elevations.

1. Handheld shower spray.
2. Controls should be accessible from outside and inside the fixture (controls may be turned on from outside the fixture and off within the fixture).
3. Vertical grab bar height is 18 inches minimum; bar should be located 4 inches maximum from side of shower.

Much like bathtubs, showers require a clear area for entering and exiting the shower. In addition, showers often include a door, in which case the space for the door swing must be considered as well. Showerheads and curtain rods are often mounted at 72 inches, although mounting heights will vary based on individual needs. See Figure 4-27a for shower clearance information. Wheelchair-accessible showers require a 30-by-48-inch clear area adjacent to the shower entry for approach and transfer as well as grab bars. See Figures 4-27b and 4-28b for these dimensions, and as stated, clear space may overlap, as shown in Figure 4-29.

When planning a wheelchair-accessible bathroom, the designer should include a full 60-inch turning radius area inside the room. This often requires more space than is available and in some cases requires taking space over from adjacent rooms or including a roll-in shower area as part of the radius. A T-shaped circulation route can serve as an alternative to the full 60-inch turning radius, as shown in Figure 4-27b. As stated, portions of clear spaces required for wheelchair access can overlap, as indicated in Figure 4-29.

Organizational Flow

A full bathroom can be seen as having three activity areas: a sink/grooming area, a toileting area, and a bathing/showering area. Effective organization of the space requires the successful linking of the three activity areas, providing appropriate clearance and access space required for each fixture as well as adequate circulation space and consideration of plumbing supply and drain lines. Circulation space within the room requires 30 to 36 inches of clear space, with a *minimum of 32 inches of clear space for wheelchair passage.*

In terms of fixture use or room organization, one rule of thumb calls for fixtures or areas used most often to be placed first (or closest to an entry), with the largest and/or least used fixtures last (or to the rear of the room). This rule puts the sink(s) in the location closest to the door and the bath or shower near the rear of the room, as shown in Figure 4-30a, thus creating a compact, economical room. Additional considerations such as number of users, spatial restrictions (or lack thereof), local climate (cold climates limit plumbed wall locations), specific fixture requirements, and general ease of use of the totality of space also become considerations for the designer when planning the room. Figure 4-30b depicts a bathroom with two plumbed walls and with the fixtures used most often placed in locations convenient to room entry. Figure 4-30c illustrates a room in which the

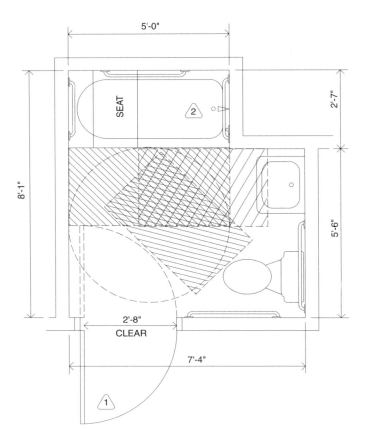

Figure 4- 29 Wheelchair clearances may overlap and may include clear areas under fixtures as shown in this diagram. This is the smallest footprint possible for an accessible bathroom; space savings have come from overlapping clearances and using a tub rather than a shower. Use of a shower is actually preferred by many wheelchair users; the addition of a shower would add a few inches to the room.

1. Given the clearances provided, the door can swing into the room; however, allowing the door to swing out (when adjacent spaces allow for it) makes the room more comfortable.
2. Note that horizontal and vertical grab bars and a transfer seat are included.

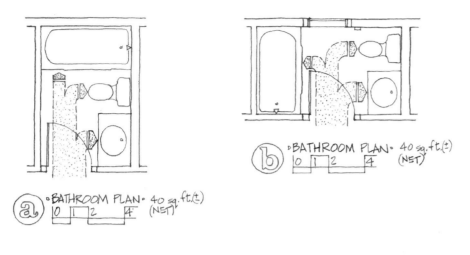

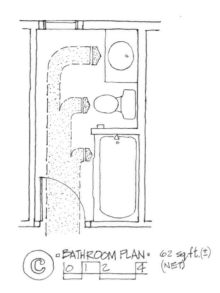

Figure 4-30 Fixture placement overview:

a. A single-wall bathroom plan with fixtures used most often placed closest to the entry and larger or those used more seldom placed at rear. The advantage of this plan is that it provides a compact and economical use of space and plumbing lines. Disadvantages include awkward access to tub/shower controls and the primary possible window area would be in the tub/shower area. In addition, making the room fully accessible would require enlarging the room to allow for greater fixture clearances, a wider doorway, and turning clearance.

b. A bathroom plan with two plumbed walls and the fixtures used most often placed conveniently in relation to the entry. This plan uses the same square footage as Figure 4-30a; however, in this plan the larger and least often used fixture (the bathtub) is not placed in the farthest position relative to the entry. This plan demonstrates the fact that two plumbed walls can provide good access to everything in a room of limited square footage and also can provide a good window location. In addition, while the door is shown as hinged and at 2 feet, 8 inches, it could easily be replaced by a pocket door of the same size or a standard 3-foot door to allow for accessibility/visitability; and the room could also be expanded in terms of width if desired. Disadvantages include the cost of plumbing two walls and the use of a smaller vanity (to keep to 40 square feet as in Figure 4-30a).

c. A single-wall bathroom plan in which the fixtures used most often are far from the room entry and that uses 50 percent more square footage than either Figure 4-30a or 4-30b. The additional square footage serves no useful purpose and creates the need to walk to the rear of the room to use the toilet or wash one's hands. One advantage to this plan is the use of tub alcove wall as a visual screen to the toilet. Generally this plan illustrates a poor use of the space.

most used fixtures are not placed in a location convenient to the entry. The drawings shown in Figures 4-31a, 4-31b, and 4-31c are examples of bathroom plans that contain problems related to organizational flow, fixture placement, ergonomics, and/or clearances.

A powder room, also known as a half bath, contains toilet and sink areas with no bathing facilities. See Figures 4-32a to 4-32d for illustrations and a discussion of fixture layout and design of this type of room.

In some bathrooms the three activity areas are included; however, a shower serves as the only bathing fixture. These are often referred to as three-quarter baths. See Figures 4-33a to 4-33c for illustrations and a discussion of fixture layout and design of this type of room.

The term full bath generally refers to a room that includes the three activity areas with bathtub and shower (separate or combined). Figure 4-34 illustrates various design considerations related to the design of full bathrooms.

In cases where there will be multiple users and/or where privacy is desired, multiple rooms or compartments can be used. Figures 4-35a to 4-35c, 4-36, and 4-37 illustrate various design considerations related to multiple room layouts.

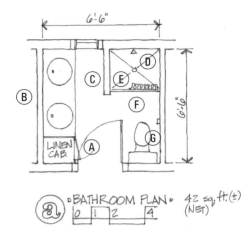

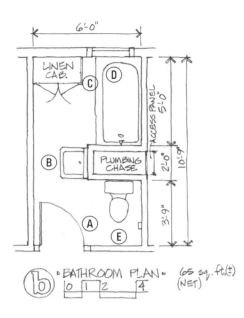

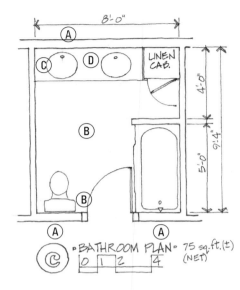

Figure 4-31a Problematic bathroom plan.

A. Door swing on linen closet conflicts with entry door because if left slightly ajar, it can block entry door; changing the hinge location to the left side would alleviate the door blockage.

B. There is space for a 5-foot vanity. This meets the recommended minimum for each sink of 30 inches per person.

C. Circulation to and clearance at sink is too tight. A minimum of 30 inches and a recommended clear space of 36 inches would be preferable (the code requires a minimum of 21 inches).

D. Showerhead location sprays directly on user while he or she is turning standard controls on. Plumbing on an exterior wall is not recommended due to freezing in cold climates, and access for repairs to shower water supply would require an exterior access panel or cutting and subsequent patching.

E. Shower size meets IRC minimum of 30 by 30 inches, but the recommended minimum size is 36 by 36 inches.

F. Not enough clear space between shower and toilet.

G. Center of toilet is not a minimum of 15 inches from the wall, as required by most codes.

Figure 4-31b Problematic bathroom plan. While this bathroom may seem economical in terms of making use of one plumbing location, it has many serious flaws in terms of clearance and building codes and is rather large given how poorly the space works functionally.

A. Location of door creates immediate sightline to toilet; this is undesirable to some homeowners.

B. Clearance at sink is too tight. A minimum of 30 inches and a recommended clear space of 36 inches would be preferable; code (IRC) requires a minimum of 21 inches. In addition, the long passageway to the tub and linen cabinet is less than ideal.

C. Access to window is compromised; more space is required by code (IRC).

D. Window location is problematic in cold climates due to moisture from the shower.

E. Not enough clear space in front of the toilet.

Figure 4-31c Problematic bathroom plan. This bathroom is large with no particular advantage granted by the extra square footage.

A. Plumbing is fragmented into three locations and does not result in any particular functional gains.

B. This area exceeds all clearance requirements to such a degree that there is wasted space; despite the space available around the toilet, it would be difficult to adapt the room for accessibility due to the door location conflicting with possible grab bar locations.

C. Plumbing on an exterior wall is not recommended and would probably come from the side wall.

D. Possible window locations on the exterior wall would conflict with mirror locations (this could be solved by clerestory windows).

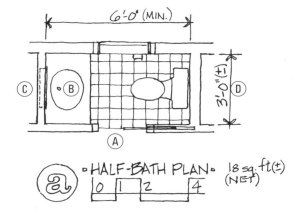

6'-0" (MIN.)

3'-0" (±)

C   B   D

A

•HALF-BATH PLAN• 18 sq. ft (±) (NET)

0 1 2 4

ⓐ

Figure 4-32a Small powder room/half-bath plan.

A. Pocket door is shown (2 feet); door could swing out or in if overall width of room is increased.

B. 3-foot vanity is shown; a wall-hung or pedestal lavatory (1 foot, 6 inches deep) could serve as an alternate and room width could be decreased to some extent.

C. Medicine cabinet with mirror is shown; other options are possible.

D. Absolute minimum dimension is 2 feet, 6 inches.

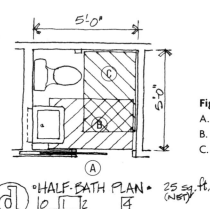

5'-0"

5'-0"

C

B

A

•HALF-BATH PLAN• 25 sq. ft. (NET)

0 1 2 4

ⓓ

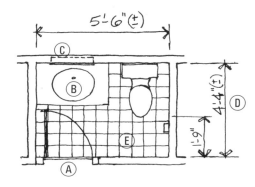

5'-6" (±)

4'-4" (±)

1'-9"

C

B   D

E

A

•HALF-BATH PLAN• 24 sq. ft. (±) (NET)

0 1 2 4

ⓑ

Figure 4-32b Small powder room/half-bath plan.

A. 2-foot door is shown.

B. 3-foot vanity is shown; a wall-hung or pedestal lavatory (1 foot, 6 inches deep) could serve as an alternate and room width could be decreased to some extent.

C. Medicine cabinet with mirror is shown; other options are possible.

D. A minimum space of 4 feet, 2 inches is required for an elongated toilet bowl; dimension could be reduced to 4 feet with smaller (round) toilet bowl.

E. A clear space of 1 foot, 9 inches is required by code (IRC).

Figure 4-32d Visitable powder room/half-bath plan with:

A. 32-inch pocket door allows for access into room.

B. 30-by-48-inch clear space in front of sink.

C. 30-by-48-inch clearance in front of toilet (parallel access).

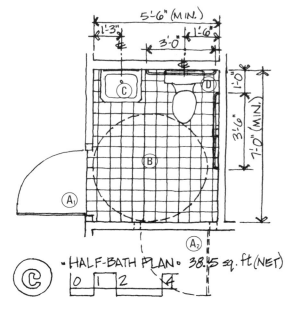

5'-6" (MIN.)

1'-3"   3'-0"   1'-6"

1'-0"

3'-6" (MIN.)

7'-0" (MIN.)

C   D

B

A1

A2

•HALF-BATH PLAN• 38.5 sq. ft (NET)

0 1 2 4

ⓒ

Figure 4-32c Wheelchair-accessible powder room/half-bath plan. Includes a full 5-foot-diameter clear turning area and 32-inch clear doorway (this requires a 3-foot swinging door, or smaller pocket door with 32-inch clear space), which requires the room be 60 percent larger than the example shown in Figure 4-32b.

A1. 3-foot door is shown; when door swings out, it allows the turning radius to exist free of door.

A2. Alternate 3-foot door location; when door swings out, it allows the turning radius to exist free of door.

B. 5-foot-diameter clear turning area.

C. 18-by-22-inch wall-hung lavatory.

D. 36-inch and 42-inch grab bars mounted 33 to 36 inches above floor.

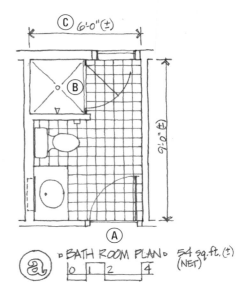

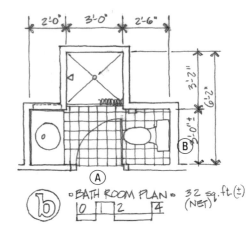

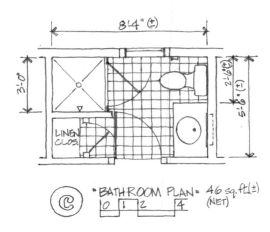

Figure 4-33a Three-quarter-bath plan.

A. 2-foot, 6-inch door is shown.

B. Using a 3-by-3-foot shower module rather than a standard 5-foot-long tub does not save space. In this example the bathroom is as large as a full bath with a shower/tub combination.

C. The 6-foot width could be decreased by 10-plus inches if the shower door is held to 24 inches maximum.

Figure 4-33b Three-quarter-bath plan. This is a very efficient shape, but the room form would not easily integrate into a configuration of surrounding rooms and the plumbing is scattered.

A. 2-foot, 6-inch door is shown.

B. This dimension *could* be reduced to 2 feet, 6 inches if a smaller lavatory and smaller door or pocket door were used.

Figure 4-33c Three-quarter bath plan. This plan contains the same elements as shown in Figure 4-33a with the addition of a linen closet. Also, the room is significantly smaller than that shown in Figure 4-33a, illustrating that by employing two plumbed walls, certain spatial economies can be gained.

Figures 4-32 through 4-37 are not intended to illustrate bathrooms designed for wheelchair accessibility, adaptability, or visitability (with the exception of Figure 4-32C). However, using a 3-foot-wide door, which would create at minimum a 32-inch clear passage through the doorway, would add greatly to the visitability of these rooms. In addition, locating a bathroom on the ground floor is considered a requirement for visitability. For specific accessibility information, please refer to Figures 4-27b, 4-28a, 4-28b, and 4-29. In addition, for information about bathroom design requirements for FHAA (Fair Housing Amendments Act), ANSI, and ADAAG, please refer to the overview presented in Chapter 1 and Appendix B.

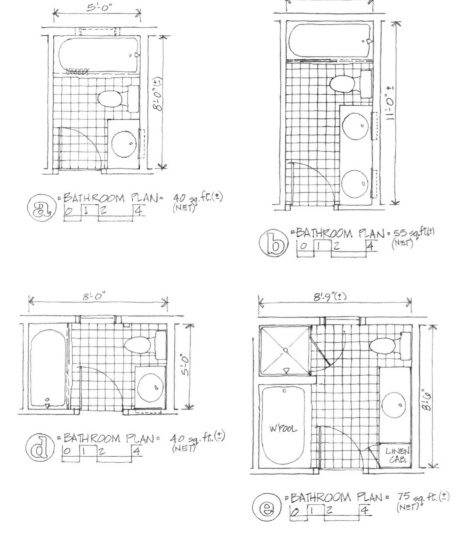

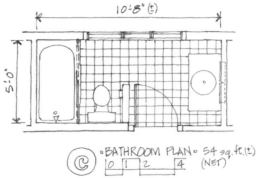

Figure 4-34 Full-bath plans. All plans show a 5-foot combination shower/tub with shower curtain or sliding doors, with the exception of drawing e, which contains separate tub and shower—requiring a sizable increase of square footage. All entry doors are shown at 2 feet, 6 inches but could be reduced to 2 feet, 4 inches or increased to 2 feet, 8 inches with some adjustment in size to plans a and b and by limiting door trim size in other plans. All plans show the sink at the first position relative to the entry door, which is convenient; however, the door location allows the door to swing into the area where a person would stand to use the sink (with plan e the exception). Adding a second sink as shown as the difference between plans a and b increases the overall space of the room by 35 percent, which increases the construction costs proportionally. Drawing illustrates a typical, post-World War II, suburban single-wall bathroom. In many climates a window placed in the shower area as shown can cause rotting in the window or within the window wall; glass block can be used in place of a standard window to alleviate this problem, or the window can be located elsewhere.

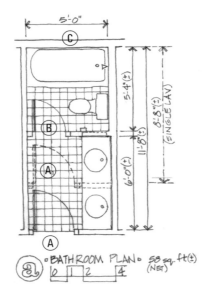

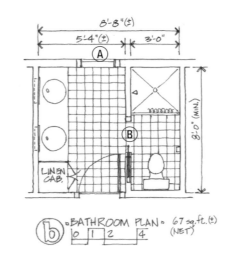

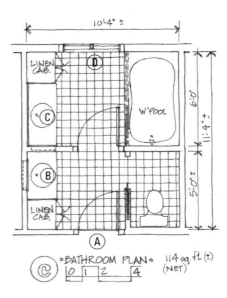

Figure 4-35a Multiple-room plan; commonly used in motel/hotel bathrooms as well as residences.

A. 2-foot, 6-inch door is shown; could be reduced to 2 feet, 4 inches. Door/wall location will vary depending on the size of the vanity and number of sinks.
   A1. Alternative door/wall location for single-sink bathroom. See note above for door size.
B. 2-foot, 4-inch door is shown.
C. Standard window not recommended in this location; standard windows are designed to resist water intrusion from the exterior, not the interior. Glass block or another suitable material could be used at such locations.

Figure 4-35b Multiple-room plan.

A. Using two plumbed walls creates an area appropriate for a window at this location.
B. 2-foot pocket door is shown.

Figure 4-35c Multiple-room plan.

A. 2-foot, 6-inch doors (shown); could easily be reduced to 2 feet, 4 inches or increased to 2 feet, 8 inches.
B. 3-foot vanity is shown.
C. 4-foot vanity is shown.
D. Larger room size and use of two plumbed walls creates a large area appropriate for windows at this location. The larger room as shown allows for a good deal of linen and other storage.
E. A 6-foot whirlpool tub/shower combination is shown; these are available in a range of sizes. Using a 5-foot tub/shower could decrease room size by 10 percent.
F. 2-foot pocket door is shown.

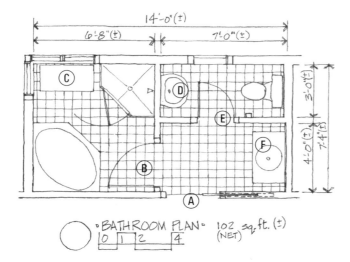

°BATHROOM PLAN° 102 sq. ft. (±)
(NET)

Figure 4-36 Multiple-room plan. This plan requires significant use of exterior walls to allow for window locations as shown. However, the plan could work successfully without exterior walls; it would then have no windows.

A. 3-foot pocket door is shown; a 2-foot, 8-inch pocket or swinging door could serve as an alternative.
B. 2-foot, 8-inch door is shown.
C. Freestanding bench/seat.
D. Small pedestal, wall-hung, or vessel sink.
E. 2-foot, 4-inch door is shown.
F. Vessel sink on freestanding console table is shown.

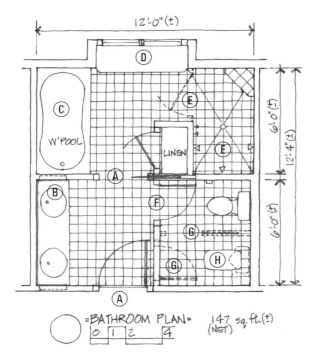

°BATHROOM PLAN° 147 sq. ft. (±)
(NET)

Figure 4-37 Very large multiple-room plan. It is as large as a bedroom and would be the most costly of all examples shown.

A. 2-foot, 8-inch door is shown.
B. Medicine cabinet to side with mirror above sink is shown—other options are possible.
C. A 6-foot-by-3-foot whirlpool tub combination is shown. A larger tub requires that the width of the room be increased accordingly.
D. Window seat.
E. Site-built shower with seat and multiple showerheads. A 2-foot, 4-inch door is shown but is not required unless shower serves as a steam room.
F. 2-foot door is shown.
G. Additional wall/compartment could be created at this location, which would require an additional door at G1.
H. Bidet or urinal location (urinal or second toilet would be enhanced by a separating partition or wall).

RELATED CODES AND CONSTRAINTS

Section R306 of the International Residential Code (IRC, 2003) covers "Sanitation" and states "Every dwelling unit shall be provided with a water closet, lavatory and a bathtub or shower" (R306.1). Section R306.4 goes on to state that all plumbing fixtures will be connected to an approved water supply and that all "kitchen sinks, lavatories, bathtubs, showers, bidets, laundry tubs, and washing machines shall be provided with hot water"; this only excludes toilets from a required hot-water supply.

Section R307 covers "Toilet, Bath and Shower Spaces" and states in item R307.2 that "bathtub and shower floors and walls above bathtubs with installed showerheads and in shower compartments shall be finished with a nonabsorbent surface. Such wall surfaces shall extend to a height of not less than 6 feet (1829 mm) above the floor." Clearly, prefabricated modular shower units made of fiberglass or acrylic meet the code requirements, as they are nonabsorbent surfaces. For showers using receptor bases and for site-built showers, a range of nonabsorbent wall surface materials can be used, including tile, stone, acrylics and other plastics, and in some installations, metals or glass.

The plumbing chapter of the IRC (Chapter 26) covers locations of waste pipes and states, "In localities having a winter design temperature of 32°F (0°C) or lower . . . a water, soil or waste pipe shall not be installed outside of a building, in exterior walls, in attics or crawl spaces, or in any other place subjected to freezing temperatures unless adequate provision is made to protect it from freezing by insulation, or heat or both" (P2603.6). This directly influences placement of plumbing lines (and fixtures) in buildings in colder climates

Chapter 27 of the IRC covers "Plumbing Fixtures" and states in Section P2705, item 5: "The centerline of water closets or bidets shall not be less than 15 (381 mm) inches from adjacent walls or partitions or not less than15 (381 mm) inches from centerline of a bidet to the outermost rim of an adjacent water closet. There shall be at least 21 inches (533 mm) clearance in front of the water closet, bidet or lavatory to any wall, fixture or door." The fixture locations and clearances illustrated earlier in this chapter meet the code as listed.

Item 6 in this same section states: "The location of piping, fixtures or equipment shall not interfere with the operation of windows or doors." This chapter goes on to state that shower compartments shall not be less than 900 square

inches and "30 inches (762 mm) in minimum dimension measured from the finished interior dimensions of the shower compartment, exclusive of fixture valves, showerheads, soap dishes and safety grab bars or rails."

In terms of shower construction, Section P2709.1 states that "shower receptors shall have a finished curb threshold of not less than 1 inch (25.4 mm) below the sides and back of the receptor." The section continues to state that "the finish floor shall slope uniformly toward the drain not less than one-fourth unit vertical in 12 units horizontal (2 percent slope) nor more than 0.5 inch (12.7 mm) and floor drains shall be flanged to provide a water-tight joint in the floor."

This portion of the code also covers site-built shower construction, requiring that they be "lined with sheet lead, copper or a plastic liner material" compliant with ASTM D 4068—or "hot mopping" as outlined in P2709.21

Additional areas of the IRC that relate to bathroom fixtures include P2712.7, which states that water closet seats shall be of a "smooth, nonabsorbent material and shall be properly sized." Section P27222 states that the "flow of hot water from the fittings corresponds to the left-hand side of the fitting." Put simply, this means that hot-water faucets belong on the left.

Section R303.3, "Light, Ventilation and Heating," states that "bathrooms, water closet compartments and other similar rooms shall be provided with aggregate glazing area in windows of not less than 3 square feet (0.279 m²), one-half of which must be openable." An exception to this requirement allows for "artificial light and a mechanical ventilation system" to serve in place of the required glazing. Such ventilation systems must be "exhausted directly to the outside." Clearly, use of this exception is commonplace.

Section R305 of the IRC covers ceiling height in detail and states that habitable rooms and "bathrooms . . . shall have a ceiling height of not less than 7 feet (2134 mm). The required height shall be measured from the finish floor to the lowest projection from the ceiling." This section contains several exceptions that are listed in Chapter 3 in the "Related Codes and Constraints" section, with the requirements illustrated in Figure 3-21 of the codes. In addition, there is an exception that is distinct to bathrooms, which reads: "Bathrooms shall have a minimum ceiling height of 6 feet 8 inches (2036cm) over the fixture and at the front clearance area for the fixtures . . . A shower or tub equipped with a showerhead shall have a minimum ceiling height of 6 feet 8 inches (2036 cm) above a minimum area 30 inches (762 mm) by 30 inches (762 mm) at the showerhead."

ELECTRICAL AND MECHANICAL

As mentioned, because the International Residential Code (Section R303.8) calls for heating to a minimum of 68°F when the winter design temperature is below 60°F, most bathrooms in the United States (with the possible exception of portions of Hawaii and Florida) require some form of heat source. The location for the heat source or its registers or diffusers, as well as those used by any air cooling source, must be considered by the interior designer as lighting, furnishings, window, and door locations are planned. The actual engineering of the heating and cooling system is, of course, done by professionals other than the interior designer.

National and local electrical codes call for the use of ground fault interrupters (GFIs) to be used for electrical outlets in bathrooms and other wet locations. These are designed to protect from electrical shock by detecting currents as minor as a few milliamperes and tripping a breaker at the receptacle or at the breaker panel to remove the shock hazard. The IRC (Section E3802.1) states that all "receptacles installed in bathrooms shall have ground-fault circuit-interrupter protection." Section E3603.4 requires that a minimum of one 20-amp branch circuit be provided to supply the bathroom receptacle outlets.

Bathroom outlet (duplex receptacle) placement is based on the organization of the room and the placement of countertops and vanities. Generally, outlets are located above countertop height, where they are needed for grooming and convenient use of small appliances and yet away from direct contact with water. The IRC (Section 3801.6) requires that "at least one wall receptacle outlet shall be installed in bathrooms and such outlet shall be located within 36 inches (914 mm) of the outside edge of each lavatory basin" and the receptacle "shall not be installed in a face up position in the work surface or counter top." Figure 4-38 conveys a simple bathroom electrical and lighting plan, which includes outlet and switching locations.

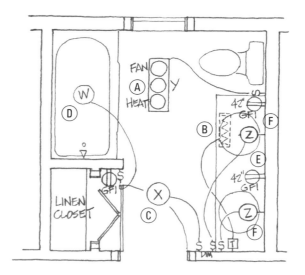

Figure 4-38 A simple bathroom electrical and lighting plan.

A. Ceiling fan (60 CFM minimum) exhaust to exterior with a nearby switch; not required by code where there is an operable window.

B. Under-counter/toe space electric heater for extremely cold climates; on a separate wall thermostat.

C. Ceiling light; not necessarily required with adequate light at other locations, shown on a dimmer switch (also not a requirement).

D. Heat lamp shown; could be combined with a fan in some locations; not required by code.

E. Ground fault interrupters (GFIs) for all outlets in order to protect from electrical shock at potentially wet locations. Per the IRC (section E3802.1), "receptacles installed in bathrooms shall have ground-fault circuit-interrupter protection." Section 3801.6 requires that at least one wall receptacle is installed in bathrooms, within 36 inches (914 mm) of the outside edge of each lavatory basin.

F. Mirror area luminaires on separate switches. This example does not allow for side-mounted luminaries as shown in Figure 4-39, due to the layout of the area around sinks.

The on/off switches for general lights are best located close to the room entry door on the latch side of the doorway when possible. In addition to lighting and power outlets, some clients request various communication lines for telephone, cable, and stereo/audio for use in bathroom or dressing areas.

As stated previously, exhaust fans are required in rooms with no glazing and are used in many bathrooms in addition to windows to aid in removing steam and odors. Some local codes may require that the fan is switched with the light; however, when that is not the case, separate switching allows someone to enter the room and turn on only the light when the fan is not needed.

In those situations when there is no window and the fan is meant to do all of the ventilation, central placement is advisable. However, in rooms with windows and fans, locating the fan requires consideration of its purpose. For example, if the fan is required to remove steam created by the shower, then placement near the shower is appropriate. When possible, it is helpful to place the fan switch near the place of use. For example, when the fan is meant to exhaust the toilet area, a switch convenient to the toilet can be helpful.

LIGHTING

Lighting for bathrooms must provide general illumination as well as task or focal lighting at mirrors, lavatories, and other locations where self-care-related tasks are performed. Traditionally, most grooming is done at the sink location in front of a mirror. Therefore, lighting this area well is crucial. Although many such areas have a single light source (or a row of lights) mounted above the mirror, this is not the ideal, as this luminaire location provides inconsistent light on only portions of the face and creates shadows.

Providing two wall-mounted luminaires on each side of the mirror (or at each sink location in larger bathrooms) of 75 watts each and mounted at roughly eye level provides cross-illumination and reduces shadows. According to Randall Whitehead in *Residential Lighting: A Practical Guide*, this manner of lighting a mirror originated in the theater, where actors applied makeup in front of mirrors surrounded by lamps. Traditional wall sconces can be used at such loca-

tions, as can more linear vertical luminaires, with such vertical fixtures providing the advantage of a cross-illumination for a variety of user heights. See Figure 4-39.

Some bathroom mirrors and grooming areas do not allow for positioning of luminaires to the side of the mirror. If the sink area is located in a small alcove, the fixtures can be mounted on adjacent walls, as illustrated in Figure 4-39. When installed in the locations described, which have the potential to become wet, the fixtures should be installed with an instantaneous circuit shutoff or GFI, as described in the preceding section. In situations where two wall-mounted fixtures are not possible, an overhead luminaire may be the only choice. In these situations, the fixture should be mounted at roughly 75 to 80 inches above the floor and contain 150 watts spread over at least 24 inches to illuminate the user as fully as possible. In such situations a glossy or light-colored countertop can be used to reflect some of the light upward.

Other areas of the bathroom require general lighting, which is often provided by overhead lights. Recessed downlights can work in bathing areas. However, these may not provide adequate ambient light and can be supplemented by wall sconces or rope lighting (or another form of concealed lighting) at counters, toe-kicks, soffits, and ledges. While unusual, locating a concealed luminaire at the toe-kick space of a vanity can create pleasant, although rather low, ambient lighting. Pendant fixtures and chandeliers can also be used depending upon bathroom size, ceiling height, and overall design.

Whether recessed or surface mounted, luminaires located in showers, directly above tubs, and in steam rooms should be listed as acceptable for use in wet locations by an approved testing agency such as UL (Underwriters Laboratory). Recently, recessed, adjustable, low-voltage fixtures have become available for use in wet areas.

Some local and state codes limit energy use by requiring particular fixtures in bathrooms. For example, California's Title 24 restricts general lighting to fluorescent fixtures only, but it does allow vanity area lighting to be incandescent or fluorescent. Title 24 also requires bathrooms with a single light source to be lit with fluorescent lighting.

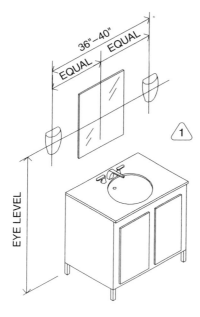

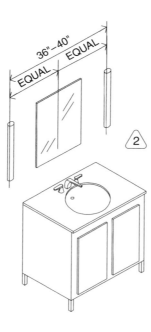

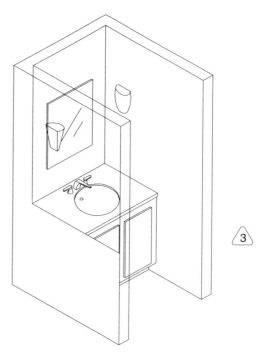

Figure 4-39 Providing wall-mounted luminaires to each side of the mirror can create attractive light for grooming.

1. Sconces placed roughly at adult eye level and spaced equally create balanced, attractive light.
2. Linear luminaires can accommodate a range of users' heights.
3. In cases where there is not room for wall-mounted luminaires at the mirror, they may be placed on adjacent walls.

BIBLIOGRAPHY

(Contains both works cited and recommended reading. Annotations where appropriate.)

Arnold, Susan. "The Right Light." *This Old House Magazine: Kitchen and Bath Guide.* Winter 2004.

Ching, Francis. *Home Renovation.* New York: Van Nostrand Reinhold, 1983.

Ching, Francis, and Cassandra Adams. *Building Construction Illustrated.* 3rd ed. Hoboken, NJ: John Wiley & Sons, 2001.

Dickinson, Mary Ann. *The Water Logue* 2, no. 5 (Fall). Sponsored by the California Urban Water Conservation Council, 2003.

Frechette, Leon. *Remodeling a Bathroom.* Newtown, CT: The Taunton Press, 2004.

Nagyszalanczy, Sandor. *Installing a Kitchen Sink.* CornerHardware.com. www.corner-hardware.com/howto/ht069.html.

Susanka, Sarah. *The Not So Big House: A Blueprint for the Way We Really Live.* Newtown, CT: The Taunton Press, 1998.

U.S. Department of Energy. *Energy Savers: Virtual Home.* www.eere.energy.gov/consumerinfo/energy_savers/virtualhome/508/toilet.html, 2004.

Whitehead, Randall. *Residential Lighting: A Practical Guide.* Hoboken, NJ: John Wiley & Sons, 2004.

CHAPTER **5**

KITCHENS

"While the house as a whole is among the more traditional and conservative elements of society, the kitchen is quickest within the house to reflect new concepts of comfort and convenience. It is here one finds technology changing fastest. Yet the kitchen's traditional role as the hub of family life remains...."

MERRITT IERLEY, *The Comforts of Home*

Residential kitchens have a rich history related to sociological, cultural, technological, and economic factors. With an open hearth, early Colonial kitchens formed the heart of the house. Later kitchens were located in the basement, at the rear of the house, or outside—depending on geography, climate, and economics. Evolving further, the kitchen later became a private, enclosed room often adjacent to a formal dining room. Various societal influences have brought about the American kitchen's common present incarnation: open to adjacent dining and entertainment areas, allowing family and guests to join in food preparation. As Ellen M. Plante, author of *The American Kitchen*, writes, "the kitchen as hearth has come full circle." See Figures 5-1 to 5-4 for images of kitchens of the past and present.

Kitchens that meet the lifestyles, culinary interests, and aesthetic preferences of owners are important components of custom home design as well as new construction and additionally generate millions of dollars in kitchen remodeling. Kitchen remodeling continues to be a significant component of the construction

Figure 5-1 A colonial kitchen hearth served as the heart of the home. Parry Mansion, Museum, New Hope, PA. Photograph courtesy of the New Hope Historical Society.

Figure 5-2 Two women standing in a kitchen of the late 1800s. The stove, sink, and cupboards are located very close to one another and the room is enclosed and separated from the rest of the house, which is rather typical of the era. Photograph courtesy of the Minnesota Historical Society.

Figure 5-3 A more open kitchen with a penninsula, on the journey to the more open kitchen popular today. Photograph dated 1952 by Norton & Peel, courtesy of the Minnesota Historical Society.

Figure 5-4 A current kitchen complete with a hearthlike cooking area, bringing the kitchen full circle. Photograph courtesy of KraftMaid Cabinetry.

industry, with the number of kitchen remodeling jobs done annually growing 50.3 percent over the past five years according to *Kitchen and Bath Business*.

Clearly, kitchen design is big business; however, as interest in kitchen design and remodeling has grown, Americans are actually eating outside of the home more than ever—4.2 times per week in 2000 according to *Restaurant News*. This has prompted some social critics to argue that today's large, well-appointed kitchen is simply a status symbol. In his book *Bobos in Paradise*, David L. Brooks writes

> When you walk into a newly renovated upscale home . . . you will likely find a kitchen so large it puts you in mind of an aircraft hangar with plumbing. The perimeter walls of the old kitchen will have been obliterated, and the new kitchen will have swallowed up several adjacent rooms. . . .You think you see the far wall of some distant great room shimmering in the distance but it could be a mirage reflected off the acres and acres of Corian countertops.

Brooks's humorous description points to the ever growing size of kitchens and their importance to many homeowners, and this importance may seem frivolous in light of the number of times people eat out and the lack of family meals actually prepared in the kitchen. However, the interest in kitchens can go beyond simply seeking status; it can also speak of the desire of some families to prepare food together, to entertain in spite of a busy schedule, and to an increased interest in food and food preparation. Perhaps people are seeking the kind of relationship to cooking that the designer Bill Stumpf discussed related to his research of Julia Child's kitchen:

> Julia was more than a cook; she had these ideas about where to be in a space while doing other things. She had a view of cooking that was essentially social . . . She was very philosophical about its central location, about the importance of sitting around the kitchen table and talking.

Kitchens and the vital social role they can play in our daily lives along with the ongoing advances in appliances and features offer designers opportunities and challenges. Much like bathrooms, kitchens have grown in terms of square footage and amenities, and well-designed kitchens require careful analysis of the homeowner's lifestyle and preferences. A thorough review of a client's requirements, lifestyle, budget, architectural parameters, and building codes may result in a kitchen design that differs from the fantasy space desired by homeowners. Perhaps, however, the well-considered kitchen will be more the active, social location sought after by Julia Child and less like Brooks's descriptions of a kitchen as an "airplane hangar with plumbing."

A review of the questions and issues shown in the "Kitchen Programming Questionnaire" sidebar will aid in the design of a useful, comfortable kitchen design and should be considered part of the programming phase of the kitchen design.

KITCHEN PROGRAMMING QUESTIONAIRE

Number of Cooks

- One
- Two people working together
- One primary cook with helper(s)
- Multiple cooks

Frequency of Meals Prepared

- Which meals are prepared at home: breakfast, lunch, dinner, other?
- Do homeowners entertain frequently and what is the typical number of guests?
- When homeowners are entertaining, what is the style of dining (for example, buffet or more formal seated dining)?

Meals Served in the Kitchen/Number of Diners

- Which meals are served in the kitchen?
- How many people should the in-kitchen seating serve?

Types of Meals Prepared

- Does the family eat a limited or wide variety of food types (this is similar to identifying the menu in commercial kitchens)?

Additional Functional Areas Required

- Do the clients require specialized work areas within the kitchen, such as baking centers?
- Do the clients require additional work areas located within the kitchen, such as sewing centers or office areas?

Level of Privacy/Visual Separation

- Is there a desire for the kitchen to be open to other areas/rooms? If so, which rooms?

ACCESSIBILITY

According to Paralyzed Veterans of America's *Kitchen Design for the Wheelchair User* by Kim A. Beasley and Thomas D. Davies, Jr.:

> For most wheelchair users, none of the functional spaces in a home is a more complex design problem than the kitchen. The process of food preparation—as well as the cleanup afterwards—involves a series of interrelated tasks requiring an array of different appliances, plumbing fixtures, storage components, food items, and utensils.

Designing a space that accommodates these interrelated tasks requires careful consideration of the user's specific needs. While American National Standards Institute (ANSI) and Uniform Federal Accessibility Standards (UFAS) standards exist for creating wheelchair-accessible residential kitchens, these do not necessarily best suit the specific needs of individual users or family groups. In most cases such standards can be modified to suit specific needs. In cases where a wheelchair user resides alone, the kitchen is best designed with counters and clear spaces that suit that individual alone. In contrast, in situations where a kitchen is shared by wheelchair users and others, a range of counter heights and accommodations is necessary. In addition, if resale and/or resale value is a concern, the kitchen design should suit a range of users. This can be accomplished with adjustable kitchen components, and wheelchair clearance spaces can be provided, as discussed later in this chapter.

Given that kitchens present significant challenges to individuals with special needs as well as to those that fall outside the range of adult averages in terms of stature, this chapter provides information about accessibility, adaptability, and universal design as these relate to appliances, fixtures, clearances, and workflow. Information on standards and guidelines that apply to certain multiple-family housing units (ANSI/UFA and FHAA) can be found in the "Related Codes and Constraints" section of this chapter, as well as in Chapter 1 and Appendix B.

FIXTURES AND APPLIANCES

The following section covers appliances and fixtures found in kitchens. An overview of appliances is presented, as well as a brief overview of considerations related to accessibility. For additional information regarding placement, mounting heights, and wheelchair clearances, please review the "Ergonomics and Required Clearances" section of this chapter.

Sinks

For many years the sink area has been seen as a primary work area in the kitchen, as it forms the base of the primary cleanup center, which often includes a dishwasher, garbage disposal, and garbage and recycling bins. Increasingly, kitchens are used by more than one cook at a time, a situation that is greatly aided by a secondary sink location. A second sink can be seen as a part of a secondary preparation and cleanup area (for use by a second cook) or as part of an entertainment/bar area. Some cooks prefer a sink adjacent to the cooktop as well as one adjacent to the dishwasher. Others require only a faucet (without a sink) near the cooktop for filling large pots

Some homeowners prefer a single-bowl (or -basin) sink because they primarily rely on the dishwasher for dish and pan cleanup, whereas other homeowners prefer a double- or triple-bowl sink because they do a good deal of dish washing by hand or a great deal of food preparation. Respondents to a 2004 survey conducted by *Plumbing and Mechanical* magazine indicated that double-bowl kitchen sinks were installed more than 79 percent of the time.

According to the National Kitchen and Bath Association's *Kitchen Basics,* standard double sinks are 33 inches and standard single-bowl models are 24 inches (2004). These can be considered standard, but a range of sizes as well as shapes are available, as shown in Figure 5-5. One-, two-, and three-bowl configurations are also readily available. Figures 5-6a to 5-6d and 5-7a and 5-7b depict various sink types and styles.

One popular option is a two-bowl configuration with one larger, deeper sink for washing and a smaller, shallower sink with a garbage disposal for cleaning and prep. Three-bowl varieties often include two larger deep sinks and one smaller shallow sink for disposal and prep. A secondary sink for a second cook or for entertaining is often smaller than the standard sink and can be found in various shapes, including square, round, and an elongated rectangular form known as a "trough sink." Figure 5-5 shows sizes of some secondary sinks.

Sinks are available in several depths, ranging from roughly 6 to 8 inches for standard sinks and 10 to 12 inches for deeper models. Deeper sinks tend to splash less than shallow sinks and obviously allow for handling larger items. Selection of the proper sink depth requires careful consideration of counter heights relative to the heights of users and to needs for accessibility. For example, taller users may find deep sinks require bending and stooping, whereas shallow sinks allow greater knee space for wheelchair users.

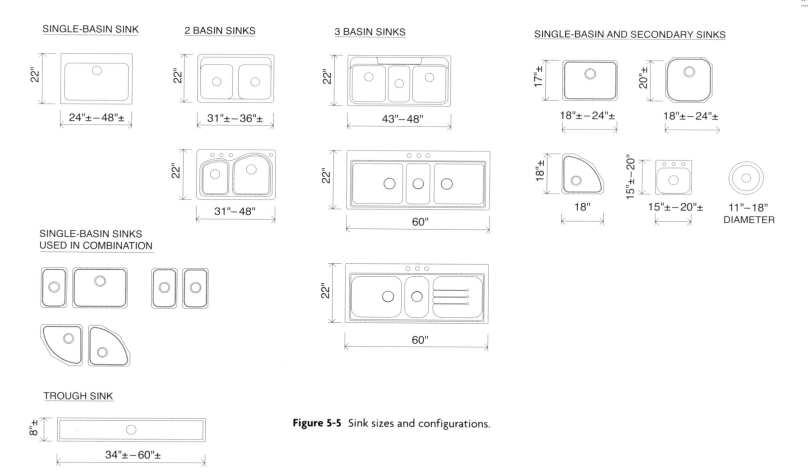

SINGLE-BASIN SINK

2 BASIN SINKS

3 BASIN SINKS

SINGLE-BASIN AND SECONDARY SINKS

22" 24"±−48"±

22" 31"±−36"±

22" 31"−48"

22" 43"−48"

22" 60"

22" 60"

17"± 18"±−24"±

20"± 18"±−24"±

18"± 18"

15"±−20" 15"±−20"±

11"−18" DIAMETER

SINGLE-BASIN SINKS USED IN COMBINATION

TROUGH SINK

8"± 34"±−60"±

Figure 5-5 Sink sizes and configurations.

Additional issues to consider in sink selection relate to the overall size and design of the kitchen. For example, in areas where counter space is limited, a sink with a cutting board that fits over the basin can be used to create a gain in usable workspace. The overall size of the kitchen, its layout, the lifestyle of the homeowner, and the project budget greatly influence sink selection.

Common materials for sink construction include stainless steel, vitreous china, fireclay, enameled cast iron, solid surfacing material, composite materials, stone, and decorative metals. The previously mentioned 2004 *Plumbing and Mechanical* magazine survey found that "stainless steel was top choice for sinks."

For sinks, stainless steel is available in a range of gauges and finishes. It does not chip or rust but can scratch (made more evident by certain finishes). Vitreous china is a ceramic product, usually with a durable glazed finish. Fireclay is also a ceramic product, fired at very high temperatures and available in high-gloss finishes. Artisan versions of ceramic sinks are available in a range of designs. Enameled cast iron is available in a wide range of colors, shapes, and configurations. Unlike stainless steel, chipping can be a problem with ceramic and enameled cast-iron sinks. Some people prefer ceramic sinks because they can be less noisy than stainless steel and enameled cast iron, although this

Figure 5-6a A double-basin cast-iron sink (self-rimming in this example). Photograph courtesy of Kohler Co.

Figure 5-6b Two single-basin cast-iron sinks used in combination (an under-counter installation in this example). Photograph courtesy of Kohler Co.

varies based on gauge and design. In addition, some sinks have noise-attenuating design features.

Solid-surface sinks are created from the same type of surfacing material used to make solid-surface countertops. Some of the sinks are available as integral to the counter surface, while others are made separately and mounted in countertops of similar or varying materials (most often mounted under the counter). These sinks tend to be quiet and offer the durability of solid-surface material. Composite sinks are a combination of stone and acrylic polymers; this material generally resists cuts, scratching, stains, and fading. These sinks are available in a range of mounting options.

Sinks are also available in materials such as stone and marble as well as terrazzo. These are used less frequently than those made of the materials discussed previously. Special artisan-created sinks in various stones and metals such as copper are also available. Often these sinks are very expensive and serve as focal points of a particular room or as secondary sinks to be enjoyed for their beauty.

Much like bathroom sinks, a range of mounting styles and options are available for kitchen sinks, including self-rimming, metal frame or rimless, under-mount, apron front, and wall-mounted sinks. See Figures 5-7a and 5-7b. As in bathrooms, the choice of countertop material and overall design determines the mounting style used.

Self-rimming sinks have a rim or lip that fits over the top surface of the counter. This type of sink is readily available in various styles, colors, and materials. One drawback with this type is that the rim prevents water to be drawn back into the

sink bowl, which can cause water and soil to collect where the rim meets the countertop, making it difficult to clean.

Metal frame or rimless sinks use a metal mounting rim and clips attached below the countertop, which hold the sink in place, as shown in Figure 5-7a. *Under-mount* sinks attach to the bottom surface of the countertop, as shown in Figure 5-6b to 5-6d.

Tile-in sinks allow tiles to be taken flush to the edge of the sink, as shown in Figure 5-7b. Apron-front sinks have an exposed panel in the front of the sink that is often the same material and depth as the sink bowl; they are called farm sinks by some people. *Wall-mounted* (also known as wall-hung) sinks feature a basin that is hung from the wall at a desired height.

As discussed in Chapter 4, "Bathrooms," wheelchair-accessible sinks require open space under the sink, as well as some form of protection from hot pipes, usu-

Figure 5-7a Cast-iron metal frame sink. Photograph courtesy of Kohler Co.

Figure 5-7b A fireclay tile-in apron-front sink. Photograph courtesy of Kohler Co.

Figure 5-6c A trough-shaped, stainless steel entertainment sink (an under-counter installation in this example). Photograph courtesy of Kohler Co.

Figure 5-6d A single-basin, vitreous china entertainment or secondary sink (an under-counter/undermount installation in this case). Photograph courtesy of Kohler Co.

ally in the form of an angled protective panel or insulation-wrapped pipes. In addition, accessible sinks are mounted lower than the standard countertop height. Some users prefer shallow sinks for better access as well.

Additional options for accessibility include sinks in adjustable countertops, as well as adaptable base cabinets with removable fronts, or with fold-back or bi-fold doors. It is worth noting that some garbage disposals can interfere with open knee space required under sinks and may not fit within protective panels. Detailed information about mounting heights and clearances for wheelchair-accessible sinks can be found in this chapter under "Ergonomics and Required Clearances."

Faucets

Faucet selection is best done in tandem with sink selection because the various types of sinks and mounting methods require differing faucet placement. Faucets come in a vast range of styles, from high gooseneck styles that make filling pots easy to low-slung models that tend to splash less and make less of a visual impact upon the room. Faucets are available with separate hot and cold controls (called *control valves*, see Figures 5-8a and 5-8b) or with single controls. Those with two separate controls may be constructed with the spout and valves grouped over a single hole, or with at least three separate holes with valves mounted 4 or 8 inches apart (often more holes are required for accessories and vacuum breaker).

Many cooks prefer single-control faucets with easy-to-use levers, because when they are preparing foods, it is easy to reach and touch a lever with a clean hand in order to wash the other dirty hand. In addition, single-lever controls are recommended for universal accessibility in kitchens, as they are more easily used by a wide range of individuals. Single-lever sinks require at minimum a single hole but may require additional holes as well for accessories such as handheld sprays or dispensers.

Self-rimming sinks generally have holes predrilled for faucets, whereas under-counter-mounted sinks often have faucet holes drilled in the countertop. Apron-front sinks vary from having predrilled holes within the body of the sink to the holes drilled into the counter. In other cases of apron sinks, faucets are wall mounted. Many wall-mounted sinks are predrilled for faucets.

Additional options that relate to sinks and faucets include *instant hot-water dispensers*, which offer instant delivery through a sink-top spout. Speed and efficiency are the primary advantages with this item, as it delivers very hot water far faster than a teakettle or microwave oven can and delivers only the water needed, with little waste. These units heat water to 190 degrees, which can easily cause severe burns in a matter of seconds. Another increasingly popular option is a *pot-filler-faucet* located at or next to the cooktop/range. These enable cooks to fill heavy pots directly at the cooking location rather than carrying them across the kitchen. These are often wall mounted.

As discussed in Chapter 4, "Bathrooms," faucet options available for universal accessibility include faucets with single-control levers, crosses, or loops (in place of other handle styles); faucets with nonslip textures; faucets with easy-to-control flow rate and/or temperature, pedal-operated options; faucets with motion-sensing activation; and side-mounted options.

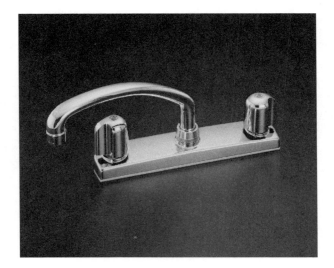

Figure5-8a A low-slung faucet with double controls. Photograph courtesy of Kohler Co.

Figure 5-8b A gooseneck faucet (double control in this example). Photograph courtesy of Kohler Co.

Garbage Disposers

Garbage disposers, also referred to as garbage disposals (or *food waste grinders* in many codes and standards), grind food scraps in a chamber with blades and use water to wash the churned-up bits down the drain. Many homeowners appreciate the convenience of being able to remove dish scraps into the sink and then directly down the drain using a disposer. There is some debate as to the ecological implications of garbage disposers: Food scraps are shifted away from landfills and into wastewater treatment systems, prompting some cities to require disposers in new homes. However, food waste in sewers can increase the burden on sewers, and septic systems generate added nitrogen and, according to some, wastewater, thus causing some municipalities to ban disposers in residences. Therefore, it is advisable to check local codes prior to installing disposers.

Disposers are available in 1/3-, 1/2-, 3/4-, and 1-horsepower models, with some models available with an auto-reverse mode for clearing jams. There are two basic feed types: continuous feed, which works as the name implies, and batch feed, which requires loading and putting a stopper in place in order to activate the blades. Batch feed types can be more costly and time-consuming but are considered safer because they keep hands out of the chamber.

Dishwashers

Dishwashers are considered part of the primary sink area because of the work required at the sink to prepare items for the dishwasher and because of the need for drainage of the dishwasher. Standard built-in dishwashers fit into a 24-inch-wide space under a kitchen countertop and are attached to a hot-water pipe, a drain, and an electrical line.

In addition to the standard built-in type, other sizes and styles are available. Compact (typically 18 inches wide) as well as larger models (30 inches wide) are also available. In addition, some manufacturers are producing double or single pull-out-drawer-style dishwashers. Portable dishwashers are available in full-size models as well as compact countertop models. KitchenAid currently manufactures a double sink with a small dishwasher located within one of the sink basins; the dishwasher elements can be removed from the sink basin to make it available for other uses. Figure 5-9 depicts dishwasher sizes.

Options for dishwashers include super-quiet operation, dirt-detecting sensors (these can aid in energy efficiency), special cycles, "turbo boosting" (for added speed or greater cleaning power depending on the manufacturer), loading flexibility, the option of a third rack, greater rack adjustability, energy and water

Figure 5-9 Dishwasher sizes.

1. Standard dishwashers fit under the counter, are roughly 24 inches wide, and have front controls.
2. Dishwashers are available with hidden controls.
3. Select models can be filled with panels to match cabinetry.
4. Drawer-style models are available as single-drawer or double-drawer models (lower drawer front can overlap toe-kick in some models/installations).

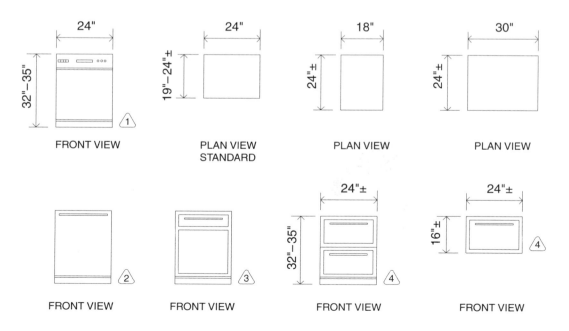

efficiency, hidden controls, and various finish options including fittings for custom panels.

Standard dishwashers require bending for loading and unloading. A higher-than-standard mounting location is required for wheelchair use or for individuals with mobility limitations. In some instances, using a compact dishwasher in a wheelchair-accessible kitchen allows for more open knee space for access to work counters, and this option is worth considering if space is at a premium. In addition, drawer-style dishwashers can be useful for some individuals with limited mobility. Additional issues to consider in terms of universal design include location of the detergent containers and simplicity and ease of reading/using controls.

Ranges

The term *range* is used to describe an appliance that combines surface cooking elements and oven functions in one unit. *Freestanding* ranges are those that are completely independent of cabinet and counter surfaces; these are generally finished on the sides. *Slip-in* ranges rest on the floor but generally line up tightly with counter and cabinet fronts; these are generally unfinished on the sides. *Drop-in* ranges rest on a drawer or cabinet frame; these are generally unfinished on the sides. See Figure 5-10 for illustrations of range types. Ranges with more than one oven are available; in some cases, a microwave or second oven is placed above the cooktop, referred to as a *high-low* range by some.

Common materials for range exteriors include porcelain enamel or stainless steel. Glass and ceramic cooking surfaces are also an option. Energy sources for ranges include electric or gas. Some homeowners prefer the more precise heat control of gas burners, while others prefer electric coil or smooth-top (heated by covered radiant elements) models. Gas ranges (and cooktops) depend on the BTUs (British thermal units) generated. Standard ranges generate from 8,000 to 10,000 BTUs per burner. Professional-style ranges, similar to those used in restaurant kitchens, generate 15,000 BTUs or more. Such high BTUs allow food to heat more quickly and allow for specialized cooking techniques such as stir-frying.

The energy source used and the number of BTUs generated are important considerations in range and cooktop selection and relate directly to the price of the unit, as well as to the need for ventilation. Ranges most commonly used in residences may be broadly divided into standard types and professional-style ranges. *Standard* electric and gas ranges, with four burners, are commonly available in 24-inch-deep by 30-inch-wide models. Smaller-size ranges—from 20 to 24 inches wide—are available as well. See Figure 5-11 for standard range sizes.

Figure 5-10 Freestanding, drop-in, and slip-in ranges.
1. Drop-in range. Rests on cabinet, base, or drawer.
2. Slip-in range. Rests on floor, unfinished on sides.
3. Freestanding. Sits independently, finished on sides.

It is worth noting that some manufacturers offer standard gas ranges with a single, high-power burner (one burner as high as 15,000 BTUs) and/or slow-simmer burners. In addition, some manufacturers offer ranges with gas burners and electric ovens (known as duel-fuel ranges), because some homeowners prefer the even heating of electric ovens, with the control and BTUs of a gas range. For addi-

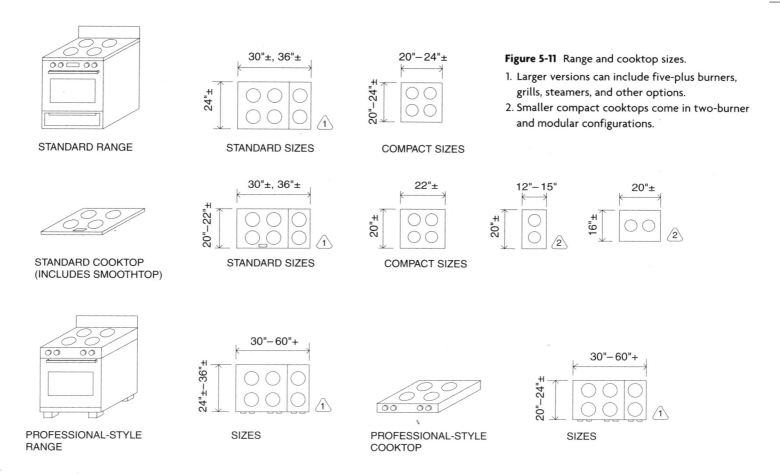

STANDARD RANGE

STANDARD SIZES

COMPACT SIZES

Figure 5-11 Range and cooktop sizes.
1. Larger versions can include five-plus burners, grills, steamers, and other options.
2. Smaller compact cooktops come in two-burner and modular configurations.

STANDARD COOKTOP
(INCLUDES SMOOTHTOP)

STANDARD SIZES

COMPACT SIZES

PROFESSIONAL-STYLE
RANGE

SIZES

PROFESSIONAL-STYLE
COOKTOP

SIZES

tional information about burners and cooking surfaces, please refer to the "Cooktops" section that follows.

As mentioned, *professional-style* ranges offer the high BTUs of commercial fixtures but generally have added insulation, which is not present in many true commercial fixtures. True commercial ranges (often with no insulation) must generally be installed as completely freestanding units a certain distance from cabinetry and other flammable elements. Professional-style ranges and cooktops look similar to true commercial models and allow very high BTUs as discussed, but can be placed within or close to cabinetry. They also require *very good ventilation*.

Although sizes are not completely standardized among manufacturers, professional-style ranges are generally available in 24-inch-deep and 30-inch-deep models, in widths of 30, 36, 48, and 60 inches, with some specialized manufacturers making larger units up to 72 inches. The widest units accommodate as many as six or eight burners, with accessories such as griddles, grills, and large double ovens. Figure 5-11 illustrates professional-style range sizes.

Another type of range, the most well known of which is made by Aga, employs radiant heat available in multiple ovens at constant preset levels, with top cooking surfaces that are also preset at consistent levels. This type of range is consistently warm at a range of settings. The temperature is controlled by selecting the oven or cooking surface location that meets the level of heat required. This type of range is available in sizes roughly 24, 29, and 59 inches wide and roughly 27 inches deep.

The designer must keep in mind that ranges require adequate ventilation. This is covered later in this chapter in the "Electrical and Mechanical" section.

Ranges are not considered ideal for use by individuals in wheelchairs because the cooking surface is too high for many seated users and because ranges require a parallel approach rather than allowing open knee space below the cooking surface. While ranges are permitted under ANSI 4.32.5.6 and UFAS 4.34.6, in order to meet these standards, controls must be mounted along the front or side of the range so that the user is not required to reach across a hot burner to adjust the controls. In most cases a cooktop with a separate built-in oven is considered best for wheelchair uses.

Cooktops

Cooktops are cooking surfaces that don't include an oven. These can be built into islands and countertops. Cooktops are available in a standard 30-inch-wide size; wider versions are also available, as are compact two-burner versions. Materials of construction include glass, porcelain enamel, and stainless steel. Professional-style cooktops are available, and these offer the same advantages and disadvantages as professional-style ranges (minus the ovens). See Figure 5-11 for cooktop sizes.

Electrical cooking elements include electric coils as well as radiant elements covered by a glass and/or ceramic surface. There are also induction units that employ a magnetic field under a smooth top, which heats when the cooktop surface comes in contact with an iron or steel pan; copper-bottomed and aluminum pans do not heat on these units. Another less common heat source employs halogen-filled glass tubes under a smooth-top surface.

In terms of cooktop surfaces, some homeowners prefer the smooth-top surface, as these are easy to clean. Others prefer gas burners, as they heat more quickly and generally allow for more precise heat control. Options with gas burners include sealed burners, which can be easier to clean than standard burners. Other options include heavy-duty cast-iron grates, as well as a single continuous grate over the entire top, allowing pots to be placed in various locations. Smooth-top models often come with indicator lights to let the users know that the burner is hot.

As with ranges, cooktops require adequate ventilation. This is covered in this chapter in the "Electrical and Mechanical" section.

As stated, cooktops can be placed in countertops with open space underneath for seated wheelchair use. Such an installation also allows for the countertop to be mounted at various heights or, in some cases, to be adjustable. The bottom of the cooktop unit must be insulated and covered in order to prevent users from being burned. Smooth-top cooktops are recommended for wheelchair users because pans can be easily moved on the smooth surface, although care must be taken to ensure that users can easily read temperature indicators in order to prevent burns, because smooth-tops do not have flames or the bright red coils of standard burners to denote heat.

Cooktop controls must be placed at the front or side of the unit for wheelchair use in order that users are not forced to reach over hot surfaces to use controls. In selecting a cooktop, the designer should give special attention to the ease of reading and using controls for users with limited eyesight or difficulty gripping. In addition, cooktops with a staggered burner arrangement or cooking elements aligned on the front of the cooktop are ideal for wheelchair users, as these minimize reaching over hot surfaces. Including an angled mirror above the cooktop surface is helpful for wheelchair users as well.

Wall Ovens

Wall ovens are available in several types and sizes and are available with gas or electric heat sources. However, the most product choice, technological advancements, and new options are available in electric models. Figure 5-12 illustrates wall oven sizes.

Conventional ovens (also called thermal or radiant ovens) cook using a combination of radiant energy from a heat source and the convection that occurs naturally from the heated air inside the oven. Such ovens can be fired by gas or electricity. Convection ovens employ an electric heating element in tandem with a fan that circulates the hot air within the oven cavity.

Some convection models have shorter interior depth due to the location of the fan, while in other models very thin, highly insulated oven walls allow for a deeper cavity. Combination ovens are also readily available; these combine conventional elements with the addition of a fan to circulate air. Combination convection/microwave ovens are also available. Wall ovens composed of a conventional oven with a warming oven are available and are becoming increasingly popular.

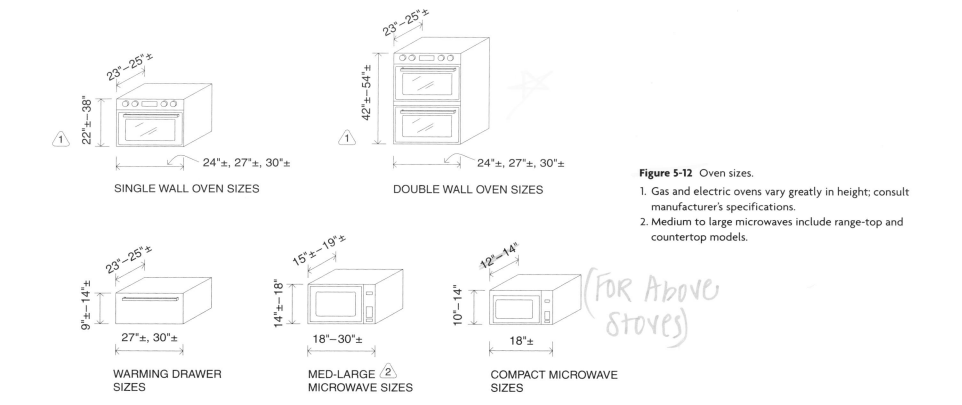

SINGLE WALL OVEN SIZES

DOUBLE WALL OVEN SIZES

Figure 5-12 Oven sizes.

1. Gas and electric ovens vary greatly in height; consult manufacturer's specifications.
2. Medium to large microwaves include range-top and countertop models.

WARMING DRAWER SIZES

MED-LARGE MICROWAVE SIZES

COMPACT MICROWAVE SIZES

(FOR Above Stoves)

Warming drawers are available in widths similar to wall ovens; these allow food to remain warm at various temperature settings and can also be used to warm plates. Figure 5-12 illustrates warming-oven sizes.

Oven height and placement for use by people using wheelchairs requires careful thought. Optimum wall-mounted oven height for universal use allows for ease of use by those in wheelchairs, as well as use by standing individuals without the need to bend to retrieve heavy objects. *Drop-front* (standard), *side-hinged,* and *double swinging door* styles offer various advantages. Side-hinged and double swinging oven doors can be helpful for seated users; these require a pull-out shelf underneath the oven for placement of hot objects (and to protect from hot spills) or a permanent ledge (such as one at the front edge of the base cabinet).

Non-self-cleaning ovens require an open knee space adjacent to the oven for cleaning access. In side-hinged models this must be on the latch side. When possible, an open knee space adjacent to the oven (often a roll-under counter space) located adjacent to the oven is helpful. The controls must be on the front or side panel of the oven. Specific information about shelf/counter placement and open knee spaces and mounting heights can be found in the "Ergonomics and Required Clearances" section of this chapter.

Microwave Ovens

Microwave ovens use radio waves, or microwaves, to heat and cook food. These ovens come in a range of sizes from compact to large; wattage on compact versions is often 600 to 800 watts, whereas larger versions offer 900 to 1350 watts. Oven capacity is another factor to consider when selecting a microwave. Larger-capacity ovens hold more food or larger items, but they also can eat up substantial counter or storage space in smaller kitchens.

Microwave ovens can be placed in various locations, such as countertop, over the range (often integrated with a hood), over the counter (attached under wall cabinets), and as a component of a double wall oven. Increasingly, homeowners are installing microwaves directly underneath countertops, especially in islands and peninsulas as part of a snack-making area (this can require bending for access and can allow children to reach controls, which is usually not a good thing). Placing a built-in microwave at countertop height but incorporated into a cabinet that sits directly on the counter is currently a popular placement as well. Microwaves are typically hinged on the left side. Counter space is needed to the right side or on top of the oven as described in the "Ergonomics and Required Clearances" section of this chapter.

According to the Center for Inclusive Design and Environmental Access (IDEA Center), microwaves placed on a counter location are "usable for the broadest population" and an adjoining counter space facilitates transfer of hot items. Simplified programming and controls as well as backlit controls make standard built-in ovens as well as microwaves most useful for a wide range of individuals.

Sizes for microwaves vary based on planned location for the oven as well as the oven capacity and special features. Compact models as well as larger countertop and above-range models are shown in Figure 5-12.

Refrigerators

Like many of the appliances discussed to this point, refrigerators are available in a variety of styles and arrangements, and with an array of options. *Freestanding* models are deeper than counter/cabinet depths. *Built-in* models are intended to fit flush or nearly flush with cabinets and counters. Some of these can be fitted with custom panels (called *overlay* models by some). *Built-in style* models are freestanding refrigerators that are just slightly deeper than counters and cabinets and offer the look of built-in models. Figure 5-13a illustrates the model types.

Freestanding models can be surrounded with cabinetry to make them appear like the more expensive built-in models (this is sometimes referred to as "framed"). Care must be taken to ensure that there is adequate clearance for doors to open fully and for ease of moving. In some cases, a wall can be recessed directly behind the refrigerator location, allowing the refrigerator to fit into the pocket created by the recess. This allows the refrigerator to align with the countertop depths.

Top-freezer, side-by-side, and *bottom-freezer* styles are the most popular refrigerator arrangements currently available in the United States. Figure 5-13b provides illustration of these configurations and sizes.

Figure 5-13a Built-in and freestanding refrigerators.

1. Freestanding. Deeper than cabinets.
2. Built-in. Flush or nearly flush with cabinets.
3. Freestanding models can be custom framed to look built-in..

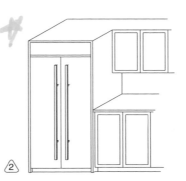
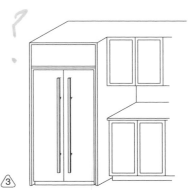

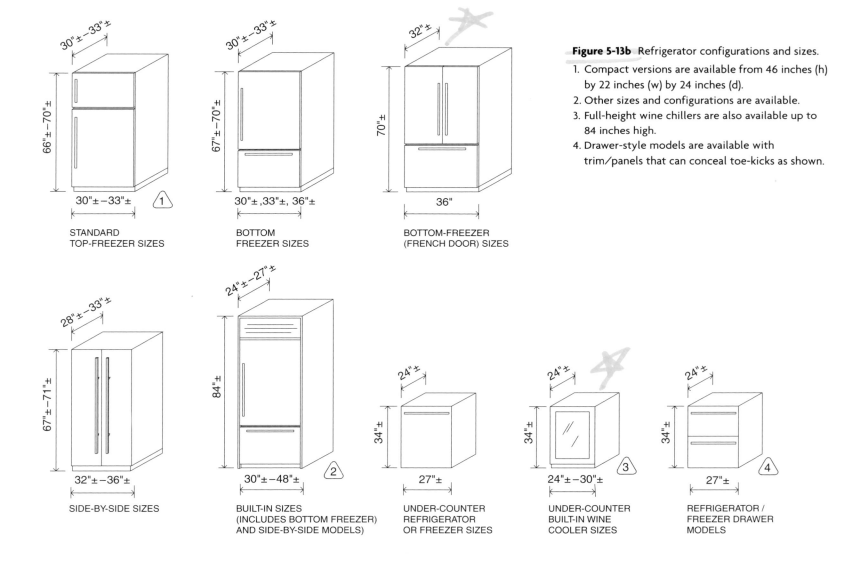

30"±−33"±

66"±−70"±

30"±−33"±

STANDARD
TOP-FREEZER SIZES

30"±−33"±

67"±−70"±

30"± ,33"±, 36"±

BOTTOM
FREEZER SIZES

32"±

70"±

36"

BOTTOM-FREEZER
(FRENCH DOOR) SIZES

Figure 5-13b Refrigerator configurations and sizes.

1. Compact versions are available from 46 inches (h) by 22 inches (w) by 24 inches (d).
2. Other sizes and configurations are available.
3. Full-height wine chillers are also available up to 84 inches high.
4. Drawer-style models are available with trim/panels that can conceal toe-kicks as shown.

28"±−33"±

67"±−71"±

32"±−36"±

SIDE-BY-SIDE SIZES

24"±−27"±

84"±

30"±−48"±

BUILT-IN SIZES
(INCLUDES BOTTOM FREEZER)
AND SIDE-BY-SIDE MODELS)

24"±

34"±

27"±

UNDER-COUNTER
REFRIGERATOR
OR FREEZER SIZES

24"±

34"±

24"±−30"±

UNDER-COUNTER
BUILT-IN WINE
COOLER SIZES

24"±

34"±

27"±

REFRIGERATOR /
FREEZER DRAWER
MODELS

Top-freezer models are currently most widely used. According to *Consumer Reports* magazine, these tend to be less expensive to purchase and more space-efficient than side-by-side models. Recently, top-freezer models have become available with through-the-door water dispensers. Side-by-side models offer narrow doors (with correspondingly narrow swings) that can be handy in tight or awkward spaces and offer through-the-door ice and water dispensers. Proportionally more of the total capacity space goes to freezer space in side-by-side models as compared to top- and bottom-freezer models.

Bottom-freezer models provide easy reach and eye-level storage for frequently used items in the refrigerator section, but they require bending or squatting to retrieve frozen items (rather than doing so to retrieve refrigerated items in other models) and generally have less area for frozen items than side-by-side models. Increasingly popular are *French-door* models, with side-by-side access to the refrigerator area above a freezer unit. Top-freezer and bottom-freezer models are commonly available with reversible handle locations, allowing the flexibility to change from left- to right-hinged doors. This is not true of all models, so the issue should be researched prior to purchase.

Under-counter models are less common than full-size models in the United States but are used widely elsewhere (as the primary cold storage space) and are increasingly used in the United States for entertainment and bar areas. Combination refrigerator/freezers as well as separate refrigerator and freezer-only under-counter models are available. Wine chillers, also known as wine coolers, are available in under-counter models as well as taller models, most often 24 inches deep, as shown in Figure 5-13b.

Several companies currently produce refrigerator and freezer *drawer* units. These can be used alone much like under-counter models or in conjunction with refrigerator and freezer units with doors. A combination of drawer and door units can create a range of customized cold storage areas throughout the kitchen.

Side-by-side models are often recommended for wheelchair accessibility because of narrow door swings and relatively easy access of large portions of refrigerator and freezer units. Some side-by-side units have exceedingly heavy doors due to in-door storage, making them difficult for some individuals to open. Slimmer built-in and built-in style units can open up floor space in front of the refrigerator for wheelchair users. Easy-to-read, simple controls as well as lighted in-door water and ice delivery can help to make side-by-side refrigerators more universally accessible. As an alternative to side-by-side models, under-counter refrigerators can be mounted in an accessible location for wheelchair users (this would place them on a toe-kick a minimum of 8 inches above the floor and create a higher-than-standard countertop).

Trash Compactors

Trash compactors compress glass, cartons, paper, plastics, and dry food waste to less than half the original volume. However, with the current mandatory and voluntary recycling programs in most areas, trash compactors are used less commonly in new-home construction and kitchen remodeling. Compactors remain desirable to some homeowners and are currently available in under-counter and freestanding units, in widths from 12 to 18 inches. A key-activated on/off switch is a safety feature that prevents children from operating the compactor.

KITCHEN STORAGE AND CABINETRY

Nowhere in a residence is the location and quality of storage more paramount to the overall usefulness of the space than in the kitchen. Food, cooking gear, small appliances, dishware, flatware, and cleaning supplies as well as trash/recycling can be found in kitchens and must be stored in a manner that makes items reasonably easy to put away, locate, and retrieve. The location and use of these items—particularly those used frequently—must be considered as kitchen work areas are designed. Specific information about kitchen work areas can be found in this chapter under "Organizational Flow."

Cabinets and shelving provide much of the storage in kitchens, and an understanding of the basic construction, production types, styles, arrangements, and available options is required. When purchasing cabinets, the designer should keep in mind that there are three production method options: stock, semicustom, and custom.

Stock cabinets are mass-produced and warehoused, awaiting quick shipment (in most cases), and come in standard sizes and finishes. This type is generally most inexpensive, most popular in terms of sales, and available in a variety of sizes shapes, styles, and wood species. But these cabinets are limited in terms of options and may not fit the desired space exactly, in which case filler strips are used to close gaps.

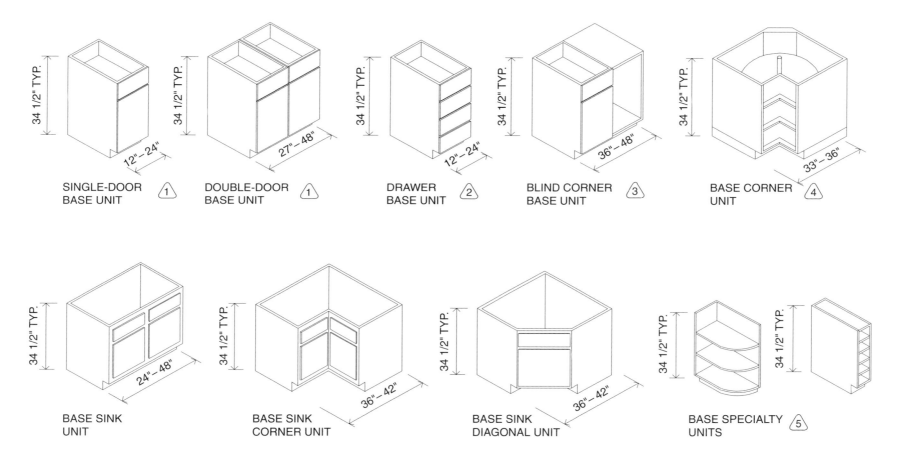

Figure 5-14a Base cabinet configurations and sizes.

1. Available with open shelves and options such as roll-out shelves.
2. A wider/deeper version is available as a cooktop base (without top drawer).
3. These have very small doors unless unit is more than 45 inches wide.
4. Not all corner units have lazy Susan devices; they are a useful option.
5. Many options are available; this is only a small sampling.

Note: Kitchen cabinet manufacturers employ a basic code for referencing cabinets in which the type of cabinet (such as base) is listed by first initial, followed by the cabinet width. Therefore, a 36-inch-wide base cabinet is referred to as a B36, whereas a 36-inch-wide sink base could be referred to as an SB36.

Stock cabinets are available in standard widths starting at 9 inches, in 3-inch increments, up to 24 inches and from 24 to 48 inches, in 6-inch increments. Standard depths are 12 inches for wall cabinets and 24 inches for base, oven, and utility cabinets. Stock cabinets are given descriptive numbers that stand for the cabinet type and measurement; for example, a W3030 describes a wall cabinet (hence the W) that is 30 inches wide and 30 inches high (hence the 3030). It is worth noting that European modular cabinets are built to different stock dimensions. Figure 5-18a illustrates standard reach and work counter height information. Figures 5-14a to 5-14d depict common stock cabinetry units.

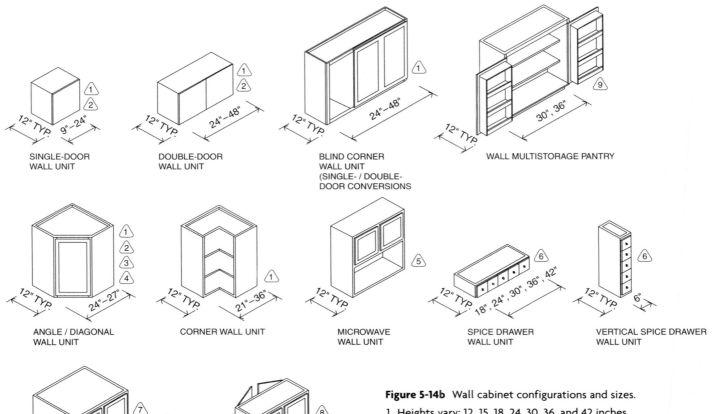

SINGLE-DOOR
WALL UNIT

DOUBLE-DOOR
WALL UNIT

BLIND CORNER
WALL UNIT
(SINGLE- / DOUBLE-
DOOR CONVERSIONS)

WALL MULTISTORAGE PANTRY

ANGLE / DIAGONAL
WALL UNIT

CORNER WALL UNIT

MICROWAVE
WALL UNIT

SPICE DRAWER
WALL UNIT

VERTICAL SPICE DRAWER
WALL UNIT

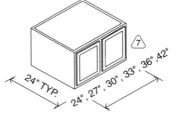

REFRIGERATOR
WALL UNIT

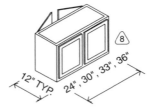

PENINSULA DOUBLE DOOR
WALL UNIT

Figure 5-14b Wall cabinet configurations and sizes.

1. Heights vary: 12, 15, 18, 24, 30, 36, and 42 inches.
2. Available with lower tambour door cabinet (in tall versions).
3. Available with drawers beneath doors and with rotating shelves/lazy Susan.
4. Special units accommodate curved doors.
5. Height varies: 36, 45, and 48 inches, depending on whether they are compact or full-size ovens. There are also other options used for microwaves.
6. Many varied options are available; this is only a small sampling.
7. Heights vary: 12, 15, and 18 inches.
8. Heights vary: 18, 24, 30, 36, and 42 inches.
9. Heights vary: 30 and 36 inches.

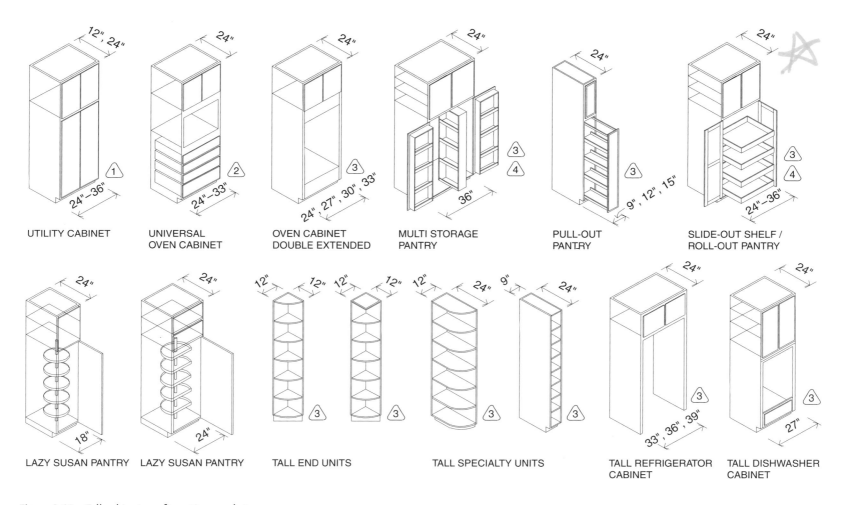

Figure 5-14c Tall cabinet configurations and sizes.

1. Heights vary: 84, 90, and 96 inches; depths vary: 12 and 24 inches. Available in single-door units: 9, 12, 15, 18, and 24 inches wide.
2. Universal unit accommodates single or double oven by eliminating drawers; microwave versions available.
3. Heights vary: 84, 90, and 96 inches.
4. Single-door versions available (24 inches wide).

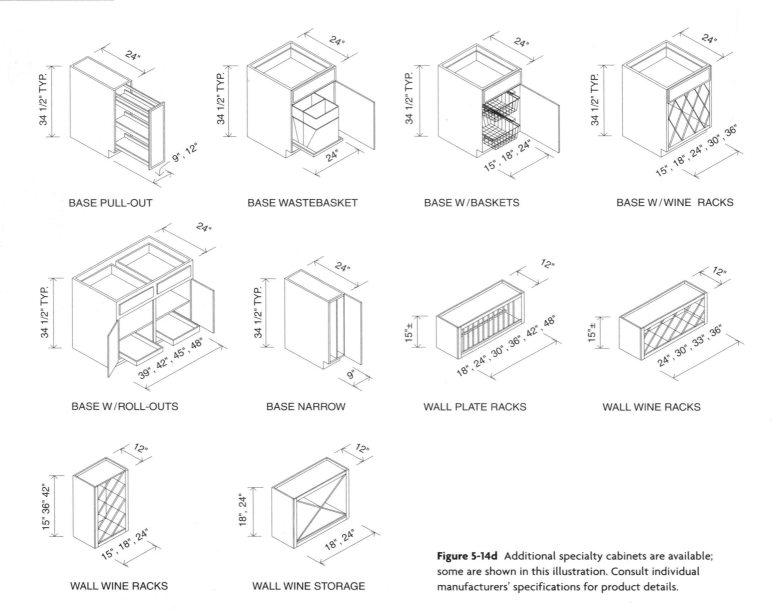

24"
34 1/2" TYP.
9", 12"
BASE PULL-OUT

24"
34 1/2" TYP.
24"
BASE WASTEBASKET

24"
34 1/2" TYP.
15", 18", 24"
BASE W/BASKETS

24"
34 1/2" TYP.
15", 18", 24", 30", 36"
BASE W/WINE RACKS

24"
34 1/2" TYP.
39", 42", 45", 48"
BASE W/ROLL-OUTS

24"
34 1/2" TYP.
9"
BASE NARROW

12"
15" ±
18", 24", 30", 36", 42", 48"
WALL PLATE RACKS

12"
15" ±
24", 30", 33", 36"
WALL WINE RACKS

12"
15" 36" 42"
15", 18", 24"
WALL WINE RACKS

12"
18", 24"
18", 24"
WALL WINE STORAGE

Figure 5-14d Additional specialty cabinets are available; some are shown in this illustration. Consult individual manufacturers' specifications for product details.

Stock base cabinets come in standard height 34½ inches tall with toe-kicks at 4 inches high. Generally, these heights work for a range of able-bodied adults of average stature; however, for smaller/taller individuals or those with mobility limitations, standard counter heights are problematic. Several cabinet manufacturers offer stock cabinets in what is sometimes referred to as universal access or universal design cabinetry, which include stock base cabinets that are 32½ inches high (without countertop) and with toe-kicks that are 9 inches high and 6 inches deep for wheelchair accessibility, as shown in Figures 5-15a to 5-15c. For additional information on counter heights, please refer to the "Ergonomics and Required Clearances" section of this chapter.

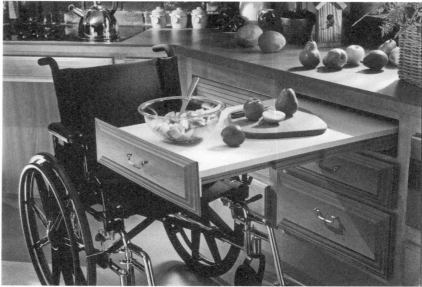

Figure 5-15b This pull-out table provides a work surface for seated use. Courtesy of KraftMaid Cabinetry.

Figure 5-15c Pull-out shelves can provide universal access to stored items. Courtesy of KraftMaid Cabinetry.

Figure 5-15a The Passport Series from KraftMaid Cabinetry is an example of universal access, stock cabinetry that allows wheelchair access. High, deep toe-kicks, lowered countertop heights, a raised dishwasher base cabinet, and lowered wall cabinets (including plate racks) allow wheelchair users better access to storage and work areas. The forward approach to the sink and cooktop is also shown, and cooktop height is adjustable. A tambour door is shown in the base cabinet next to the cooktop. Courtesy of KraftMaid Cabinetry.

Semi-custom cabinets are also preassembled but are typically constructed when the order is final in order to make custom modifications, which increases delivery times. The second most popular type of cabinet in terms of sales, semicustom cabinets can allow greater flexibility than stock cabinets in terms of cabinet size, construction materials, color, and various options. Widths start at roughly 9 inches, with 3-inch incremental increases up to roughly 48 inches. Depths can be reduced and increased from standards as required—within manufacturers' guidelines. This type is more costly than stock and is generally not accepted for return if they do not fit.

Those known as *custom* cabinets are built to completely custom specifications—either by a craftsperson or manufactured on a made-to-order basis. There are few limitations in terms of size, design, arrangement, construction materials, color, wood species, and options. Custom cabinets can be quite expensive depending upon materials and construction techniques used. Being built to precise custom dimensions and specifications can make for a long delivery time. However, custom cabinetry remains an option for certain clients and can offer excellent results.

Stock, semi-custom, and custom cabinets are production techniques and *do not refer directly to cabinet quality*; overall quality is determined by the construction of the cabinet box. The quality and thickness of the material chosen for construction as well as the joinery and bracing all contribute to the overall quality of the cabinet box.

Two additional terms related to cabinet construction describe general cabinet structure or assembly: framed (or face framed) and frameless. *Framed* cabinets are the most common style in North America and consist of a frame (referred to as a *face frame*) that is attached to the front of the cabinet box with doors attached to the frame. This frame is composed of horizontal members (known as rails) and vertical members (known as stiles). Typically, double cabinets wider than 24 inches have a center stile, although these may also be found on smaller cabinets. Figure 5-16a illustrates framed and frameless cabinets.

Various door and drawer styles can be used on framed cabinets, including those that are inset within the face frame and sit flush with the edges of the frame. These can be expensive, as their construction and installation require great precision. In addition, *traditional overlay* door/drawers rest against the frame, overlaying it and exposing at least a portion of the frame.

Full overlay doors/drawers completely cover the face frame with less than ⅛ inch between the door/drawer and frame and have concealed hinges. Figure 5-16b illustrates a range of door styles.

Frameless cabinets (also know as *European* or *Euro-style*) have no face frame on the front of the cabinet box. Without the frame and the center stile (on two door cabinets), frameless cabinets provide more open access to interior contents. Hinges are concealed on frameless cabinets and doors cover the entire opening—these are known as *full-overlay* doors/drawers. Frameless cabinets were invented in Europe and in most cases have predrilled holes at 32-millimeter increments for shelf pegs, hinges, and slides, making them easy to modify. Refer to Figure 5-16a for illustrations of frameless cabinets and Figure 5-16b for door styles.

Another type of door known as a tambour works similarly to the rolling portion of a roll-top desk. It uses separated pieces or strips attached to a backing sheet and set in a track, allowing it to roll up. This type of door is helpful in areas where a door should remain open without getting in the way, such as for an appliance garage.

Both framed and frameless cabinets can be found in stock, semicustom, and custom production. Cabinet doors are also available in a range of specialty options, including curved doors (generally called *radius doors*). Doors without center panels can be inset with glass or with mullions (thin strips of wood) and glass. See Figure 5-16b for specialty door styles. It is also worth noting that drawers are increasingly replacing doors in many kitchens. Drawers work well to contain a range of utensils, tools, and cookware and also work effectively behind doors as roll-outs for pans, canned goods, and other items. Drawers installed at appropriate heights and locations can work well for wheelchair users

Cabinet hardware includes hinges, latches, pulls, and knobs. Hinge choices can be limited depending on manufacturer's standards (this is not usually an issue in custom installations), whereas pulls (also called handles) and knobs are available in a vast array of designs, materials, and finishes. The selection of pulls and knobs can greatly impact the visual quality of cabinetry and therefore requires consideration of size, shape, and finish as part of the total composition of the design. In addition, functional issues such as the relative size and position of these will impact day-to-day use of the cabinet. In terms of universal design, larger U-shaped pulls are considered most useful for a wide range of individuals.

A variety of interior accessories and fittings are available for use in stock cabinetry. In semicustom and custom cabinetry, the options are endless. The "Ergonomics and Required Clearances" section of this chapter describes some additional accessories and adaptable/adjustable cabinets for wheelchair users.

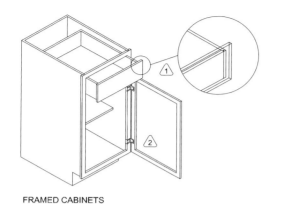

FRAMED CABINETS

Figure 5-16a Framed and frameless cabinets.

1. Door and drawer fronts can be inset within frame or overlaid.
2. Hinges attach to frame.
3. Hinges attach inside box.
4. Predrilled holes for shelf supports.
5. Can be set on leveling legs.

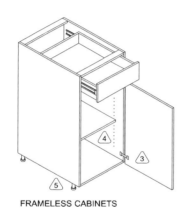

FRAMELESS CABINETS

DOOR / DRAWER TYPES

INSET INTO FACE FRAME

OVERLAY / HALF OVERLAY

FULL OVERLAY DOORS

Figure 5-16b Cabinet door and drawer styles.

1. Can be used on framed cabinets.
2. This is the only door/drawer option for frameless cabinets.
3. Recessed panels are available in a variety of style options.
4. Raised panels are available in a variety of style options.

Note: Door styles listed include matching panels for hoods and refrigerator and dishwasher doors.

DOOR/DRAWER STYLES

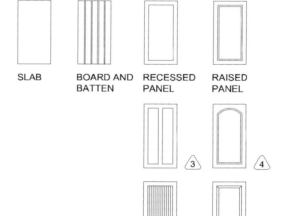

SLAB

BOARD AND BATTEN

RECESSED PANEL

RAISED PANEL

SPECIALTY DOORS

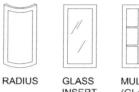

RADIUS

GLASS INSERT

MULLION (GLASS)

THE PANTRY

While in and out of favor over the years, many homeowners currently desire pantries. The term *pantry* can refer to quite an assortment of storage units: tall (deep or shallow) cabinets within the kitchen, small closets lined with shelves, or separate walk-in rooms with cabinets, shelves, and bins. Each type of pantry brings with it advantages and disadvantages, as discussed in the following paragraphs.

Located in cabinets within the kitchen, pantries are available in stock and custom cabinetry. Stock cabinets that serve as pantries are available with a range of options and fittings as described and illustrated in the previous section. In some cases multiple tall cabinet units can be used to provide extensive storage. Stock pantries located within the kitchen provide handy access to items for cooking and cleaning.

Closet-style pantries can be equipped with shelves alone, as well as with shelves, cabinets, and bins for such things as garbage and recycling. Shelf depths of 10 or 12 inches work well to contain various sizes of food packaging (from cereal boxes to canned goods); some designers find that deeper shelves simply obscure stored items, making items difficult to see and retrieve. Dinnerware, serving items, glassware, and appliances often require deeper shelving, and shelving depths may therefore vary accordingly.

Shallow shelves (10 to 12 inches as noted) in closet-style pantries allow users to see all contents with just one quick look. When placed very close to or within the kitchen, such pantries afford a convenient storage solution. This type of pantry can also be placed farther from the kitchen. In such instances, the items stored tend to be those used less frequently in day-to-day cooking. See Figure 5-17 for pantry options.

Walk-in pantries have the advantage of containing the most actual storage space, allowing for an array of storage options such as shelves, cabinets, work areas, and storage bins. Like the closet-style versions, walk-in pantries containing infrequently used items can be located well outside of the kitchen, whereas those containing frequently used food preparation items are best located immediately adjacent to the kitchen.

Some walk-in pantries are outfitted with exquisite cabinetry to display beautiful dishware and/or collections, while others are more utilitarian in terms of materials/finishes and are meant primarily as functional storage areas. A recent trend involves placing pantry rooms so that they can be used as future elevator shafts in multi-story homes so that owners may age in place. See Figure 5-17.

Creative use of space by designers and architects often results in pantries placed in locations not mentioned to this point. For example, hallways can be designed, with some modest additional width, to accommodate an additional 10 to 12 inches of floor-to-ceiling shelving for use as a pantry area. This is most commonly done with open shelving as a space-saving device, but as space allows, hallway pantry storage can be provided with doors, drawers, bins, and shelves. In areas such as mudrooms, storage may include space for pantry items along with outerwear and shoes.

ERGONOMICS AND REQUIRED CLEARANCES

The specialized nature of kitchens requires that designers consider ergonomics and required fixture clearances in order to design useful, comfortable kitchens. Because a good percentage of the work of daily living is performed in the kitchen, ergonomics, workflow, and clearance requirements must be considered in the design of a successful kitchen.

Cabinets and Work Counters

As discussed, stock cabinetry comes in standard counter heights that can work for adults of average size; however, in seeking universal design of kitchen elements or to tailor a kitchen to a particular user, careful consideration of reaching heights, comfortable standing, and seating work heights is required. Related words of caution are required: Standard dimensions are a compromise meant to meet the needs of "average" adults. Therefore, veering greatly from standards can affect resale value, which is a reason to explore adaptable design features such as adjustable counters and/or varying counter heights. Figure 5-18a illustrates standard reach and work counter height information. Figure 5-18b illustrates clearances at cabinets and counters. Figure 5-18c shows reach and work counter information for seated/wheelchair users. Figure 5-18d shows dimensional information for dining surfaces.

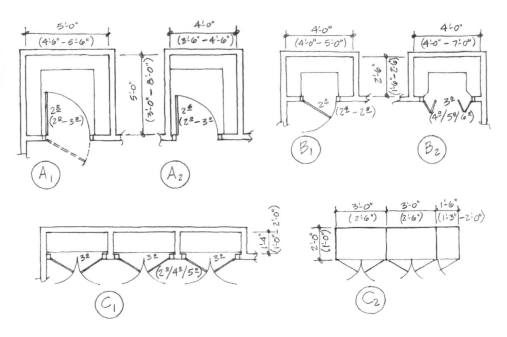

Figure 5-17 Pantry plans and configurations.

A1 and A2 are walk-in pantries with adequate storage and access space; these require a minimum of 2 feet circulation/aisle space. B1 and B2 are reach-in pantries. C1 is a reach-in pantry housed in tall cabinetry. C2 is built in, reach-in pantry cabinets (see also Figure 5-14c).

STANDARD REACH AND WORK DIMENSIONS

TYPICAL STOCK CABINET DIMENSIONS

Figure 5-18a Standard reach and work counter information and stock cabinet dimensions.

1. High shelf. Adult reach: back 4 feet, 11 inches plus.
2. Adult reach radius. 1 foot, 11 inches to 2 feet, 3 inches plus.
3. Work counter clearance. 1 foot, 3 inches to 1 foot, 8 inches; 1 foot, 6 inches recommended minimum.
4. Depth of work counters. 1 foot, 9 inches to 2 feet; 2 feet is standard.
5. Low comfortable reach. 9 inches.
6. Work counter height. 3 feet is standard.
7. High counter.

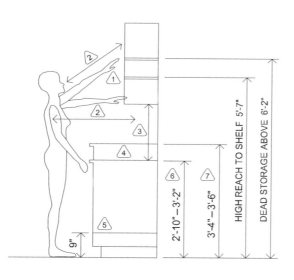

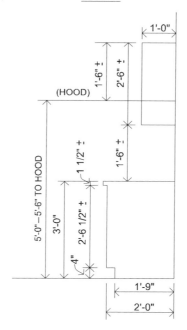

CLEARANCES AT COUNTERS

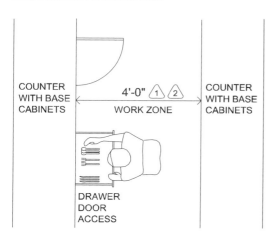

CLEARANCES AT COUNTERS

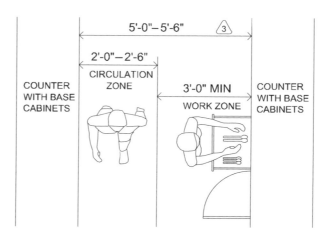

Figure 5-18b Clearances at cabinets and counters.

1. Work zone minimum between cabinets with no additional through-traffic circulation.
2. This clearance is also useful between counter/cabinet and nearest physical obstruction.
3. Total clearance of 5 feet minimum required between cabinets when the work zone is combined with (required) through-circulation.

Figure 5-18c Wheelchair-accessible storage, reach, and work dimensions.

1. Accessible handles/pulls should be at top edge of base cabinets and lower edge of wall cabinets.
2. Obstructed side reach is 10 to 24 inches maximum from side of wheelchair.
3. Storage at these locations can be provided with stacked wall cabinet, tilt-out drawers, stacked drawers, plate racks, and/or other accessories.
4. As much storage as possible should be located between 2 to 4 feet above floor; provide an adaptable device for items out of this range.
5. Low reach from wheelchair is 1 foot, 3 inches above floor.
6. Provide minimum clear space 1 foot, 7 inches deep by 2 feet, 6 inches wide for knee space.
7. Counter height for seated users varies from 2 feet, 4 inches to 2 feet, 8 inches and in some cases as high as 3 feet; this range allows for variations in user/armrest height and for a 1½-inch counter thickness.
8. For front approach, provide toe clearance 9 inches high by 6 inches deep (maximum).
9. Clear knee space at this location may be used as part of maneuvering clearance/turning space.

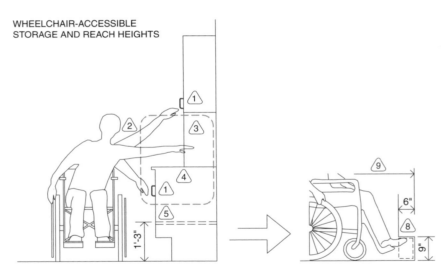

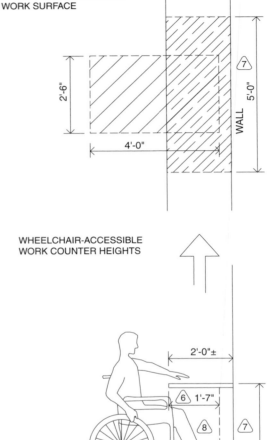

When planning dining surfaces such as eating islands, bars, and peninsulas, the designer should not only follow dimensional requirements but provide spaces that foster conversation and interaction. This means that meeting minimum dimensional requirements is important but considering how those eating will interact with one another is also important. It is important to go beyond simply creating a row of diners and instead consider how they will interact. Curving the dining surface and providing two-sided dining are both ways to foster interaction.

As stated, in some cases adjustable countertops are a good idea. Multiple users of varying abilities, including wheelchair users, benefit from adjustable work surface, sinks, and cooktops. There are several methods for creating this type of adaptable countertop, as shown in Figures 5-19a to 5-19c. Creating pull-out cutting or work boards at an appropriate height is another way to provide additional work areas for seated users. These are a very cost-effective way of creating universal design in the kitchen and are illustrated in an earlier section of this chapter.

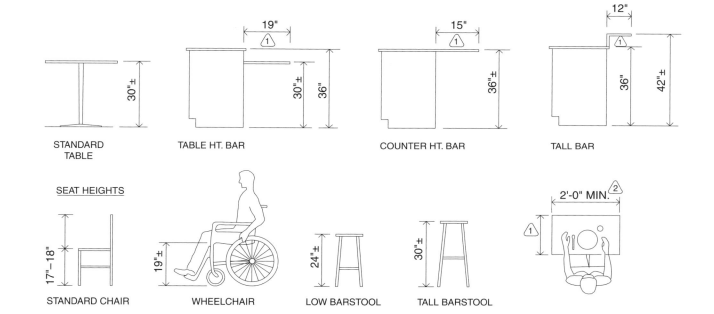

Figure 5-18d Dimensional information for dining/eating. Additional dining-related information may be found in chapter 6.

1. Depth for eating area varies based on the nature of the meal consumed; the narrow dimension shown is for snacking, while the deeper dimensions may be appropriate for dining with plate/placemats.
2. Width per person should be at least 24 inches.

30"±
STANDARD TABLE
19"
1
30"±
36"
TABLE HT. BAR
15"
1
36"±
COUNTER HT. BAR
12"
1
36"
42"±
TALL BAR
SEAT HEIGHTS
17"–18"
STANDARD CHAIR
19"±
WHEELCHAIR
24"±
LOW BARSTOOL
30"±
TALL BARSTOOL
2'-0" MIN.
2
1

Figure 5-19a Adjustable counter.

1. An adjustable counter can be attached by means of wood support strips or an apron, supported by heavy-duty shelf brackets or supported by tracks mounted to walls.
2. Floor and wall finishes continued under counter.

1
2

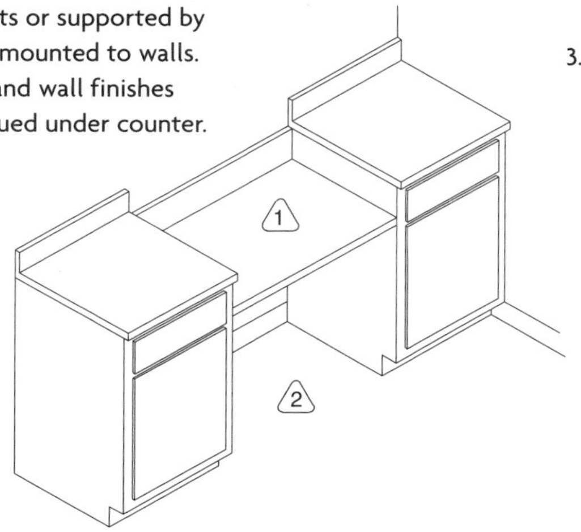

Figure 5-19b Adjustable/adaptable counter and cabinet.

1. An adjustable counter as shown in Figure 5-19a.
2. Swinging retractable doors allow for wheelchair access.
3. Hinged/fold-up cabinet bottom allows for wheelchair access

1
3
2

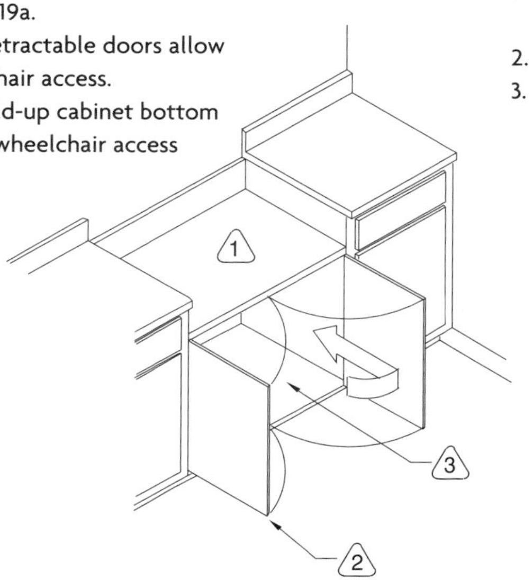

Figure 5-19c Adjustable/adaptable counter and cabinet.

1. An adjustable counter as shown in Figure 5-19a.
2. Special removable base cabinet.
3. Floor and wall finishes continued under cabinet.

1
3
2

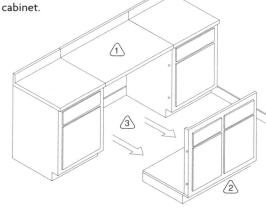

Figure 5-19d The EZ Shelf, distributed by Häfele, allows for the shelf to be pulled down by wheelchair users and some individuals with mobility limitations. Photograph courtesy of Häfele America.

Another accessible/adaptable kitchen feature is a pull-down shelf, shown in Figure 5-19d.

Other considerations for creating counters for universal use include using contrasting values or colors at countertop edges to aid in visual location. In addition, using contrasting colors in floor areas to aid in visual location of elevation changes or to highlight certain portions of work areas can be helpful. Nonslip flooring is another option that should be considered in the design of kitchens for universal use.

In addition to considering dimensions of work and storage or reach areas, the designer must consider adjacent counter space for each appliance for preparation, cooking, and cleanup. Clear floor space for access as well as clear areas to allow

for operation of appliances—such as opening and shutting doors—is required. The following are descriptions of required clearances and required counter space at major appliances.

Sinks

When planning primary sink areas, the designer must consider the space required to approach and use the sink. Sinks also require clear counter space adjacent to the sink for use in food preparation and for washing/drying. A portion of the counter should be the same height as the sink, as shown in Figure 5-20a

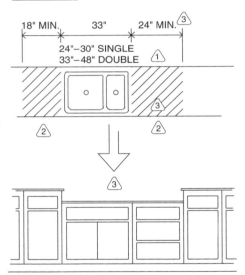

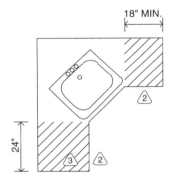

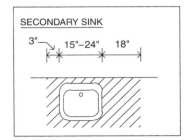

Figure 5-20a Standard sink clearances.
1. Sizes vary; see sink sizes in Figures 5-5.
2. Areas adjacent to sink accommodate D.W./trash/recycling.
3. 24-inch clear area should be the same height as sink.

FORWARD APPROACH (KNEESPACE)

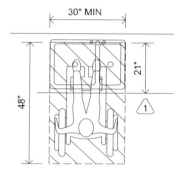

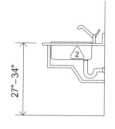

NO KNEE SPACE

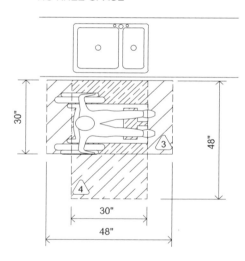

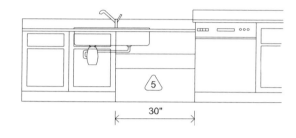

Figure 5-20b Sink clearances for wheelchair users. Forward approach with knee space is recommended, though not shown in all images.

1. Additional clear space is helpful to the side of the sink.
2. Counter height for seated users varies, around 34 inches and in some cases higher; this range allows for variations in user/armrest height and for a 1½-inch counter thickness (while ANSI/ADA call for 27-inch clear height for knee spaces, individual residential preferences may differ). Sink bowl depth varies (while the ADA calls for a maximum depth of 6½ inches, individual preferences vary). As stated previously, single-family residences need not meet ADA/ANSI. These requirements are given for reference only.
3. Parallel approach is not ideal, as it does not allow access to controls or for user to roll under the sink.
4. Front approach with no knee space provided does not allow wheelchair user to work comfortably at sink.
5 Garbage disposers can be included by locating clear space under one bowl of sink and the disposer under the second bowl behind a cabinet.

Secondary sinks (those used by a second cook or for entertainment/snack areas) also require clearance space the same height at the sink, as shown in Figure 5-20a. Sinks intended for use by those in wheelchairs require specific clearances in approach and must allow the user to access the clear space under the sink for a forward approach. Figure 5-20b illustrates an accessible sink.

Dishwashers

Dishwashers must be considered in relationship to an adjacent sink and convenient to storage for frequently used utensils and dishes. For standard use, a minimum of 21 inches of clear floor space should be allowed for using the dishwasher, or more for wheelchair users. In larger kitchens, placing the dish-

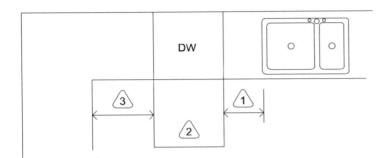

Figure 5-21a Standard dishwasher clearances.

1. Maximum from edge of dishwasher to sink is 36 inches; closer is better.
2. Location of door should not conflict with doors of opposite appliance (when open).
3. 21 inches of clear floor space is helpful between the edge of the dishwasher and a corner (this allows another person access to the corner).

washer so that it may be used by more than one person at a time is useful. See Figure 5-21a for illustrations of dishwasher clearance and counter space requirements.

While standard under-counter dishwashers are made to fit under a standard 36-inch-high counter, this is not a useful arrangement for wheelchair users. Placing the dishwasher higher than standard, often on a raised toe-kick (a minimum 8 inches above the floor), can make all interior racks accessible for various users and require less bending and stooping for standing users as well. Obviously, such a placement raises the countertop above a workable height for those using wheelchairs or standing; therefore, this is generally done in larger kitchens or those with adequate counter space (in other areas). Dishwashers require clear space for the user to access controls, as well as a clear parallel approach for the user to unload dishes, as shown in Figure 5-21b.

PARALLEL CLEAR SPACE
REQUIRED AT DISHWASHER

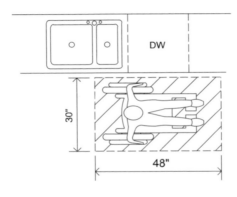

DISHWASHER MOUNTING HEIGHT

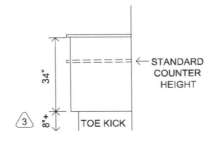

FORWARD-APPROACH CLEAR SPACE
REQUIRED TO LOAD/UNLOAD DISHWASHER

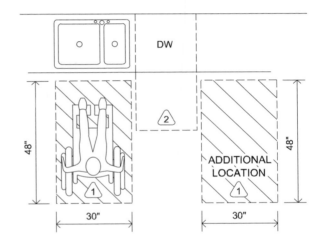

Figure 5-21b Wheelchair dishwasher clearances.

1. Knee space (not shown) under counter can also serve as clear space. Additional clear space (shown) can be included in cases where room allows; provides space for two individuals to use dishwasher/sink.
2. Open dishwasher door should not obstruct clear space for nearby appliances.
3. Minimum mounting height is 8 inches above floor; maximum 18 inches above floor.

Ranges and Cooktops

Providing adequate counter areas adjacent to each side of the cooktop or range allows for ease of use and allows the cook to slide a heavy pot directly from the burner to the counter area without lifting in case of emergency. With this in mind, such adjacent countertops must be the same height as the cooktop and should be fabricated of heat-resistant materials. Figure 5-22a illustrates standard cooktop/range clearances and clear counter spaces required. Figure 5-22b shows wheelchair-accessible cooktop/range clearances and clear counter spaces required.

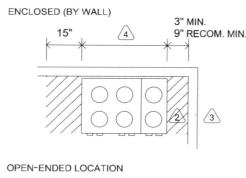

Figure 5-22a Standard range/cooktop clearances.

1. Island/peninsula locations require 9 inches minimum behind cooktop.
2. Required clearance space should be the same height as cooktop/range as shown in lower elevation illustration.
3. Minimum 3-inch clearance required at end wall with flame-retardant surface.
4. Sizes vary; see Figure 5-11.

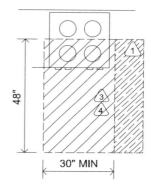

RECOMMENDED KNEE SPACE AT COOKTOP

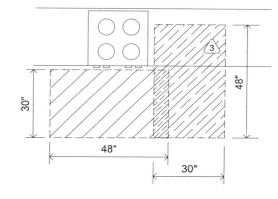

CLEAR SPACE AT RANGE PARALLEL APPROACH

Figure 5-22b Range/cooktop clearances for wheelchair users.

1. Additional space at side(s) preferred.
2. Height for seated users varies from 2 feet, 4 inches to 2 feet, 8 inches and in some cases, 3 feet to allow for variation in armrest height and for variation in countertop thickness.
3. Access to controls must not require reaching over burners.
4. Knee space allows access; the knee space must be insulated to protect from burns, abrasions, and electrical shocks.

Proper location of ventilation system requires that there is adequate clearance between cooking surface and the hood. In cases where there is not a hood or flame-resistant surface above, more clearance is often required, as shown in Figure 5-23. Cooking surfaces should not be placed below an operable window unless there is proper clearance and a protected wall surface behind and above the cooking surface, as shown in Figure 5-23.

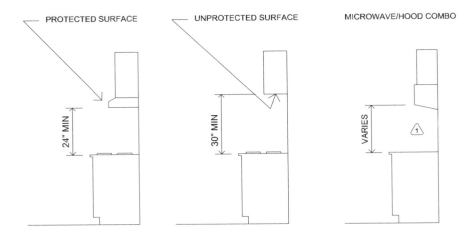

PROTECTED SURFACE   UNPROTECTED SURFACE   MICROWAVE/HOOD COMBO

24" MIN   30" MIN   VARIES

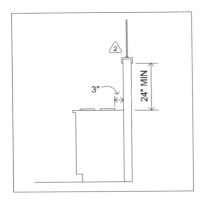

3"   24" MIN

Figure 5-23 Clearance for hoods and windows at range/cooktop.

1. Manufacturer suggested clearances for protected surfaces such as micro/hood combinations may be less than 24 inches as shown in the first drawing—access for oven/rear burners must be considered.
2. Cooking surfaces should not be located below an operable window unless these minimum dimensions are met.

Ovens and Microwaves

Wall ovens should be placed so that open oven doors do not dangerously protrude into high-traffic areas and so that hot items may be easily transferred to a resting space on the adjacent counter surface or another nearby counter surface that is removed from major traffic areas, as shown in Figure 5-24a. Ovens are not ideally located directly next to refrigerators. In cases where this occurs, counter space should be provided next to the refrigerator and next to/across from the oven. Oven heights vary depending on whether single, double, or combination ovens are used.

As discussed previously, wall ovens are well suited for wheelchair users; see Figure 5-24b. Side-hinged and swinging doors require a pull-out shelf (which pulls out a minimum of 10 inches deep) underneath the oven or a permanent shelf (such as one at the front edge of the counter). In cases where the oven is not self-cleaning, an adjacent counter with open knee space is required (on the latch side). Non-self-cleaning ovens with drop-front doors also require an adjacent counter with open knee space below, as shown in Figure 5-24b. In self-cleaning models, adjacent clear knee space is recommended where possible. For many seated users, ovens installed with the cavity between 30 to 40 inches above the floor work well, but this varies based upon the individual.

WALL OVEN/MICROWAVE CLEARANCES

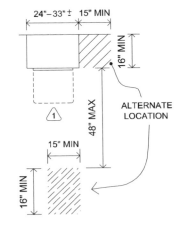

24"–33"± 15" MIN   16" MIN   48" MAX   ALTERNATE LOCATION   15" MIN   16" MIN

Figure 5-24a Standard wall oven/microwave clearances. For information about built-in wall oven cabinets, see Figure 5-14c.

1. Door should not open into major traffic aisle.
2. Bottom of microwave oven should be 24 to 48 inches above floor; heights vary based on location/users.
3. 15 inches of clear space is required above, below, or adjacent to microwave.

MICROWAVE MOUNTING HEIGHTS

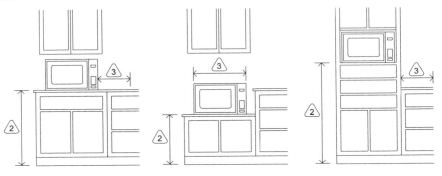

ACCESSIBLE OVENS/MICROWAVES

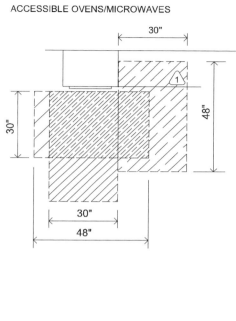

FOLD-DOWN OVEN DOOR

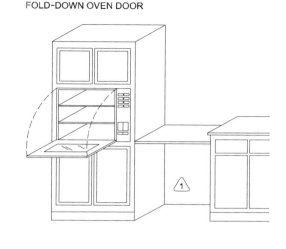

SIDE-HINGED OVEN DOOR

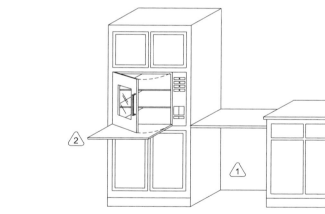

Figure 5-24b Wall oven/microwave for wheelchair users.

1. Non-self-cleaning ovens require an adjacent 30-inch open knee space (on latch side of side-hinged doors); this clear space is helpful for self-cleaning models as well.
2. Side-opening doors require a shelf that pulls out (10 inches minimum).
3. Counter location is best for microwaves for a range of users; however, this placement does eliminate clear counter space.
4. Clear counter space required adjacent to microwave.

Generally, microwave ovens are comfortably located with the oven bottom between 24 and 48 inches above the floor, although those set at counter height (36 inches) or slightly lower are considered best for many wheelchair users. Microwave units that are part of built-in ovens or over cooktops are sometimes higher than the 48 inches mentioned. Microwaves require open adjacent counter space or open space below or above the oven. See Figures 5-24a and 5-24b.

Refrigerators

Refrigerator placement requires thought about the swing of the door(s) and the need for clear counter space nearby. Single-door units require clear counter space next to the refrigerator or across from the refrigerator. In two-door models, where open space is not available to both sides of the refrigerator, it is important to have the available open counter space accessible to the fresh food (refrigerator) section,

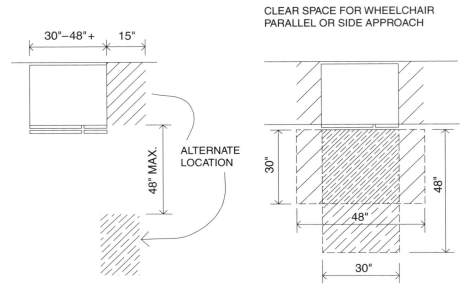

CLEAR SPACE FOR WHEELCHAIR
PARALLEL OR SIDE APPROACH

Figure 5-25 Standard and accessible refrigerator clearances. A minimum of 15 inches of clear counter space should be provided on the latch side of single-door refrigerators, or at an alternate location that is not more than 48 inches from the refrigerator. Side-by-side models require this clear counter space convenient to the fresh food section or in an alternate location as shown.

as this is used more often. The refrigerator door side should be hinged so that the flow of food to counters and work centers takes precedence over the freezer section As stated previously, side-by-side models offer best access for wheelchair users; one rule of thumb calls for 50 percent of freezer space below 54 inches for universal access. Figure 5-25 illustrates standard and accessible refrigerator clearances.

ORGANIZATIONAL FLOW

Many publications covering kitchen design describe three major kitchen work centers that are anchored by appliances:

1. *Primary sink center*, for food preparation (such as washing) and cleanup. This could be considered the most heavily used area of the kitchen, and its location therefore provides an important base or anchor for the other work centers.

2. *Primary refrigerator center*, for storage of perishable foods. Food is received into this area and then removed for preparation and cooking; therefore, reasonable access to entry/exit areas should be considered, as should the relationship to the sink center. The National Kitchen and Bath Association (NKBA) and others describe this as part of a preparation and mixing center and therefore indicate that mixing utensils should be stored in this location. The authors argue that preparation is often done in other locations and is sufficiently important to be considered a center or entity separate from the refrigerator center.

3. *Cooktop/range* center for cooking and serving food (in terms of placing it in serving platters, bowls, etc.).

Generally, discussion of these work centers describes a "work triangle," which is an imaginary triangle linking each of the work centers, with each leg of the triangle greater than 4 feet and less than 9 feet and with the total of the three legs combined to total at least 12 feet and no greater than 26 feet. Interestingly, the cumulative total (recommended maximum) has grown from 22 to 26 feet over the years. Such minimum and maximum footage recommendations are guidelines meant to aid in creating a kitchen that is not cramped but also not so spacious as to require excess movement to complete basic tasks. In general, a built-in oven is not considered part of the work triangle, as it is not part of either of the three work centers.

Storage should be planned at each of the work centers so that adequate storage is provided in order to support work performed. Items used most frequently should be readily available, whereas those used seldom may be placed in more remote locations. For example, everyday dishes and glassware should be placed conveniently to the sink area/dishwasher as well as to the areas where items are served, whereas serving pieces used only for holiday meals may be placed in more remote locations.

Based upon the notion of the work triangle, basic kitchen configurations have been identified: *single wall* (which contains a flattened triangle), *corridor* (also known as parallel or galley), *L-shaped*, *U-shaped*, and *G-shaped*, all of which are illustrated in Figure 5-26.

The notion of the kitchen triangle was developed over 50 years ago based on research done at the University of Illinois (the Small Homes Council) and Cornell University, and a great number of changes have occurred in appliances, technolo-

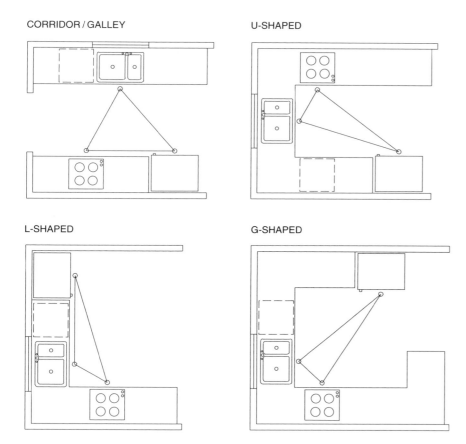

CORRIDOR / GALLEY

U-SHAPED

L-SHAPED

G-SHAPED

Figure 5-26 Corridor or galley, L-shaped, U-shaped, and G-shaped kitchens are designed based upon a standard single "work triangle" linking the sink center, refrigerator center, and cooking center.

gy, and lifestyle in the ensuing years. The addition of a second cook, a second sink, and frequent use of microwave ovens, just to name a few changes, have greatly impacted the way kitchen work is done and the organization of the kitchen.

A survey done in 1992 by NKBA found "the work triangle to be valid" (BASICS) in a large percentage of kitchens, and NKBA guidelines were updated in 1992 (based on research conducted by NKBA, the University of Illinois, and the University of Minnesota). Updated guidelines provide detailed guidance for count-

er space, cabinetry, clearances, and kitchen organization. However, these guidelines provide only cursory information about how to integrate a second cooking area or accommodate some of the newer appliances.

The authors believe that the one-cook kitchen may be improved through inclusion of a *major preparation/work area*. We find that providing a major preparation/work area in a single contiguous counter space, rather than several chopped up counter locations, creates a useful kitchen. This major preparation/work area anchors a secondary triangle linking the refrigerator and sink. This secondary preparation/work triangle aligns with one leg of the standard work triangle; the authors refer to this configuration as the "*double work triangle*." See Figure 5-27a, where a secondary triangle is anchored by a major prep area.

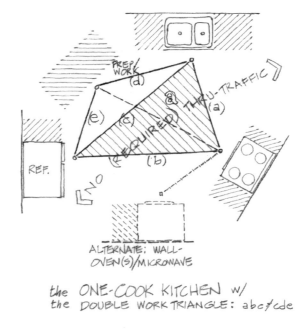

the ONE-COOK KITCHEN w/ the DOUBLE WORK TRIANGLE: abc≠cde

Figure 5-27a The one-cook kitchen can be designed based on double work triangles; those are a primary triangle (a,b,c) connecting the major centers and a secondary triangle (c,d,e) connecting a preparation/work area (36 inches wide minimum) with the sink and refrigerator. As shown here, the secondary triangle is anchored by the major prep area. Any given side, (a) or (b) or (c), should be more than 4 feet but less than 9 feet. The sum of all the sides, (a) + (b) + (c), should be more than 12 feet but less than 26 feet.

Increasingly, more than one cook is involved in the family kitchen. A work triangle for the secondary cook is worth including when possible. In order to provide a true secondary work triangle, a secondary sink is generally necessary. In addition, the work triangle provided for the second cook should not cross the primary work triangle but may align with one leg of it. Taking the idea of the double work triangle mentioned in the previous paragraph and adding these to the two primary work triangles can form *double-double work triangles,* shown in Figure 5-27b.

The notion of double work triangles is a new way of considering the organizational flow of the kitchen and a way of planning for the manner in which homeowners currently cook. It is a bit radical and perhaps deserves a more serious name; however, providing a major preparation space and/or a second complete work triangle for a secondary cook is highly useful and worth considering.

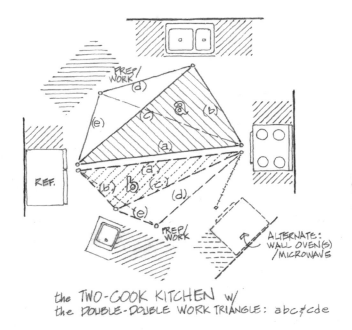

Figure 5-27b The two-cook kitchen can be designed based on two double work triangles consisting of two triangles connecting the major centers (using two sinks) and with two secondary triangles connecting 36- inch-wide preparation/work areas with the sink and refrigerator. These can be referred to as double-double work triangles.

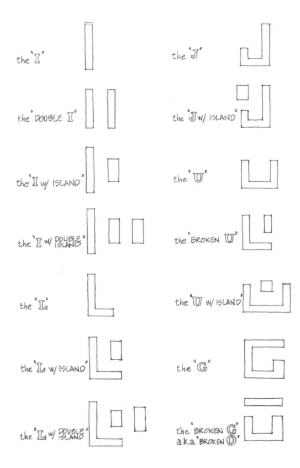

Figure 5-28 Prototype kitchen types.

It is also worth noting that the L-shaped, corridor, and U-shaped kitchens shown in many publications do not reflect the variations and options available in the design of work islands and peninsulas, which are extremely popular in new construction and home remodeling—kitchen islands were favored by 71 percent of respondents in the NAHB survey entitled "What 21st Century Home Buyers Want." In order to accommodate kitchen islands and peninsulas as well as secondary work triangles and two-cook kitchens, the authors have identified 13 kitchen configurations or prototypes shown in Figure 5-28 and detailed in later figures.

Detailed prototypes have been developed to illustrate workflow, work triangles, and basic clearances, and to introduce readers to various advantages and disadvantages of certain design choices and layout options. Each kitchen prototype is detailed in an illustration showing the location of appliances, work triangles, and dimensions. Appliances and fixtures are shown in a range of sizes—all with the goal of meeting clearance standards mentioned previously.

Each kitchen prototype shows the primary work triangle and either a second major preparation area triangle forming double triangles, or a double-double set of triangles with adjacent preparation triangles. A 1-foot-square floor grid is also displayed to give a sense of scale to each kitchen. Primary sinks in the prototypes are generally shown in window locations, but this is not required by code and is not always feasible, especially in multifamily housing or remodeling situations.

Additional notes about the prototypes include a general caution about avoiding inside corners for primary sink areas—when possible—as one cook in the corner location blocks access to substantial cabinetry. Islands and peninsulas used as seating/eating bars are shown in many prototypes, with a focus on grouping people in a way that fosters interaction and discussion rather than as a line-up, where interaction can be difficult.

Figures 5-29a through 5-29d are variations on the single-wall or I-shaped kitchen. The L-shaped prototypes are shown in Figures 5-30a to 5-30c. J-shaped kitchens are shown in Figures 5-31a and 5-31b. U-shaped plan prototypes are illustrated in Figures 5-32a to 5-32c. Figure 5-33a and 5-33b illustrate G-shaped plans.

Not shown in the prototypes are specialized items and work centers requested by some homeowners. For example, baking centers, which generally have a relationship to the mixing center or oven, work well located between the refrigerator and oven. Home offices or desk areas and craft/hobby areas can be included but should be located outside of work triangles. Some homeowners desire indoor, wood-fired ovens. These often form a strong focal point, but they also have very specific spatial and ventilation requirements and may need to be located outside of the primary work triangle.

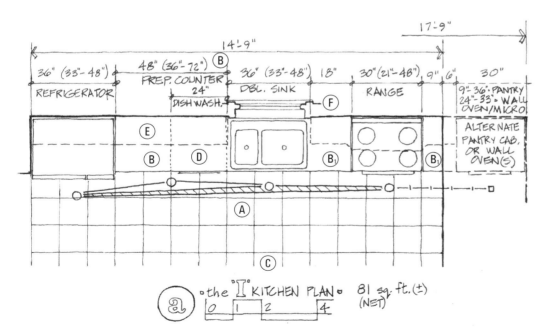

Figure 5-29a The "I" kitchen.

A. This is a one-cook kitchen that involves a lot of steps for the cook. The work triangle becomes a virtual straight line that can easily exceed recommended maximum travel distance, as noted in B below.

B. Increasing the prep area to the full 72 inches will cause the work triangle to exceed the recommended 26-foot maximum.

    B1. When expanded, the total overall counter space still falls short of what is recommended.

C. If the kitchen is open to adjacent spaces, it forces the cook to stand facing away from family/guests. Where a wall exists at C, the room becomes long and tunnel-like

D. Primary preparation center is 8 feet from the range, and clear counter space at the range is very limited.

E. Location for dish storage in wall cabinet is convenient to cleanup area.

F. Shown as an exterior wall with a window, but this would not be required when the kitchen is open to an adjoining room with operable window (natural ventilation and daylight are provided) or when mechanical ventilation and artificial illumination are provided.

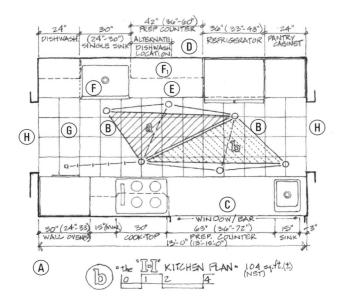

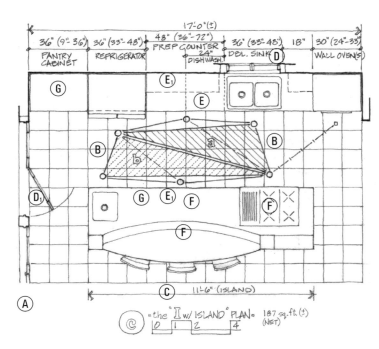

Figure 5-29b The "double I" kitchen (also known as a corridor, galley, or Pullman kitchen).

A. This can work as a two-cook kitchen, providing reasonable counter and cabinet storage; it packs a lot of kitchen into a relatively small area with generally efficient double triangles.

B. Work triangle: (a) 14 feet, 6 inches (lineal feet), (b) 15 feet, 6 inches (lineal feet).

C. Window/bar as shown can be an informal dining bar, a pass-through, a window on an exterior wall, or a wall with wall cabinets.

D. An interior or exterior wall (with a window possible at sink).

E. Preparation center also serves as part of cleanup center.

F. Cleanup center has convenient wall cabinets for dish storage (F1).

G. Width of work "corridor" is 4 feet (as shown); 3 feet, 6 inches is the minimum; 5 feet is a good rule-of-thumb maximum. Excessive width only leads to more steps between major work/appliance stations.

H. Mandatory through traffic is to be avoided; this type of kitchen works best with major circulation routes located outside of the kitchen.

Hatched triangle(s) indicate(s) primary work triangles (a and b); secondary adjoining triangles are anchored by a major prep area. Dimensions given in parentheses indicate a range of possible dimensions.

Figure 5-29c The "I with island" kitchen.

A. This works as a two-cook kitchen, providing room for others to gather and contribute to meal preparation. The double triangles in this layout are not as efficient as other layouts but are reasonably efficient.

B. Work triangle: a. 19 lineal feet, b. 18 lineal feet.

C. Kitchen is very open to adjacent spaces, allowing interaction with family and guests.

D. Standard location for a window (and preferred by many clients) but not required or necessary at exact location shown.

D1. French doors shown; or substitute window.

E. Prep center also serves as part of cleanup center.

E1. Cleanup center has convenient wall cabinets for dish storage, with additional storage in island (drawers).

F. Island contains a 36-inch range with downdraft vent, small secondary sink and a work/preparation center (36 inches above floor), curved shelf 42 inches above floor, and room for an informal eating area that allows for conversation.

G. Open-island-based kitchens often provide limited storage due to limited wall cabinets. This can be compensated through the use of pantry cabinets and/or dish storage drawers.

Hatched triangle(s) indicates primary work triangles (a and b); secondary adjoining triangles are anchored by a major prep area. Dimensions given in parentheses indicate a range of possible dimensions.

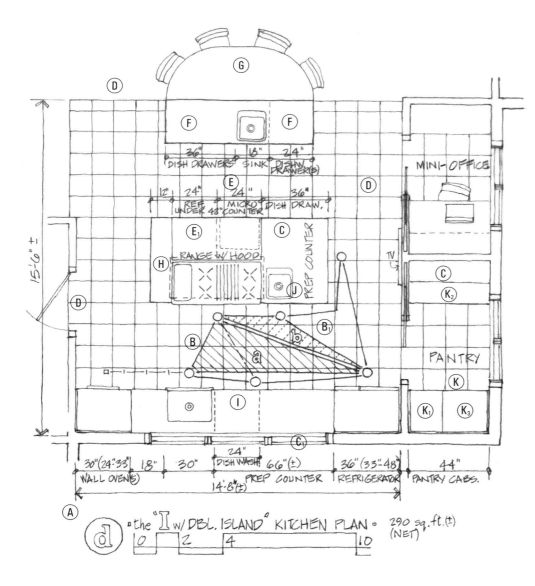

the "I w/ DBL. ISLAND" KITCHEN PLAN   290 sq. ft. (±)
(NET)

Figure 5-29d The "I with double island" kitchen.

A. This works as a two-cook kitchen, with the second island serving as a snack/preparation area for a third cook. It is a very large kitchen, two or three times the size of more efficient layouts.

B. Work triangle: a. 18 lineal feet, b. 15 lineal feet. The triangle B1 (secondary triangle) is not composed of straight lines and requires moving around the corner of the island to fully access the prep from the side.

C. Islands and exterior windows would provide a very spacious feeling but result in very few wall cabinets; this must be offset with a pantry and dish storage drawers.

C1. Some of the windows could be replaced with wall cabinets.

D. Traffic through the primary work triangles can be avoided by taking alternate routes.

E. A snack/sandwich preparation area with sink, under-counter refrigerator, and under-counter microwave oven are readily available.

E1. A 42-inch A.F.F. (for above finished floor) counter with refrigerator and microwave raised (6 inches) to a more accessible/visible height.

F. A second cleanup area with dishwasher or dishwasher drawers and adjacent dish storage drawers.

G. Informal dining at 29 inches, /36 inches or 42 inches A.F.F., with dish cleanup and storage close at hand (see F above).

H. Suitable for open shelves under counter for cookbooks, decorative accessories, collectibles, and so on.

I. Primary cleanup area, especially for pots, utensils, and large items.

J. Preparation counter with small sink (and garbage disposal); convenient for filing pots with water.

K. Pantry suitable for any/all of the following:

K1. Pantry cabinets

K2. Base cabinets

K3. Small upright freezer

Hatched triangle(s) indicates primary work triangles (a and b); secondary adjoining triangles are anchored by a major prep area. Dimensions given in parentheses indicate a range of possible dimensions.

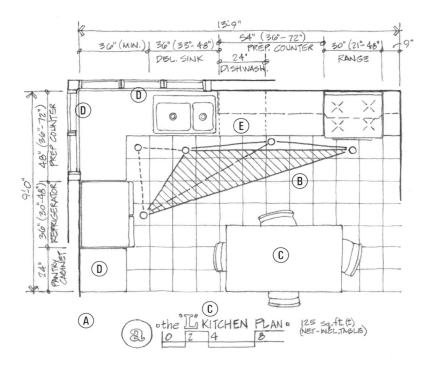

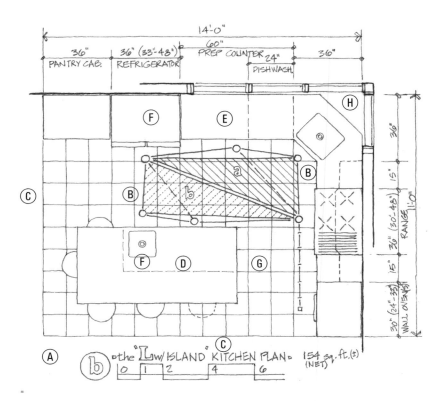

Figure 5-30a The "L" kitchen.

A. The kitchen is, as shown, a one-cook kitchen with a relatively large work triangle.

B. Work triangle: a. 20 lineal feet.

C. This prototype yields a natural spot for in-kitchen informal dining. As shown, the kitchen is open to other spaces but the cook would have his or her back to others. Often L-shaped kitchens are enclosed by a wall or walls to create a less open space than that shown.

D. Corner windows provide plentiful daylight for a secondary work/preparation area; however, wall cabinet storage is lost in the use of many windows—the use of a pantry or additional storage can offset the loss.

E. This preparation/work center can serve as part of the cleanup center; convenient dish storage is provided near sink and dishwasher.

Hatched triangle indicates a primary work triangle (a); secondary adjoining triangles are anchored by a major prep areas. Dimensions given in parentheses indicate a range of possible dimensions.

Figure 5-30b The "L with island" kitchen.

A. This kitchen, at 154 square feet, is roughly average in size (for an American home) and accommodates two cooks with two (nearly equal) efficient triangles.

B. Work triangle: a. 16 feet, 6 inches (lineal feet), b. 16 feet, 6 inches (lineal feet).

C. As shown, the kitchen is open to two adjoining spaces combined with the open island and windows—wall cabinet storage is lost—and dish storage would have to be provided by pantry and/or island drawer storage.

D. This prototype accommodates a very generous work/eating island; a sink installed at this location allows for a second work triangle/cook.

E. Dish storage would be required in base cabinets due to the small quantity of wall cabinets.

F. The open nature of this design combined with easy acces to the second sink and the refrigerator result in minimal traffic intrusion into the work triangles.

G. An alternative workstation, conveniently located to range and oven(s).

H. Corner sink location creates a space here that is useful for some clients and annoying for others.

Hatched triangle(s) indicates primary work triangles (a and b); secondary adjoining triangles are anchored by a major prep area. Dimensions given in parentheses indicate a range of possible dimensions.

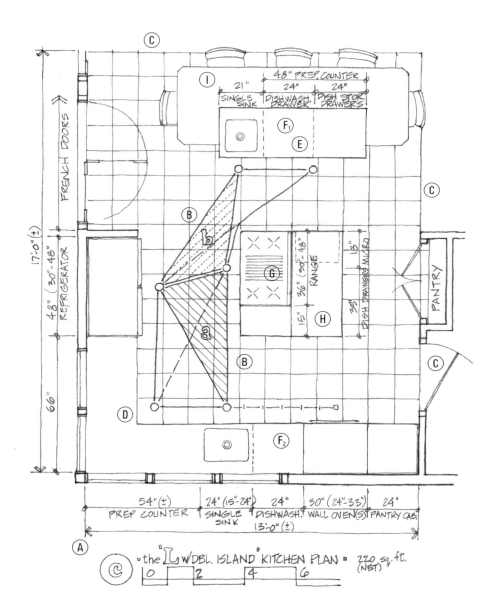

Figure 5-30c The "L with double island" kitchen.

A. This kitchen allows for two cooks and multiple helpers; it can be a social center with guests/family eating, drinking, and helping.

B. Work triangle: a. 14 lineal feet, b. 12 feet, 6 inches (lineal feet).

C. As shown, the kitchen is set into a large alcove, open to adjoining spaces yet set apart. Through traffic can be avoided by creating alternate routes to adjoining areas/exits.

D. A prep/work center with abundant daylight results in a significant loss of wall cabinets.

E. A secondary prep/cleanup center.

F. Two dishwasher locations are shown; F1 for primarily dishes (with dish storage nearby) and F2 for cooking utensils, pans, and bowls as needed.

G. 48-inch range with hood, with limited adjacent clear counter space.

H. Counter is 48 inches A.F.F. (above finished floor), with microwave under counter (at a convenient height) and room for dish storage drawers; counter at this height has limited use but allows for standing, eating, and drinking.

I. Counter shown at 29 inches A.F.F., with seating at chairs; it could, alternatively, be a 36- or 42-inch-high counter with stool (24 or 30 inches) seating.

Hatched triangle(s) indicates primary work triangles (a and b); secondary adjoining triangles are anchored by a major prep area. Dimensions given in parentheses indicate a range of possible dimensions.

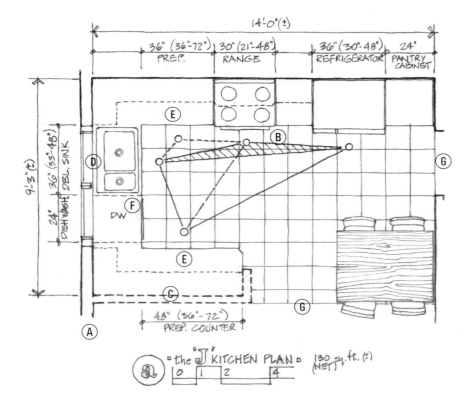

"the "J" KITCHEN PLAN

Figure 5-31a The "J" kitchen.

A. This "J" kitchen is a modestly sized, one-cook kitchen that includes an eat-in kitchen table.

B. Work triangle: a. 16 lineal feet.

C. The degree of openness to adjoining spaces varies in relation to the wall at this location; for example, only wall cabinets with no full wall or a partial wall to 42 inches above the floor with wall cabinets or a full wall with cabinets.

D. Placing windows only at the sink, as shown, maximizes space for wall cabinets. However, this window placement minimizes daylight at the other end of the room (table).

E. There are two prep/work centers (one small and one large) but only one primary work triangle, making this less than ideal for two cooks. The distance between work centers is 5 feet, 3 inches, plus or minus, to accommodate the space required for the sink and dishwasher.

F. The cleanup center and convenient dish storage (in wall cabinets) can be screened by C from adjoining rooms for clients that desire this visual separation.

G. Through circulation/traffic does not require penetration of the work areas.

Hatched triangle indicates a primary work triangle (a); secondary adjoining triangles are anchored by major prep areas. Dimensions given in parentheses indicate a range of possible dimensions.

Figure 5-31b The "J with island" kitchen.

A. This is a larger-than-average two-cook kitchen (170 square feet); the length required for the kitchen relates directly to the size of the island, which incorporates a cooktop to better serve two cooks.

B. Work triangle: a. 15 feet, 6 inches (lineal feet), b. 12 feet, 3 inches (lineal feet).

C. The room is open to adjoining spaces with limited screening provided by a 42-inch-high shelf/bar.

C1. Dish storage in suspended wall cabinets with doors on both sides (C2).

D. As shown, there is available daylight only from the window at the sink; this maximizes space for wall cabinets.

E. Space must be provided for loading the dishwasher; while the minimum space is provided, this location could be awkward (see Figure 5-31a for an alternative sink/dishwasher configuration).

F. In addition to two primary preparation/work counters (F1), there are two other smaller work centers (F2).

G. 42-inch-high bar/counter with three 30-inch-high barstools.

H. Cooktop with downdraft vent instead of hood to maintain visual connection to adjoining areas.

I. Single sink with high wall cabinets (mounted at 60 inches above the floor).

J. Centrally located refrigerator is convenient but can create a circulation problem, especially with dishwasher door open.

Hatched triangle(s) indicates primary work triangles (a and b); secondary adjoining triangles are anchored by a major prep area. Dimensions given in parentheses indicate a range of possible dimensions.

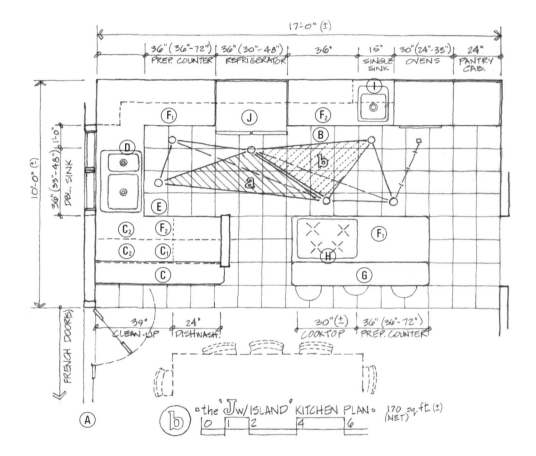

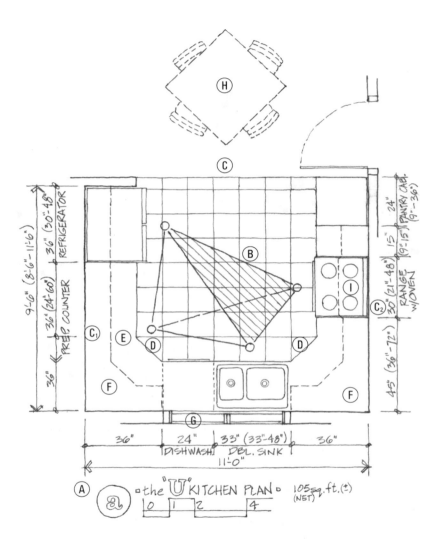

Figure 5-32a The "U" kitchen.

A. This is small and efficient for one cook; though small, it provides plentiful wall and base cabinet storage and counter frontage in relatively small square footage (105 square feet); there is no through traffic/circulation.

B. Work triangle: (a) 16 feet, 6 inches (lineal feet).

C. The room is open on one side only, separating the cook from adjoining spaces (some clients prefer this, while others find it isolating). Depending on the design of adjoining rooms, walls could be partially opened at C1 and C2 (with the range adjusted); in both cases, this would drastically reduce quantity of wall cabinets

D. There are two inside corners, and while these aid in efficiency for a single cook, a second person in the room at these locations blocks access to a disproportionate amount of storage and counter space.

E. Counter space is divided into unequal segments in order to create a major prep/work center.

F. A lazy Susan at these locations is useful. Additionally countertop appliances, TV, and so on can be located here in these relatively inaccessible (to reach) corners.

G. Sinks are shown in the traditional location under windows; windows are not required by code at this location.

H. Optional adjoining dining area (formal or informal).

I. Standard 30-inch range with vent/hood mounted under raised wall cabinet.

Hatched triangle indicates a primary work triangle (a); secondary adjoining triangle is anchored by major prep area. Dimensions given in parentheses indicate a range of possible dimensions.

Figure 5-32b The "broken U" kitchen.

A. This is a small, efficient layout, and with the addition of a secondary sink, it can function as a two-cook kitchen. It provides plentiful wall and base cabinet storage and counter frontage.

B. Work triangle: a. 13 feet, 6 inches (lineal feet), b. 14 feet, 6 inches (lineal feet).

C. Shown with two doorway openings; an alternate route should be provided for circulation/traffic outside of kitchen.

D. This inside corner has disadvantages/issues discussed in Figure 5-32a, items D and F.

E. Dish storage is close to but not immediately above dishwasher.

F. Two work centers are provided; the larger also serves as part of the cleanup center (F1).

G. Width of work corridor is at recommended maximum of 5 feet.

H. Windows at sink may create a pleasing vantage point but introduce daylight only to the far end of the room.

I. Range placement does not provide recommended clear counter space to the left of the cook; however, this placement allows a larger, more useful preparation counter/work center (F2).

Hatched triangle(s) indicates primary work triangles (a and b); secondary adjoining triangles are anchored by a major prep area. Dimensions given in parentheses indicate a range of possible dimensions.

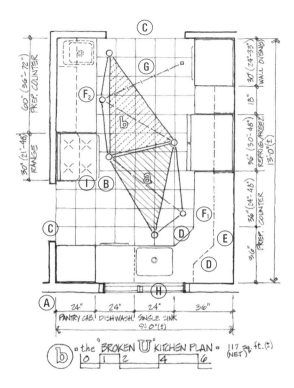

Figure 5-32c The "U with island" kitchen.

A. Accommodates two cooks with an imbalance in the work triangles (one large, one small); it provides plentiful wall/base cabinet storage, and counter frontage is provided in part by the island.

B. Work triangle: a. 21 lineal feet, b: 12 lineal feet.

C. This plan demonstrates the dilemma of creating an island within a U-shaped plan; as the size of the island increases, the size of the room necessarily increases; it can quickly reach the point where the work triangle(s) become too big. As shown, the room is open to adjoining spaces on one side only and a modest amount of windows provide adequate daylight.

D. Work/prep centers are modest in size; an additional work center (D1) could be shared with the cleanup center.

E. Cleanup center has convenient base and wall cabinets for dish storage.

F. 36-inch vent/hood mounted under raised cabinet.

   F1. Secondary sink is well placed for filling pots and drawing water at range, but it eliminates recommended counter space at one side of the range.

G. Inside corners have disadvantages/issues discussed in Figure 5-32a, items D and F.

H. Work/eating island is 36 inches high and is not large enough to include a range or sink and still provide, as shown, adequate counter space to the kitchen at large.

Hatched triangle(s) indicates primary work triangles (a and b); secondary adjoining triangles are anchored by a major prep area. Dimensions given in parentheses indicate a range of possible dimensions.

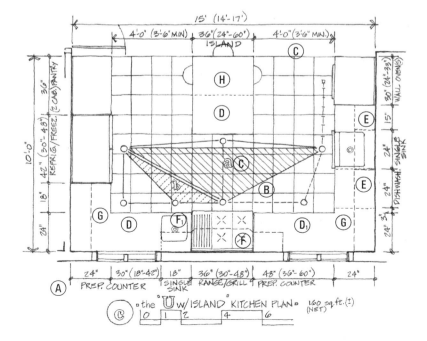

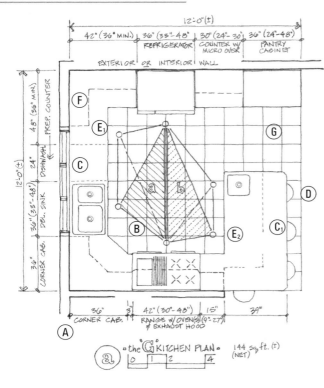

the "G" KITCHEN PLAN · 144 sq. ft. (±) (NET)

Figure 5-33a The "G" kitchen.

A. This is a medium-sized kitchen (144 square feet) and accommodates two cooks; it provides plentiful wall and base cabinet storage and counter frontage.

B. Work triangle: a. 16 lineal feet, b. 16 feet, 6 inches (lineal feet).

C. As shown, windows at cleanup center also provide daylight/view for the counter/bar seating.

D. Room is open to adjoining spaces on one side only; however, the enclosing walls provide abundant location(s) for appliances and storage.

E. Work/prep center (E1) receives direct daylight, while E2 allows for interaction (and exposure) to diners; both locations contain inside corners and related disadvantages/issues discussed in Figure 5-32a, items D and F.

F. Dish storage cabinets are convenient to dishwasher but remote from the dining counter (C1).

G. A single opening to kitchen can become a bottleneck with heavy traffic; the only route to triangle a is though triangle b.

Hatched triangle(s) indicates primary work triangles (a and b); secondary adjoining triangles are anchored by a major prep area. Dimensions given in parentheses indicate a range of possible dimensions.

Figure 5-33b The "broken G" kitchen.

A. This is medium-sized, accommodates two cooks, and has adequate base and wall cabinet storage and counter frontage. However, one of the work triangles can be interrupted by through traffic, making it less useful than other plans for some clients.

B. Work triangle: a. 13 feet, 9 inches (lineal feet), b. 16 feet, 3 inches (lineal feet).

C. As shown, the room is open on one side to adjacent rooms.

D1 and D2. Work centers; part of D1 also serves as cleanup center.

E. Cleanup center has convenient dish storage in wall cabinets, which also allows convenient pass-through to eating area(s).

F. Limited window area could be expanded at the expense of convenient wall cabinet storage.

G. 30-inch cooktop with downdraft/exhaust.

H. Wall is recessed to accommodate a deep refrigerator and allow refrigerator doors to be flush with front of cabinets.

I. Sink location (close to corner) can block access (by others) to adjacent cabinets when sink is in use.

J. Casual eating bar 42 inches high with three 30-inch stools at 27 inches on center; 15 inches minimum knee space is required.

Hatched triangle(s) indicates primary work triangles (a and b); secondary adjoining triangles are anchored by a major prep area. Dimensions given in parentheses indicate a range of possible dimensions.

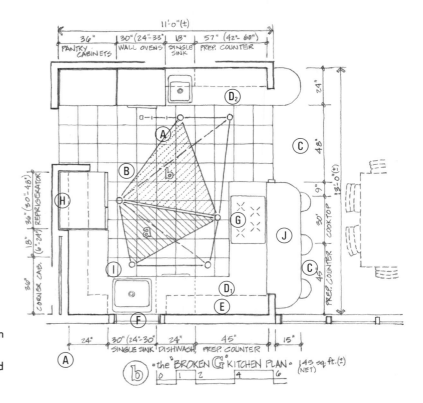

the "BROKEN G" KITCHEN PLAN · 145 sq. ft. (±) (NET)

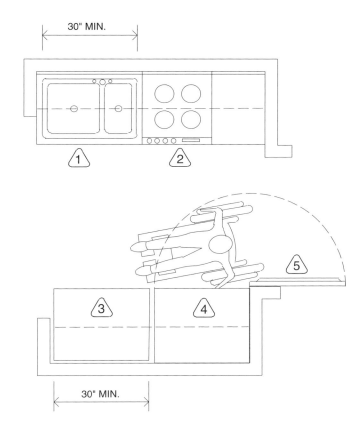

30" MIN.

30" MIN.

Figure 5-34 A prototype of a minimum-size ANSI/UFAS-compliant kitchen; this is not ideal, merely compliant. While this kitchen is wheelchair accessible, it may be inadequate for many disabled or nondisabled people because of its small size. This kitchen would be suited for small efficiency apartments only. Design courtesy of the Ability Center of Greater Toledo, Ohio.

1. Adjustable height sink.
2. Range with front controls (only allows a parallel approach).
3. Adjustable height work counter.
4. ANSI/UFAS-compliant refrigerator with 50 percent of storage within reach ranges.
5. Recommended position for single-handled door; position refrigerator so door can swing back 180 degrees, a side-by-side is recommended but not possible in such a small space.

Another specialized residential kitchen is the kosher kitchen, which requires the separation of items used in the preparation and serving of dairy and meat items. Depending on the level of observance, kosher kitchens may require two separate sinks, two disposals, two sinks, two ovens, or the separation of storage and prep areas, with the sink and cooktop centered between the two. Clearly, designing these kitchens requires specialized expertise not detailed in this chapter.

Prototypes of fully accessible kitchens can be found in Figures 5-34 and 5-35a to 5-35b; these have been provided by the Ability Center of Greater Toledo, Ohio.

Figures 5-36a, 5-36b, and 5-36c illustrate negative examples of kitchen design in which there are significant problems with planning, organization, and/or flow.

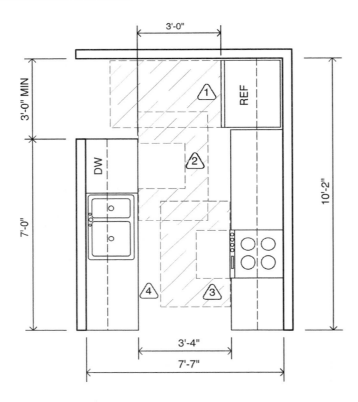

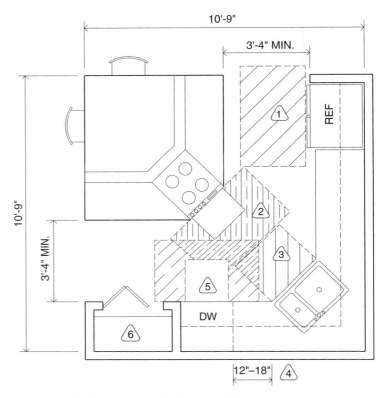

Figure 5-35a A wheelchair-accessible, small-corridor kitchen prototype; this is not an ideal plan, as it allows only parallel approach to sink and cooktop. Providing knee space at cooktop, sink, and work counter would make the kitchen more useful and would require more space (a wall oven would replace range). Design courtesy of the Ability Center of Greater Toledo, Ohio.

1. Because there is no opposing counter/cabinet, the refrigerator may encroach on the 3 feet, 4 inches required by ANSI/UFAS. When space allows, a side-by-side model is recommended.
2. This space provides a parallel approach to the dishwasher/counter surface.
3. Space for parallel approach to range.
4. Parallel approach centered on sinks permits a forward approach to dishwasher baskets when pulled out of dishwasher.

Figure 5-35b A wheelchair-accessible, "broken U" kitchen prototype. Design courtesy of the Ability Center of Greater Toledo, Ohio.

1. Parallel approach to refrigerator (side-by-side models are recommended when possible).
2. Parallel approach to range with front-mounted controls (range as shown does not provide knee space as a cooktop might.
3. Corner sink with knee space allows for full forward approach.
4. 12 to 18 inches minimum required to position dishwasher to provide access with knee space for loading/unloading dishwasher.
5. Dishwasher may be placed at a raised height.
6. Although not required, due to shallow depth of pantry, 32-inch door width is preferred for full access. In place of pantry, this would also be a possible location for a wall oven if a knee space were provided at cooktop.

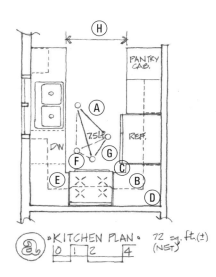

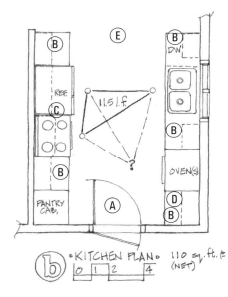

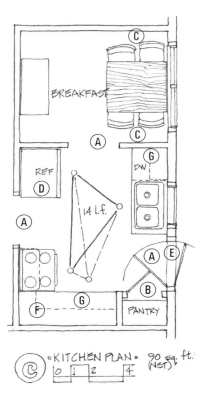

Figure 5-36a Problematic kitchen plan.

A. Primary work triangle totals less than 9 feet—too small.

B. Counter is inaccessible; work space is behind refrigerator and over a range.

C. Inaccessible base cabinet storage.

D. Difficult-to-access wall cabinet over the range.

E. Counter space area totals 24 square feet, but it is fragmented and difficult to access typically.

F. Dishwasher and oven doors will conflict.

G. Refrigerator and oven doors will conflict.

H. Main aisle width is minimal and reduced even further by refrigerator.

Figure 5-36b Problematic kitchen plan.

A. Mandatory through traffic should be avoided; here it is required (through to door).

B. Counter space is fragmented into equal small pieces and there is no major preparation/work counter.

C. Refrigerator and range should not be immediately adjacent (conflicting heat/cold appliances).

D. Not a useful counter space—a dead corner; would be better located elsewhere.

E. 5-foot, 6-inch width is wider than necessary but gains little other than more steps unless it's done to partially accommodate through traffic.

Figure 5-36c

A. This is a small kitchen that is made less effective because multiple doorways chop up the room/work areas and create mandatory through-traffic, which interrupts the primary work triangle.

B. Door swings conflict; pantry door left ajar may prevent exterior door from opening.

C. Tight for two people.

D. Refrigerator isolated with no clear counter to serve as "landing space" for items.

E. Direct, abrupt entrance from exterior; especially problematic in cold climates.

F. Relatively inaccessible—requires reaching over a hot range.

G. Inadequate counter frontage, base, and wall cabinet space.

RELATED CODES AND CONSTRAINTS

Many of the constraints related to kitchen design have been covered in previous discussions of recommended appliance and fixture clearances. As stated in previous chapters, all code information provided here is presented for general information based on the International Residential Building Code. The designer should always consult local codes, as they may vary.

The International Residential Code defines "habitable space" to include spaces for "living, sleeping, *eating* or *cooking* . . ." which includes kitchens. Section R303.1 requires that all habitable rooms "shall be provided with aggregate glazing area of not less than 8 percent of the floor area of such rooms. Natural ventilation shall be through windows, doors, louvers or other approved openings to the outdoor air." This section of the code includes kitchens and continues by stating, "The minimum openable area to the outdoors shall be 4 percent of the floor area being ventilated." Exceptions to this rule state that adequate mechanical ventilation and artificial light may serve as a substitution for natural ventilation in certain rooms (such as kitchens) not requiring an escape opening. Additionally, in cases where kitchens are open to adjoining rooms, they may share approved natural ventilation, contingent upon the degree of separation of the rooms.

The required ventilation discussed covers room ventilation, not the ventilation of the range or cooktop. A detailed discussion of ventilation of cooking surfaces can be found in the next section, including additional International Residential Code (IRC) requirements related to cooking ventilation.

Section R304 ("Minimum Room Areas") allows kitchens to be the exception to the requirement for all habitable rooms to have a floor area of not less than 70 square feet (R304.2), as well as the exception to the requirement for a room to be less than 7 feet in any horizontal dimension (R304.3).

Section R305 of the IRC covers ceiling height in detail and states that habitable rooms " . . . shall have a ceiling height of not less than 7 feet (2134 mm). The required height shall be measured from the finish floor to the lowest projection from the ceiling." An illustration of this requirement is shown in Figure 3-21. This section contains several exceptions related to beams, soffits, and sloped ceilings, as discussed in Chapter 3.

Section R306.2 ("Kitchens") states that "each dwelling unit shall be provided with a kitchen area and every kitchen area shall be provided with a sink." Section R306.4 states that "all plumbing fixtures shall be connected to an approved water supply. Kitchens . . . shall be provided with hot and cold water." Section P2706.3

prohibits plumbing fixtures from receiving the discharge of an indirect waste; however, the exception is that "a kitchen sink trap is acceptable for use as a receptor for a dishwasher."

Section M1502 of the IRC covers range hoods and indicates that "they shall discharge to the outdoors through a single-wall duct"—with exceptions based upon natural and mechanical ventilation provided through other sources.

Section M1502 of the IRC shows minimum requirements for ventilation in kitchen to be 100 cfm (cubic feet per minute) for intermittent ventilation or 25 cfm for continuous ventilation. Additional information on range and cooktop ventilation can be found in the next section of this chapter.

As stated in a previous chapter, multiple-family dwellings must meet accessibility guidelines required by the Fair Housing Amendments Act (FHAAG), which require "usable kitchens . . . such that an individual in a wheelchair can maneuver about the space." This generally requires *wheelchair-turning clearance* in U-shaped kitchens and 36-inch clearance at all passageways and circulation areas, but the guidelines do not address counter heights.

UFAS requires a 40-inch clearance between kitchen cabinets (providing knee space) and opposing walls, appliances, and cabinets, as well as specific parallel or front clearance requirements at appliances and adjustable or 34-inch-high counters. See Appendices A and B for comparative information about ANSI and UFAS related to kitchen design.

ELECTRICAL AND MECHANICAL

The work done in a kitchen brings smoke, odors, grease, and toxic fumes (in gas ranges and cooktops). With newer homes, increasingly airtight due to improvements in construction and insulation, proper ventilation of cooking equipment is an ongoing necessity.

Four cooking area ventilation choices are available: a ventilating hood over the cooktop vented to the outside, a ductless hood with a recirculating fan, a downdraft range/cooktop that draws contaminants into connected duct work downward and then outside, and a wall fan that exhausts to the outside. According to the NKBA's *Kitchen Basics: A Training Primer for Kitchen Specialists*, the ductless hood and wall fan are the least effective, with the vented hood the best option. The limitations of the downdraft system can involve tall pots and pans limiting ventilation and the dependence on the proximity to the substances being vented.

Both the vented hood and downdraft systems work to filter out grease, odors, and smoke, whereas the other options primarily move the air only.

Downdraft systems may vent directly outside or utilize ducting running beneath the floor between joists. Ventilated hoods may exhaust outside: vertically through the roof, directly through an exterior wall, or horizontally through a soffit or through exposed ductwork. Sizing the ventilation hood and fan requires careful thought. According to NKBA, hoods should be roughly 3 inches wider on each side than the cooking surface, although in the authors' experience, this is seldom seen in standard residential construction.

According to NKBA, ventilation of 150 cfm is recommended for surface cooking appliances. This recommendation exceeds that required by the code and may vary from that called for by manufacturers; therefore, careful consultation with manufacturers' guidelines is imperative. The length of ductwork, how many bends are required, and its location all affect the sizing of the ventilation fan. Location of ductwork in uninsulated attics in some colder climates may require that the ductwork be wrapped with insulation.

Because the IRC (Section R303.8) calls for heating to a minimum of 68°F when the winter design temperature is below 60°F, most kitchens in the United States (with the possible exception of portions of Hawaii and Florida) would be required to have some form of heat source.

The location for the heat source or its registers or diffusers, as well as those used by any air-cooling source, must be considered in relationship to the location of appliances and counters. The actual engineering of the heating and cooling system is, of course, done by professionals other than the interior designer. However, it's worth noting that in colder northern climates, heat is often delivered low—for example, at toe spaces—and on outside walls. Conversely, in warmer climates, cool air can be delivered at higher locations on interior walls.

The National Electrical Code calls for use of ground fault interrupters, or GFIs, to be used for electrical outlets in kitchens and other wet locations. These are designed to protect from electrical shock by detecting currents as minor as a few milliamperes and tripping a breaker at the receptacle or at the breaker panel to remove the shock hazard.

Most electrical guidelines call for two 20A-120V circuits for kitchens; these are for small-appliance use. In addition, special single-outlet circuits are required for larger appliances such as ranges/cooktops and ovens. In some cases, these are directly wired to a junction box. In other cases, a heavy-duty receptacle (and plug

for the appliance) are used. Further information about the electrical system can be found in Chapter 1.

Kitchen outlet (duplex receptacle) placement is based on the organization of the room and the location of countertops and appliances. Generally, outlets are located above countertop height, where they are needed for appliances, and at wall locations for general use. One rule of thumb requires duplex receptacles every 4 feet along counters at roughly 6 to 8 inches above counter height (depending on backsplash height) to a maximum height of 48 inches above the floor. This rule provides a helpful guideline; however, specific conditions vary widely and may require different outlet placement. It is also generally useful to place outlets to one side of the sink and cooktop. Where counters are lower than the standard 36 inches, especially at accessible counters, outlets should be a maximum of 3 feet, 6 inches from the floor—often lower. Figure 5-37 illustrates outlet/receptacle placement.

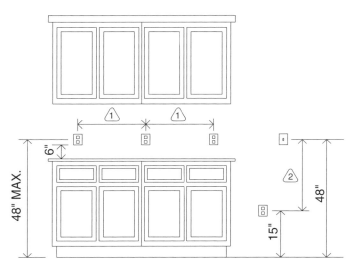

Figure 5-37 Kitchen outlet and control placement.

1. As a general rule, outlets can be placed 48 inches apart above counters or specifically located as required; local codes may vary.
2. The best height for wheelchair users (or limited mobility) is 24 to 48 inches above floor. However, counters may obstruct reach of wheelchair users.

Note: Wall-mounted outlets and switches should be 15 to 48 inches above the floor (to center of actual controls, not bottom of plates).

The on/off switches for general lights are best located close to the room entry door on the latch side of the doorway when possible. In addition to lighting and power outlets, some clients request various communication lines for telephone, cable, and stereo/audio for use in kitchen areas.

LIGHTING

Kitchens can be places of work, entertainment, and relaxation. Lighting a space where such varied activities take place can require providing a range of light sources at various heights and locations.

Providing task lighting for areas where work is done as well as general or ambient lighting for the room makes the kitchen attractive and useful. Creating soft ambient light will make people and food appear more attractive; doing this generally requires more than a single centrally located downlight. Also, a person working at a counter can block the light coming from a single centrally located downlight, causing a darkened work area—the opposite of helpful task light. Some lighting designers find that using only a series of recessed downlights can create rather harsh shadows, which is less than ideal in lighting a kitchen. Figure 5-38 illustrates some kitchen lighting concepts.

Adding under-cabinet lighting helps create ambient light and can serve as task lighting at countertop areas. Such lighting does not put those working at the counters in a position to cast shadows. Under-cabinet lighting can be provided by linear fluorescent or incandescent luminaires and/or spot luminaires (called puck lights because of their shape), which are available in incandescent (including halogen and xenon). In some cases, incandescent luminaires produce enough heat to affect food inside of cabinets. Location of food and luminaires should be planned accordingly.

Under-cabinet luminaires should be mounted so that they are not visible from seated locations, which can happen when they are placed at the rear of the cabinet (without some type of concealing trim) or when they are not recessed into the bottom of the cabinetry. See Figure 5-39. Under-cabinet fixtures can be a problem in cases where countertop materials are highly reflective, as this can create significant glare. In such instances, a different type of luminaire may be a better choice.

Linear luminaires may be placed above cabinets to create indirect overhead lighting. This is often done with fluorescent fixtures. Some cabinets with deep top framing or molding allow for the installation of luminaires that are not seen from a standing position, while others require the addition of trim pieces in order to

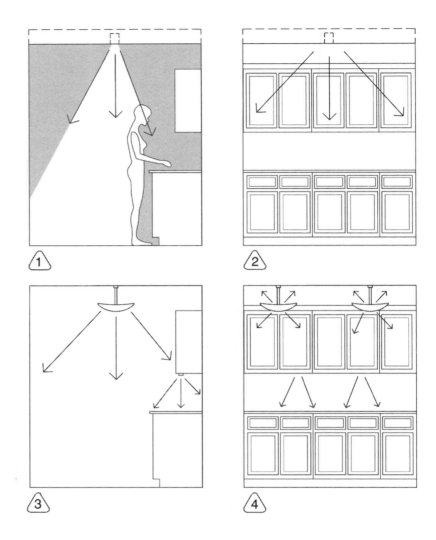

Figure 5-38 Kitchen lighting concepts.

1. A person working at a counter can block light cast by a single/centrally located downlight.
2. Downlights can create dark areas under cabinets.
3. Under-cabinet lighting washes the counter and backsplash with light.
4. Multiple pendants combined with under-cabinet lights provide ambient lighting and some task lighting at counters.

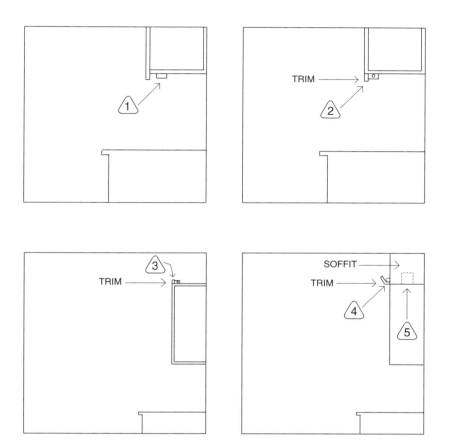

Figure 5-39 Under-cabinet and above-cabinet lighting.

1. Small surface-mounted spot or "puck" (also known as "puc") lights, as well as linear fluorescent or incandescent luminaires, may be used under cabinets.
2. Linear under-counter fixtures may require concealing trim (as will deeper puck lights).
3. Luminaires may be placed above cabinets to supply indirect uplighting; trim may be required.
4. Luminaires may be placed at soffits to supply indirect uplighting; trim may be required. Sconces may also be used at these locations, if the vertical dimension of the soffit is adequate.
5. Recessed luminaires or other downlights may be helpful at soffit/ceiling locations above sink.

cover existing soffits above cabinets. These can be fitted with crown molding to accommodate linear luminaires and strip luminaires. See Figure 5-39.

While under-cabinet luminaires can provide excellent task lighting, certain locations, particularly the sink area and areas such as islands and peninsulas, may require a different approach. Many clients prefer downlights at the primary sink area; depending upon the size and design, one or two incandescent downlights in the sink area may work well. Islands and peninsulas that serve as dining or conversation areas are often lit with downlights, with pendant fixtures, or with a combination of the two.

Pendants in such areas are currently popular, and a variety of fixtures are available that can enhance the dining experience and provide an interesting aesthetic component. Height, location, and design of pendant fixtures must be well considered in order to avoid creating glare at seated eye level, as well as uneven lighting, and so that the fixtures do not block vision or cause people to bump into them.

Some kitchens require accent lighting in order to display art and collections or to show off appliances. Adjustable downlights, track or canopy fixtures, and wall washers can provide accent lighting. Enhancing certain areas to the desired effect requires careful consideration of fixture placement, and beam spread of these fixtures requires careful study of product information. Figure 5-40 shows an electrical/lighting plan, illustrating some of the lighting choices discussed.

The discussion of lighting to this point has included using a variety of fixtures because using a range of luminaires at a variety of mounting heights can create attractive ambient light and task light and can add visual interest to the room. However, some clients are focused on energy efficiency, and some states and municipalities have codes that regulate energy use; these may limit the type and number of fixtures used. California's Title 24 requires that the first switch reached in a kitchen must operate a fluorescent fixture or have an efficacy of 40 lumens per watt. Title 24 also states that in cases where there is one light for the kitchen, it must be fluorescent. This includes rooms where the under-cabinet lighting is the only light source. Figure 5-41 illustrates some Title 24 limitations related to kitchen lighting and energy efficiency.

In cases where fluorescent fixtures are used, color rendition is important in making food look appetizing. Lamps at 3000 K and with a CRI of 80-plus will render food and beverage colors more pleasing than will those used in areas where color rendition is less important. However, as stated, local codes may restrict lamp choices. Additional lighting information can be found in Chapter 1.

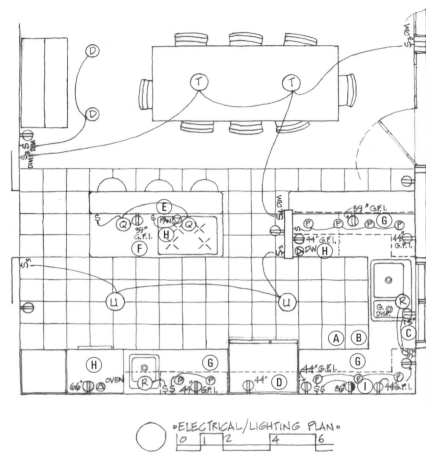

ELECTRICAL/LIGHTING PLAN
0   1   2   4   6

Ⓟ UNDER CAB. LOW VOLT. QUARTZ HALOGEN

Ⓠ INCAND. PENDANT FIXT.

Ⓡ RECESSED INCAND. SOFFIT FIXT.

Ⓓ RECESSED ADJUSTABLE DOWNLITE

Ⓣ INCAND. PENDANT FIXT.

Ⓤ FLUOR. CEILING FIXT.

Figure 5-40 Sample kitchen electrical and lighting plan.

A. The IRC (section E3801.4.1) states, "A receptacle outlet shall be installed at each counter wall space 12 inches (305 cm) or wider. Receptacles shall be installed so that no point along the wall line is more than 24 inches (610 cm) measured horizontally from a receptacle outlet in that space."

B. The IRC (section E3802.6) states, "All 125-volt, single-phase, 15- and 20-ampere receptacles that serve countertop surfaces shall have ground fault interrupter protection. . . ."

C. Switched outlet for garbage disposal inside base cabinet in this example, not required if disposal is wired directly.

D. Separate 15-amp circuit for refrigerator/freezer is a good practice (not required by IRC or many other codes).

E. Downdraft exhaust fan with switch.

F. Duplex convenience outlet set horizontally to fit in between the two counter heights. The IRC (E3801.4.2) states that "at least one receptacle outlet shall be installed at each island counter space with a long dimension of 24 inches (610 cm) and a short dimension of 12 inches (305 cm) or greater. A duplex receptacle is also required at peninsula counters."

G. Referred to by some as puck or puc lights.

H. Dishwasher, fan, and oven are wired directly.

I. A switched, split-wired duplex outlet placed on wall above cabinets for a variety of possible uses (such as lighting or decorative elements).

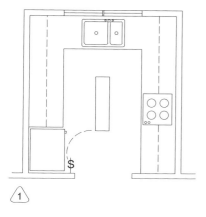

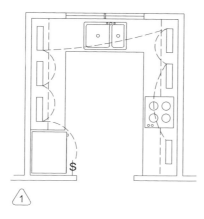

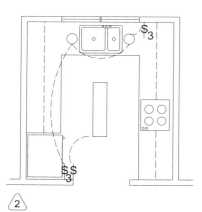

Figure 5-41 Title 24 kitchen concepts.

1. California's Title 24 requires either the overhead or under-cabinet luminaire to be fluorescent.

2. California's Title 24 requires a center fluorescent luminaire in kitchens with two or more light sources. It is helpful to include a switch at sink locations (not required as part of Title 24).

BIBLIOGRAPHY

(Contains both works cited and recommended reading. Annotations where appropriate.)

Ability Center of Greater Toledo. *Usable Kitchens*. www.abilitycenter.org.

Beasley, Kim A., and Thomas D. Davies. *Kitchen Design for the Wheelchair User*. Washington, DC: Paralyzed Veterans of America (PVA), 1999.

Bouknight, Joanne Kellar. *The Kitchen Idea Book*. Newtown, CT: The Taunton Press, 2001. Contains beautiful examples and many helpful ideas.

————. *The Storage Idea Book*. Newtown, CT: The Taunton Press, 2003. Contains helpful examples and innovative ideas.

Brooks, David. *Bobos in Paradise*. New York: Simon & Schuster, 2000. The quotation may be found on page 87.

Ching, Francis, and Dale E. Miller. *Home Renovation*. New York: Van Nostrand Reinhold, 1983. A great reference for renovation and residential construction.

Ching, Francis, and Cassandra Adams. *Building Construction Illustrated*. 3rd ed. Hoboken, NJ: John Wiley & Sons, 2001.

Consumer Reports Online. *"Refrigerators: Opening New Doors."* July 2005. www.consumerreports.org/cro/appliances/refrigerators/reports/how-to-choose.htm?resultPageIndex=1&resultIndex=8&searchTerm=opening%20doors.

Galvin, Patrick K., and Ellen Cheever. *Kitchen Basics: A Training Primer for Kitchen Specialists*. E. Windsor, NJ: Galvin Publications, 1998. A kitchen guide sponsored by the National Kitchen and Bath Association that covers principles and standards for kitchen design, with limited information about multiple-cook kitchens.

Ierley, Merritt. *The Comforts of Home: The American Modern House and the Evolution of Modern Convenience*. New York: Three Rivers Press, 1999.

International Code Council. *International Residential Code 2003*. Florence, KY: Thomson Delmar Learning, 2003.

Karlen, Mark, and James Benya. *Lighting Design Basics*. Hoboken, NJ: John Wiley & Sons, 2003.

Kitchen and Bath Business Online. July 2005. www.kitchen-bath.com/kbb.

McGowan Maryrose, and Kelsey Kruse. *Interior Graphic Standards*. Hoboken, NJ: John Wiley & Sons, 2003.

"The Metropolis Observed: Kitchen Confidential." *Metropolis Magazine*, November 2004, Volume 24, Number 3. An interview with designer Bill Stumpf.

National Association of Home Builders. "Housing Facts, Figures, and Trends 2004: What 21st Century Home Buyers Want." Washington, DC: NAHB Advocacy/Public Affairs and the HAHB Economics Group, 2004.

Newmark, Norma, and Patricia Thompson. *Self, Space, and Shelter: An Introduction to Housing*. New York: Harper & Row, 1977. This is an excellent survey of environmental psychology and social history related to the residential environment. Out of print, but worth a search.

Pile, John, F. *Interior Design*. 2nd ed. Englewood Cliffs, NJ: Prentice Hall, 1995.

Plante, Ellen M. *The American Kitchen: 1700 to the Present: From Hearth to Highrise.* New York: Facts on File, 1995.

Rumberger, Janet, ed. *Architectural Graphic Standards for Residential Construction.* Hoboken, NJ: John Wiley & Sons, 2003.

State University of New York at Buffalo. "Technical Report: Accessible Appliances Universal Design." August 8, 1996.

Smith, Steve. *Plumbing and Mechanical Magazine.* "Special PM Survey: Kitchen Plumbing." April 2004, http://www.pmmag.com/CDA/Archives/44ea61cba20d 7010VgnVCM100000f932a8c0

Susanka, Sarah. *The Not So Big House: A Blueprint for the Way We Really Live.* Newtown, CT: The Taunton Press, 1998.

Whitaker, Ellen, Colleen Mahoney, and Wendy Jordan. *Great Kitchens: At Home with America's Top Chefs.* Newtown, CT: The Taunton Press, 2001.

Whitehead, Randall. *Residential Lighting: A Practical Guide.* Hoboken, NJ: John Wiley & Sons, 2002.

CHAPTER 6

LEISURE SPACES

Living room, gathering room, great room, family room—all of these terms describe a space where people gather to interact and take part in various forms of entertainment, from reading to computer work/games and television viewing. For many current homeowners, a formal living room—"where no one ever goes"—is no longer desired. Instead, a great room or gathering room where all family members can gather and take part in a range of activities is preferable. However, some homeowners do still desire a room for more formal events, and there may be a desire for a room used for the adults in the family, with younger family members using a separate room—often called a family room or den. Similarly, formal dining rooms are not favored by some current homeowners; these people often prefer a more casual eating area that is open or partially open to the kitchen, forming a cooking, eating, and entertainment area.

The NAHB survey *What 21st Century Homebuyers Want* found that respondents most often prefer "kitchens adjacent to family rooms and want the two rooms to be visually open or divided with a half wall." A majority of new homes include a fireplace, with 54 percent of homes built in 2003 having one fireplace and 5 percent having two or more. As discussed later in this chapter, fireplaces can serve as a focal point for leisure spaces. Additional trends mentioned in the survey include an interest in media rooms and home gyms.

Formal living rooms and parlors, casual youth-oriented entertainment rooms, informal and/or formal dining areas, and media rooms (including home theaters) are all places where people gather for interaction and entertainment. Careful client interviews and programming are required in order to design spaces that reflect family interests and support interaction. In planning such spaces, the first steps involve a thorough review of the owner's spatial requirements, day-to-day activities, and interests. Armed with a clear understanding of a homeowner's actual needs and activities, the designer can undertake the design of such places.

Although the various leisure spaces differ in terms of formality, size, and to some degree activities undertaken, they all share the primary need for furniture groupings that support interaction (such as conversation). Interestingly, while dining areas can be seen as supporting very different functions than, say, formal parlors, they share the similarity of seated activities being the focus of the experience conducted in the room. Therefore, we can see all of these rooms as being based to some degree on the organization of seating and related furnishings.

Media rooms (including home theaters) and home gyms are increasingly favored by homeowners, particularly those with large residences and/or those involved in large-scale renovation and building additions. The design of home theaters and some media rooms require an understanding of equipment and acoustics that goes beyond the limitations of this book: Refer to the bibliography of this chapter for information on publications that cover home theater design. The design of home theaters and media rooms has become a design specialty, with a number of firms and studios available for design or design/build services. Home gym design and layout varies, dependent upon room size, equipment used, and manufacturers' suggested clearances.

Spaces that are specifically meant to support conversation require seating and/or furniture that can accommodate a certain number of people, arranged at appropriate distances for speaking and discussion. In addition, such spaces, as well as all others used for leisure activities, require adequate circulation. Additional information about furniture layout and clearances is provided later in this chapter.

In addition to furniture placement supportive of interaction and appropriate circulation, many leisure spaces are designed in relation to some focal point. A fireplace or wood stove; window(s); or views of adjoining spaces, television, or artwork may become focal points and therefore major influencing factors on the design of the space and the layout of furnishings.

The discussion of room design in this chapter is less technical and in some ways more general than discussions of most other rooms covered in this book. This was done in order to adapt to the many types of rooms, situations, and architectural parameters that may present themselves in the design of leisure spaces. In this chapter, we approach leisure spaces broadly, in order to aid in the design of a wide range of spaces and a wide range of room types and combinations that may present themselves in current design practice. Therefore, readers will find fewer illustrations of specific room designs and prototypes than in previous chapters and a more general discussion of the design of leisure spaces.

Regardless of the relative size of the room or the specialized nature of the room, there are some general rules that can be of help in planning leisure spaces. Areas that are meant to support interaction are best planned for a *minimum of six* seated individuals. This is not true for dining spaces but generally holds true for other rooms where other forms of interaction take place. When there is not room for six actual seats—such as in the cases of small rooms or rooms used for a range of purposes—it is helpful to find an area for standing interaction for six. This could be done by providing four seats plus room for two people to stand. Another option is to allow space for pulling up a small chair or chairs.

The authors have found that it is best to cluster seating arrangements in seating groups of six people, when possible. We have found that groups larger than six tend to splinter into smaller conversations, dividing the larger group into *conversation clusters*. We have also found that dividing larger leisure spaces into a series of areas for smaller-group interaction (groups of six and smaller) also provides for better acoustics, because groups are clustered away from one another. Because of the limits of human hearing and issues of territoriality, furniture within the cluster should be spaced from 4 to 10 feet apart. Depending on furniture size and room configurations, the actual area of conversation clusters should be roughly 12 feet to 13 feet in diameter to best support interaction. Figure 6-1 illustrates conversation clusters with a range of seating options.

Conversation clusters may be created within larger spaces by simply arranging furniture into separate groupings. When possible, architectural elements such as alcoves can serve as the setting for conversation clusters. Alcoves also work well to articulate areas in which different activities take place—for example, a home office or computer space works well set into an alcove within a larger room. In addition to architectural features that reinforce clusters of seating, rooms may be divided into clusters based on focal points such as windows, fireplaces, or televisions, or on other uses, such as a game table area. Figure 6-2 illustrates a room with two seating clusters with different functions and/or focal points.

As with all spaces described in this book, the overall square footage, general layout, and activities engaged in will greatly alter the furnishings within the space. The most basic seating cluster will consist of varied forms of seating, such as a sofa and two chairs or two sofas and a chair plus some type of table upon which to place items such as drinks, reading material, and remote controls. Specialized areas such as game areas, very small rooms, and media rooms will require furnishings other than those mentioned.

In many ways dining areas offer fewer options for laying out spaces than do other leisure spaces because they are typically focused on a single table with appropriate seating. Generally, the only options dining rooms present are the size and shape of the table and, in some cases, table location. Room size, shape, and the level of formality required will influence table shape and other furnishing selections. Views and window locations and the existence of some other focal point—such as a fireplace—will also influence table shape and location. Also, as noted in the "Lighting" section later in this chapter, the table shape and location can influence—or be influenced by—decorative lighting location(s).

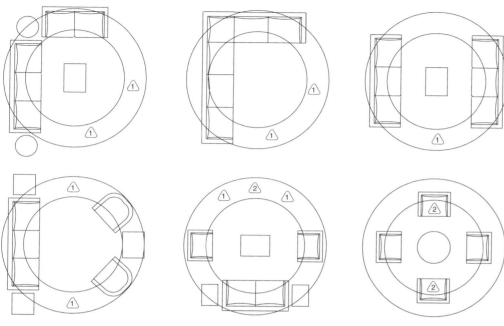

Figure 6-1 Large groups tend to break into smaller groups of four to six people, creating *conversation clusters*. Conversation clusters of roughly 12 feet to 13 feet diameter support interaction. The outer dash on each illustration depicts the outer limits of furniture arrangement that will allow for successful interaction; limits "for face-to-face" interaction are indicated by the inner dashed circle, roughly 4 feet to 10 feet.

1. Room for standing interaction or for seating to be pulled up on occasion.
2. Could be a seating location or a focal point.

For dimensions of furniture, see Figures 6-3, 6-4, and 6-5.

Figure 6-2 Furniture can be arranged into separate groups or clusters within the larger space. This room contains two seating clusters with differing functions and different focal points.

A. Access to bedroom(s).
    A1. Access to dining/kitchen/utility spaces beyond.
B. Through traffic is straightforward and does not go through any of the activity/furniture clusters.
C. Focus of the seating cluster is a fireplace and/or television (location of the television above fireplace is too high for some clients).
    C1. Keep a fireplace low (hearth at floor level); a wood-burning fireplace requires a noncombustible hearth 18 inches from fire area opening.
    C2. Hearth shown extends to the sidewalls; this is not required.
D. Bookshelves.
E. Game table or library/study/homework table.

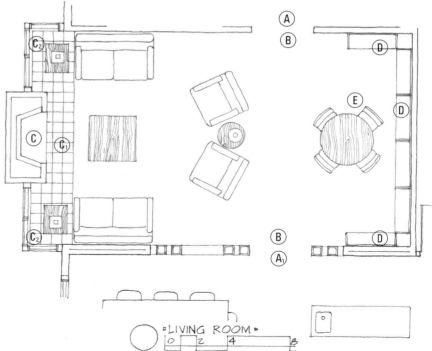

LIVING ROOM

Round tables can nurture conversation within smaller groups of four to six people and work well in small alcoves such as breakfast coves and for game tables. Placement of additional furnishings such as buffets and china hutches generally involves consideration of circulation space and location of walls or corners (for use of corner hutches). These issues are discussed further in the "Ergonomics and Required Clearances" and "Organizational Flow" sections later in the chapter.

Actual furniture sizes and ergonomics must be considered as arrangements are designed. Furniture sizes have kept up with the ever increasing size of American houses, with larger and oversized leisure-space furnishings becoming increasingly popular. Figure 6-3 depicts a range of sizes for various types of seating for non-dining areas. Figure 6-4 depicts sizes of some tables and storage units for leisure rooms. Figure 6-5 depicts sizes of some dining furnishings. For additional information on furniture arrangement and layout of specific types of spaces, please refer to the "Ergonomics and Required Clearances" and "Organizational Flow" sections of this chapter.

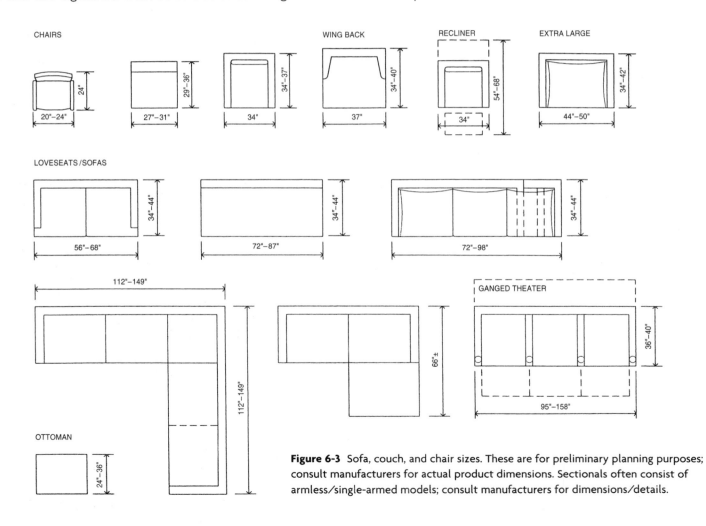

Figure 6-3 Sofa, couch, and chair sizes. These are for preliminary planning purposes; consult manufacturers for actual product dimensions. Sectionals often consist of armless/single-armed models; consult manufacturers for dimensions/details.

OCCASIONAL TABLES

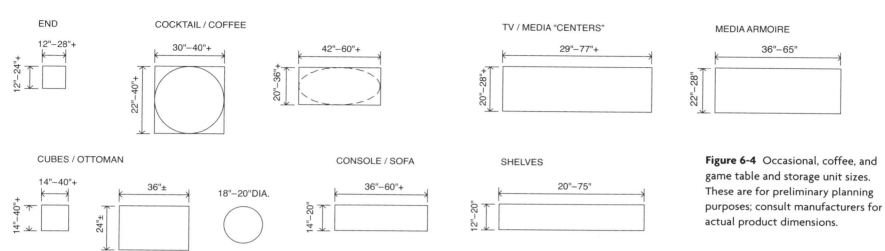

END

COCKTAIL / COFFEE

TV / MEDIA "CENTERS"

MEDIA ARMOIRE

CUBES / OTTOMAN

CONSOLE / SOFA

SHELVES

Figure 6-4 Occasional, coffee, and game table and storage unit sizes. These are for preliminary planning purposes; consult manufacturers for actual product dimensions.

Figure 6-5 Dining table, chair, and storage furniture sizes.

1. Tables shown have the potential for extensions and leaves, which will add to overall dimensions (or in some cases reduce the table size). Extensions and leaves vary in size—often adding 10 inches to 18-plus inches for each extension. These are for preliminary planning purposes; consult manufacturers for actual product dimensions.

2. The smaller dimension indicated seats the smaller number of people indicated.

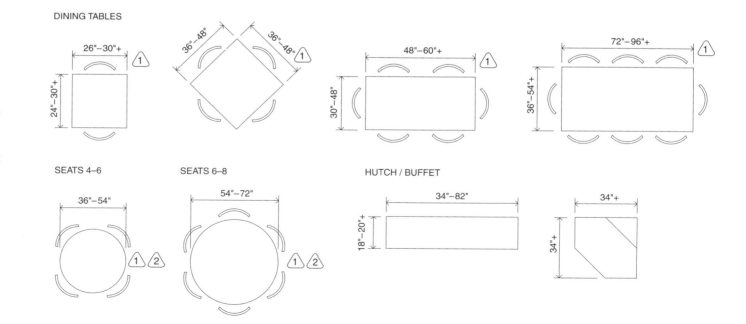

DINING TABLES

SEATS 4–6

SEATS 6–8

HUTCH / BUFFET

ACCESSIBILITY

In contrast to chapters on other spaces covered in this book, there is very little technical information that must be conveyed regarding accessibility of leisure spaces. In contrast to kitchens and baths, leisure spaces tend to have fewer built-in cabinets, as well as other elements that can create barriers to those using wheelchairs or walkers, or with mobility limitations. However, access to and enjoyment of leisure spaces by all requires careful planning of circulation routes, locations of switches and controls, and arrangement of furnishings. These issues are addressed in this chapter in the appropriate sections.

Making sure that access to the leisure space requires no steps is a major factor in making the space wheelchair-accessible as well as visitable. It is also worth noting that selection of furnishings must be made with special attention to the ease of sitting in and getting out of chairs and sofas, which can be an issue for a range of individuals of various heights and those with mobility problems. Huge, overstuffed chairs with low or unsupportive seats can be very difficult to get up and out of for individuals with mobility limitations. With an aging population, this will be an increasing problem.

ERGONOMICS AND REQUIRED CLEARANCES

Planning leisure spaces requires consideration of providing adequate space for each individual to sit and conduct the desired activity (for example, television viewing or conversing while playing games) as well as adequate circulation. Figure 6-6 illustrates the room required for comfortable adult seating.

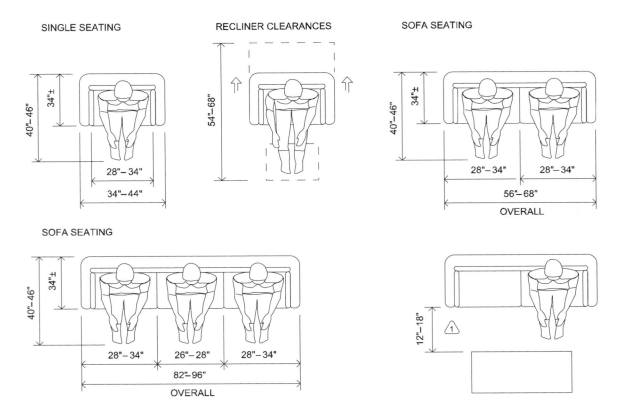

Figure 6-6 Space required for adult seating (sizes shown are for upholstered pieces). The space requirements shown are based on male and female adult averages. The 12-inch dimension shown (1) is a minimum and only possible in cases where the table length is also minimal; longer tables, such as that shown, require greater access space for comfortable movement

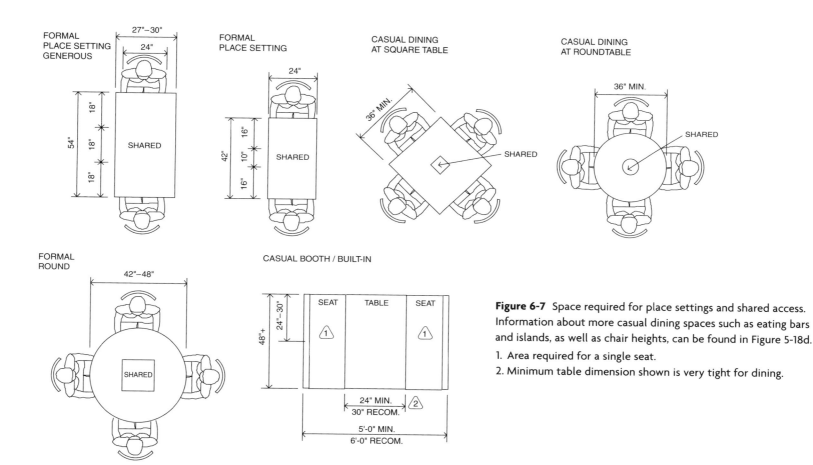

FORMAL
PLACE SETTING
GENEROUS
27"–30"
24"
18"
18"
18"
54"
SHARED

FORMAL
PLACE SETTING
24"
16"
10"
16"
42"
16"
SHARED

CASUAL DINING
AT SQUARE TABLE
36" MIN.
SHARED

CASUAL DINING
AT ROUNDTABLE
36" MIN.
SHARED

FORMAL
ROUND
42"–48"
SHARED

CASUAL BOOTH / BUILT-IN
SEAT   TABLE   SEAT
① ①
24"–30"
48"+
24" MIN.
30" RECOM.
②
5'-0" MIN.
6'-0" RECOM.

Figure 6-7 Space required for place settings and shared access. Information about more casual dining spaces such as eating bars and islands, as well as chair heights, can be found in Figure 5-18d.

1. Area required for a single seat.
2. Minimum table dimension shown is very tight for dining.

Dining tables require adequate space for each seated individual as well as for serving pieces, dishes, and table decorations. The areas allotted for serving pieces, dishes, and decorations are considered shared-access zones. More formal dining areas generally require more space in the access zone in order to accommodate more formal dining as well as room for more formal place settings. Peninsulas and dining bars generally have minimal shared-access zones due to the casual nature of the dining experience. These are covered in detail in Chapter 5, "Kitchens." Figure 6-7 shows required spaces for place settings and shared-access zones for various table shapes. Figure 6-8 illustrates clearances for dining areas, including necessary space for circulation to and within the area.

Figure 6-8 Required clearances at and for circulation to and around dining areas.

1. Required clearance from table edge to wall or obstacle to allow access to chair and clearance for chair movement; total dimension is dependent upon chair size. The use of round tables can allow for a minimum of 30 inches, as shown on lower left illustration, but this varies depending on chair size and room form.

2. Required clearance for circulation and seating.

3. This shows the minimum required for seating space (18 inches) and the minimum required for chair movement and body placement (18 inches, which allows for seated individuals to pull away from the table to relax); total dimension is dependent upon chair size.

4. 24 inches is required for forward movement in addition to clearance required for seating (18 inches minimum).

5. Minimum room width.

6. Minimum clearance for standing activity, such as buffet line.

7. Minimum casual or breakfast room dimensions—round table.

8. Eye level varies greatly; 27 inches is at the low range and 34 inches is at the high range; hanging luminaires should be placed above this height or be adjustable.

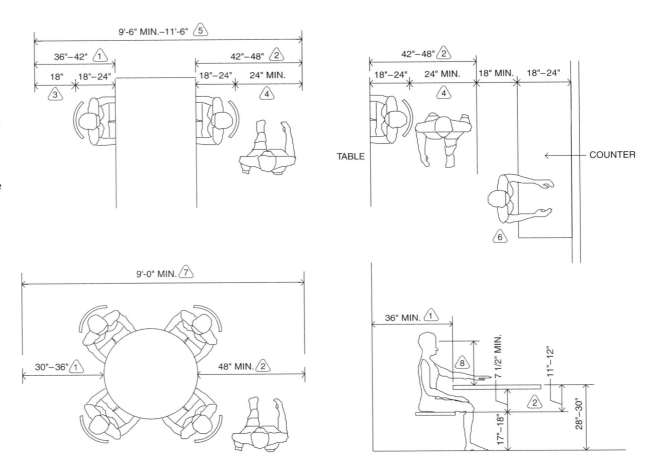

ORGANIZATIONAL FLOW

Circulation and flow through leisure spaces is dependent upon the relationship of doors and the related circulation patterns that flow from doors and doorways to adjacent rooms, spaces, and furnishings. Put simply, the locations of doors/passageways influence the flow through a leisure space and the related arrangement of furnishings. Numerous doorways and passageways into leisure spaces can negatively impact furniture arrangement, as can location of poorly placed doors, as shown in Figures 6-9a to 6-9c. Additional influencing factors in organizing leisure spaces include the relationship of furnishing groupings to windows, additional architectural elements, and focal points, as well as a consideration of conversation clusters, as previously discussed.

Doors and passageways can also have a negative impact upon dining room furniture arrangement because doors dictate the circulation through the room and because the dining table often occupies a central location within the room, as shown in Figures 6-10a to 6-10c. In temperate climates and/or certain building sites, a door leading to the exterior from leisure and dining spaces can be desirable. The location of such doors requires consideration of circulation patterns and furniture arrangements.

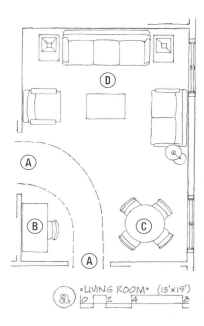

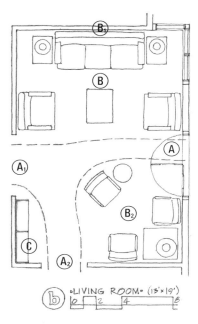

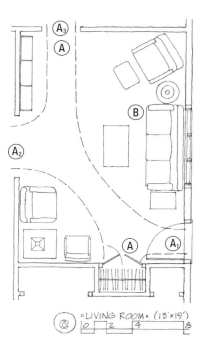

Figure 6-9a Door and passageway placement has an impact upon furniture arrangements and conversation clusters.

A. Through traffic originating from two adjacent walls allows for a range of options in seating arrangements.
B. A desk for computer/writing/reading in a corner that is not suited for much more.
C. A game table corner for study/games/projects.
D. Seating cluster for 6; as shown, there is no focal point; seating could be rearranged, allowing for a focal point.

Figure 6-9b Door and passageway placement has an impact upon furniture arrangements and conversation clusters.

A. Although traffic to French or sliding doors leading to a patio or deck may be sporadic, it is necessary to locate furniture in a manner that will leave an access route open.
   A1. Access to dining/kitchen and secondarily to utility spaces.
   A2. Access to bedrooms.
B. The larger of two seating clusters could be turned 180 degrees and allow for a focal point (B1); cluster (B2) is quite tight and limited in terms of arrangement possibilities.
C. Shelves.

Figure 6-9c Door and passageway placement has an impact upon furniture arrangements and conversation clusters.

A. Traffic moving from end to end of a rectangular space is most disruptive and leads to a very constrained situation in terms of options for arranging furniture.
   A1. House entrance; very minimal in terms of space provided for the transition from outside and for receiving guests.
   A2. Access to dining/kitchen and secondarily to bedrooms.
   A3. Access to owner's suite (called master bedroom by some).
B. While this room shape is similar to that shown in Figures 6-9a and b, the door locations significantly limit options for furniture arrangement and, as arranged, the room is not particularly comfortable.

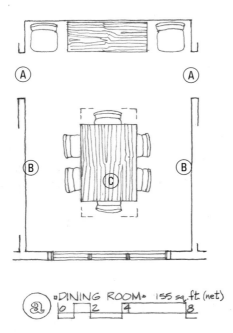

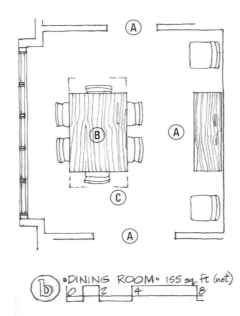

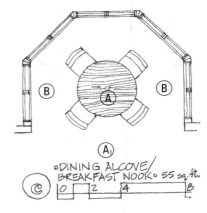

Figure 6-10a Door and passageway placement has an impact upon furniture locations in dining areas.

A. Any required through-circulation is straight across the short dimension of the room.

B. At 10 feet, 6 inches wide, there is not sufficient room for auxiliary furniture on either side of table.

C. Table shown is 5 feet long by 3 feet, 6 inches wide but could be longer (6 to 7 feet). A pendant fixture centered in the ceiling could work well in this room, as the layout dictates a centrally placed table.

Figure 6-10b Door and passageway placement has an impact upon furniture locations in dining areas.

A. Door openings that are located centered in the walls create a more meandering path of travel through the room than those shown in Figure 6-10a.

B. A light fixture placed in the center of this room will not fall in the center of this table. In situations such as this, it is important that the designer convey the desired location of the pendant luminaire or chandelier so the luminaire does not end up (by default) poorly located.

C. Table shown is 5 feet long by 3 feet, 6 inches wide but could be longer (6 to 7 feet).

Figure 6-10c Door and passageway placement has an impact upon furniture locations in dining areas.

A. The table shown is 42 inches diameter; this comfortably accommodates 4 adults and would be a tight fit for 5. Increasing the table size may be possible but would require that the table extend outside of the room (A1), where the appropriate amount of space would be required but may not be available.

B. Chair locations work best at the angles shown for ease of movement and seated comfort.

As mentioned, increasingly, homes contain "great rooms" or "gathering rooms" that include dining, entertainment, and kitchen areas all within a single open space. As with other types of spaces mentioned, the location of doors in these large open areas requires careful consideration. While often fewer doors are required than for individual rooms, the placement of openings and doors in such rooms has a significant impact upon the use of the room and the placement of furnishings, as shown in Figures 6-11a and 6-11b.

Figure 6-11a Door and passageway placement has an impact upon room use and furniture locations in large, open "great rooms."

A. Primary entrance to house.
A1. Generous entry corridor with convenient coat storage and view of
    adjoining areas/exterior views.
    A2. Access to owner's suite.
    A3. Access to utility spaces.
    A4. French-door access to patio/deck.
B. Seating cluster.
C. Gas fireplace with raised hearth (C1) shown extending to each side.
D. Television.
E. Work area for computer/mail center/desk or hobby area.

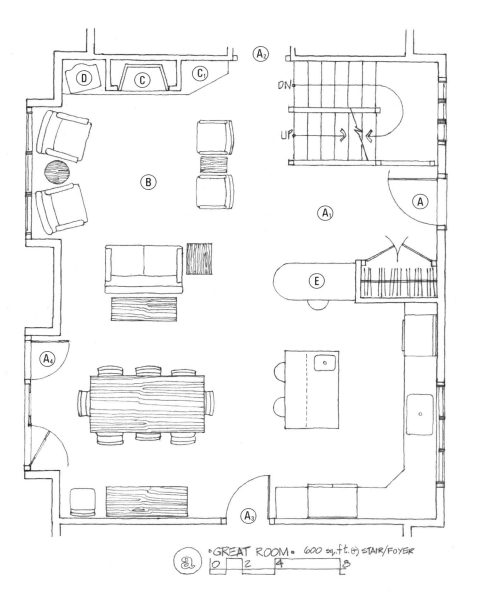

     GREAT ROOM. 600 sq.ft. (±) STAIR/FOYER
     0 2 4 8

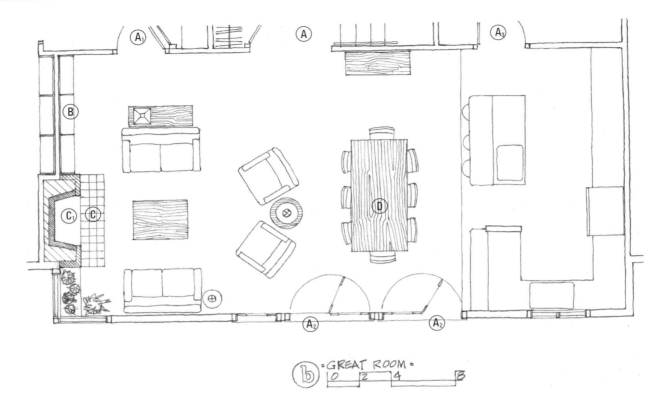

Figure 6-11b Door and passageway placement has an impact upon room use and furniture locations in large, open "great rooms."

A. Access to foyer/stairs.
   A1. Access to owner's suite.
   A2. French-door access to patio/deck.
   A3. Access to utility spaces.
B. Shelves.
C. Wood-burning fireplace with floor hearth.
   C1. Flat-screen television above mantel.
D. Dining table seats 8 with plenty of space to expand to 10.

Well-designed residences often provide a hierarchy of experience, with the great room, gathering room, or living room (and less often the dining room) providing a culminating experience that can be seen as the *height of experience* within the building. This is often done through the use of a focal point, such as a view or fireplace, through enhanced spatial definition such as a raised or specialized ceilings or floors, or through the special use of materials and finishes. Thought should be given to the hierarchy of experience within the structure and the role of the leisure space in this hierarchy.

Often an important leisure space that serves as the culmination of the building hierarchy has an adjacent or significant relationship to the building entry or foyer and related hallways and circulation spaces to the rest of the building. There is often a strong relationship between the building entry, the "most important" room or rooms (in terms of hierarchy), and the major circulation corridors.

It is also worth stating that some balance of room size and quantities should be considered. For example, a home with several large leisure spaces is best balanced with an appropriate number of bedrooms, bathrooms, general storage, and kitchen facilities to make use of the entertainment potential provided by the generous leisure spaces. This is not only an issue of supporting leisure spaces with appropriate kitchen, storage, and toilet facilities, but it can be an issue for the resale value of the property as well. For publications that provide information about design related to hierarchy of space and plan balance, please refer to the bibliography of this chapter.

RELATED CODES AND CONSTRAINTS

Many of the constraints related to the design of leisure spaces have been covered in previous chapters covering habitable spaces. The International Residential Code (IRC) includes "living rooms" as habitable spaces. Section R303 of this code (IRC, 2004) covers "Light, Ventilation, and Heating." Section R303.1 states that "all habitable rooms shall be provided with aggregate glazing area of not less than 8 percent of the floor area of such rooms. Natural ventilation shall be through windows, doors, louvers, or other approved openings to the outdoor air. Such openings shall be provided with ready access or shall otherwise be readily controllable by the building occupants. The minimum openable area to the outdoors shall be 4 percent of the floor area being ventilated."

The exception to these requirements allows for rooms to be provided with acceptable mechanical ventilation systems. In addition, there may be exceptions or broader requirements in some state and local codes. Regardless of possible exceptions, it is a good general rule to meet or exceed the ventilation and daylight requirements.

As described in previous chapters, Section R304 of the IRC covers minimum room areas and states that "every dwelling unit shall have at least one habitable room that shall have not less than 120 square feet (11.2 m²) of gross floor area" (2004). This largest required room can be the living space or major leisure space. The code goes on to state that after the required standard of the 120 square foot room is met, "other habitable rooms shall have a floor area of not less than 70 square feet (6.5 m²)." In addition, "habitable rooms shall not be less than 7 feet (2143 mm) in any horizontal dimension." This is a very minimal code requirement and is easy to meet or exceed in most rooms used for leisure spaces.

Section R305 of the IRC covers ceiling height in detail and states that habitable rooms ". . . shall have a ceiling height of not less than 7 feet (2134 mm). The required height shall be measured from the finish floor to the lowest projection from the ceiling." This section contains several exceptions related to beams, soffits, and sloped ceilings, as discussed in Chapter 3, "Bedrooms," and illustrated in Figure 3-21.

Issues that relate to leisure spaces located in basements are covered in the IRC under "Emergency Escape and Rescue Openings" in Section R310. Detailed descriptions of code requirements for basements with habitable spaces are covered in Chapter 3 and detailed in Figure 3-22.

The code issues mentioned to this point relate to single-family homes only, which are governed by the International Residential Code. State or local codes may be more stringent.

ELECTRICAL AND MECHANICAL

Unlike some other rooms in a home, most leisure spaces are not influenced to any large degree by plumbing or unusual electrical requirements. Mechanical provisions for such spaces are rather straightforward. Because the International Residential Code (Section R303.8) calls for heating to a minimum of 68°F when the winter temperature is below 60°F, most leisure spaces in the United States are required to have some form of heat source.

The location for the heat source or its registers or diffusers, as well as those used by any air-cooling source, must be considered by the interior designer as lighting, furnishings, window, and door locations are planned. The actual engineering of the heating and cooling system are, of course, done by professionals other than the interior designer. However, it is worth noting that in colder, northern climates, heat is often delivered low on or near exterior walls. In warmer climates, cool air can be delivered at higher locations at interior walls or ceiling diffusers near the center of the room.

There are some general rules for locating electrical switches and convenience outlets, and these are discussed in Chapter 1 and illustrated in Figure 1-9. Figure 6-12 shows outlets and switching locations for a larger leisure space.

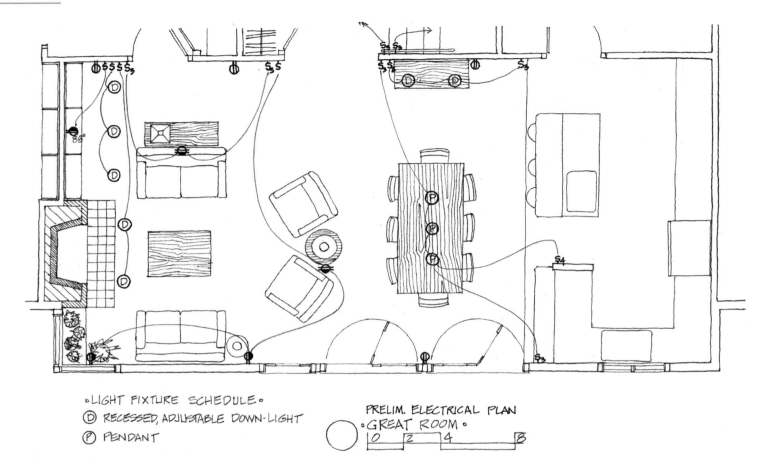

°LIGHT FIXTURE SCHEDULE°
Ⓓ RECESSED, ADJUSTABLE DOWN-LIGHT
Ⓟ PENDANT

PRELIM. ELECTRICAL PLAN
°GREAT ROOM°
0   2   4   8

Figure 6-12 Outlet and switching location for the space illustrated in Figure 6-11b; switching/lighting for kitchen area is not shown (see Figure 5-40 for a kitchen outlet and switching example). In this room, switching is included at the multiple room entry points for convenience and safety.

LIGHTING

One key to planning lighting for leisure spaces is to properly identify the activities the space is meant to support and to provide some level of flexibility for special occasions. For example, a space meant primarily for conversational interaction and occasional reading will require ambient lighting to support conversation and task lighting for reading. Flexibility in such a space could be provided through the use of dimmers, and additional focal lighting could be provided by wall washers (for lighting artwork or special room locations). Other options for flexibility are to place adjustable recessed luminaires that adjust to accommodate changes in both furniture and artwork.

Layering lighting within living rooms, gathering rooms, dens, and family rooms so that ambient lighting, task lighting, and focal lighting is provided and is somewhat flexible is a goal worth trying to achieve. Simply placing fixed downlights above seating areas in leisure spaces is not a good choice because it can create harsh shadows and make people look quite unattractive. Ceiling height is a major factor in making luminaire selection and placement choices.

Standard 8-foot ceilings are rather low for pendant fixture placement because of clearance limitations and the actual limitations of the fixture height. In rooms with lower ceilings, wall sconces can provide attractive ambient lighting. Freestanding torchères are another option in such areas, although the lighting they provide tends to be less balanced than that provided by two well-placed sconces. Both sconces and torchères work best in pairs to create even ambient

lighting. Uplights such as torchères provide the most illumination when directed up at light- or white-colored ceilings.

Rooms with higher ceilings allow for more options in luminaire selection and placement; ceilings that are 9 feet or higher allow for pendant placement, as well as cove lighting or perimeter lighting, which can create attractive ambient lighting. Sloped and beamed ceilings offer the opportunity to place lighting on top of beams and on tall walls (often using sconces or concealed fixtures). Figure 6-13 illustrates lighting for leisure spaces in rooms with varied ceiling heights.

Task lighting is most often supplied through the use of portable table and floor luminaires, as these bring the light down to the appropriate height. For reading, luminaires with shades that direct light down onto the reading surface are generally best; these often offer some degree of adjustability so that the height

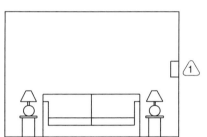

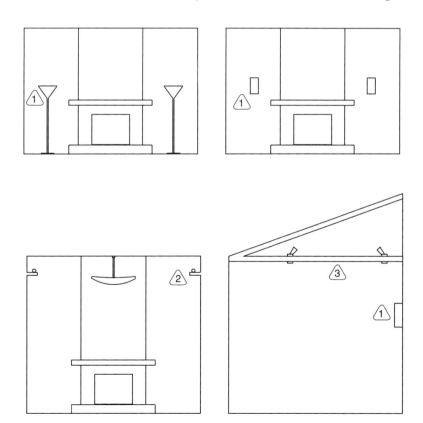

Figure 6-13 Ceiling height has an impact upon luminaire selection for ambient light in leisure spaces.

1. Sconces and torchères can provide comfortable ambient light in rooms with 8-foot ceilings (as well as those slightly higher).

2. Cove lighting can work well in ceilings over 9 feet high, as can multiple pendant luminaires.

3. Structural beams can serve as mounting surfaces for luminaires (on top or bottom surface of beam); sconces can be used to light higher portions of wall. Pendants can also be hung from ceiling surface (not shown).

Regardless of room height, adjustable recessed downlights and wall washers can provide accent lighting, as can track lighting (in situations where using other fixtures is not possible).

can be adjusted to accommodate various users. Standard table and floor models also provide light at a lower height for reading but may not direct light to the reading surface and may provide overwhelming bright spots of light at various locations throughout the room. In cases where reading lamps and other portable luminaires are used in the middle of a room, installing floor outlets solves the problem of stepping over cords. Locating such floor outlets requires that a variety of furniture arrangements are considered, so that the use of the room is not limited for future furniture arrangements—or to only one furniture arrangement.

As in many rooms, accent lighting may be provided with wall washers, recessed downlights, recessed adjustable downlights, and track lighting. Many lighting designers currently employ adjustable recessed downlights because they provide a level of flexibility that is very helpful in leisure spaces. Track lighting is not the first choice of many lighting designers, although it is used where constraints prevent adjustable, recessed downlights and wall washers. Using track lights around the perimeter of the room much like one would lay out wall wash-

ers can work in situations where using downlights or wall washers is not possible. Track lights allow flexibility, but the tracks can become a highly visible element.

Lighting design in dining rooms is very much like that described for other leisure spaces in that it requires layering of ambient and accent lighting (some types of accent lighting may also serve as task lighting in buffets and cocktail bar areas). The one element that makes dining areas different is the largest piece of furniture in most dining rooms: the table.

Traditionally, a decorative luminaire such as a chandelier is hung in a prominent central position above the dining table. This continues to be a preferable choice for many homeowners, while others prefer a more flexible approach that allows them to move the table around a bit. Locating a decorative luminaire a bit higher than a standard chandelier, or installing it in a raised portion of the ceiling, makes it a less conspicuous design element and can allow some flexibility with table placement.

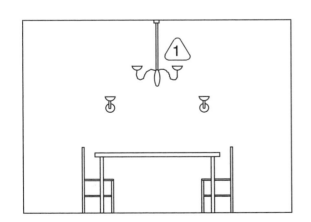

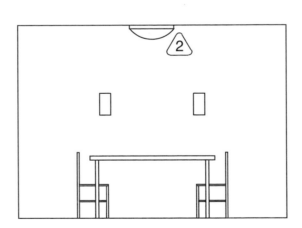

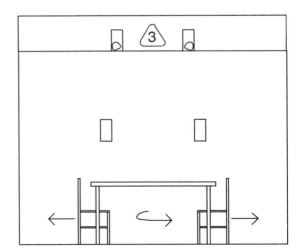

Placing a chandelier requires consideration of the proportions of the room as well as possible future locations for the dining table. Central placement can create such a strong visual presence in the room that it creates a "visual expectation" that the table be centered directly under it. If the table appears in another location, the chandelier can seem awkward and out of place. Chandelier or pendant placement height above the table requires consideration of the eye levels of those seated at the table (see Figure 6-8).

Use of a centrally placed, decorative luminaire does not eliminate the need for additional ambient light sources. Currently many lighting designers are employing adjustable recessed downlights in dining areas both as sources of fill light, used with a decorative luminaire, and as the primary source of ambient light in the room. When used as the primary source, the lights should not be pointed directly down, as this creates harsh shadows. Instead, the light should be directed to cross-illuminate various areas within the room. Sconces also work particularly well to supplement the light provided with a centrally placed decorative luminaire. See Figure 6-14 for illustrations of some dining area lighting design options.

Figure 6-14 Selected dining area lighting options.

1. Central chandelier and/or pendant placement can limit table placement options; as such, placement creates a "visual expectation" that the table be placed directly under the luminaire. In addition, luminaire height must be carefully considered so that it does not obscure vision of diners or create a physical barrier to movement. Wall sconces add pleasant fill light.

2. A luminaire mounted tightly to the ceiling surface in a central dining room location allows for greater flexibility with table placement; this location doesn't create the same "visual expectation" and allows for a variety of table locations. With this placement wall sconces can be added as at 1.

3. Recessed adjustable luminaires can provide cross-illumination, making people and food appear attractive, with fewer hard shadows than those created with fixed downlights. With this placement wall sconces can be added as at 1.

BIBLIOGRAPHY

(Contains both works cited and recommended reading. Annotations where appropriate.)

Alexander, Christopher, et al. *A Pattern Language*. New York: Oxford University Press, 1977.

Briere, Danny, and Pat Hurley. *Home Theater for Dummies*. Hoboken, NJ: John Wiley & Sons, 2003. A general guide.

Castle, Steve, and Phillip Ennis. *Great Escapes: New Designs for Home Theaters by Theo Kalomirakis*. New York: Harry N. Abrams, 2003. A lavish, coffee-table book covering the work of Theo Kalomirakis; not a planning guide but instead a review of home theaters for the very wealthy.

Ching, Francis. *Home Renovation*. New York: Van Nostrand Reinhold, 1983.

Jacobson, Max, Murray Silverstein, and Barbara Winslow. *The Good House: Contrast as a Design Tool*. Newtown, CT: The Taunton Press, 1990. This publication contains wonderful sketches and drawings and follows up on some issues raised in *A Pattern Language*. What the authors refer to as "studies of contrast" provide some guidance to hierarchy of experience and plan balance.

Karlen, Mark, and James Benya. *Lighting Design Basics*. Hoboken, NJ: John Wiley & Sons, 2004.

Panero, Julius, and Martin Zelnik. *Human Dimension and Interior Space*. New York: Whitney, 1979.

Leslie, Russell, and Kathryn Conway. *The Lighting Pattern Book for Homes*. Troy, NY: Rensselaer Polytechnic Institute, 1993.

Susanka, Sarah. *The Not So Big House: A Blueprint for the Way We Really Live*. Newtown, CT: The Taunton Press, 1998.

Whitehead, Randall. *Residential Lighting: A Practical Guide*. Hoboken, NJ: John Wiley & Sons, 2004.

CHAPTER 7

UTILITY SPACES

The *term utility* space can be used to describe a range of areas with practical uses. This chapter details such spaces, as well as the related items that may be found in them.

Garages and carports are used to store cars and other vehicles, as well as lawn and garden equipment. They may also provide general household storage and work/hobby areas. Garages and carports have a direct relationship to streets and/or alleys, as well as to an entry door or doors (and in many cases a mudroom). They may be attached to the home or freestanding. As with many of the rooms mentioned previously, garages (and garage doors) in North America have evolved to be larger over time. This has occurred due to the increasing number of cars owned by many families, as well as increased purchasing of recreational vehicles and lawn maintenance equipment. Many new homes are built with three- and four-car garages.

Some homes have equipment rooms/spaces that contain items such as the furnace, one or more hot-water heaters (some large homes require more than one), electrical panel(s), and water treatment equipment. These may be located in a basement, on a ground floor, or in the case of a furnace, perhaps in an attic space.

Hobby/craft/sewing rooms may be found in homes where people are involved with specific hobbies. These are often former bedrooms that have been fitted with appropriate work counters and storage elements to support the work being done. In the case of custom homes, such rooms may be designed and located to specifically support some important hobby or activity. In some cases such rooms are combined within a larger laundry room, in which case the issues mentioned in the following paragraphs may apply.

Laundry rooms/spaces contain laundry equipment and related storage, and when possible, spaces for related activities such as sorting, folding, and possibly ironing (and much less frequently sewing). In contrast to other types of utility spaces, laundry rooms/areas are used very frequently by occupants, particularly in large households and those with young children. Given the daily use of these spaces and the varying lifestyles of homeowners, laundry room/area placement varies greatly.

Placement of laundry rooms near bedrooms allows clothes to be kept in the area where they are removed for cleaning, sorting, and putting away. For many homeowners placement on a second floor near bedrooms (rather on a ground floor many steps from where clothes are removed and stored), is the most desirable laundry room location. Another common location for laundry rooms is near a second entrance, often a service entry or mudroom. Often such areas are adjacent to a garage and serve as a buffer between public and private realms of a home (such placement is discussed as it relates to circulation in the chapter that follows).

Location of laundry spaces within a kitchen, or just off a kitchen, is also common. This adjacency allows the person doing work in the kitchen to have easy access to the laundry. In older homes with basements, laundry areas are often located in the basement, although there is currently a remodeling trend that moves laundry areas to a top floor (near bedrooms) in such homes. In new custom home design, location of laundry rooms is often based on homeowner preferences, whereas in existing homes or new tract housing, options for laundry room placement may be quite limited by existing plumbing locations and space availability.

Another major limitation to the design and location of laundry areas is restricted space. Smaller homes, apartments, condominiums, and townhomes may simply not offer the space required to create a separate room for laundry-related activities. In such cases, laundry areas may be combined with kitchens, bathrooms, hallways, and mudrooms or second entrances. Often when part of other rooms, laundry areas are neatly hidden behind some type of door or visual screen, nicely shielding untidy items from view. Stacking appliances, which have greatly improved in performance in recent years, allow for stacked washer and dryers to take up a limited footprint, making space available for storage and folding counters or reducing the spatial requirements for the room.

In terms of homeowner's preferences, the previously mentioned NAHB survey "What 21st Century Home Buyers Want" found that home shoppers were "divided over the preferred location for their clothes washer and dryer, with 26% preferring a location near bedrooms, 26% near the kitchen, 23% in the basement, and 10% in the garage." The range of preferences most probably has to do with owner's lifestyle preferences, whether there are children in the home, the age (and level of mobility) of the respondents, as well as simply what people are accustomed to in their own homes.

Clearly, deciding on the best location and room design requires careful consultation regarding homeowner's preferences and a careful review of the overall building design. Location of the room relative to other areas of the home is also discussed in the "Organizational Flow" section of this chapter.

ACCESSIBILITY

Generally, designing utility spaces for wheelchair users requires providing adequate circulation space to the various areas, with no steps (changes of floor level) along the way, and providing enough wheelchair turning space and clear space for wheelchair access in front of appliances and work areas. In designing accessible garages, thought must be given to creating no steps between the garage and most immediate entrance, as well to allowing 32 inches of clear circulation space for all portions of the path of travel.

For laundry areas, front-loading appliances work very well for wheelchair users. Controls must also be within reach limitations. In addition, all appliances require clear access space. While some front-loading washers and dryers are stackable, a side-by-side arrangement allows much easier seated use and facilitates transferring laundry. In case where front-loading versions are not used, assistive devices are available for wheelchair users and those who have mobility limitations; however, this is not an ideal design solution. Accessible laundry room shelves and counters must be located within the comfortable reach range for seated users. For more information on actual clear space requirements and mounting heights, please see the "Ergonomics and Clearances" section of this chapter.

APPLIANCES

Washing machines come in a variety of loading types including front-loading and top-loading models. Front-loading models are gaining in popularity due to their good washing performance, large capacity, and efficient use of energy and water. In response to this, manufacturers have developed top-loading models that offer some of the advantages of the front loaders. All types of washing machines have become more efficient due to consumer demand as well as stricter Federal Department of Energy standards regulating water and energy use.

Both front-loading and top-loading models are available in full-sized models that are roughly 27 inches wide. Considering size is critical for fitting into cabinetry, closets, and small rooms. Compact models are typically 24 inches wide and can be stacked with compact dryers of the same width. Information on appliance sizes can be found in Figure 7-1.

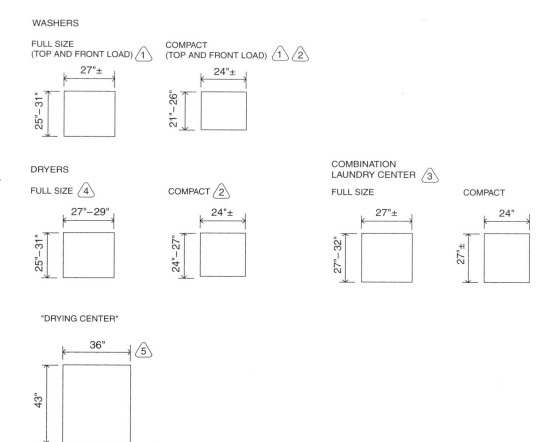

Figure 7-1 Washer and dryer sizes (plan views).

1. Front-load models are typically 34 to 38 inches high, with matching pedestals available that raise door height to prevent stooping and bending; pedestals often offer storage and are roughly 12 inches. Top-load models are typically higher than front-load models, at roughly 36 to 42 inches high.
2. Compact models are roughly 33 inches plus-or-minus high and can fit under standard countertops.
3. Heights vary from 71 to 75 inches, plus or minus.
4. Heights vary from 36 to 42 inches, plus or minus.
5. Heights vary from 71 to 75 inches, plus or minus.

Clothes dryers may use gas or electricity to heat the air. Additionally, dryers vary in how sensors are programmed to shut off, which can be done by way of a thermostat or moisture sensors. Full-sized models measure between 27-inch and 29-inch widths, and as with washers, size is critical. Front-mounted controls on some models allow stacking the dryer atop a front-loading washer.

Some manufacturers offer a "drying center," which consists of a standard dryer surrounded by hanging drying areas. These are generally quite large (36 inches wide, 40-plus inches deep, and roughly 75 inches high).

Compact models are generally electric and are roughly 24 inches wide, with a drum capacity roughly half that of full-sized models. They can be stacked atop a companion washer. Some compact dryers operate on 120 volts, while others require a 240-volt outlet (as do full-sized electric dryers). Gas dryers are more costly to purchase but may result in lower energy costs long term (this will vary based on world energy costs).

A combination washer and dryer, a single appliance, similar to stacked units, is another space-saving option. These are available with gas or electric dryers in

Figure 7-2 Kitchen cabinet manufacturers make laundry room cabinets that are similar to kitchen cabinets in size and construction. In addition, cabinets in special sizes and with special laundry-related fittings such as hampers and foldout ironing boards are available. The wall cabinets shown are deeper and taller than standard kitchen wall cabinets, to accommodate a front-load washer and dryer on a pedestal. Photograph courtesy of KraftMaid Cabinetry.

full-sized and compact sizes. Space saving is also supplied by units that combine washing and drying in a single unit. Such models use the same drum for washing and drying.

One additional consideration in washer/dryer utility spaces is noise. In small living spaces, or those where the utility space is in close proximity to leisure or sleeping spaces, quiet models should be selected. Front-loading washers are generally considered less noisy than top-loading models, but this varies with the model selected. Appliance noise is less of an issue when appliances are located in a separate room with a door.

Compact washer and dryer models are typically available in heights that allow them to sit under standard counter height.

Storage provided by cabinetry can be much like that discussed for kitchens and baths. Laundry rooms/areas are made much more useful with the inclusion of work counters for folding and sorting clothing. In addition, storage for laundry products and other household items can be provided with built-in cabinetry. Generally speaking, cabinets designed for kitchen use can be used in laundry and hobby/craft/sewing rooms. Manufacturers of kitchen cabinets make fittings and specialty units for use in utility rooms; these include hampers, ironing boards, and special height/depth wall cabinets that accommodate front-load washers/dryers on pedestals (see Figure 7-2).

ERGONOMICS AND REQUIRED CLEARANCES

Generally, laundry rooms require appropriate space for the desired appliances as well as clear space in front of appliances to access them. Figure 7-3 illustrates standard clearances for washers, dryers, and ironing boards, as well as wheelchair clearances and reaching heights for laundry rooms.

Garages and carports require space for circulation around the car, as well as room for door clearance and, of course, room enough for the car itself. These spaces should allow a range of car sizes. Carports may be designed to include storage spaces, and these may provide secure storage (when locked) for items often stored in garages, such as sporting and lawn equipment. Figure 7-4 illustrates a range of car sizes and minimum clearance spaces recommended for garages and carports. Figure 7-5 illustrates additional issues related to garage sizes, clearances, and design.

STANDARD CLEARANCES

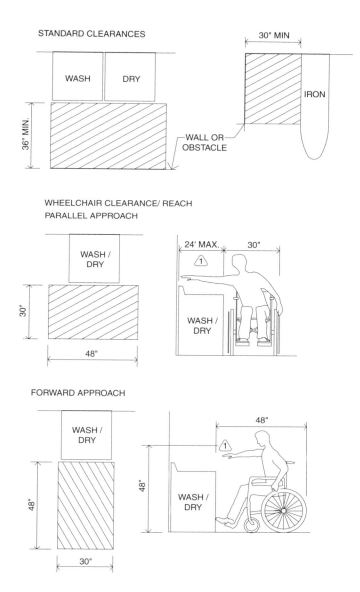

WHEELCHAIR CLEARANCE/ REACH
PARALLEL APPROACH

FORWARD APPROACH

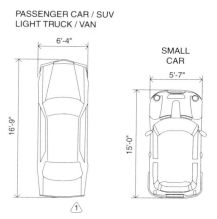

PASSENGER CAR / SUV
LIGHT TRUCK / VAN

SMALL
CAR

Figure 7-4 Car sizes and garage/carport clearances.

1. Some SUVs and pickup trucks may be up to 17 feet, 9 inches long.

2. To increase this dimension sufficiently to allow wheelchair access would require a 22-foot-wide (minimum outside dimension) garage; 24 feet would be preferable. See double car garage example in Figure 7-5.

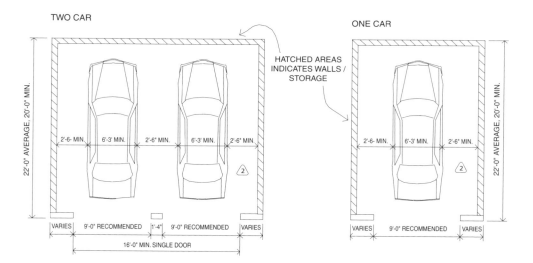

TWO CAR

ONE CAR

HATCHED AREAS INDICATES WALLS / STORAGE

Figure 7-3 Standard and wheelchair clearances for laundry room/space items.

1. Equipment controls must be within this zone (controls must be within reach height of wheelchair user, typically on the top/front of a front-load model for comfortable access).

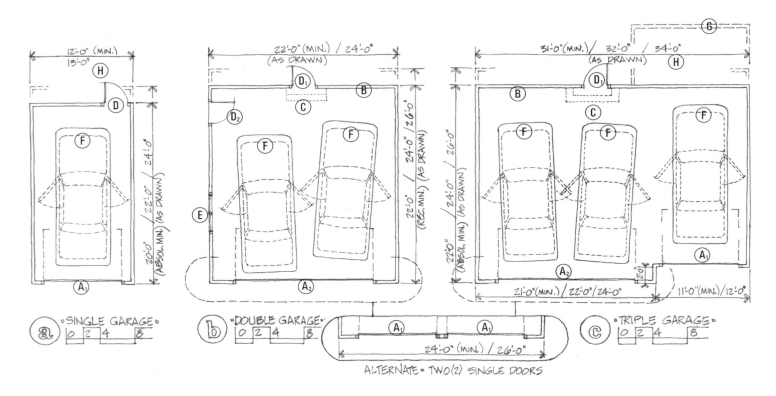

Figure 7-5 Dimensional requirements for one-, two-, and three-car garages.

A1. Single, 9-foot-wide minimum by 7-foot/8-foot height.

A2. Double, 16-foot-wide minimum by 7-foot/8-foot height. Alternative, larger doors; as large SUVs have become more common, homeowners may desire taller doors. Wider doors have also become more common:
- Single: 10 feet wide by 8 feet high.
- Double: 18 feet wide by 8 feet high.

B. As noted in the "Related Codes and Constraints" section, in attached garages fire-rated walls and doors are required between the house and garage, as is a fire-rated ceiling if there is habitable space above the garage.

C. Houses that are built over basement or crawl spaces will require steps up from the garage (floor) level to the house floor level; this is generally provided by a minimum of two steps that are 7 inches, plus or minus, each.

D. Passage doors (2 feet, 6 inches to 3 feet).

D1. Although not a requirement, garage-to-house door will generally swing into the house.

D2. Garage-to-exterior door can swing in or out, but commonly swings in. There is no requirement for this door except in code jurisdictions where a second exit out of the house can be through the garage; in such cases the overhead garage door would not be a legal exit.

E. Windows. None required; but if provided, select windows that relate visually to those used in the house.

F. Vehicle icons show a small car (dashed line) and a larger car (solid line); the solid line represents the footprint of vehicle such as an SUV or van.

G. Ancillary space for storage can be achieved by adding depth (front to back) to the garage, or in some cases, the footprint of the attached house may allow space for an alcove (this can be used for shop or storage).

H. Use of larger doors (such as 10-foot width for single and 18-foot for double) will typically require larger building width.

ORGANIZATIONAL FLOW

As stated previously, laundry room placement varies greatly and relates to adjacent spaces and their uses, as well as overall spatial limitations and constraints. Laundry room design also varies greatly in items included and overall space used. Clearly, there is quite a range of workable possibilities. Some reasonable options are illustrated here to convey various possible room and space sizes. Figure 7-6 shows some small utility rooms and closets.

Figures 7-7 and 7-8 illustrate larger utility rooms, some of which serve combined purposes. These larger rooms are shown with a bubble diagram of adjacent spaces in order to convey spatial relationships within the residence.

Figure 7-6 Utility closets.
A. Stacking washer and dryer.
B. Small base cabinet with door.
B1. Wall cabinet for laundry supplies.
C. Counter (at 36 inches high) with clothes hamper below.
D. Utility sink.
E. Electrical service panel requires (per the IRC) a 3-foot by 2-foot, 6-inch (width) by 6-foot, 6-inch (height) clear space (E1) in front of the electrical panel for service access.
F. Floor drain for water heater and condensate from furnace/air conditioner.
G. Return air to furnace; ideally mixing with some outside, tempered, fresh air.
H. Sliding doors on three tracks.
Note: Water heater and furnace equipment vary greatly in terms of size; items shown are average sizes.

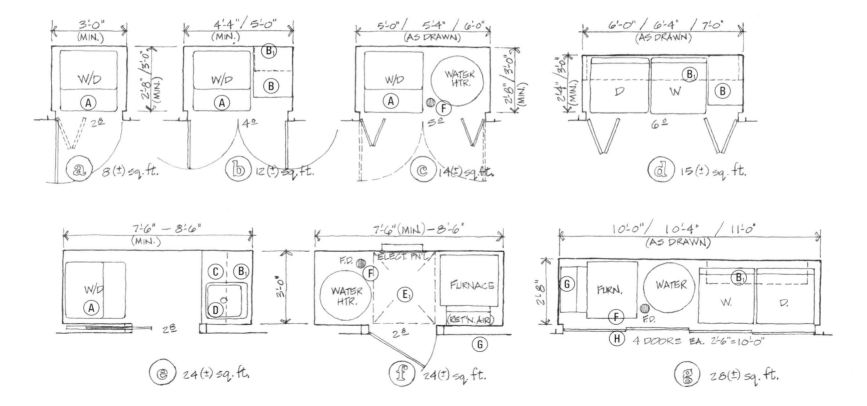

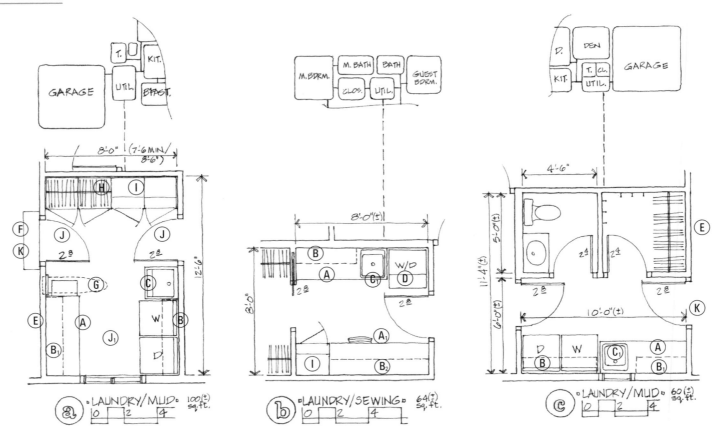

Figure 7-7 Laundry rooms.

A. Work counter for sorting and folding clothes with hamper below. Lower work
counter required for sewing (28-inch height, shown at A1).

B. Wall cabinet for laundry/cleaning supplies and so on.

B1. General storage.

B2. Sewing supplies.

C. Utility sink.

C1. Deep utility sink in base cabinet.

D. Stacking washer/dryer.

E. As noted in the "Related Codes and Constraints" section, in attached garages, fire-
rated walls and doors are required between the house and garage, as is a fire-rated
ceiling if there is habitable space above the garage. See "Related Codes and
Constraints" for additional information.

F. Steps to garage, as required.

G. Semi-recessed fold-down ironing board, with fixed bench below.

H. Wardrobe cabinet.

I. Pantry-style cabinet for laundry/cleaning supplies and equipment and/or remote
food storage.

J. Through circulation; this is a short distance and the circulation avoids laundry work
areas (J1).

K. Door leads to the garage as shown; an alternate design would allow exit directly to
the exterior (exterior steps may be required).

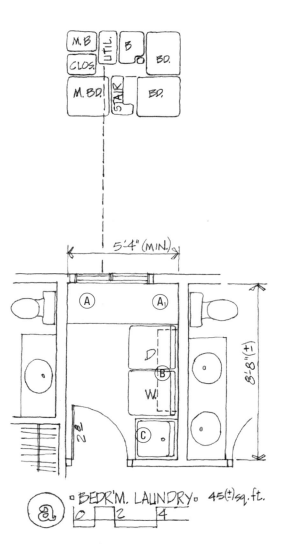

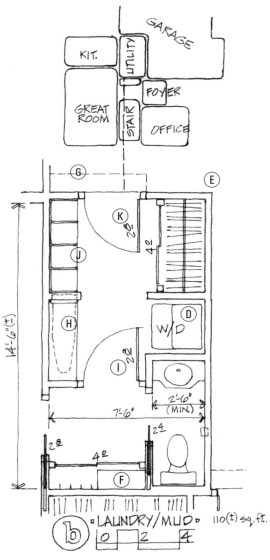

Figure 7-8 Laundry rooms.

A. Work counter for sorting and folding clothes with hamper below. The disadvantage of this arrangement is dead corners below at A1.

B. Wall cabinet for laundry/cleaning supplies.

C. Utility sink.

D. Stacking washer/dryer.

E. As noted in the "Related Codes and Constraints" section, in attached garages, fire-rated walls and doors are required between the house and garage, as is a fire-rated ceiling if there is habitable space above the garage. See "Related Codes and Constraints" for additional information.

F. Closet (12 inches deep, with sliding doors) for laundry/cleaning supplies and equipment.

G. Steps to garage, as required.

H. Semi-recessed fold-down ironing board, with fixed bench below.

I. A door can be useful at this location; serves as an acoustic and visual barrier.

J. Cubbyholes/open storage for outerwear, boots, and so on.

K. Door leads to the garage as shown; an alternate design would allow exit directly to the exterior (exterior steps may be required).

RELATED CODES AND CONSTRAINTS

According to the International Residential Code, laundry rooms and utility spaces are not considered habitable rooms and therefore need not meet previously mentioned requirements such as minimum room dimensions and window requirements. Most codes related to laundry areas relate to electrical and plumbing and are covered in the section that follows. Local codes may require second-floor (or higher) clothes washers to sit on an overflow pan (laundry tray) to prevent water overflow from pouring onto the floor and intruding into the ceiling below.

Section R309 of the IRC governs garages and carports and requires that "the garage shall be separated from the residence and its attic area by not less than ½ inch (127 mm) gypsum board applied to the garage side" (R309.2). This section also calls for garages beneath habitable rooms to be "separated from habitable rooms above by not less than ⅝ inch (15.9 mm), Type X gypsum board or equivalent." This section of the code also requires that the floor surface in garages be of "approved noncombustible material" and should be sloped to facilitate draining. The IRC also requires that, if installed, automatic door openers "be listed in accordance with UL 325"(R309.6). Carports are required to be open on a minimum of two sides, with a noncombustible, sloped floor surface (R309.4).

ELECTRICAL AND MECHANICAL

Section E3603.3 of the International Residential Code requires a minimum of "one 20 ampere-rated branch circuit" for receptacles in the laundry area, and these "shall serve only receptacle outlets located in the laundry area." In addition to these items required by code, an electric dryer may require a 240-volt circuit.

Continuing the IRC, Section E3801.5 states that "appliance receptacle outlets installed for specific appliances, such as laundry equipment, shall be installed with-in 6 feet (1829 mm) of the intended location of the appliance"; and E3801.8 states, "At least one receptacle outlet shall be installed to serve laundry appliances." This code also requires that basements and garages have at least one receptacle outlet in addition to any provided laundry equipment (E3801.9).

Regarding storage and equipment spaces, Section E3803.4 states, "in attics, under-floor spaces, utility rooms and basements, at least one lighting outlet shall be installed where these spaces are suited for storage or contain equipment requiring servicing." The section continues by stating that the required lighting outlet "shall be controlled by a wall switch or shall have an integral switch."

Dryers vent heat and water vapor, including some lint, through a duct that must attach to the machine and carry exhaust to the building exterior. *Consumer Reports* states that flexible dryer ducts made of foil or plastic can prove problematic because they can sag and allow lint buildup at low points. For this reason it is best to select rigid metal or flexible metal ducts.

LIGHTING

In most cases, utility room lighting is rather utilitarian in nature, providing minimal general lighting, especially in equipment rooms, storage areas, and garages. Because they are rooms in which a range of visual tasks is performed, laundry rooms are made more pleasant, useful, and comfortable with well-designed lighting features. Laundry room and hobby/craft/sewing room cabinetry and work counters are similar to those in kitchens, and therefore room lighting for these is much like that in kitchens. Under-cabinet lighting can provide helpful task lighting, while top-of-cabinet lighting as well as pendant luminaires can create pleasant ambient lighting, making the many hours spent doing laundry more pleasing. Reviewing information in Chapter 4 about kitchen area lighting can aid in planning laundry and hobby/craft/sewing rooms. Figure 7-9 is an electrical/lighting plan illustrating some options for utility area lighting.

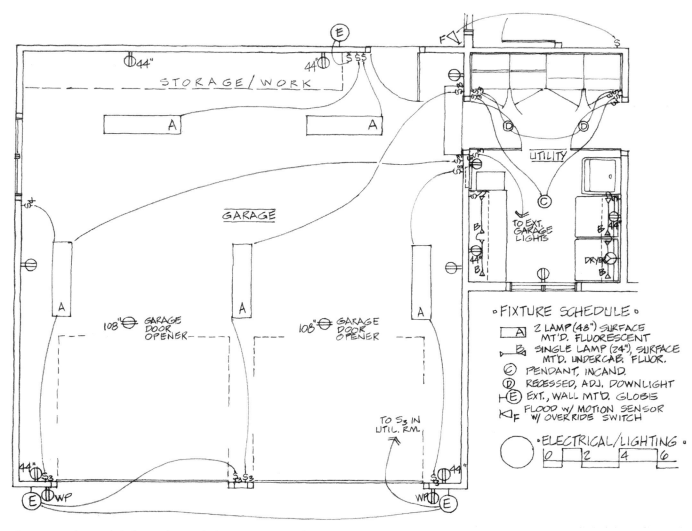

Figure 7-9 Electrical/lighting plan. Includes some options for utility area lighting as well as related exterior fixtures.

BIBLIOGRAPHY

(Contains both works cited and recommended reading. Annotations where appropriate.)

Consumer Reports. "Buying Advice: Clothes Dryers." February 27, 2006. http://www.consumerreports.org/cro/appliances/clothes-dryers/reports/how-to-choose/

International Code Council. *International Residential Code 2003.* Florence, KY: Thomson Delmar Learning, 2003.

National Association of Home Builders. "Housing Facts, Figures, and Trends 2004: What 21st Century Home Buyers Want." Washington, DC: NAHB Advocacy/Public Affairs and the HAHB Economics Group, 2004.

Rumbarger, Janet, and Richard Vitullo, eds. *Architectural Graphic Standards for Residential Construction.* Hoboken, NJ: John Wiley & Sons, 2003.

CHAPTER 8

CIRCULATION SPACES

Circulation refers to the areas provided for movement within and along spaces. Providing adequate space for movement is essential and requires careful consideration of ergonomics, scale, and organizational flow. In addition to allowing for physical movement, circulation spaces provide for psychological transition from one type of space to another and/or from one territory to the next. The way we move from one place to another colors our experience of that place and therefore is a significant contributing factor to the quality of designed environments.

Much has been written about the significance of the main entry in residential design in terms of providing a symbolic transition space between public and private domains. Writing in *A Philosophy of Interior Design*, Stanley Abercrombie states, "In our own culture, rather than plunge directly into the heart of an interior, into its living room full of conversation . . . we prefer some transitional area." He also writes that entrances are "a physical transition point, obviously, and also a mental one, the entrant bringing into the interior memories of the exterior. . . ." In this discussion Abercrombie is pointing out the role the entry plays symbolically, as well as how important the design of the space is in terms of articulation of the entry area relative to the architectural form of the building.

The seminal book *A Pattern Language* by Christopher Alexander et al. explores entrances and circulation space in detail. Several of the patterns relate directly to building entry. For example, Pattern 112 reads:

"Buildings, and especially houses, with a graceful transition between the street and the inside, are more tranquil than those which open directly off the street.

The experience of entering a building influences the way you feel inside the building. If the transition is too abrupt there is no feeling of arrival, and the inside of the building fails to be an inner sanctum."

Also, in discussing entry area design, the authors of *A Pattern Language* continue with the description of a space that allows people "to settle down completely into the more intimate spirit appropriate to a house."

Clearly, the placement, location, and physical qualities of entry areas can provide not only an aesthetic experience—an adequate, safe passage area—but also a psychological barrier or symbolic transition between the outside world and the inner sanctum of a home. As stated in the introductory chapter, there are zones of intimacy related to public and private territories within the home, and the entry area is the key buffer zone between the most public portions of a home and the more private areas, as shown in Figure 8-1.

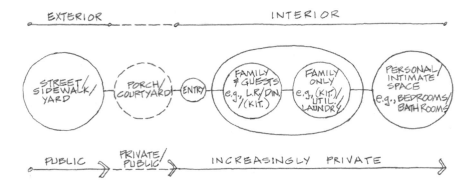

Figure 8-1 Bubble diagram illustrating public and private realms, with the entry area serving as a transition between the two realms.

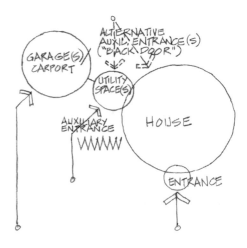

Figure 8-2 Bubble diagram illustrating main and adjacent entry areas.

An understanding of issues of privacy and territoriality can shape the design of the building entrance or entrances; however, additional cultural, geographic, and site-related issues impact the design and location of residential entrances. For example, in some locales, entering through the rear or back door of the house is common; neighbors and guests come to the back door to enter the house rather

than approaching the front. This is particularly true when the building has an alley serving the rear portion of the house. In cases where the homeowners wish to receive guests only through the front, the design of the house can enforce such an entrance by screening auxiliary entrances (as shown in the diagram in Figure 8-2).

In climates with extreme weather, a mudroom is often required not only for family members but in some cases for guests as well, and use of this room must be considered as entrances are designed. Additionally, depending on the design, homeowners enter houses through the garage. In such instances, a buffer or transition area can be created between the garage and other rooms of the house. This can be done with a room or series of rooms that serve utility purposes, as shown in Figure 8-2. Locating a coat closet and/or additional storage in such a room proves helpful as a place to shed outer clothes, shoes, bags, and so on and aids in the transition from public to private space or from "messy" to "tidy," depending on the situation.

Movement within a structure such as a residence can be horizontal (hallways/corridors); entirely vertical (elevators, fireman's pole), mostly vertical (ladders and circular stairs), or a combination (most stairs). Any of these can become strong design elements, facilitating the drama of movement. Vertical movement has the potential of being more interesting than horizontal; stairs are generally more dramatic than ramps (with notable exceptions, such as Wright's Guggenheim Museum). Steps are often used as a staging device in dramatic productions (for example, the use of steps and stairs on the set of the television show *Cheers* is familiar to more than one generation of television viewers). There is little visible drama in moving vertically in an elevator, unless it is a glass elevator, and then the drama is increased exponentially.

Much like the building entrance, the stairs should be one of the first things to be considered and remain a priority throughout the entire design process. Because they take up a significant amount of space, they dictate flow and need careful consideration from the beginning. The interior designer should be comfortable in manipulating stairs as easily as any other space. In order to gain such a comfort level, an understanding of the variations of vertical movement is required. Toward that end, an overview of the various means of vertical movement follows.

Forms of vertical circulation vary from fully upright ladders (at 90°) to gently sloping ramps at 4°, as shown in Figures 8-3 and 8-4. Each form of vertical movement has advantages and disadvantages related to use of space and ease of use, with some types clearly most useful in a residential setting, as described in the following paragraphs as well as in the captions for Figures 8-3 and 8-4.

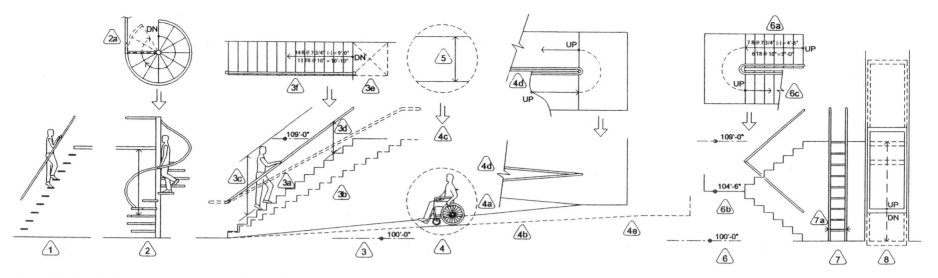

Figure 8-3 Graphic depiction of a wide range of possibilities for vertical movement; all examples are shown with a 9-foot floor-to-floor height, although a wide range of floor-to-floor heights is possible. Those shown are residential examples with two exceptions: public building requirements (per ADAAG) for a stair and a ramp, to show their more restrictive requirements. Shown here are ranges of configurations required for functions that involve vertical and/or horizontal movement as well as the generally accepted angle limits of each mode of vertical movement. For additional codes information see the "Related Codes and Constraints" section of this chapter.

1. Ships ladders. Not a legal egress stair in most codes; some local codes may allow use in access to and egress from attics and/or limited-size open lofts. The angle (slope) of a ship's ladder can vary a great deal: 50 to 75 degrees (see Figure 8-4); the example shown is 65 degrees (10 inches [−] R [riser] and 4½ inches [+] TR [tread]).

2. Spiral stairs. The steepest of the legal residential stairs (IRC R311.5.8); risers can be as much as 9½ inches (9 inches is shown) and minimum width can be 26 inches. The number of risers must be sufficient (of sufficient height) to create sufficient headroom (6 feet, 6 inches minimum) within three-fourths of a circle, so the user does not hit his head on the landing above (which almost always occupies one-fourth of the full circle; see 2a). The footprint of a spiral stair can be as small as 22 square feet, without exceeding the maximum riser criteria and with meeting the minimum tread depth requirement of the applicable code.

3. Straight-run stairs: maximum horizontal movement of all the stairs shown.
   3a. Profile shown is at a maximum slope for a residential stair (IRC): 7¾-inch risers; 10-inch treads (37-plus degrees).
   3b. Profile shown (with dotted line) is at maximum slope for stair that is accessible to the public. 7-inch risers; 11-inch treads; (32 [+] degrees) per ADAAG and IBC.
   3c. Required headroom (stair and landings). 6 feet, 8 inches, measured from the plane of the nosings.
   3d. Required handrail(s). 34- to 38-inch height (vertically from nose); 35 inches is shown.

3e. Required landing (top and bottom). 36 by 36 inches (minimum).
3f. Always one fewer tread than riser.

4. Ramps:
   4a. Residential. Profile shown is maximum slope for residential use: 1:8 slope (7-plus degrees), (12.5 percent); see also the "Related Codes and Constraints" section of this chapter. This slope will require assistance for many wheelchair users.
   4b. Public. 1:12 slope is the maximum slope mandated by ADAAG; together with the required handrails and landing, intended for independent (unassisted) use by most wheelchair users.
   4c. Required headroom (at ramp and landings). 6 feet, 8 inches (necessary for ambulatory users).
   4d. Required handrails similar to stairs.
   4e. Maximum ramp length (between landings). 30 feet (per ADAAG).

5. Hallways. 36-inch minimum width; no legal maximums.

6. "U" stairs, aka "scissor" or "switchback" stairs:
   6a. Profile shown is at maximum slope (per IRC); thus, each run: 7 R @ 7¾ inches = 4 feet, 6 inches (total rise to landing) 6 TR @ 10 inches = 5 feet (run).
   6b. The landing splits the 9-foot floor-to-floor height exactly in half (not a requirement); the landing should occur at a point where both runs of the stair will have identical, individual riser dimensions.
   6c. The break line is used to break the "up" run.

7. Vertical ladder. Rungs 12 inches plus or minus O.C., width 18 inches (7a); results in the smallest footprint necessary to go from floor to floor (with the exception of a firefighter's pole); it is not a legal stair in a residence. These require descending backwards (facing the ladder). Rungs and side rails used for hand grip. 24 inches (width) required if confined by sidewalls.

8. Elevators. An increasingly common mode of residential floor-to-floor travel for those who have trouble negotiating stairs (including, but not limited to, wheelchair users). A modest footprint of 16 to 24 square feet is required for the clear inside hoistway.

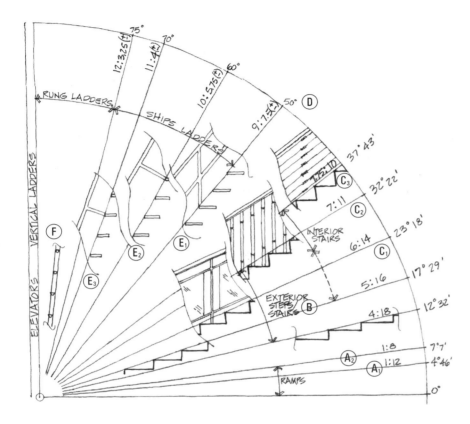

Figure 8-4 The range of configurations required for functions that involve vertical and/or horizontal movement, as well as the generally accepted angle limits of each mode of vertical movement; for example, answering the question, when is a stair a stair rather than a ladder?

A. Ramps

   A1. 1:12 slope (1 unit or vertical rise/drop in 12 units of horizontal distance); legal maximum slope for unassisted wheelchair use per ADAAG; with appropriate width: 4 feet; landings (5 feet) at 30 feet maximum apart; and handrails on both sides.

   A2. 1:8 slope; suitable for small vertical rises in *residences*; minimum width: 3 feet;

handrails required on at least one side. For use by the ambulatory who have difficulty with steps and by wheelchair users—most of whom will need assistance at the 1:8 slope (see also the "Related Codes and Constraints" section of this chapter).

B. Exterior steps/stairs. Slope can vary a great deal; the limits of range of slope shown is not absolute but is a good rule-of-thumb range. For example:

   4-inch riser with an 18-inch tread

   5-inch riser with a 16-inch tread

   6-inch riser with a 14-inch tread

   7-inch riser with an 11- to 12-inch tread

The tread surface should slope slightly (1 to 2 percent) to shed water. The exact tread/riser ratio of the exterior steps is often influenced by the slope of the adjacent ground slope and how much horizontal space is available (to spread out) to accomplish the vertical transition.

C. Interior steps/stairs (with appropriate/required handrails). 23(+) degrees − 37(+) degrees.

   C1. 6:14 represents a reasonable, working minimum slope (there is no legal minimum); a lesser slope would require an inordinate amount of space (e.g., a 5-inch R/15-inch TR stair would take 33 feet of horizontal distance [with required top and bottom landings] to handle a modest 9-foot floor-to-floor height [total vertical rise]).

   C2. 7:11 represents the maximum slope for a stair in a public building (ADAAG and IBC requirements).

   C3. 7.75:10 represents the maximum residential stair slope allowed by code (IRC), the exception being spiral stairs. Certain local codes may allow an 8-inch riser (maximum) and 9-inch tread (minimum).

D. 50 degrees; generally considered to be the point at which even an able-bodied, well-coordinated adult can no longer go up or down the stair without assistance of handrails. However, all stairs are required to have at least one handrail, so the point becomes moot.

E. Ladders are allowed by some codes (not IRC) for access to open lofts of limited size or attics, or in some cases, as an access in addition to a legal exit stair. Examples of ship's ladders (50 to 70 degrees) follow:

   E1. 9 inches R − 7½ inches TR.

   E2. 10 inches R − 5¾ inches TR.

   E3. 11 inches R − 4 inches TR.

F. Vertical, or near vertical, rung ladders have rungs 12 to 13 inches O.C.; minimum width of ladder: 18 inches (24 inches if confined by walls).

Elevators and spiral stairs and ladders require the smallest footprint and generally involve little or no horizontal movement while making the vertical transition from level to level. The traveler moves up to the destination level, directly above or below where he or she started. Stairs and ramps can move the traveler a goodly distance horizontally (for example, one can start the trip from floor to floor on one side of the house and wind up on the other). The use of a "switchback" stair or ramp (also known as scissor stairs) will more closely emulate a spiral stair because the traveler winds up on the destination floor approximately above or below where they started.

Generally speaking, ramps are seldom used in the interiors of a residence except for small vertical changes or in those cases where the design of the house is centered around movement (for example, a linear house that "cascades" down a hillside, with the ramp becoming the spine of the house). Ramps consume significant space and are therefore largely relegated to the exterior, where there is more space.

An understanding of the various terms related to stair design and construction is necessary, as these terms are very specific and have significant design implications. Stair *treads* are the horizontal upper surfaces where the foot is placed,

while *risers* are the vertical face of a step/stair. The edge of a stair tread that extends over the riser is referred to as the nosing or nose. The nosing is often rounded, which makes it less likely to cause feet to catch and decreases the risk of tripping, and more comfortable when in contact with the body. The sum of all treads is referred to as the total *run* of the stair, while the rise is the sum of all risers. Figure 8-5 provides an illustration of stair elements, terms, and constructions.

Figure 8-5 An illustration of stair elements, terms, and construction.

A. The term "step" can be somewhat ambiguous, since there is, in any given run of stairs (between floors/landings), *always one fewer tread than riser*. As a general rule, refer to the number of risers when describing rudimentary information about any stair.

B. The riser dimension is from tread surface to tread surface, and it should always be constant in any given run of stairs.

C. The sum of all the risers is the rise of the stair, which will be the floor-level-to-floor-level (or landing-to-landing) dimension.

D. The tread dimension is measured from nose to nose, rendering the "tread surface" (almost always) larger (see also "Ergonomics and Required Clearances" section of this chapter).

E. The sum of all tread dimensions equals the "run" of the stair.

F. The odds of a safe trip up (or especially down) the stair are enhanced by the ability to steady oneself with a hand on a suitable handrail during those times, during each step, that support is only on one foot. The handrail needs to be stable (sturdy) and either/or:

> Wall mounted (on a wall or half wall)
> Open balusters

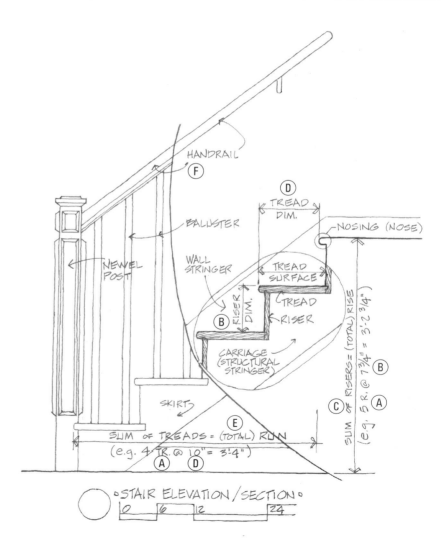

A stair landing is, as the term implies, a place to "land" if you were to fall. The IRC calls for a landing every 12 feet of vertical rise and a 36-inch landing at the *top and bottom* of every stair run. Obviously the top landing is required because it is not a good idea to reach the top of a stair only to be knocked back down by running into a wall 18 inches away. For more information on codes, refer to the "Related Codes and Constraints" section of this chapter.

It is worth noting that vertical movement on stairs can be hazardous; it would be an unusual person who has never had a fall of some sort on a stair. Approximately 50,000 people are hospitalized each year in the United States for accidents occurring on stairs; thousands more are injured and not hospitalized. Given such statistics, safety should be a significant consideration in stair design. One safety rule of thumb: The steeper the ascent and descent, the more risk is involved, making ladders more dangerous than stairs. Ramps create the least potential for accidents in terms of vertical circulation.

Most of us can think back to our own incidents with stairs and note that when accidents have occurred, they likely did so in the act of descending the stair rather than ascending. Older people often take to traversing stairs in their homes by descending the stairs backward (like younger people would come down a ladder). This is done because such an approach offsets many of the risks inherent in descending stairs. Please refer to the "Ergonomics and Required Clearances" section for a more complete analysis of this phenomenon.

Interestingly, one- and two-step stairs prove more hazardous than multiple steps; this is not because one falls as far as a full floor-to-floor stair, but because fewer stairs are more difficult to see—and the most dangerous steps/stairs are the ones you don't see. This does not mean that such configurations should be avoided, but they require strong visual cues to the user. Such visual cues can be provided through a change of flooring materials, the sloping appearance of handrails, a change of color/texture/materials, and of course, adequate lighting.

In terms of safety, it is important to see the stairs, but once movement within the stairs is in process, there should not be any surprises. In fact, one of the first rules of stair design is to create no surprises. An example of a hidden surprise, one that is not likely discernible from the initial assessment, is a difference in riser height or tread depth from step to step. Nothing will trip up the stair user faster than a shift in anticipated rhythm.

While spiral and curved (also known as winding) stairs do not have treads that are uniform in depth (across the width of the stair), users tend to compensate for that phenomenon by perhaps being more careful and counting on the fact that treads are all the same shape (or consistency). The principal safety issue with spiral stairs is the difficulty of meeting another user coming in the opposite direction, forcing one of the users toward the inside where the treads are at their narrowest. This potential hazard can be avoided by one user waiting for the other to complete the trip.

Specific information about required clearances and dimensions for vertical and horizontal circulation can be found in the "Ergonomics and Required Clearances" section of this chapter, whereas information about traffic flow and organization can be found in the "Organizational Flow" section. For the most part, this chapter covers circulation related to moving from one room or space to the next, rather than circulation within rooms. Information about circulation within rooms and spaces can be found in the individual chapters; for example, bedroom circulation is covered in Chapter 3, "Bedrooms."

ACCESSIBILITY

Designing accessible spaces requires that adequate circulation be provided. Indeed, allowing universal entrance into a home is a key element of visitable design, as is allowing accessible circulation to a ground-floor bathroom. These are generally accomplished by providing 32 inches of clear space at doorways and 36 inches of clear space at hallways. Throughout the ground floor, providing adequate clear space for wheelchair movement is required, as is allowing for adequate turning space or space that allows for changing direction for the wheelchair.

In designing accessible vertical circulation, ramps or elevators must be provided, as stairs are problematic for wheelchair users and those with mobility limitations and significant difficulty with balance. It is also worth noting that many people benefit from the use of well-designed handrails as a component of vertical circulation. Handrails provide stability for a range of users throughout their life span. They should therefore be incorporated into the design of stairs and ramps. In addition, most codes require them. For detailed information about required clearances, spatial requirements, and dimensional information for accessible circulation, see the "Ergonomics and Required Clearances" and "Related Codes and Constraints" sections of this chapter.

ERGONOMICS AND REQUIRED CLEARANCES

Hallways and stairs are designed for the average adult. In motion, the average adult will have a 24- to 26-inch pace and require a clear space a minimum of 22 inches wide. That rule of thumb has become a moving target in an age of plentiful food, where the average adult size keeps growing—in both directions (see Figure 8-6). Wheelchair-accessible circulation routes (hallways) should be 36 inches minimum width except as noted in Figure 8-6.

The code minimum in a residential setting is 36 inches wide for a hallway or stair. However, this is not optimum, as persons meeting in such a space will have to pause, slow down, and possibly turn sideways. In the case of stairs, one of the

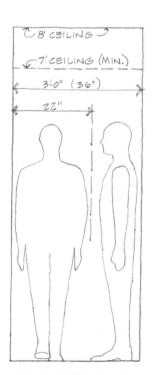

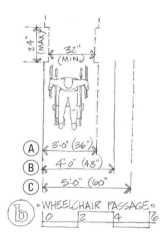

Figure 8-6 Hallway/horizontal circulation clearances.

A. Clear width of an accessible route.
B. Required space for one wheelchair and one ambulatory person.
C. Required space for two wheelchairs.

persons may need to wait at the head or foot for the other person to complete the trip. It is a relatively minor inconvenience that many occupants/owners are willing to put up with in a residential setting. In contrast, this minimal dimension is too intimate as well as time-consuming for circulation within a public building, where the minimum widths of stair and corridor passages are 44 to 48 inches (depending on specific code jurisdiction). There are additional passage requirements for wheelchair users, as shown in Figure 8-6.

If stairs are designed for the pace and ambulatory capabilities of an average adult, then it can also be said that they are not designed for small children. They will have to flex and struggle a bit to handle adult stairs. On the other end of the spectrum, stairs are also not designed for the tall and/or athletic adult, who will often compensate by taking two steps at a time on the ascent. Also, they are *not* designed for the old, arthritic, or inflexible, even though stair riser maximums have been, over time, reduced. That is the paradox: People, and consequently average strides, are getting bigger, but the population is also getting older. What used to be the maximum riser in a nursing home stair (i.e., 7 inches) is now the maximum for all public stairs (IBC and ADAAG), and residential stair riser maximums have dropped $1/4$ to $1/2$ inch (for example, the IRC now requires $7\,3/4$ inches maximum).

The typical stair user can, generally speaking, handle a larger riser as he or she ascends the stair; a smaller riser would be desirable on the descent. It can be argued that the ideal, but of course impractical, stair system would have larger risers for the ascent, smaller for the descent, thereby requiring two sets of steps. Anecdotal evidence is provided by the fact that people can be frequently seen climbing a stair two steps (risers) at a time and often without railing support, but rarely do you see anyone descend a stair two steps at a time and even more rarely without the aid of a handrail.

Therefore, a compromise is struck in favor of the descent. The descent is inherently the more hazardous. The feet are in much more stable positions on the ascent and if a fall occurs, the person falls into the plane of the stair—a relatively short trip. As stated previously, those with mobility limitations and/or difficulty with balance often feel safer descending a stair backward, just as people typically descend a ladder.

A person can move up or down a hallway or ramp at any step increment (pace). This is much different than stairs, which must be traversed at the pace determined by the designer. A person can take two steps at a time, but one cannot take a half step or a $1\,1/4$ step, for example. So, it is important that the pace be comfortable for the average user, and in most cases such a pace is more likely to be safe. It is also important that every stair, although certainly not identical, be designed within reasonable pace parameters. The average indoor stride translates to a commonly used formula for proportioning riser/tread ratios (in the equation, R stands for riser, T for tread):

$$2R + T = 25 \text{ inches (24 inches min. – 26 inches max.)}$$

Following are a few examples:

7-inch risers / 11-inch treads: 2×7 inches + 11 inches = 25 inches

$7\frac{1}{2}$-inch risers / 10-inch treads: $2 \times 7\frac{1}{2}$ inches + 10 inches = 25 inches

$7\frac{3}{4}$-inch risers / 10-inch treads: $2 \times 7\frac{3}{4}$ inches + 10 inches = $25\frac{1}{2}$ inches

Maximum   /   Minimum (IRC)

In ascending a stair, it is not necessary to place any or all of the heel on the tread surface. However, in a descent mode, there must be room on the tread surface for the heel to rest (lightly or heavily). This means that the tread size must not be too small and that the stair nose be limited in size and be detailed in a manner that will not easily catch a stair user's heel in the descent mode (see Figure 8-7).

Furthermore, too small a tread will put the toe too far out beyond the nosing and compromise the footing. Even an adequate (legal) tread may prove to be difficult for people with very large feet, as they may be forced to set the foot askew on the tread to get full support. Consideration of headroom at stair locations is required for safety and comfort and by most codes. Headroom is defined as the clear vertical space from a stair tread (at the nosing) to any overhead obstruction, as shown in Figure 8-8.

Another safety consideration relates to materials used for the tread surface and especially the nosing. These must not be slippery or become slippery with wear. Slippery surfaces are likewise to be avoided on ramps; the steeper the ramp and the more exposed to the elements (rain/ice/snow), the more care that is required of the designer regarding suitable material selection.

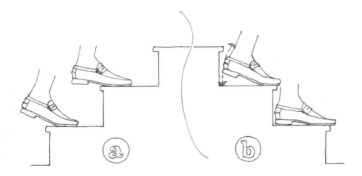

Figure 8-7 Ascending and descending stairs. In ascending a stair, heels are not necessarily placed on the entire tread surface. However, descending requires room on the tread surface for the heel to rest fully, requiring that the tread size must not be too small and that the stair nose be limited in size and be detailed in a manner that will not easily catch a stair user's heel in the descent mode; too small a tread will put the toe too far out beyond the nosing and compromise the footing.

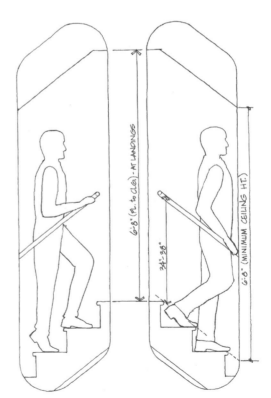

Figure 8-8 Headroom clearances at stairs and landings, and handrail heights at stairs.

Figure 8-9 A range of handrail/railing design options that meet code requirements that do not allow passage of a sphere 4 inches or more in diameter of clear/open railing space (as described in the "Related Codes and Constraints" section of this chapter).

A. Cable and turnbuckle with wood or metal handrail.
B. Glass and steel with wood or steel handrail.
C. Wood balusters and handrail.
D. Wood or metal handrail mounted on a "half wall" with metal rail brackets.
E. Pipe railing; handrail: 1 ¼ to 2 inches diameter.

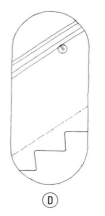
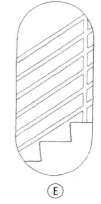

Ⓐ Ⓑ Ⓒ Ⓓ Ⓔ

A stable and easily graspable handrail is the final component in the design of a safe and comfortable stair/ramp to ascend and descend. A well-placed handrail will ensure that the user will always have the possibility of at least two points of body support (a hand and a foot) at any point in time. The designer should ascertain the best railing height in any given setting, within the parameters set by the code: generally 34 to 38 inches vertically above the nose (see Figure 8-8). While there are distinct code requirements for handrails, balusters, and railings, a variety of design and material options can meet requirements. Some are shown in Figure 8-9. For additional information, see the "Related Codes and Constraints" section of this chapter.

Figure 8-10
A. Diagram depicting single-loaded circulation flow.
B. Diagram depicting double-loaded circulation flow and the efficiency thereof vis-à-vis single-loaded circulation.
C. Diagram depicting single-loaded circulation flow that is enhanced visually through the creation of views or emphasis.

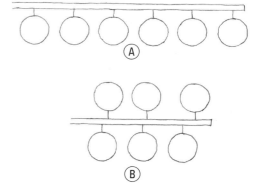
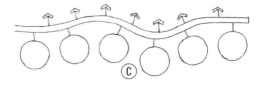

ORGANIZATIONAL FLOW

Space that is devoted exclusively to circulation is often regarded as nonproductive and is to be minimized. The exceptions would be found in those residences where the design statement is principally about circulation—the drama of movement, where the pleasure of the use of the residence is found in moving around in it.

Single-loaded circulation, as shown in Figure 8-10 (item A), is twice as long and takes twice the time to negotiate as double-loaded circulation, shown in Figure 8-10 (item B). This is true whether the circulation delivers access to rooms or simply to other items such as equipment or furniture. Thoughtful design of the circulation space itself may involve the shape of the space, features along the way such as a view to the outside, an elevated view of other rooms, a gallery of artwork, the play of artificial or natural light, and so on. In creating views, in turn, circulation becomes more than a long, deadly corridor, as shown in Figure 8-10 (item C).

The drama of movement, especially vertical movement, is a powerful tool in a designer's arsenal. The level of drama in vertical movement, for the observer as well as the mover, can be related to the relative speed of ascent or descent. For instance, stairs are generally more dramatic than ramps, a firefighter's pole more dramatic than a stair (but, unfortunately, it works in one direction only). Vertical movement is also more hazardous than horizontal movement, an important issue for the designer. See the "Related Codes and Constraints" section of this chapter for a more complete discussion of safety issues.

Stair design, in any given circumstance, is driven (at a minimum) by the following factors:

Flow within the residence
Floor (level) to floor (level) vertical distance
Minimum requirements of the applicable code(s)

Within those parameters, the stair can be a design statement in and of itself—a piece of "sculpture" or fine woodwork/metalwork that becomes a dominant and memorable element in the residence.

Hallways (corridors) will, obviously, move the occupants horizontally from one part of the residence to another and, in the process, control direction of flow. Ramps will do much the same thing, albeit with modest vertical gains or losses. Movement between floors (a full story) is seldom done with ramps because of the inordinate amount of space they take. For example, to move 9 feet floor to floor would take a 1:12 ramp (required to move unassisted in a wheelchair), 125-plus lineal feet including landings every 30 feet, and (approximately 400 total square feet).

Well before that point, it becomes less expensive to build a shaft (plus-or-minus 25 square feet) and install a small residential elevator. As compared to most stairs that involve some horizontal movement (to the other side of the house in the case of straight-run stair), one can enter and exit an elevator in the same relative horizontal position; in other words, you can enter and exit through the same wall of the shaft and find yourself directly above (or below) where the trip was started. It is also possible to enter through any given shaft wall and exit through the opposite or adjacent shaft wall (thereby necessitating a 90-degree turn). It has become increasingly common in recent years for clients to request framing a rough opening for future installation of an elevator. Often the future shaft is used as a closet or pantry on the floors where the elevator will stop in the future.

A spiral stair comes close to an elevator in terms of virtually no horizontal movement for the floor-to-floor traveler and a minimal footprint (20-plus square feet for a minimal spiral stair, which is 5 feet diameter). But unlike an elevator, a spiral staircase is obviously not suitable for wheelchair use. That, coupled with the problem of moving large objects, such as furniture, up and down, relegate its use to secondary stairs or where there is access to open balconies (lofts, etc.) that provide an alternative route (albeit difficult) for moving furniture. The "Related Codes and Constraints" section of this chapter contains spiral stair examples.

For the curve to be created in a curved monumental stair, each tread must vary (identically to all other treads) from one end to the other, but the tread/riser ratio should ideally be reasonable at both ends of each tread. This likely will result in a large radius to the curve of the stair (e.g., 24-plus feet). This, in turn, leads to a modest (less than 90 degrees) change in direction from the top to the bottom (see Figure 8-11, item D). A larger range of change in direction (0 to 180 degrees) of a stair can be achieved with the use of landings, as shown in Figure 8-11.

Figure 8-12 highlights some common errors and bad practice in stair design and delineation. In this example the stairs occupy "prime" real estate within the home: They use exterior walls that might be better used for some exterior exposure/windows for light and air for the interior of the house, and a central location for the stairs is often preferable, from the standpoint of ease of circulation. Additionally, the example shows stairs that do not stack directly, one over the other, resulting in greater horizontal travel distance. For example, the travel distance from basement to second floor involves an extra-long transfer distance (through two rooms) on the first floor.

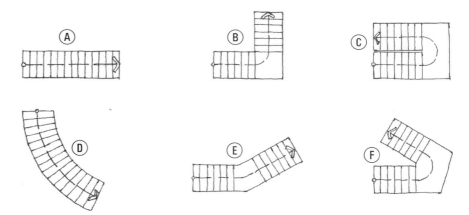

Figure 8-11 Stairs used to control direction of flow in the residence.
A. Straight-run stair; no change in direction.
B. An "L" stair; 90-degree change in direction.
C. Single "U" stair; 180-degree change in direction.
D. A curved (monumental) stair will yield a 30-degree to 90-degree change in direction.
E. 0- to 90-degree change in direction.
F. 90- to 180-degree change in direction.

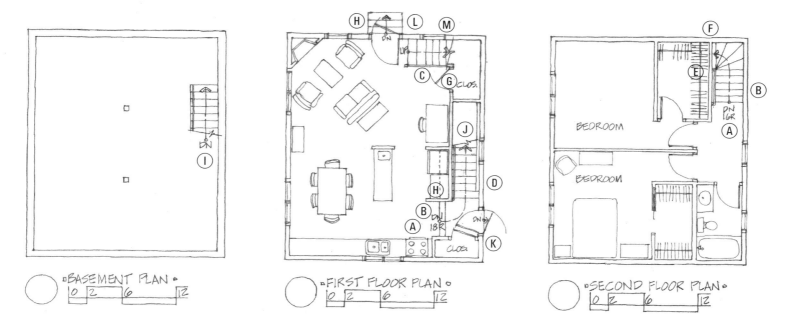

Figure 8-12 This is a negative example to serve as an illustration of some common errors and/or bad practice in stair design and delineation. The stairs shown occupy "prime real estate" within the home, including exterior walls that might be better used for some exterior exposure/windows for light and air for the interior of the house. A central location for the stairs is often preferable, from the standpoint of ease of circulation. Stairs that do not stack directly, one over the other, result in greater horizontal travel distance; for example, the travel distance from basement to second floor involves an extra-long transfer distance (through two rooms) on the first floor.

A. The likelihood of there being more steps to the basement (18 R) (first floor to basement) than to the second floor (16 R) is minimal; 16 R indicates that the first floor ceiling is likely 9 feet (plus or minus). Though possible, 18 R (10 feet, plus or minus), floor to floor, is not common for a basement.

B. Tread depth is insufficient; 10 inches will be the required minimum.

C. Treads need to be a uniform depth in any given run of stair, not changed partway into the run.

D. The basement walls will likely be 2 to 6 inches thicker than the first-floor exterior walls; a basement stair that starts out at (a legal minimum) 3 feet wide becomes too narrow as the stair descends.

E. "Winder stairs" need a prescribed minimum tread depth at the narrow end (see the "Related Codes and Constraints" section of this chapter).

F. Insufficient head clearance (6 to 8 feet required); the floor will have 12 inches plus or minus of thickness and the head must clear the bottom-most portion of the floor structure.

G. Doors under stairs; check height available. In this case, the door would have to be shorter than a standard 6- to 8-foot door.

H. Handrail not required by some codes (when less than four risers), but it would be considered good practice to install a handrail in this situation.

I. Directional arrows (and notation: "UP"/"DOWN") should point from the floor level that is being shown; in this case, an "up" arrow should be shown starting at the bottom of the stair.

J. No break line should be shown on the "down" run of a stair; all the risers will be shown, or they will disappear under a floor/wall or the "up" run of another stair.

K. If there are steps at the "front door," it's almost a virtual certainty, in the example shown, that steps will be necessary at the "back door" also; the maximum step from a secondary door to the ground: 7¾ inches (see the "Related Codes and Constraints" section of this chapter).

L. Exterior steps. 3 feet by 3 feet (minimum) landing required; 3-foot-wide steps minimum (or as wide as the door); handrails required.

M. Windowsill may not be able to be as low as the window on the other side of the "front door"; stair may partially block it.

Figures 8-13 to 8-15 provide examples of houses with different floor-to-floor heights, and each illustrates a different type of stair. As shown, common ceiling heights of 8 feet, 9 feet, and 10 feet are going to result in floor-to-floor heights of 9 feet plus-or-minus, 10 feet plus-or-minus, and 11 feet plus-or-minus, respectively. The floor thickness will vary, but a 12-inch thickness is a good preliminary assumption, and all of the examples use that assumption. In most projects the floor thickness is frequently, but certainly not always, in the 11- to 14-inch range.

Most stairs involve horizontal movement as well as the sought-after vertical movement. As shown in Figure 8-13, a straight-run stair involves the most horizontal movement; in a modest-sized house, the stair will carry the user to the other side of the house. Then, to continue to another level, the user doubles back

Figure 8-13 Straight-run stairs. Most stairs involve horizontal movement as well as vertical movement; a straight-run stair requires the most horizontal movement. In a modest-sized house, the stair will carry the user to the other side of the house, and then, continuing to another level involves doubling back to the head or foot of the next stair, thereby requiring dedicated circulation space on the mid (transfer) level(s).

A. Movement from the second floor to basement (or vice versa) will require circulation space at the middle level (first floor in this case) to be able to get to the head or foot of the next stair; at a minimum, the total footprint (stair and first floor circulation and landings at the top and bottom of each stair) can easily amount to more than 100 square feet (115 square feet in this example).

B. Required head clearance. As much as 6 to 8 feet in most codes.

C. Alternate ceiling, to reduce stair volume and consequent maintenance.

D. First-floor-to-second-floor stair total rise. 9-foot ceilings/10-foot (120 inches) floor to floor.

  • 120 inches divided by 15 risers = 8 inches each riser (may still be legal in some codes, not the IRC).
  • 120 inches divided by 16 risers = 7.5 inches each riser (a suitable choice).
  • 120 inches divided by 17 risers = 7.06 inches each riser (an easier stair to climb but will add 26 inches of length to the total run).

E. First-floor-to-second-floor stair total run:

  (2 R + T = 25);

  $2 \times 7.5 + T = 25$

  $T = 25 - (2 \times 7.5)$

  T = 10 inches each tread

Total run: 15 treads @ 10 inches = 150 inches (12 feet, 6 inches)

F. Break line—shown in all "up" runs.

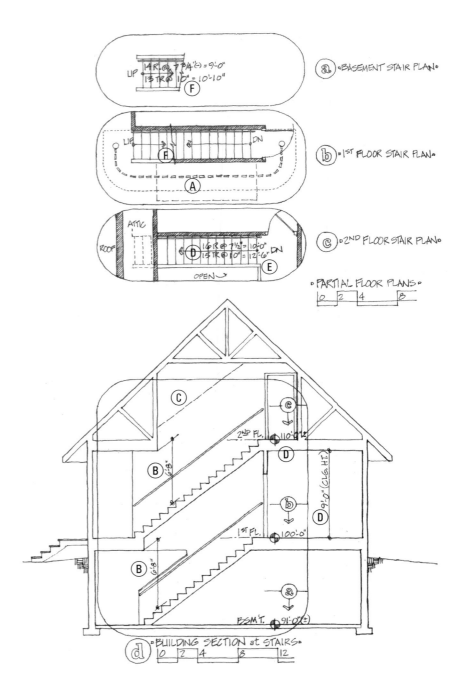

to the head or foot of the next stair, thereby requiring dedicated circulation space on the mid (transfer) level(s).

The L-shaped stair shown in Figure 8-14 creates a 90-degree change in direction that can be used, in certain situations, to the designer's advantage to improve the circulation in the whole residence. The transition distance (and space dedicated to it) on the first floor, to move from one stair to the other, is somewhat less than the straight-run stair.

U-stairs, also known as scissor stairs and shown in Figure 8-15, take a 180-degree turn over roughly half a floor. This, of course, means that the stair user winds up directly above or below where he or she started (every full story traveled), not unlike a spiral stair. The resultant stair shape is quite square, as compared to the straight-run or L-shaped stair. The mid levels can be as small as 3-by-6-foot (plus-or-minus) landings or as large as need be, to accommodate the total design of the residence. Figure 8-15 shows equal runs: seven risers/seven risers on all the stair runs. This is *not* a requirement, as the 14 risers (floor to floor) could be divided into eight risers/six risers, nine risers/five risers, and so forth.

Any residential stair is often the dominant factor in the flow throughout the entire residence; it is imperative that the designer consider the stair not as an afterthought but as a critical element that can be as important as any other space in the residence. Bad decisions regarding a stair can ruin an otherwise fine design.

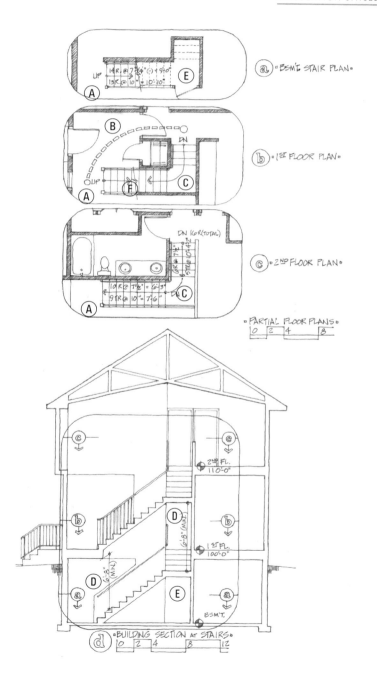

Figure 8-14 The L-shaped stair creates a (90-degree) change in direction, which can be used to the designer's advantage to improve the circulation throughout the residence in certain situations. Less space is required to move from one stair to the other, on the first floor, than the straight-run stair.

A. The two runs forming the "L" need not be identical in length.

B. Circulation route required at the first-floor level to be able to move easily to all three levels.

C. Minimum landing: 36 by 36 inches; minimum stair width: 36 inches.

D. Minimum head clearance at stair and landings: 6 feet, 8 inches in most codes.

E. Door(s) located under stairs; check door height (in this case the maximum door height would be about 5 feet, 8 inches).

F. Break line on the "up" run; steps above can be shown with dashed line, if doing so helps with the drawing's clarity.

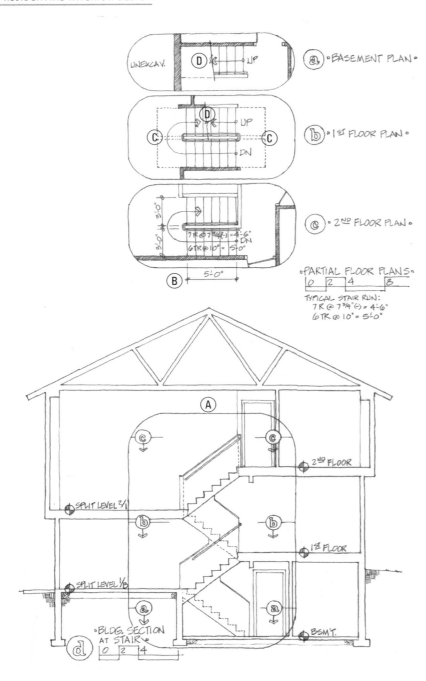

Figure 8-15 "U" stairs, also known as scissor stairs, take a 180-degree turn every half (plus-or-minus) floor; therefore, the stair user winds up directly above or below where he or she started (every full story traveled). The resultant stair shape is quite square, as compared to the straight-run or "L" stair. The midlevel landings can be as small as 3 feet by 6 feet (plus or minus); conversely, landings can be as large as need be to accommodate the total design of the residence (for example, to become part of a room that is at the landing level). The example shows equal runs: seven risers/seven risers on all the stair runs; this is not required, as the 14 risers (floor to floor) could be divided: eight risers/six risers, nine risers/five risers, and so on.

A. Circulation path between all levels is the shortest of any of this set of examples.
B. Minimum footprint of (all) steps: 6 feet by 5 feet (30 plus-or-minus square feet) is comparable to a 6-feet-diameter spiral stair with a comparable 3-foot tread width: 28 plus-or-minus square feet.
C. Landings. 36 by 36 inches required minimum landing at the top and bottom of each run. The stair minimum footprint, including landings, is 67 square feet.
D. Break line shown on all "up" runs; "down" runs are shown in their entirety—until they disappear under the floor or the stair above.

RELATED CODES AND CONSTRAINTS

Interior ramps, stairs, hallways, and exterior doors may at some point in the life of the structure need to be used as a means of emergency egress from the residence. That egress needs to be safe and must therefore comply with applicable portions of the code. Stairs are also an inherently hazardous element in the residence during normal daily use as well as when used for emergency egress. For these reasons, building codes are quite specific and rigorous in their delineation of minimum requirements for those elements (doors, hallways, stairs, and ramps) that facilitate or impede movement.

Regarding hallway width, IRC Section R311 "Means of Egress" states that "the minimum width of a hallway shall be not less than three (3) feet (914 mm)" (R 311.3). The section continues with R311.4.2, which indicates that a dwelling should not have less than one exit door that opens directly to the exterior (or, in the case of apartments, to a fire-rated corridor). That exit door needs to be "not less than three (3) feet (914 mm) in width and six (6) feet, eight (8) inches (2032 mm) in height." Some codes may require a secondary door as well as bedroom egress windows (see Chapter 3, "Bedrooms").

The section continues: "There shall be a floor or landing on each side of each exterior door . . . the floor or landing at the exit door . . . shall not be more than

1.5 inches (38 mm) lower than the top of the threshold." Also, "the width of each landing shall not be less than the door served. Every landing shall have a minimum dimension of 36 inches (914 mm) measured in the direction of travel" (R 311.4.3). Figure 8-16 illustrates these code restrictions at landings.

The following is a list of code-related requirements as well as health/life safety considerations and suggestions related to the design of stairs and stairways. Figures 8-16 to 8-20 illustrate the items.

- As stated previously in this chapter, avoid designing stairs that are too steep. Some codes may allow a riser to be as much as 8 inches. The IRC maximum is 7¾ inches. The corollary tread is 9 inches minimum in some codes; 10 inches minimum in the IRC.
- Avoid slippery tread surfaces; the stair nose is a particularly critical surface.
- Provide adequate width, enough that it is possible for two average adults to meet and pass on the stairs and not necessitate contortions, on the part of one or both, sufficient to force them off balance.
- Provide adequate headroom. A residence is required to have 6 to 8 feet of head clearance at doors/doorways. That should be matched on a stair. The possibility of the user bumping his or her head while traversing a stair is, obviously, to be avoided.
- Avoid built-in tripping hazards. The nosing detail is critical in minimizing this hazard.
- Provide lateral support for the upper body. Support, in the form of a handrail, is mandatory. The rail needs to be easily graspable, sturdy, and at an optimal height.
- In order to eliminate falls off the side of a stair, railings need to be either solid or the components need to be spaced close together enough to disallow the passage of a small child's or baby's head. The actual dimensions for this vary by code, but they are consistent in concept and are often roughly described by not allowing the passage of a sphere 4 inches (6 inches in some codes) or more in diameter through the clear/open railing space (see Figure 8-18).
- Limit the potential falling distance. Provide landings at no more than every 12 feet of vertical distance; provide a substantial landing (3 feet by 3 feet minimum) (IRC R311.5.4).
- Provide good illumination for the stair. The IRC minimum is one foot-candle at the center of every tread and landing.

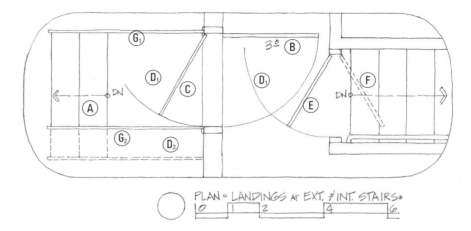

PLAN◦ LANDINGS ᴀᴛ EXT. ≠ INT. STAIRS◦

Figure 8-16 An illustration of various code regulations for entry steps and doors, as well as landings and doors at stairs.

A. The number of steps will vary to accommodate the site and the type of house construction (such as basement/no basement); in many geographic areas, no exterior steps will be necessary.

B. Required 3-foot (minimum) residential entrance/exit door.

C. Screen/storm door is a climatic requirement only.

D1. 3-foot-by-3-foot (minimum) landing or floor on each side of each exterior door (IRC R311.4.3).

D2. Extra width (beyond minimum) is desirable; it serves as a place for the user to stand while opening an out-swinging door.

E. "There shall be a floor or landing at the top and bottom of each stairway. A floor or landing is not required at the top of an interior flight of stairs, provided a door does not swing over the stairs. The width of each landing shall not be less than the stairway served. Every landing shall have a minimum dimension of 36 inches (914 mm) measured in the direction of travel" (IRC R311.5.4).

F. DO NOT swing a door *into* a stair at the top of a flight of stairs.

G1. "Porches, balconies or raised floor surfaces located more than 30" (762 mm) above the floor or grade below shall have guards not less than 36" (914 mm) in height. Open sides of stairs with a total rise of more than 30" (762 mm) above the floor or grade below shall have guards not less than 34" (864 mm) in height measured vertically from the nosing of the treads."

G2. Railing not required in this case (stoop is approximately 24 inches above grade), but good practice would call for installation of a railing—especially in this case where the stoop is code minimum width.

Figure 8-17 An illustration of stair calculation/design.

Note: Common ceiling heights (where there is another floor level above) are 8 feet, 9 feet, 10 feet, and occasionally 7 feet; floor structure thickness (1 foot plus or minus) added to that will set the floor-to-floor height, which in turn sets one of the main parameters for the final stair design.

A. Stair design. Given floor-to-floor height of 10 feet (120 inches).

   A1. Estimate the number of risers required: 120 inches (floor to floor) divided by 7¾ inches (maximum legal riser) = 15.48 (number of risers).

   A2. Number of risers has to be a whole number, so check the following:

   120 inches divided by 15 risers = 8 inches (too large)
   120 inches divided by 16 risers = 7.5 inches (OK)
   120 inches divided by 17 risers = 7.06 inches (OK also)

   A3. Select 16 risers; calculate an appropriate "matching" tread:

   2 R + T = 24 to 26 inches
   Try 2 × 7.5 inches + 10" (T) = 25 (OK)
   Try 2 × 7.5" + 11" (T) = 26 (OK)

   A4. Select tread: 10 ½ inches ; 15 treads @ 10½ inches = 157.5 inches (13 feet, 1½ inches; total run).

B. Stair width. 3 feet (36 inches) minimum (IRC R311.5.1).

C. 3 feet x stair width (in this case the minimum, 3 feet) required landing top and bottom (IRC R311.5.4).

D. Terminate handrail at newel post or return to wall, at a point directly above lowest and highest riser (IRC R311.5.6.2).

E. One handrail (minimum) is required in any stair with four or more risers (IRC R311.5.6). Railing (guard) required on open side of stair (IRC R312.1).

F. Railing at wall. Optional in this case; cannot project more than 4½ inches into the required minimum width of stair: 3 feet (IRC R311.5.1).

G. Handrail height. Minimum 34 inches, maximum 38 inches; measured vertically from a typical nose (IRC R311.5.6).

H. Stair headroom. 6 feet, 8 inches (minimum); measured vertically from the plane of the nosings or any landing (IRC R311.5.2).

I. Hallways. 3 feet wide (minimum) (IRC R311.3).

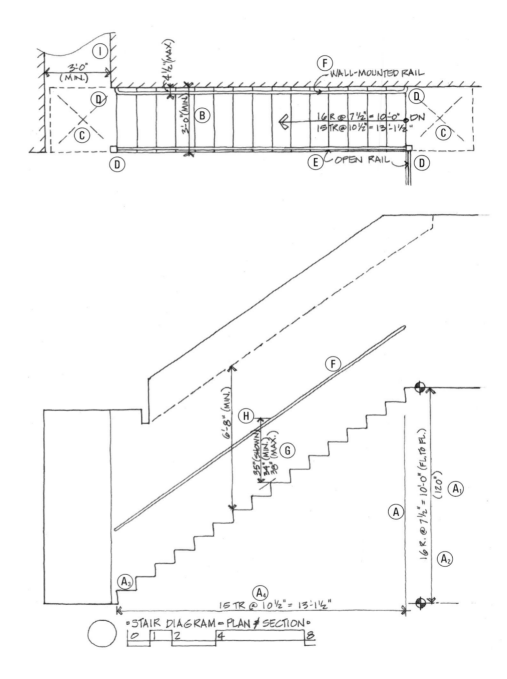

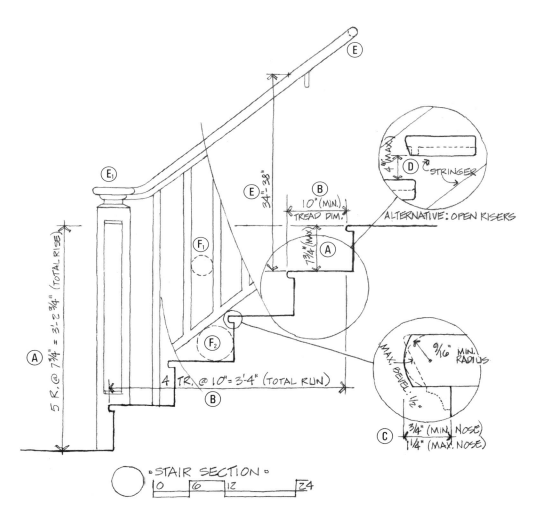

STAIR SECTION

Figure 8-18 An illustration of code regulations related to riser, tread, handrail, nosing, and railing code requirements.

A. Riser height. "The <u>maximum</u> riser height shall be 7¾ inches (196 mm)" (IRC R311.5.3.1). There is no absolute <u>minimum</u>, but a good rule of thumb working minimum is 7 inches, plus or minus.

B. Tread depth. "The <u>minimum</u> tread depth shall be 10"" (IRC R311.5.3.2). The depth of the tread should increase as the riser decreases (refer to the "Ergonomics and Required Clearances" section of this chapter).

C. Nosing. ". . . the radius of curvature at the leading edge of the tread shall be no greater than 9/16 inch (14.3 mm). A nosing not less than ¾ inch (19 mm) but not more than 1¼ inches (32 mm) shall be provided on stairways with solid risers" (IRC R511.3.3). A nosing is not required where the tread depth is a minimum of 11 inches or more.

D. "Open risers are permitted, provided that the opening between treads does not permit the passage of a 4 inch diameter (102 mm) sphere. The opening between adjacent treads is not limited on stairs with a total rise of 30 inches (762 mm) or less" (IRC R311.5.3.3).

E. Handrail height. 34 inches minimum, 38 inches maximum (IRC R311.5.6.1 and R311.5.6.2). "Handrails for stairways shall be continuous for the full length of the flight, from a point directly above the top riser of the flight to a point directly above lowest riser of the flight. Handrail ends shall be returned or shall terminate in newel posts or safety terminals. Handrails adjacent to a wall shall have a space of not less than 1½" (38 mm) between the wall and the handrails. Handrails shall be permitted to be interrupted by a newel post at the turn. The use of a volute, turnout, starting easing or starting newel shall be allowed over the lowest tread" (see E1).

F. "Required guards on open sides of stairways, raised floor areas, balconies, and porches shall have intermediate rails or ornamental closures which do not allow passage of a sphere 4 inches (102 mm) or more in diameter" (see F1). "<u>Exception</u>: The triangular openings formed by the riser, tread and bottom rail of a guard at the open side of a stairway are permitted to be of such a size that a sphere 6 inches (150 mm) cannot pass through" (see F2).

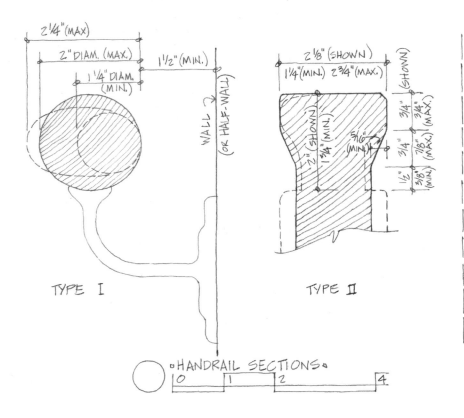

Figure 8-19 An illustration of the requirements for "graspability" described in the International Residential Code (IRC). Type I handrail requirements are relatively straightforward. The possible profiles for type II are much more varied, and the figure only delineates a very limited interpretation of the code requirements described in IRC 311.5.6.3.

"Type I Handrails with a circular cross section shall have an outside diameter of at least 1¼ inches (32 mm) and not greater than 2 inches (51 mm). If the handrail is not circular it shall have a perimeter dimension of at least 4 inches (102 mm) and not greater than 6¼ inches (160 mm) with a maximum cross section of dimension of 2¼ inches (57 mm).

"Type II Handrails with a perimeter greater than 6½ inches (160 mm) shall provide a graspable finger recess area on both sides of the profile. The finger recess shall begin within a distance of ¾ inch (19 mm) measured vertically from the tallest portion of the profile and achieve a depth of at least 5/16 inch (8 mm) within ⅞ inch (22 mm) below the widest portion of the profile. This required depth shall continue for at least ⅜ inch (10 mm) to a level that is not less than 1¾ inches (45 mm) below the tallest portion of the profile. The minimum width of the handrail above the recess shall be 1¼ inches (32 mm) to a maximum of 2¾ inches (70 mm). Edges shall have a minimum radius of 0.01 inches (0.25 mm)."

The design of ramps is similar to stairs in terms of the need and standards for handrails and for landings (3 feet by 3 feet). There is a significant difference between what is allowed in public accommodations versus private residences in terms of slope, width, length, and landing size of any ramp. The IRC allows a slope up to 12.5 percent (one vertical unit in eight horizontal units). This steeper-than-public-buildings slope will necessitate assistance for many wheelchair users. The amount of space consumed by a ramp (the footprint) should not be underestimated. It will be significant, and the designer should take that reality into account in the initial stages of the design process.

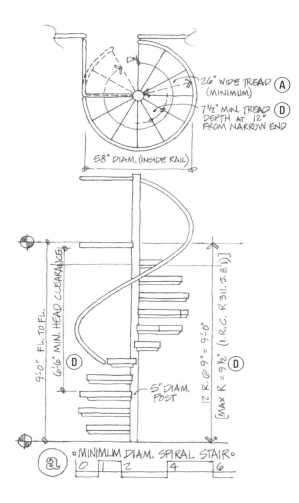

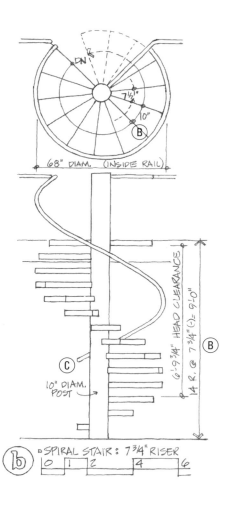

Figure 8-20 An illustration comparing two very similar spiral stairs. Stair a meets the minimum requirements of the IRC. The 10-inch-diameter increase (58 to 68 inches) shown in Stair b results in a much more comfortable, and arguably safer, stair to ascend/descend. The examples shown are for a 9-foot floor-to-floor height. Obviously, the floor-to-floor height varies with the specific residence design.

A. Stair a shows the code minimum (diameter) spiral stair.

B. Stair b shows a more comfortable spiral stair with risers similar to a straight run stair (i.e., 7 ¾ inches maximum) and a tread dimension of 10 inches at the centerline of travel (presumed centerline of travel: 11 inches in from railing).

C. Balusters not shown—for clarity and ease of drawing.

D. "Spiral stairways are permitted, provided the minimum width shall be 26" (660 mm) with each tread having a 7 ½" (190 mm) minimum tread depth at 12" from the narrower edge. All treads shall be identical, and the rise shall be no more than 9 ½" (241 mm). A minimum headroom of 6 feet 6 inches (1982 mm) shall be provided" (IRC R311.5.8.1).

ELECTRICAL AND MECHANICAL

Much like other areas of the home, circulation areas require general electrical outlets at minimum for cleaning and maintenance. Following general rules of thumb for outlet spacing and placement will suffice in most instances; these can be found in Figure 1-9. Keep in mind, however, that specialized situations may require additional outlets or unusual placement or mounting heights.

LIGHTING

Lighting for circulation spaces varies greatly based on the type of space involved. For example, decorative lighting for an elegant open stair located in or near an entry foyer may be supplied by a chandelier and layered with additional ambient light provided with wall sconces or adjustable downlights. On the other hand, lighting in more utilitarian circulation spaces may be provided without decorative

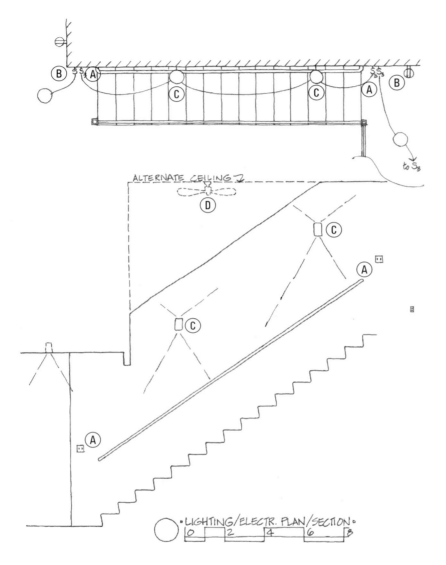

ALTERNATE CEILING

·LIGHTING/ELECTR. PLAN/SECTION·
0 2 4 6 8

Figure 8-21 Lighting/electrical plan and section at a stairwell.

A. Stair lighting requires a switch (S3 three-way switch) at both the head and foot of every stair.

B. Hallway lighting should also be switched at each end of any hall.

C. Light distribution is important. Wall sconces are shown providing up and down light (in this case mounted at 6 feet, 8 inches A.F.F. (above finished floor).

D. If the HVAC system requires a ceiling fan, a high ceiling in a stairwell can be an unobtrusive location.

fixtures and supplied instead by recessed downlights, surface-/ceiling-mounted luminaries, or cove- or soffit-mounted fluorescent fixtures.

Given the range of types of circulation spaces within most houses, careful consideration of any desired aesthetic effects as well as the use and requirements of each space must occur. Great drama may be provided in some foyer/entry areas and hallways through the use of chandeliers, pendant fixtures, and wall sconces, and in fact many such spaces with higher-than-standard ceilings call for this kind of decorative lighting. In some homes, long hallways serve as gallery spaces, and these are well served by accent lighting in addition to general/ambient lighting. In other cases, hallways and other circulation spaces may benefit from a simple approach to lighting that provides adequate light levels for safe passage in a way that makes a minimal visual impact.

The previous two paragraphs point to a need of establishing lighting design criteria for circulation spaces. This requires noting any specific visual or aesthetic requirements for each space as well as the basic functional requirements of adequate lighting for safe passage, in addition to the architectural parameters, and making design decisions accordingly.

Because circulation spaces are designed to facilitate movement, the location of switches and controls provided in such spaces must work to support that movement. This often requires providing switching at both ends of any particular circulation space, for example, at the top and bottom of a run of stairs and at each end of a hallway, as shown in Figure 8-21. It is not uncommon for central controls or for home security system controls to be placed within a circulation space, although this varies based on layout and design.

BIBLIOGRAPHY

(Contains both works cited and recommended reading. Annotations where appropriate.)

Abercrombie, Stanley. *A Philosophy of Interior Design.* New York: HarperCollins, 1991.

Alexander, Christopher, et al. *A Pattern Language.* New York: Oxford University Press, 1977.

International Code Council. *International Residential Code 2003.* Florence, KY: Thomson Delmar Learning, 2003.

Rumberger, Janet, ed. *Architectural Graphic Standards for Residential Construction.* Hoboken, NJ: John Wiley & Sons, 2003.

Whitehead, Randall. *Residential Lighting: A Practical Guide.* Hoboken, NJ: John Wiley & Sons, 2004.

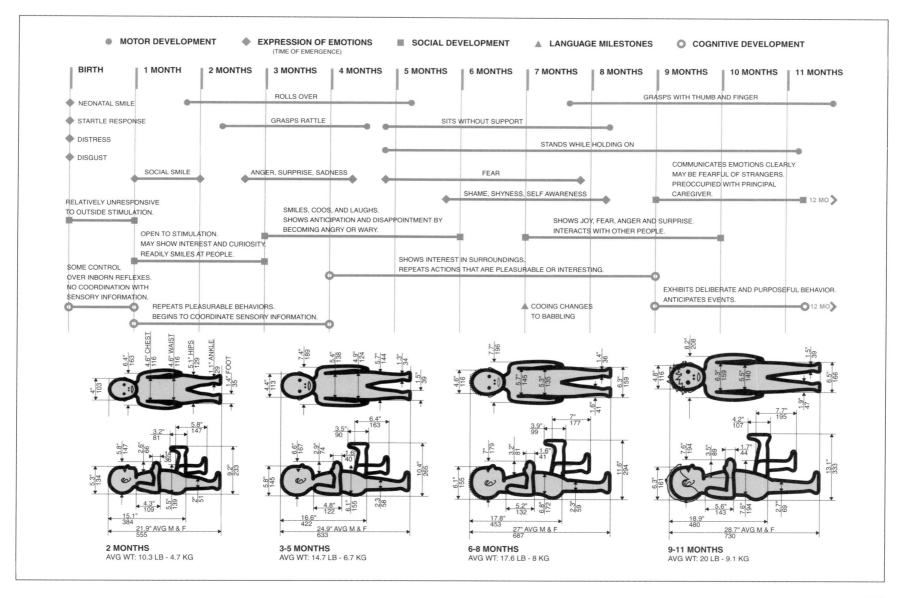

● MOTOR DEVELOPMENT ◆ EXPRESSION OF EMOTIONS (TIME OF EMERGENCE) ■ SOCIAL DEVELOPMENT ▲ LANGUAGE MILESTONES ○ COGNITIVE DEVELOPMENT

| BIRTH | 1 MONTH | 2 MONTHS | 3 MONTHS | 4 MONTHS | 5 MONTHS | 6 MONTHS | 7 MONTHS | 8 MONTHS | 9 MONTHS | 10 MONTHS | 11 MONTHS |

ROLLS OVER

GRASPS WITH THUMB AND FINGER

NEONATAL SMILE

STARTLE RESPONSE

GRASPS RATTLE

SITS WITHOUT SUPPORT

DISTRESS

STANDS WHILE HOLDING ON

DISGUST

SOCIAL SMILE

ANGER, SURPRISE, SADNESS

FEAR

COMMUNICATES EMOTIONS CLEARLY.
MAY BE FEARFUL OF STRANGERS.
PREOCCUPIED WITH PRINCIPAL
CAREGIVER.

SHAME, SHYNESS, SELF AWARENESS

12 MO

RELATIVELY UNRESPONSIVE
TO OUTSIDE STIMULATION.

SMILES, COOS, AND LAUGHS.
SHOWS ANTICIPATION AND DISAPPOINTMENT BY
BECOMING ANGRY OR WARY.

SHOWS JOY, FEAR, ANGER AND SURPRISE.
INTERACTS WITH OTHER PEOPLE.

OPEN TO STIMULATION.
MAY SHOW INTEREST AND CURIOSITY.
READILY SMILES AT PEOPLE.

SHOWS INTEREST IN SURROUNDINGS.
REPEATS ACTIONS THAT ARE PLEASURABLE OR INTERESTING.

SOME CONTROL
OVER INBORN REFLEXES.
NO COORDINATION WITH
SENSORY INFORMATION.

EXHIBITS DELIBERATE AND PURPOSEFUL BEHAVIOR.
ANTICIPATES EVENTS.

12 MO

REPEATS PLEASURABLE BEHAVIORS.
BEGINS TO COORDINATE SENSORY INFORMATION.

COOING CHANGES
TO BABBLING

2 MONTHS
AVG WT: 10.3 LB - 4.7 KG

3-5 MONTHS
AVG WT: 14.7 LB - 6.7 KG

6-8 MONTHS
AVG WT: 17.6 LB - 8 KG

9-11 MONTHS
AVG WT: 20 LB - 9.1 KG

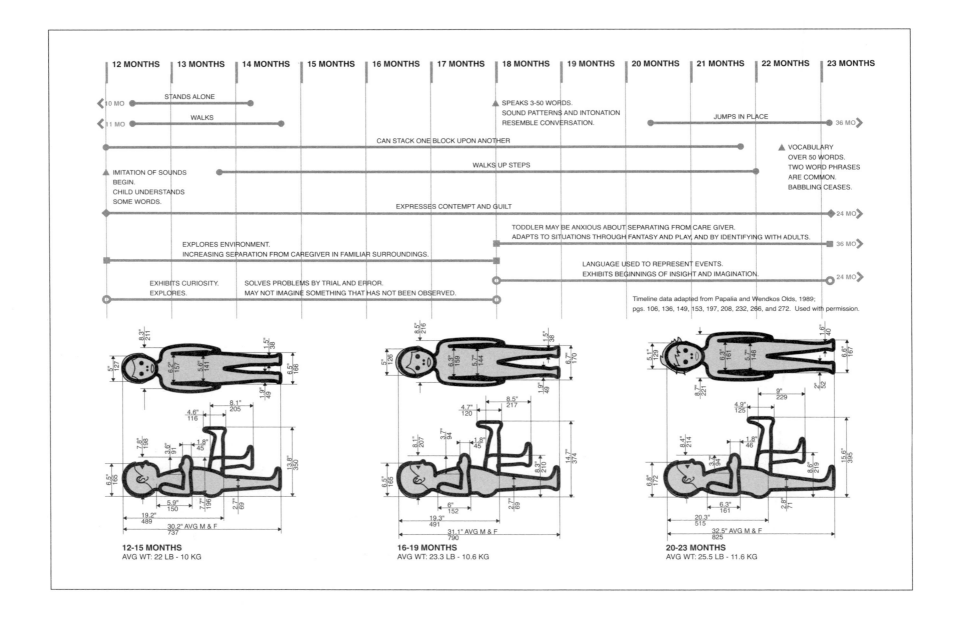

| 12 MONTHS | 13 MONTHS | 14 MONTHS | 15 MONTHS | 16 MONTHS | 17 MONTHS | 18 MONTHS | 19 MONTHS | 20 MONTHS | 21 MONTHS | 22 MONTHS | 23 MONTHS |

10 MO STANDS ALONE

11 MO WALKS

SPEAKS 3-50 WORDS. SOUND PATTERNS AND INTONATION RESEMBLE CONVERSATION.

JUMPS IN PLACE 36 MO

CAN STACK ONE BLOCK UPON ANOTHER

VOCABULARY OVER 50 WORDS. TWO WORD PHRASES ARE COMMON. BABBLING CEASES.

WALKS UP STEPS

IMITATION OF SOUNDS BEGIN. CHILD UNDERSTANDS SOME WORDS.

EXPRESSES CONTEMPT AND GUILT

24 MO

TODDLER MAY BE ANXIOUS ABOUT SEPARATING FROM CARE GIVER. ADAPTS TO SITUATIONS THROUGH FANTASY AND PLAY, AND BY IDENTIFYING WITH ADULTS.

EXPLORES ENVIRONMENT. INCREASING SEPARATION FROM CAREGIVER IN FAMILIAR SURROUNDINGS.

36 MO

LANGUAGE USED TO REPRESENT EVENTS. EXHIBITS BEGINNINGS OF INSIGHT AND IMAGINATION.

24 MO

EXHIBITS CURIOSITY. EXPLORES.

SOLVES PROBLEMS BY TRIAL AND ERROR. MAY NOT IMAGINE SOMETHING THAT HAS NOT BEEN OBSERVED.

Timeline data adapted from Papalia and Wendkos Olds, 1989; pgs. 106, 136, 149, 153, 197, 208, 232, 266, and 272. Used with permission.

12-15 MONTHS
AVG WT: 22 LB - 10 KG

16-19 MONTHS
AVG WT: 23.3 LB - 10.6 KG

20-23 MONTHS
AVG WT: 25.5 LB - 11.6 KG

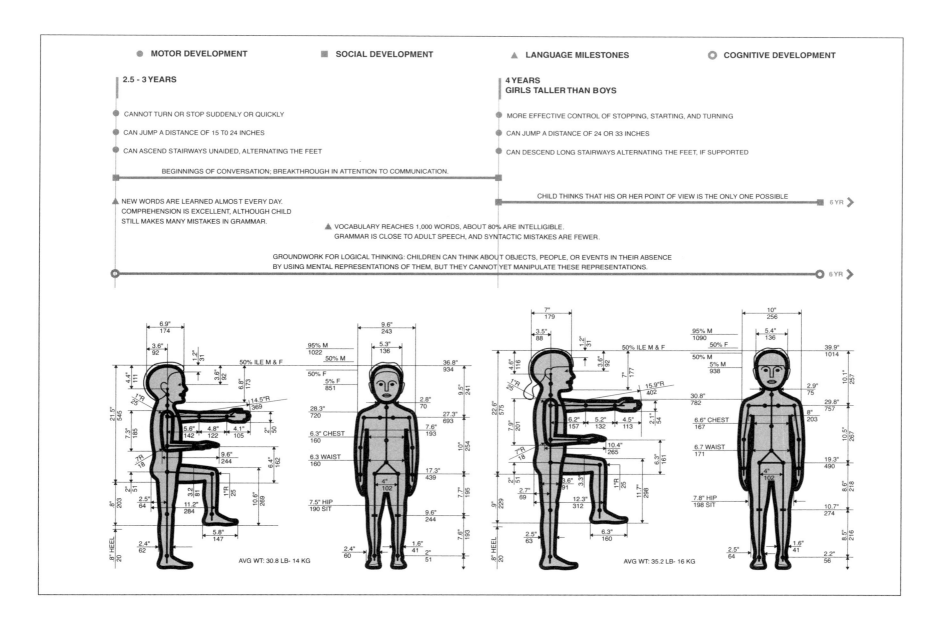

● MOTOR DEVELOPMENT   ■ SOCIAL DEVELOPMENT   ▲ LANGUAGE MILESTONES   ○ COGNITIVE DEVELOPMENT

2.5 - 3 YEARS

● CANNOT TURN OR STOP SUDDENLY OR QUICKLY

● CAN JUMP A DISTANCE OF 15 T0 24 INCHES

● CAN ASCEND STAIRWAYS UNAIDED, ALTERNATING THE FEET

■ BEGINNINGS OF CONVERSATION; BREAKTHROUGH IN ATTENTION TO COMMUNICATION.

▲ NEW WORDS ARE LEARNED ALMOST EVERY DAY.
COMPREHENSION IS EXCELLENT, ALTHOUGH CHILD
STILL MAKES MANY MISTAKES IN GRAMMAR.

▲ VOCABULARY REACHES 1,000 WORDS, ABOUT 80% ARE INTELLIGIBLE.
GRAMMAR IS CLOSE TO ADULT SPEECH, AND SYNTACTIC MISTAKES ARE FEWER.

○ GROUNDWORK FOR LOGICAL THINKING: CHILDREN CAN THINK ABOUT OBJECTS, PEOPLE, OR EVENTS IN THEIR ABSENCE
BY USING MENTAL REPRESENTATIONS OF THEM, BUT THEY CANNOT YET MANIPULATE THESE REPRESENTATIONS.

**4 YEARS
GIRLS TALLER THAN BOYS**

● MORE EFFECTIVE CONTROL OF STOPPING, STARTING, AND TURNING

● CAN JUMP A DISTANCE OF 24 OR 33 INCHES

● CAN DESCEND LONG STAIRWAYS ALTERNATING THE FEET, IF SUPPORTED

■ CHILD THINKS THAT HIS OR HER POINT OF VIEW IS THE ONLY ONE POSSIBLE   6 YR ❯

○ 6 YR ❯

AVG WT: 30.8 LB- 14 KG

AVG WT: 35.2 LB- 16 KG

5 YEARS

- CAN START, TURN, AND STOP EFFECTIVELY IN GAMES
- CAN MAKE A RUNNING JUMP OF 28 TO 38 INCHES
- CAN DESCEND LONG STAIRWAYS UNAIDED, ALTERNATING THE FEET

6 YEARS

- GIRLS ARE SUPERIOR IN ACCURACY OF MOVEMENT.
  BOYS ARE SUPERIOR IN FORCEFUL, LESS COMPLEX ACTS.
- CAN THROW WITH PROPER WEIGHT SHIFT AND STOP

4 YR — CHILD THINKS THAT HIS OR HER OWN POINT OF VIEW IS THE ONLY ONE POSSIBLE

CHILD LEARNS NOT ONLY BY SENSING AND DOING, BUT BY THINKING AS WELL.
3 YR — BASIC UNDERSTANDING OF CAUSE AND EFFECT.

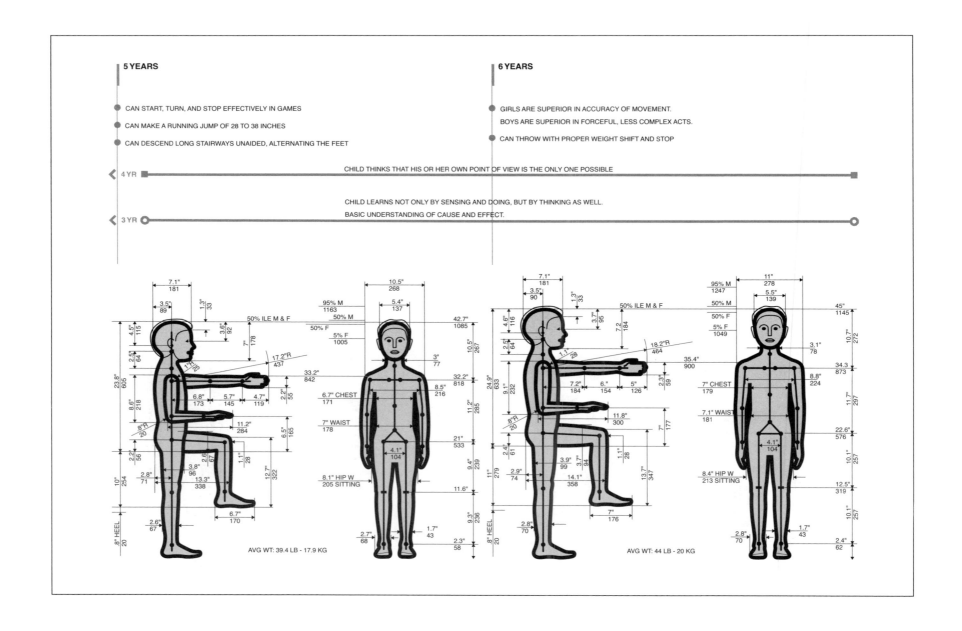

AVG WT: 39.4 LB - 17.9 KG

AVG WT: 44 LB - 20 KG

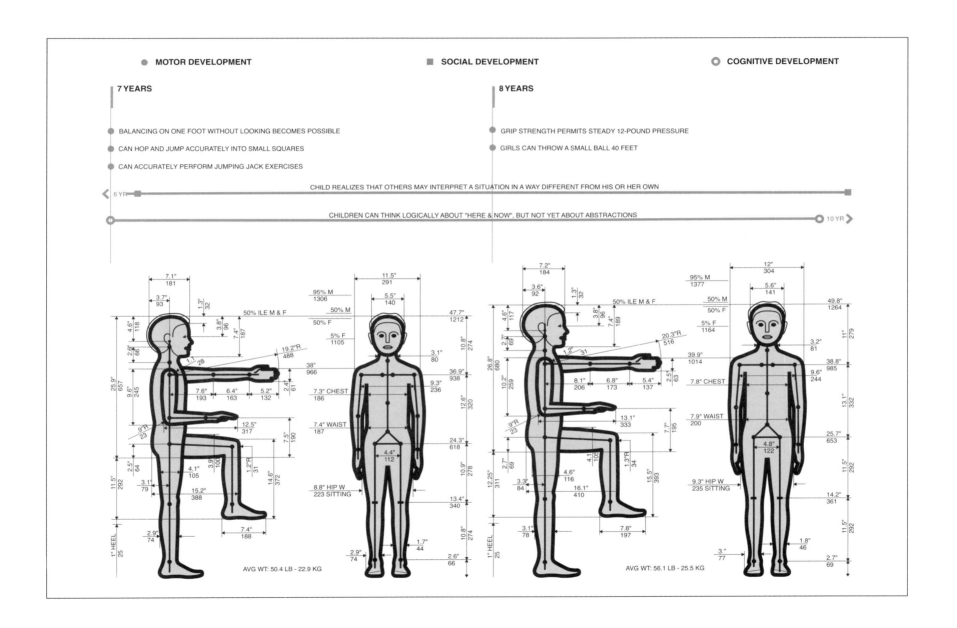

● MOTOR DEVELOPMENT   ■ SOCIAL DEVELOPMENT   ○ COGNITIVE DEVELOPMENT

7 YEARS

● BALANCING ON ONE FOOT WITHOUT LOOKING BECOMES POSSIBLE

● CAN HOP AND JUMP ACCURATELY INTO SMALL SQUARES

● CAN ACCURATELY PERFORM JUMPING JACK EXERCISES

8 YEARS

● GRIP STRENGTH PERMITS STEADY 12-POUND PRESSURE

● GIRLS CAN THROW A SMALL BALL 40 FEET

6 YR ── CHILD REALIZES THAT OTHERS MAY INTERPRET A SITUATION IN A WAY DIFFERENT FROM HIS OR HER OWN ──

CHILDREN CAN THINK LOGICALLY ABOUT "HERE & NOW", BUT NOT YET ABOUT ABSTRACTIONS ── 10 YR

AVG WT: 50.4 LB - 22.9 KG

AVG WT: 56.1 LB - 25.5 KG

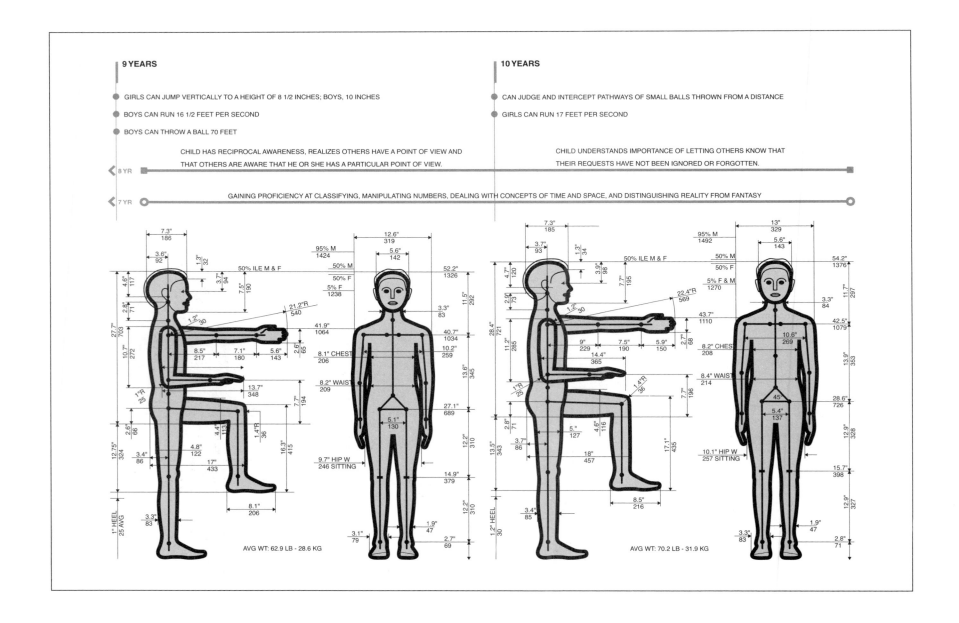

9 YEARS

- GIRLS CAN JUMP VERTICALLY TO A HEIGHT OF 8 1/2 INCHES; BOYS, 10 INCHES
- BOYS CAN RUN 16 1/2 FEET PER SECOND
- BOYS CAN THROW A BALL 70 FEET

CHILD HAS RECIPROCAL AWARENESS, REALIZES OTHERS HAVE A POINT OF VIEW AND THAT OTHERS ARE AWARE THAT HE OR SHE HAS A PARTICULAR POINT OF VIEW.

8 YR

7 YR GAINING PROFICIENCY AT CLASSIFYING, MANIPULATING NUMBERS, DEALING WITH CONCEPTS OF TIME AND SPACE, AND DISTINGUISHING REALITY FROM FANTASY

10 YEARS

- CAN JUDGE AND INTERCEPT PATHWAYS OF SMALL BALLS THROWN FROM A DISTANCE
- GIRLS CAN RUN 17 FEET PER SECOND

CHILD UNDERSTANDS IMPORTANCE OF LETTING OTHERS KNOW THAT THEIR REQUESTS HAVE NOT BEEN IGNORED OR FORGOTTEN.

AVG WT: 62.9 LB - 28.6 KG

AVG WT: 70.2 LB - 31.9 KG

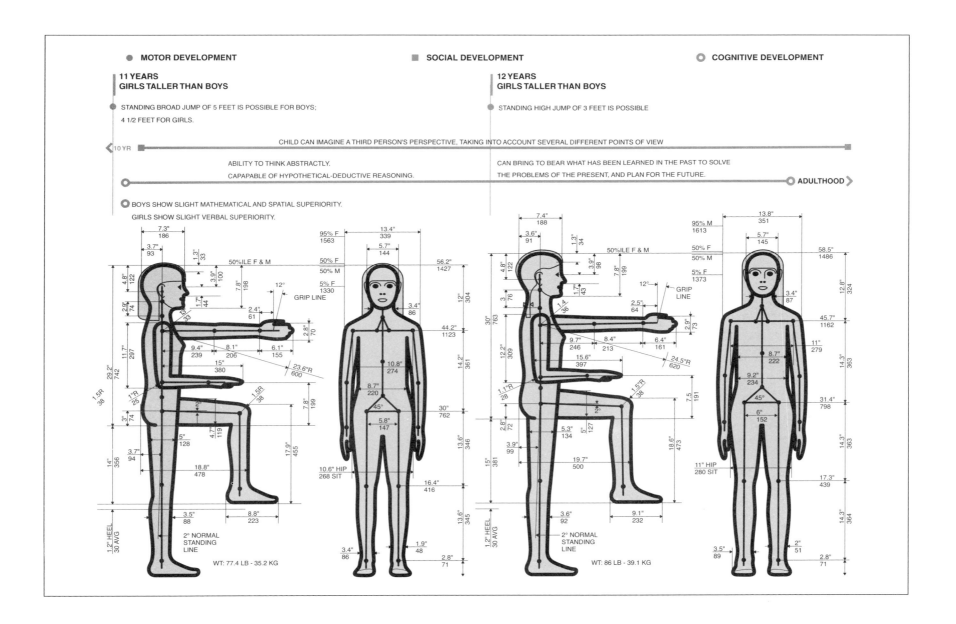

- ● MOTOR DEVELOPMENT
- ■ SOCIAL DEVELOPMENT
- ◎ COGNITIVE DEVELOPMENT

11 YEARS
GIRLS TALLER THAN BOYS

● STANDING BROAD JUMP OF 5 FEET IS POSSIBLE FOR BOYS;
4 1/2 FEET FOR GIRLS.

12 YEARS
GIRLS TALLER THAN BOYS

● STANDING HIGH JUMP OF 3 FEET IS POSSIBLE

◁ 10 YR   CHILD CAN IMAGINE A THIRD PERSON'S PERSPECTIVE, TAKING INTO ACCOUNT SEVERAL DIFFERENT POINTS OF VIEW

ABILITY TO THINK ABSTRACTLY.
CAPAPABLE OF HYPOTHETICAL-DEDUCTIVE REASONING.

CAN BRING TO BEAR WHAT HAS BEEN LEARNED IN THE PAST TO SOLVE
THE PROBLEMS OF THE PRESENT, AND PLAN FOR THE FUTURE.   **ADULTHOOD** ▷

◎ BOYS SHOW SLIGHT MATHEMATICAL AND SPATIAL SUPERIORITY.
GIRLS SHOW SLIGHT VERBAL SUPERIORITY.

WT: 77.4 LB - 35.2 KG

WT: 86 LB - 39.1 KG

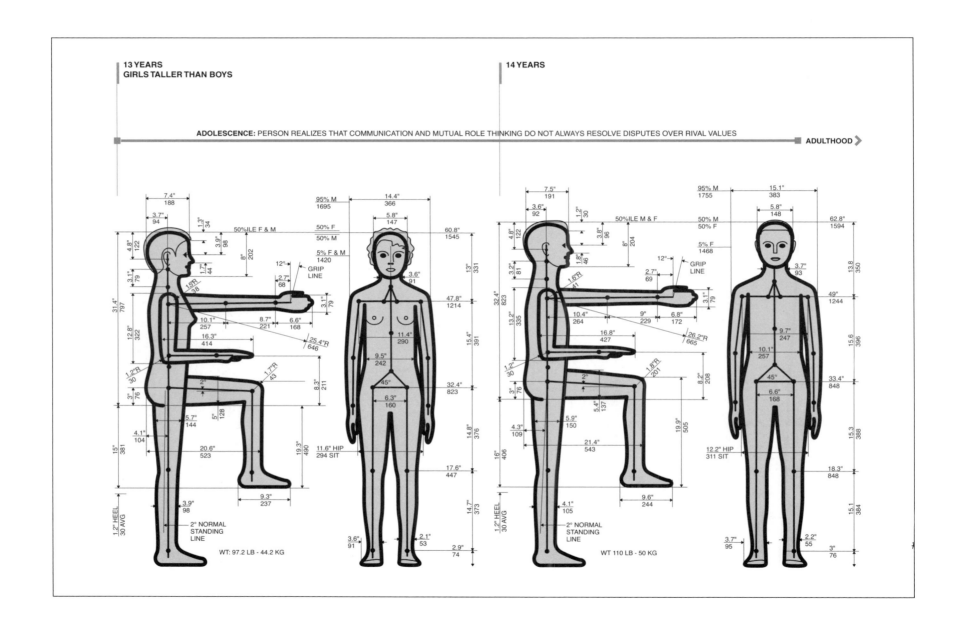

13 YEARS
GIRLS TALLER THAN BOYS

14 YEARS

ADOLESCENCE: PERSON REALIZES THAT COMMUNICATION AND MUTUAL ROLE THINKING DO NOT ALWAYS RESOLVE DISPUTES OVER RIVAL VALUES   **ADULTHOOD** ➤

WT: 97.2 LB - 44.2 KG

WT 110 LB - 50 KG

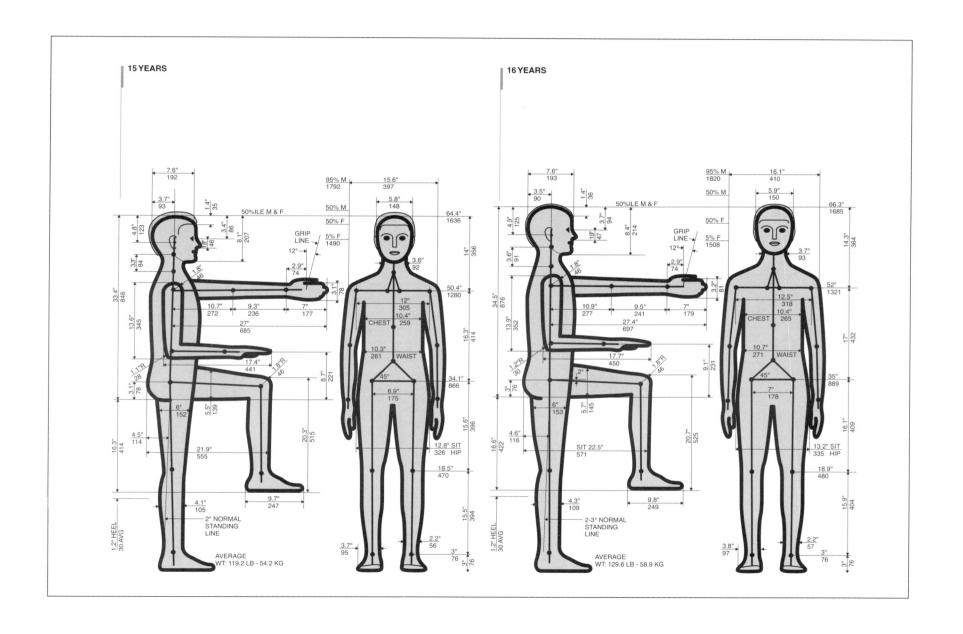

15 YEARS

50%ILE M & F

GRIP LINE

27"
685

17.4"
441

AVERAGE
WT: 119.2 LB - 54.2 KG

2° NORMAL
STANDING
LINE

1.2" HEEL
30 AVG

16 YEARS

50%ILE M & F

GRIP LINE

27.4"
697

17.7"
450

AVERAGE
WT: 129.6 LB - 58.9 KG

2-3° NORMAL
STANDING
LINE

1.2" HEEL
30 AVG

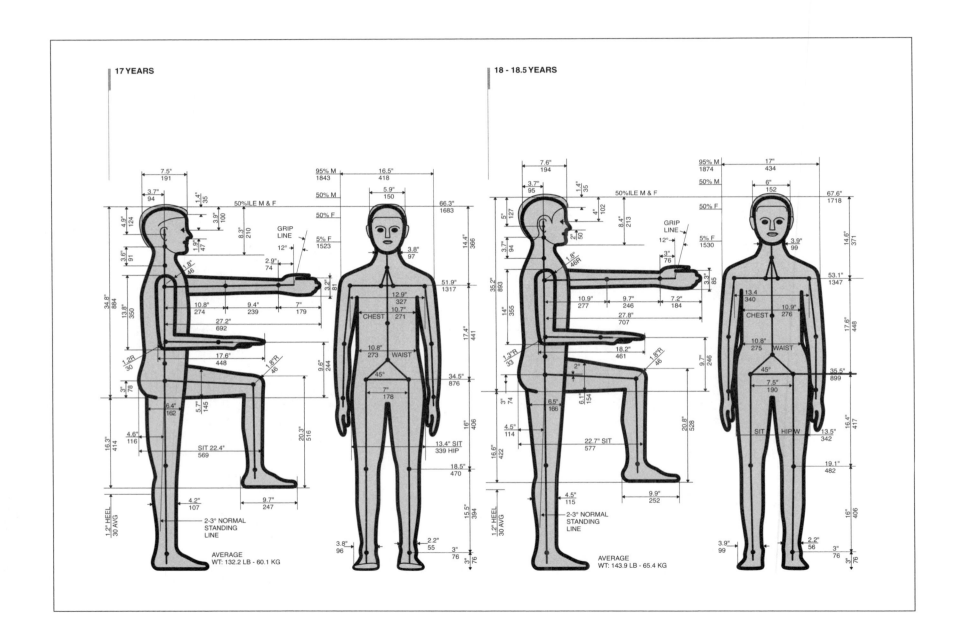

17 YEARS

AVERAGE
WT: 132.2 LB - 60.1 KG

18 - 18.5 YEARS

AVERAGE
WT: 143.9 LB - 65.4 KG

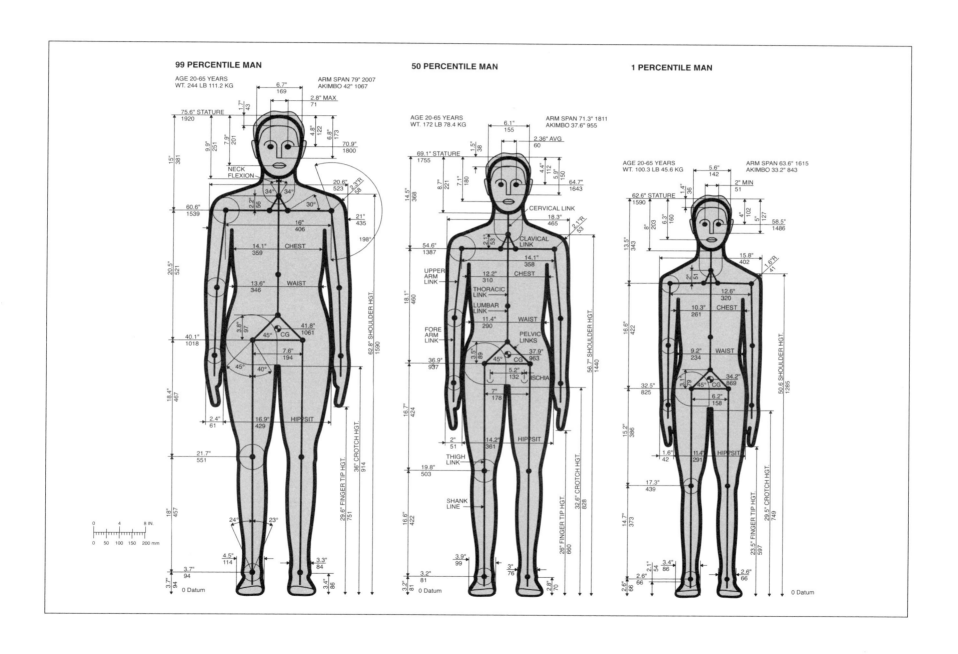

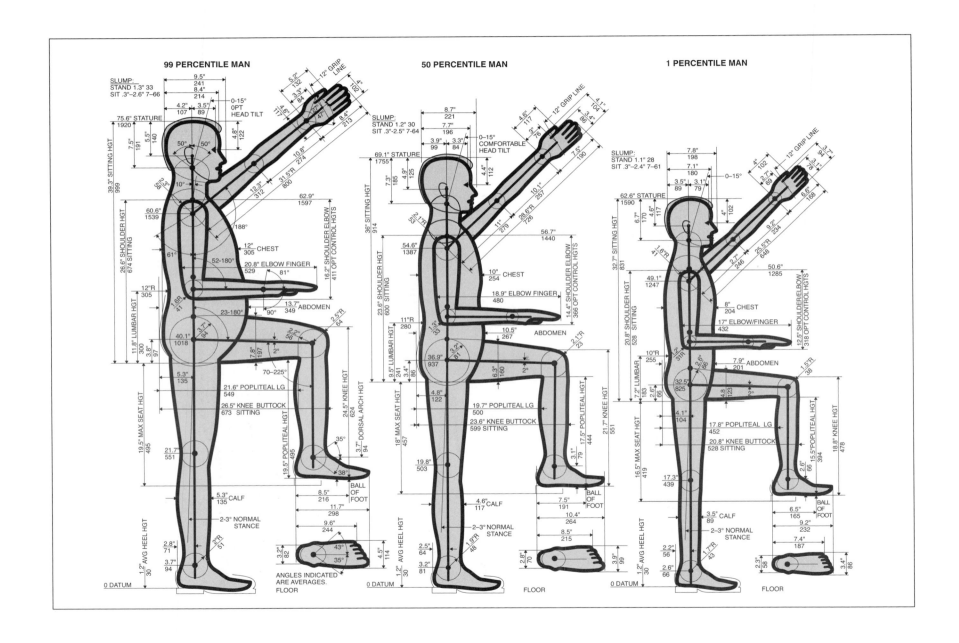

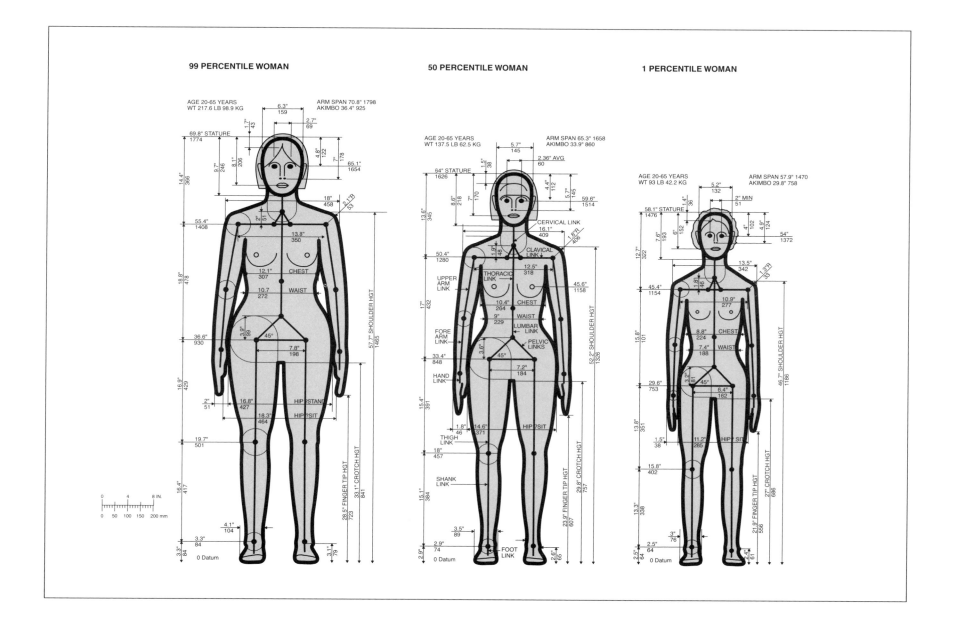

99 PERCENTILE WOMAN

50 PERCENTILE WOMAN

1 PERCENTILE WOMAN

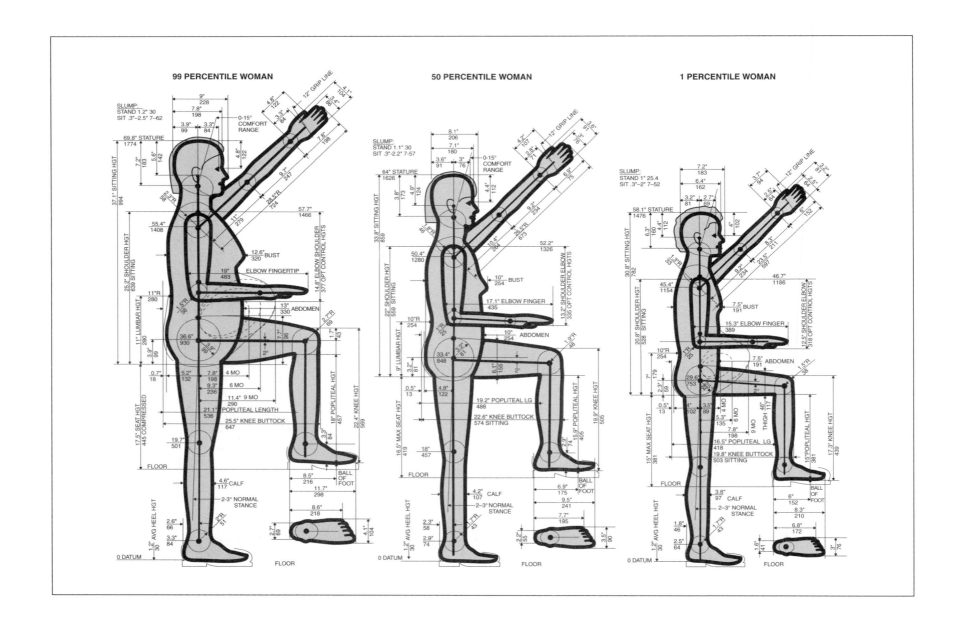

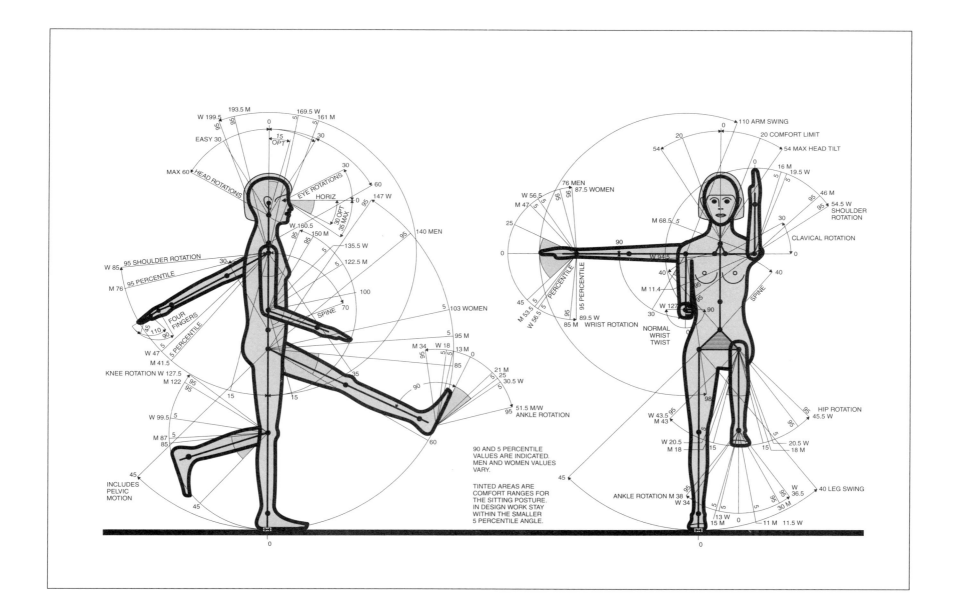

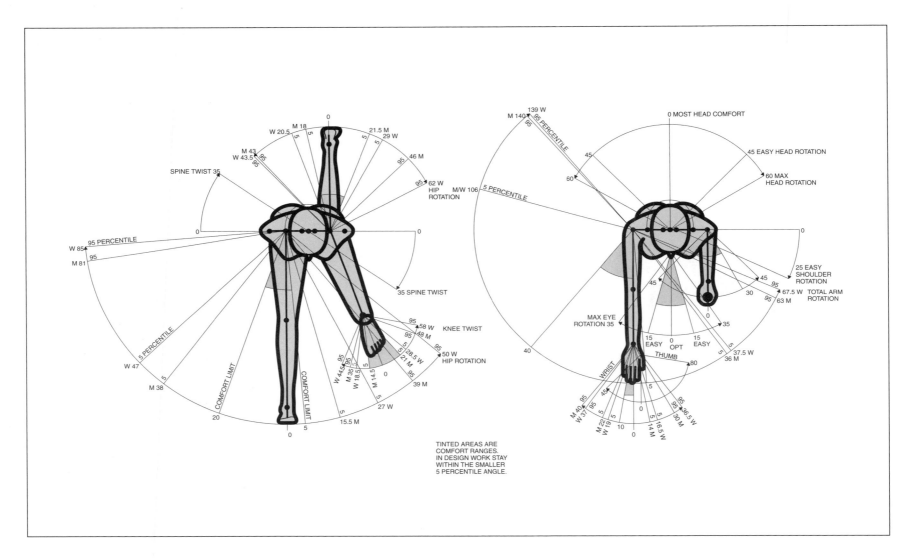

Adapted from Henry Dreyfuss Associates, *The Measure of Man and Woman* (Alvin R. Tilley, Ed.). John Wiley & Sons, Hoboken, 2001, for *Interior Graphic Standards* (Maryrose McGowan, Ed.), John Wiley & Sons, Inc., Hoboken, 2003.

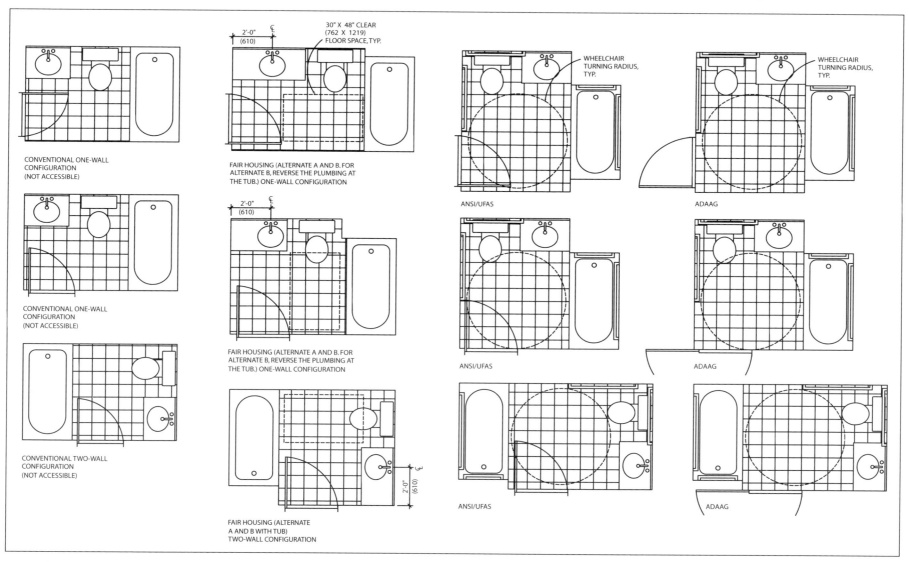

30" X 48" CLEAR (762 X 1219) FLOOR SPACE, TYP.

2'-0" (610)

CONVENTIONAL ONE-WALL CONFIGURATION (NOT ACCESSIBLE)

CONVENTIONAL ONE-WALL CONFIGURATION (NOT ACCESSIBLE)

CONVENTIONAL TWO-WALL CONFIGURATION (NOT ACCESSIBLE)

FAIR HOUSING (ALTERNATE A AND B. FOR ALTERNATE B, REVERSE THE PLUMBING AT THE TUB.) ONE-WALL CONFIGURATION

2'-0" (610)

FAIR HOUSING (ALTERNATE A AND B. FOR ALTERNATE B, REVERSE THE PLUMBING AT THE TUB.) ONE-WALL CONFIGURATION

2'-0" (610)

FAIR HOUSING (ALTERNATE A AND B WITH TUB) TWO-WALL CONFIGURATION

WHEELCHAIR TURNING RADIUS, TYP.

WHEELCHAIR TURNING RADIUS, TYP.

ANSI/UFAS

ADAAG

ANSI/UFAS

ADAAG

ANSI/UFAS

ADAAG

From *Architectural Graphic Standards Tenth Edition* (AIA: Ramsey/Sleeper). John Wiley & Sons, Hoboken, 2000.

ANSI/Fair Housing Kitchens

NOTE

A U-shaped counter arrangement must include a 5-foot clearance between the opposing counters (or appliances or walls) in order to comply with ANSI or UFAS standards. FHAA guidelines require a 5-foot clearance if a sink, range, or cooktop is installed in the base leg of the U. If the base leg fixture includes a knee space or removable base cabinets, the 5-foot clearance is not required.

NOTE

ANSI and UFAS require 40 inches of clearance between kitchen cabinets and opposing walls, cabinets, or appliances where the counters provide knee space. In other instances, an accessible route is required. The FHAA guidelines, however, require a 40-inch clearance in all cases. Passage widths between opposing counter sides or walls and counter sides are not specifically addressed in the FHAA guidelines. If this passage's length does not exceed 24 inches, ANSI or UFAS permits the width to be a minimum of 32 inches.

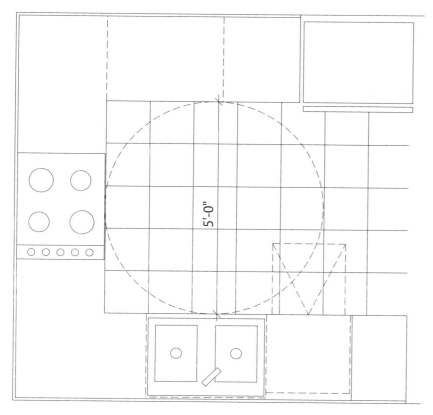

U-SHAPED KITCHEN PLAN

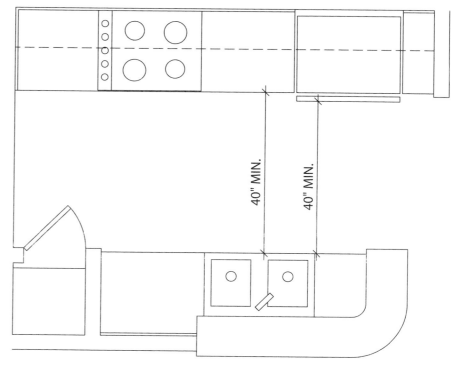

GALLEY KITCHEN PLAN

Floor Space and Knee Space Requirements for Fixtures and Appliances

Appliance	Requirement	Fair Housing	ANSI/UFAS
Sink	Approach Knee space	Parallel No	Parallel or front Yes
Range/cooktop	Approach Knee space	Parallel No	Parallel or front Optional
Work space	Approach Knee space	Not required No	Front Yes
Refrigerator	Approach Knee space	Parallel or front No	Parallel or front No
Dishwasher	Approach Knee space	Parallel or front No	Parallel or front No
Oven (self-cleaning)	Approach Knee space	Parallel or front No	Front No
Oven (non-self-cleaning)	Approach Knee space	Parallel or front No	Front Yes (offset)
Trash compactor	Approach Knee space	Parallel or front No	Parallel or front No

NOTE

Fair Housing guidelines and most building code standards require a clear floor space at most kitchen fixtures and appliances. This space can permit a parallel or a perpendicular (front) wheelchair approach, depending on the fixture or appliance selected or the decision of the designer. HUD has interpreted its FHAA guidelines to require centering of the clear floor space on the appliance or fixture. This is not a requirement of the building codes, however, and may exceed the 1986 ANSI "safe harbor" for FHAA.

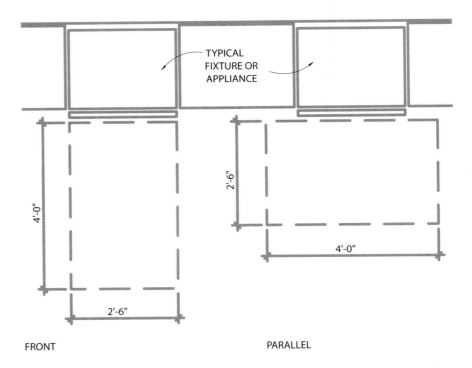

FRONT   PARALLEL

APPROACH DIAGRAM FOR FIXTURES OR APPLIANCES

NOTE

Locating the kitchen sink next to the dishwasher has accessibility benefits as well as functional advantages. The sink knee space provides convenient access for a wheelchair user to the adjacent dishwasher. The sink itself should be a shallow unit with easy-to-operate faucets. A tall spout and a pull-out spray attachment are also recommended. Garbage disposals must be offset in order to provide full knee space under the sink.

NOTE

The design of kitchen storage space for wheelchair users should provide both visual and physical access to wall and base cabinets, drawers, and pantries. Base cabinets, for example, can be specified to include pull-out shelves or drawers that will provide easy access to items stored in the back of the cabinets. Similarly, shelf racks on pantry doors make it easier for the user to find and reach stored items.

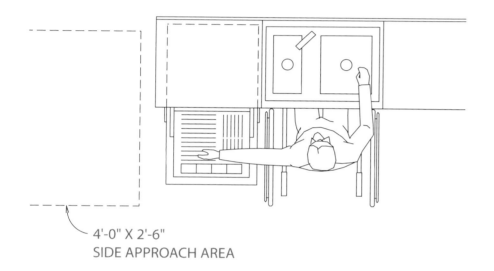

4'-0" X 2'-6"
SIDE APPROACH AREA

KITCHEN SINK AND DISHWASHER

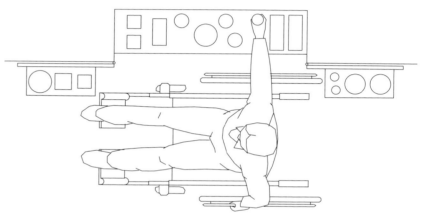

KITCHEN STORAGE

NOTE

A range or cooktop should have front- or side-mounted controls so the seated user does not need to reach over the heated surfaces. A smooth cooktop surface allows pots to be slid rather than lifted on and off the burners. Separate cooktop and oven units allow the alternative of providing knee space below the cooking surface, although this arrangement can also create safety issues.

NOTE

Side-by-side models offer the user both freezer and refrigerator storage at all height levels from the floor to the top shelf. Over-and-under models can also be a satisfactory choice for many wheelchair users. Models with narrower doors are easier to operate, and the desired parallel access is easier to provide if the refrigerator doors swing back a full 180 degrees.

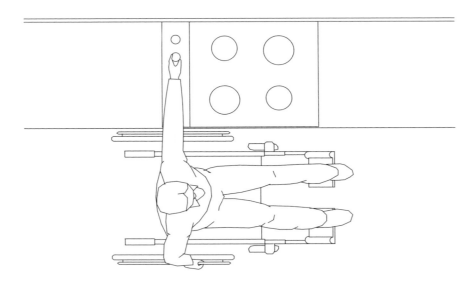

STOVES AND COOKTOPS

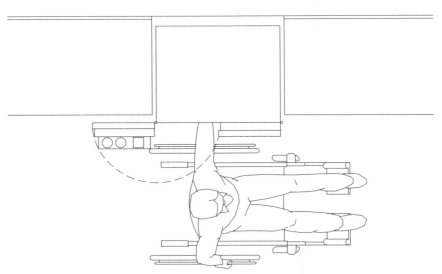

REFRIGERATORS

From *Architectural Graphic Standards Tenth Edition* (AIA: Ramsey/Sleeper).
John Wiley & Sons, Hoboken, 2000.

INDEX